THE GENDERED REPUBLIC

Jeffersonian America

Charlene M. Boyer Lewis, Annette Gordon-Reed,
Peter S. Onuf, Andrew J. O'Shaughnessy, and
Robert G. Parkinson, Editors

THE GENDERED REPUBLIC
Reimagining Identity in the New Nation

Edited by
Craig Thompson Friend
and Lorri Glover

University of Virginia Press • Charlottesville and London

The University of Virginia Press is situated on the traditional lands of the Monacan Nation, and the Commonwealth of Virginia was and is home to many other Indigenous people. We pay our respect to all of them, past and present. We also honor the enslaved African and African American people who built the University of Virginia, and we recognize their descendants. We commit to fostering voices from these communities through our publications and to deepening our collective understanding of their histories and contributions.

University of Virginia Press
© 2025 by the Rector and Visitors of the University of Virginia
All rights reserved
Printed in the United States of America on acid-free paper

First published 2025

9 8 7 6 5 4 3 2 1

Library of Congress Cataloging-in-Publication data is available for this title.

ISBN 978-0-8139-5372-4 (hardback)
ISBN 978-0-8139-5373-1 (paperback)
ISBN 978-0-8139-5374-8 (ebook)

Cover art: Clockwise from top: "A Woman chained to a Girl, and Man in irons at work in the field," *Illustrations of the American anti-slavery almanac for 1840* (New York), broadside (Ephemera Collection, Portfolio 248, Prints and Photographs Division, Library of Congress, Washington, DC); "American CItizens," by Thomas Waterman Wood, oil on canvas, 1867 (T. W. Wood Gallery & Arts Center, Montpelier, VT); "Elizabeth Freeman," by Susan Anne Livington, miniature portrait, watercolor on ivory, 1811 (Massachusetts Historical Society, Boston); "A new touch on the times: Well adapted to the distressing situation of every sea-port town. / By a daughter of liberty, living in Marblehead," by Molly Gutridge 33 × 21 cm broadside, c. 1779 (The New York Historical, 48257); "Lewis and Clark at Three Forks" by Edgar S. Paxson, oil on canvas, 1912, Mural in the Montana State Capitol (Montana Historical Society, Don Beatty, photographer)
Cover design: Kelley Galbreath

CONTENTS

Introduction — 1

Reframing the Early Republic — 5

The Formation of Chickamauga Towns: A Study of Cherokee Gender, Kinship, and Resistance in the Revolutionary Era — 7
Jamie Myers

Missionary Models of Evangelical Manhood and Womanhood — 21
Ashley E. Moreshead

"First White Man Sets Hisself Inside That Rail Fence Gets It from the Gun": Firearms, Fatherhood, and Slavery in the South — 46
Antwain K. Hunter

Reimagining Citizenship — 69

The Slave, the Concubine, and the Unnatural Beauty: Depictions of the Other and the Constriction of Women's Rights in American Magazines, 1790–1800 — 71
Jacqueline Beatty

Squaring for a Fight in the Early Republic: *Silvia Dubois, a Biografy of the Slav Who Whipt Her Mistres and Gand Her Fredom* — 95
Kenneth E. Marshall

Gender, Race, and Missionization in Antebellum Indian Territory — 119
Steven Peach

Thinking About Intersectionality — 141

"Scorned by Every Man of Honour": The Middleton Family, Divorce, and Masculine Respectability — 143
LYNN KENNEDY

"It's Possible That He Is the Author of the Poor Thing's Being": Interracial Sex and the Battle with Honor — 163
SHANNON C. EAVES

The "Black Douglass" and the "White Douglas": Embodying Sectional Politics in Late Antebellum America — 185
JOSHUA A. LYNN

Reading Bodies — 211

Reading the Gendered Body in Early America — 213
RACHEL WALKER

Fifth Avenoodles: Effeminate Dandies in Antebellum New York — 243
RACHEL HOPE CLEVES

Black Women, Illness, and Refinement in Antislavery Literature — 264
STEPHANIE J. RICHMOND

Historiographies — 287

Histories of Women in the Early American Republic — 289
LORRI GLOVER AND AMI PFLUGRAD-JACKISCH

Men and Manhood in the Historiography of the Early American Republic — 320
CRAIG THOMPSON FRIEND AND TIMOTHY J. WILLIAMS

Notes on Contributors — 351

Index — 355

THE GENDERED REPUBLIC

INTRODUCTION

WHAT DOES it mean to study early American history through gender? In a simple way, it insists that definitions of womanhood and manhood have histories and that those definitions change, sometimes subtly and slowly, sometimes dramatically and quickly. In more complex ways, gender history requires us to interrogate how and why societal understandings of manhood and womanhood evolved over time and varied across cultures, what historical forces fostered—or obstructed—changes in gender roles and experiences, how gender influenced individuals' understandings of their lives and world, and what roles gender played in shaping historical events.

The essays in this collection reflect vibrant ways in which historians have employed gender to understand the early American republic. Some authors study women and/or men, while others employ gender as an interpretive lens to explore themes such as race, citizenship, gentility, and family. They all build on a half-century of gender historiography. Beginning in the 1970s, scholars of women's history and then, in the 1980s, gender history, and by the 1990s men's studies fundamentally altered historical understanding of topics previously ungendered or reflexively assumed to be in the realm of men alone, including civic life, diplomacy, and war. Historians reinvigorated studies of economy, religion, and print culture. They sparked new lines of inquiry into sexualities and the body, and they uncovered histories previously obscured by scholars' perceptions of what drove societal and cultural change, how citizenship was defined, and how power is manifested. Along the way, gender historians innovated with women-centered and expanded chronologies, fresh geographies, and intersectional analyses, transforming our understandings of society, culture, citizenship, politics, and power in the American republic.

No subfield of early American history went unchanged by the growing sophistication of gender studies over the past half-century. The essays that follow illuminate the state of this wide-ranging, influential, fascinating, and sometimes unwieldly approach to studying the past. We have grouped them to reflect leading trends in gender histories: the questions scholars ask, the evidence they study, the methods they use, and the conclusions they reach. Together, the essays showcase the transformative impact of gender history, suggesting new chronological and geographic frameworks, broadening understandings of politics and citizenship, highlighting the complexities of intersectional identities, and exploring new approaches that center bodies and sexualities.

In part 1, "Reframing the Early Republic," Jamie Myers, Ashley E. Moreshead, and Antwain K. Hunter open the collection with revealing studies that recenter the geographies and chronologies of the early republic. Myers focuses on the centrality of gender to social order and power dynamics among the Chickamauga in the 1770s and 1780s, asking us to stretch our vision of the early republic beyond its traditional East-Coast orientation, richly illuminating how the Revolutionary War precipitated internal struggles among Indigenous Americans and foregrounding geopolitics different from the perspective of the "founding fathers." Moreshead centers White women and men missionizing beyond the nation's territorial boundaries, revealing how transnational experiences and narratives shaped Christian ideals of gender and the development of an American national identity. Hunter's study of gun use and ownership stretches the traditional chronological framing of the early republic beyond the Civil War. These essays—and others in the collection—provoke questions of where and when the early American republic emerged and ended, and what mattered in between.

In "Reimagining Citizenship," this volume's second part, Jacqueline Beatty, Kenneth E. Marshall, and Steven Peach also contribute to reframing the American republic as their essays reveal the power of gender history to broaden understandings of citizenship and national identity. Beatty expands the traditional understanding of "prescriptive literature" to highlight how White women's rights relied on "Othering" non-White women. Marshall employs the biography of a Black woman to challenge long-held assumptions about the meaning of citizenship in an increasingly democratic society. And Peach adopts a Creek and Seminole women-centered chronology and a methodology that locates Removal as the signal event in redefining citizenship and identity in the mid-nineteenth century.

In part 3, "Thinking About Intersectionality," Lynn Kennedy, Shannon C. Eaves, and Joshua A. Lynn offer opportunities to see how gender was just one of multiple defining characteristics for individuals. The intersections of different influences and identities are central to the stories that each author tells: Kennedy's study of a well-to-do White man and his rather mysterious immigrant wife; Eaves's exploration of an enslaved woman, a White southern man, and their biracial child; and Lynn's analysis of two nationally significant political figures, the formerly enslaved Frederick Douglass and the "Little Giant" Stephen Douglas. All three essays invite questions about relationships among gender, race, and nationality in defining people and framing how they interacted with others.

In "Reading Bodies," part 4 of the book, three essayists—Rachel Walker, Rachel Hope Cleves, and Stephanie J. Richmond—pursue one of the most recent and fruitful innovations of gender historians: reading bodies. Walker's essay intersects with sexuality and science/pseudo-science; Cleves's with sexuality and material culture; and Richmond's with science, medicine, and literature. All three challenge traditional perceptions of authority, both in terms of cultural power and historical sources. Who created sources? Who claimed scientific knowledge? Who commanded moral, political, and cultural influence?

Vigorous debates pervade the primary source–based essays in the volumes' first four parts, and a close reading reveals many complexities and occasional disagreements over evidence and interpretations. Cleves and Lynn, for example, see masculinity in the late antebellum era in different lights. Kennedy and Beatty offer divergent takes on marital infidelities and divorce. Myers and Peach reveal both the differences between Chickamauga and Creek and Seminole cultures and the two authors' approaches to those nations' histories.

The final two essays in this collection are historiographical and explain the deep methodological and interpretative contexts for the preceding original research essays. They help readers see the many, intersecting schools of thought and subfields pursued by these authors (as well as many other topics undertaken by gender historians). Readers will see that in their takes on the existing historiography, Lorri Glover and Ami Pflugrad-Jackisch and Craig Thompson Friend and Timothy J. Williams do not always see eye to eye. That is the nature of scholarship and the inspiration for further, fresh inquiries.

Of course, because the topics and interpretations connect and diverge in varied ways, our decisions about grouping the essays and our historiographical framings for the collection might fruitfully be questioned. The works could proceed in a strict chronology or be organized around historical events or topics, such as politics, religion, law, or popular culture. They could be arranged according to the race or region of the people studied or the authors' evidentiary bases or their methods (for example, biography, microhistory, ethnohistory). We hope readers, including teachers and their students, will contemplate such alternative structures to further advance their understanding of how gender shaped the lives of people in the early American republic, and how those people in turn experienced and redefined gender and, with it, their communities, cultures, laws, families, and nations.

REFRAMING THE EARLY REPUBLIC

THE EARLY AMERICAN REPUBLIC, like most periodization in United States history such as the American revolutionary era, Civil War and Reconstruction, and the New Deal era, began as a political designation within a nation-state framework. The Society for Historians of the Early American Republic (SHEAR) is, for example, "dedicated to exploring the events and the meaning of United States history between 1776 and 1861."[1] Women's and gender historians, alongside scholars studying race, ethnicity, and intersectionality, broaden and challenge those assumptions about how we define historical periods to expand beyond events driving national political changes in the United States.

The essays in this section reframe the early American republic in three distinct yet interconnected—and enriching—ways. Jamie Myers, working in the early phases of the long revolutionary era, resituates the divisions wrought by the Revolutionary War away from Anglo-American patriots and loyalists on the eastern seaboard to center Cherokee matrifocal communities and clans. As Myers reveals, the emergence of Chickamauga towns in the 1770s, amid a spiraling international war (which too often gets reduced to a struggle for patriot independence), cannot be understood without analyzing gender values. Ashley E. Moreshead, like Myers, explores masculinity and femininity in tandem, but she adopts a global rather than a North American continental framework, and her study illuminates how early Americans, operating in Protestant evangelical missions in Burma, India, and West Africa, took gendered ideals and power dynamics across the globe. Antwain K. Hunter utilizes a more familiar geography, the US South, but his study of Black fatherhood and firearms presses us to see the legacy of early republic traditions beyond the Civil War. All three authors also employ innovative research methods to foreground the perspectives of women and men whose histories they recovered from limited, fraught, and sometimes biased sources.

Collectively, these three essays suggest important questions about the traditional chronology and geography of the early American republic.

What is gained when historians move from a narrow, nation-state origins story toward transnational approaches—either continental, Atlantic, or global? How can scholars recover the voices and perspectives of people often obscured in the surviving archives? How does centering the experiences of women and men of color alter understandings of how gender worked in the new nation?

Note

1. "About Us," SHEAR, https://www.shear.org.

The Formation of Chickamauga Towns

A STUDY OF CHEROKEE GENDER, KINSHIP, AND RESISTANCE IN THE REVOLUTIONARY ERA

Jamie Myers

IN MARCH 1775, a group of Cherokee headmen sold approximately 27,000 square miles of land to Richard Henderson, a lawyer and representative of the Transylvania Land Company. Both the Cherokee headmen and Henderson ignored the ban on Indian land sales to private individuals established by the Royal Proclamation of 1763. Henderson received most of present-day Kentucky, and the Cherokee headmen who signed the deed received some £10,000 in trade goods. Not all Cherokees were pleased with the agreement. Unable to stop what became known as the Sycamore Shoals Treaty, some Cherokees decided to forge their own path, forming new towns in present-day southeastern Tennessee, northeastern Alabama, and northwestern Georgia to pursue their own anticolonial policies, including violent resistance, and to express their displeasure with accommodationist leaders and land sales and cessions. Their towns, referred to as Chickamauga towns, reached seven hundred warriors and provided a base for violent resistance to American colonialism until 1794.[1]

During the era of Chickamauga resistance, on 29 February 1792, an "Eagle-tail dance was held . . . which was also danced with all the forms of a war-dance, exulting over the scalps."[2] Through such rituals, Cherokee communities exalted male spiritual power derived from shedding enemies' blood, and social structures affirmed this derivation of masculine power. While the dances venerated the gendered activities of men, women importantly also participated in rituals after warriors returned. According to Cherokee oral tradition:

> On their return from war, the scalp dance was attended to. In this the women first danced. . . . They moved in a stooping posture, and stepped slowly or not according to the beat of the drum. . . . They sometimes raised their hands, and made motions as if striking some enemy. The men then joined. . . . One man with a scalp, or scalps on a stick, held the stick by each end, with a woman at his side, and both danced round the fire, as before, halfbent. They moved their feet at the sound of the drum. . . . These two persons now danced up to others, who arose and joined, till at length many, if not all, were engaged in the dance side by side.[3]

Even though men were responsible for engaging in battle, women played an essential role in choosing the spoils of war. As leaders of their clans, Cherokee women encouraged male kin to seek revenge when a family member died unnaturally, and they decided captives' fates. In communal rituals such as the eagle-tail dance, women danced first, a symbolic recognition of the importance of their roles. Men and women later danced as pairs, another symbolic act meant to illustrate how women shared the act of warfare with men. Community involvement manifested in the eagle-tail dance as eventually all were encouraged to join, just as entire communities dealt with decisions to go to war.

The bigendered nature of Cherokees' decision-making was central to ways in which they negotiated and survived the American revolutionary era and the early American republic. This essay analyzes how masculine ideals centered on clan responsibilities informed the relocation of some Cherokees to new towns where they became "Chickamaugas" and engaged in violent resistance to settler colonialism. However, rather than focusing solely on warriors, this essay also considers women's roles as the definers of clan responsibilities, and how they actively participated in decisions to relocate and engage in war. As the eagle-tail dance illustrated, warfare in eighteenth-century Cherokee society was not solely a male responsibility. Rather, Cherokee women played influential and decisive roles in the prosecution of war. The Chickamaugas offer unique insights into the active role women played in a male-gendered occupation.

A lack of sources complicates historians' understanding of women's behind-the-scenes influences in political affairs.[4] Much of the existing scholarship on Cherokees who inhabited Chickamauga towns focuses on men, specifically Dragging Canoe, the warrior who led the Cherokees in warring against European colonials and then US settlers. While

Chickamauga men undoubtedly expressed masculinity as war leaders and diplomats in their towns, Cherokee women acted as the heads of their matrilocal households. As a result, men experienced subtle pressures to conform to household politics that influenced their political decisions.[5] Although individual Cherokee women are not named in surviving sources, matrilineages and kinship connections demonstrate the decisive role female clan members played in the formation of Chickamauga towns and the militant politics of those villages.

For several decades, scholars have explored the gendered dynamics of Cherokee society but have largely neglected how such patterns manifested among the Chickamaugas. Theda Perdue's seminal 1998 book, *Cherokee Women,* elucidated the power of women. Other historians, including Susan M. Abram and Nathaniel Sheidley, illuminated the expectations of masculine expressions beyond hunting and warfare.[6] This essay builds on their scholarship to explore gendered motivations in Chickamauga towns and the masculine and feminine impulses that informed political decisions. Scholars of kinship and gender in the revolutionary era and early American republic have drawn attention as well to ways in which intimate relationships in Native communities informed diplomatic interactions with White American colonists and their governments.[7] The Chickamaugas' story enters those broader conversations by advancing understanding of borderland spaces and warfare. Emphasizing the domestic considerations of Chickamauga Cherokee men who engaged in borderland violence provides insights into Chickamauga Cherokee women's political desires and machinations. As a result, a more complete picture of the inner workings of Chickamauga Cherokee society emerges, with women centered and men operating as more than simply "warriors," offering a clearer example of the complementary character of Cherokee gender roles.

In Cherokee cosmology, Selu and Kana'ti, the first woman and first man, had gendered occupations. Selu, which also means "corn," provided corn and beans for her family. Kana'ti, the great hunter, complemented Selu's contributions by providing protein for the family's diet. The creation story instituted and reflected Cherokee communities' divided responsibilities and specified that women held power through their abilities to create life (human and plant) and men through their ability to take life (human and animal). Creating and taking life relied on the shedding of blood: menstruation as a sign of women's giving of life, and the blood of war and the hunt as symbolic of men's taking of life. Blood provided the source of both female and male power.[8]

Historic Cherokees respected and feared the potency of blood, as numerous rituals and oral traditions attest. For example, before raids commenced, Cherokee men ritually prepared themselves for battle through scratching, using bone and animal teeth to scrape their skin until they bled. Anthropologist Raymond D. Fogelson asserted that through such acts men sought to capture the power of menstruating women. When warriors returned from raids, they remained beyond their villages for a specified period to perform cleansing rituals. Their recent contact with blood put them at the height of their power, so returning to their homes put other household members at risk. Such beliefs mirrored how women experienced the height of their power when they shed blood, protecting their households during their menses and childbirth by confining themselves to huts beyond their villages. In contrast to men, however, women's blood was potent because of its creative forces.[9]

Cherokee women's ability to procreate reflected in the matrilineal nature of their society, their gendered occupations, and their status in their homes. Dwellings were extremely feminine places, and men were expected to recognize and respect the authority of household women. Because women outnumbered men in the home, they easily enforced household priorities. Once sons came of age and married, they moved to their wives' homes, which meant that husbands and an occasional older maternal uncle were the only men present. Cherokee women used their numerical superiority and domestic authority to influence men's political participation, their influence radiating from the domestic domain. This is not to suggest a model of "separate spheres" applies to historic Cherokee people. Women's influence and presence exceeded the walls of the household. Although they did not act as political representatives, they served important functions in diplomatic meetings.[10] Women fed visiting traders and diplomats, and they performed rituals that incorporated outsiders as fictive kin. Such ceremonies solemnized relationships and proved crucial to the success of alliances and trading relationships.

In 1775, when several Cherokee headmen signed the Sycamore Shoals Treaty, women were also present. The actions of Dragging Canoe, however, overtook the historical narrative. A war leader in his late thirties from Big Island Town, Dragging Canoe contended that the sale (much like previous land cessions) had satisfied White settlers for only a short time. Colonists continued to demand land, and Dragging Canoe feared that eventually the Cherokees would have no more land of their own. Unable to stop the sale, he disgustedly walked out of negotiations and into history as a preeminent leader of an anticolonial Cherokee resistance.

For the resistance movement, the crux of the issue was land. Loss of territory undermined Cherokee men's abilities to hunt, which threatened their identity as men. The sale at Sycamore Shoals deprived Cherokee men of approximately 20 million acres teeming with game, constricting men's abilities to perform a fundamental expression of their gender and inhibiting their abilities to provide for family or acquire trade goods. Consequently, such land cessions threatened to make young Cherokee men less attractive mates to women. In the eighteenth century, Cherokee society offered no viable alternatives to their standard rites of passage. Some accommodationist headmen attempted to placate younger warriors with gifts, hoping that such distributions of gifts as status symbols would persuade the men to acquiesce to land cessions and treaties. The solution proved inadequate to men whose masculine ideals depended on actively achieving distinction through blood power.[11]

Outbreak of war between Britain and its North American colonies in 1775 amplified disagreements among Cherokees. In early 1776, Dragging Canoe complained to Deputy Indian Superintendent Henry Stuart about the continued demand for Cherokee land. Stuart responded that the Indians themselves were to blame because they had ignored the king's proclamation and made private sales to people like Richard Henderson. Dragging Canoe retorted that "he had no hand in making these Bargains." He echoed the statement he had made at Sycamore Shoals: that "some of their Old Men who were too old to hunt" had made those land sales and cessions, but for "his part he had a great many young fellows that would support him and that they were determined to have their land." Later that spring, agitation among the Cherokees peaked when a Shawnee and Mohawk delegation visited. After the delegates arrived, "every young Fellow's face in the Overhills Towns appeared Blackened, and nothing was . . . talked of but War." As the northern representatives argued for war, it was Dragging Canoe who received belts of wampum from the Shawnee and Mohawk delegations.[12]

Beginning on 1 July 1776, Cherokee warriors attacked the borderlands of the southern colonies from Virginia to Georgia. Peace-minded Cherokees attempted to distance themselves from the warriors' actions to pursue their own course, many signing treaties with American officials, exchanging land for promises of peace. In May 1777, Cherokees from the Lower, Middle, and Valley towns signed the Treaty of Dewitts Corner, which ceded Cherokee lands in present-day South Carolina. Two months later in July, Overhill Cherokees signed the Treaty of Long Island of Holston, which ceded Cherokee lands in present-day Tennessee.

The cessions disrupted life in Cherokee towns and resulted in a diaspora of Cherokee people from ancestral villages. Dragging Canoe's relocation proved the most notable as he and other like-minded Cherokees, refusing to pursue a policy of peace with the Americans, moved southward and settled on Chickamauga Creek, taking on the designation as Chickamaugas. According to one observer familiar with the political situation in Cherokee regions, Cherokees "were moving, so as to take the situation which best suited their wishes and disposition for war or peace."[13]

Despite conciliatory Cherokees' efforts to disassociate themselves from the Chickamaugas, in the years between 1779 and 1782 American militias conducted eight different campaigns against Cherokee towns in all regions, including Chickamauga town sites, forcing Chickamaugas to eventually establish new town sites that became known as the five Lower Towns along the Tennessee River around present-day Chattanooga: Crow, Lookout Mountain, Long Island, Nickajack, and Running Water. From these locations, the Chickamauga warriors attacked American settlements. As Dragging Canoe's words and the events of 1776 and 1777 make clear, land was the central issue for the men who became Chickamaugas.[14]

Cherokee women were also heavily affected by land sales, and given the matrilocal nature of Cherokee society, women certainly became necessary participants in decisions to relocate, perhaps even directing them. Although the Sycamore Shoals sale impacted hunting lands rather than village sites, the treaties in the spring and summer of 1777 dispossessed Cherokee households of their cornfields. Women's power and influence in Cherokee society rested in part on their gender roles as farmers, so the loss of farmlands threatened their ability to sustain those roles, undermining the intimate and subtle influence women had at varying levels of Cherokee political life. Thus, Cherokee women also wanted to "have their land."[15]

Relocation promised Chickamauga women could continue as farmers without threat of additional land cessions, and men could feel secure access to the hunt—gendered occupations that held practical and symbolic implications for Chickamauga residents. But such foundational practices became more vulnerable with continued American militia raids and other abuses. Chickamauga concerns over the extinction of their way of life peaked, eliciting an offensive response, such as raids on White American settlements. Attacks by Chickamauga warriors, then, may be interpreted as more than attempts to preserve land. The attacks defended historic gender roles and occupations. American observers reported numbers of warriors in Chickamauga towns as the threat facing them, but women, children, and the elderly resided in the Lower Towns as well, performing tasks appropriate to age and gender as part of a larger community response.[16]

Although men actively participated in prosecuting war, women played a role through demanding male relatives take part in attacks and raids. Most often, such encouragement arose from the desire to avenge the unnatural death of kin. Given the frequency of violence during the revolutionary era, women, through their status as clan leaders and expressing their desires through their public displays of grief, increasingly requested clan vengeance. Again, blood became central: the practice of clan revenge dictated that kin lost to acts of violence must have their "crying blood" quieted. When warriors returned to a village with captives, Cherokee women, calculating how to restore balance to the clan, made decisions regarding their fates: adoption into the clan or death. The matrilineal nature of Cherokee society required Cherokee women's participation and concession to adoption, so they held the fate of every captive in their hands.[17] Clan vengeance, then, provided increasingly more numerous opportunities for Chickamauga men and women to perform historically appropriate gender roles during wartime.

Some Cherokee warriors who did not permanently settle among the Chickamaugas occasionally joined them in raids before returning to their own villages. A "countryman," or White man living among the Cherokees, reported "that many of the young men of every part of the nation discovered an inclination to join the war party of the Lower towns." Younger and unmarried, such Cherokee men did not need to consult wives about possibly relocating a household. Instead, they had the freedom to travel to Chickamauga towns and return to the homes of their mothers, sisters, or maternal uncles. As visiting warriors in Chickamauga raiding parties, they demonstrated the continued importance of expressing spiritual power through familiar gendered behaviors and achieving manhood in a historically acceptable way: through war. Their actions empowered many Cherokee women as well. Although most Cherokee women did not relocate among the Chickamaugas, many took advantage of the situation and adopted captives taken in raids by their male kin.[18] Cherokee participation in Chickamauga vengeance continued throughout the revolutionary era, and although not all raiding Cherokees resettled among the Chickamaugas, clan revenge was a powerful motivator in decisions to join the resistance and relocate.

The killing of Old Tassel in 1788 also fueled relocation and resistance. A Cherokee headman from Toqua, an Overhill town located in present-day eastern Tennessee, Old Tassel frequently called for peace between Cherokees and Americans. Unfortunately, White settlers flouted existing treaty boundaries and settled in Cherokee territory. In 1788, Colonel John Sevier, the governor of a planned state named Franklin in western North Carolina, led an attack on Cherokee towns, forcing the Cherokees to abandon villages east of the Cumberland Mountains. As Cherokees evacuated en masse, Sevier and his men burned Big Island, Chilhowie, Chota, Coyatee, Hiwassee, Settico, Talassee, and Tellico. According to a Cherokee spokesperson, "Flourishing fields of corn and pulse [peas or beans] were destroyed and laid waste; some of their wives and children were burnt alive in their town houses."[19] Sevier's attacks struck at the heart of the historic Overhill Cherokee settlements. Chota, for example, long considered a capital city, had served as a residence for many leading political figures.

The ferocity and political implications of Sevier's campaign provoked responses throughout Cherokee towns as men and women experienced the impacts of the attack, whether through the death of kin or the lingering threats of future attacks. As Sevier's forces attacked women and children, their horrific deaths emasculated the kinsmen responsible for their safety. Beyond women's bodies, however, the destruction of women's expressions of spiritual power—their crops—had a practical and psychological impact on survivors. In response, a group of Cherokee men attacked a White family who had encroached beyond the agreed-upon boundary. The father, John Kirk, and one son were away. Eleven members of the Kirk family died at the hands of Cherokee warriors. In response, Americans requested Old Tassel and other headmen council with them in Chilhowie. As Old Tassel entered the village, the Americans raised a white flag but it was a trap. American militiamen barred all exits, and John Kirk killed Old Tassel with a hatchet.[20]

While relatives of Old Tassel had not moved to Chickamauga towns prior to his death, after his murder most of his kin relocated and became leading figures in the resistance. For example, John Watts Jr., Old Tassel's maternal nephew, became a war leader and prominent political representative among Chickamaugas after his uncle's death. Watts was not the only member of his matrilineage involved in the Chickamauga resistance after the death of his uncle. Two of Old Tassel's brothers, Doublehead and Pumpkin Boy, moved into the Lower Towns to participate in clan vengeance. The latter ultimately lost his life fighting against White settlers. Additional clan members who relocated to Chickamauga towns included Old Tassel's two sisters, his nephew Whiteman Killer, and his niece Wurteh and her sons.[21] This genealogy of resistance testified to women's centrality in deciding on war and vengeance. Reaction to Old Tassel's murder took shape through the connections and participation of his sisters and niece.

The overlapping layers and strands of kinship in Chickamauga towns illuminate ways that Cherokee women provided the nexus of an anticolonial resistance movement, including seeking retribution for the deaths of kin. Frequent attacks on Cherokee towns by Sevier and others, and the undisputed presence of women in the Chickamauga resistance, attest to the decisive role that clan and matrilineal affiliations held in shaping peoples' political decisions to move.[22]

Perhaps the greatest evidence of the role matrilineages played in decisions to relocate can be traced to Dragging Canoe and his kin. One of Old Tassel's sisters, Nancy, was the wife of Dragging Canoe's brother The Badger. The Badger and Dragging Canoe's other siblings—Little Owl (or White Owl's Son), Turtle-at-Home, and a sister whose name has been lost to us—lived in Chickamauga towns. The Badger and Little Owl relocated with Dragging Canoe in 1777 to Chickamauga Creek and then to the Lower Towns. Turtle-at-Home resided at Running Water, Dragging Canoe's village, and apparently became the headman of that village after the death of his brother. Their sister's son, Black Fox, was a Chickamauga warrior and later a principal chief of the Lower Towns.[23]

Despite their renowned warring prowess, Dragging Canoe and other men could not decide to move without the consent of their household women. The sheer number of Dragging Canoe's kin in Chickamauga towns suggests that, rather than merely consenting to a relocation, Cherokee women initiated the moves. Although surviving historical records do not evidence the voices of Dragging Canoe's sister or other female kin, the mention of "Oconostota's wife" and her actions signal the impact that Cherokee women had in shaping such political decisions.

Oconostota, a famed warrior and prominent headman from the town of Chota, was a leading participant in the events at Sycamore Shoals. When the negotiating parties worked out the treaty details and signed the document, Oconostota's wife learned of the events from a trader. She became visibly upset and reportedly "went away . . . to acquaint some of the Chiefs with it."[24] Although the kinship relations of Oconostota's wife remain shrouded in mystery, the episode demonstrates ways in which Cherokee women inserted themselves into decisions that impacted land. Perhaps aware of Dragging Canoe's dramatic exit the day before, she sought out the discontented war leader and other like-minded individuals. She certainly would have actively sought to influence sons, brothers, and nephews to respond to colonial dispossession.

Matrilineages and extended kinship networks impacted people's decisions to leave and return to historic town sites. According to one Cherokee warrior, Tuskegetchee (or Long Fellow, as he was also known) initially moved with Dragging Canoe to the Chickamauga towns and "Loved War." However, at the urgings of Joseph Martin, a US Indian agent, Tuskegetchee moved from the Chickamauga towns and endeavored to promote peace. It seems unlikely that an outsider like Martin could so effectively dissuade a Cherokee man from his gendered and clan obligations, but Martin was no typical American. He had married Elizabeth "Betsy" Ward, maternal niece of Tuskegetchee. Through marriage, Betsy Ward enveloped Martin into her kinship networks. Additionally, Tuskegetchee's sister Nancy Ward was the most influential Cherokee woman at the time and an advocate for peace. Nancy and Betsy Ward exerted subtle but authoritative political pressures. Tuskegetchee, knowing his connection to another man would resonate more with an American audience, credited his kinship connections to Martin instead of the Ward women.[25]

Although histories of the formation of Chickamauga towns have traditionally focused on warriors and Dragging Canoe specifically, there is far more to the story. Cherokee men acted on clan responsibilities, including gendered concerns grounded in the land. If we consider historic Cherokee gender ideals and expectations, then the importance of matrilineages and clans, and by extension their female members, becomes evident. Formation of Chickamauga towns depended on household relocations in which women necessarily played a principal part. Intimate connections among Chickamaugas, centered on the matrifocal, motivated relocation and resistance. In their historic gender roles, as clan leaders and heads of households, Chickamauga Cherokee women exerted tremendous influence over Cherokee men, their patterns of war, and the future of the Cherokee nation. Recognizing and inspecting such connections allows us to see beyond colonialism's record of men's activities, providing a more nuanced, multifaceted, and human understanding of the Chickamaugas.

Questions to Consider

1. Even though Chickamauga women did not physically engage in battles, how did they participate in warfare?
2. How does the consideration of women's roles impact our understanding of Chickamauga masculinity?

Notes

1. Colin G. Calloway, *The American Revolution in Indian Country: Crisis and Diversity in Native American Communities* (New York: Cambridge University Press, 1995), 189–90; Jon W. Parmenter, "Dragging Canoe (Tsi'yugunsi'ni): Chickamauga Cherokee Patriot," in *The Human Tradition in The American Revolution,* ed. Nancy L. Rhoden and Ian K. Steele (Wilmington, DE: SR Books, 2000), 118–20, 130–31. According to historian Cynthia Cumfer, characterizations of Dragging Canoe and other Chickamaugas as simply militants opposed to American settlers ignores how, throughout the so-called Chickamauga War, Chickamauga politicians treated with American governments; see Cumfer, *Separate Peoples, One Land: The Minds of Cherokees, Blacks, and Whites on the Tennessee Frontier* (Chapel Hill: University of North Carolina Press, 2007). American records of the Chickamauga War demonstrate how militancy was a key component of Chickamauga diplomatic strategies. The willingness of Chickamaugas to attack American settlements to achieve political goals set them apart from the diplomatic strategies of other Cherokees who were unwilling to embrace violence. Although the Chickamaugas were culturally Cherokee, source materials from the era differentiated those engaged in attacks on American settlements from Cherokees who desired peace. Once the

Chickamauga Cherokees ended their resistance in 1794, they did not remain a distinct political unit from the rest of the Cherokee Nation and contemporaries returned to referring to them as Cherokee.
2. David Craig to William Blount, report, 15 March 1792, in *American State Papers: Documents, Legislative and Executive, of the Congress of the United States*, vol. 4, *Indian Affairs* (Washington, DC: Gales and Seaton, 1832), 264.
3. John Howard Payne, *The Payne-Butrick Papers*, vol. 3, *Cherokee Customs and Antiquities*, ed. William L. Anderson, Jane L. Brown, and Anne F. Rogers (Lincoln: University of Nebraska Press, 2010), 255.
4. There are few Native-authored sources from the eighteenth century. Most of the primary sources were by colonizers, who were typically uninterested in the activities of women, so Native women's voices are scarce in the historical record.
5. Raymond D. Fogelson, "On the 'Petticoat Government' of the Eighteenth-Century Cherokee," in *Personality and the Cultural Construction of Society*, ed. David K. Jordan and Marc J. Swartz (Tuscaloosa: University of Alabama Press, 1990), 161–81.
6. Theda Perdue, *Cherokee Women: Gender and Culture Change, 1700–1835* (Lincoln: University of Nebraska Press, 1998); Susan M. Abram, *Forging a Cherokee-American Alliance in the Creek War: From Creation to Betrayal* (Tuscaloosa: University of Alabama Press, 2015); Abram, "Real Men: Masculinity, Spirituality, and Community in Late Eighteenth-Century Cherokee Warfare," in *New Men: Manliness in Early America*, ed. Thomas A. Foster (New York: New York University Press, 2011), 93–116; Abram, "'Souls in the Treetops': Cherokee War, Masculinity, and Community, 1760–1820" (PhD diss., Auburn University, 2009); Nathaniel Sheidley, "Hunting and the Politics of Masculinity in Cherokee Treaty-Making, 1763–75," in *Empire and Others: British Encounters with Indigenous Peoples, 1600–1850*, ed. Martin Daunton and Rick Halpern (New York: Routledge, 1999), 167–85; Sheidley, "Unruly Men: Indians, Settlers, and the Ethos of Frontier Patriarchy in the Upper Tennessee Watershed, 1763–1815" (PhD diss., Princeton University, 1999). For works including but not exclusively focusing on the Cherokee, see Tyler Boulware, "'We Are MEN': Native American and Euroamerican Projections of Masculinity during the Seven Years' War," in Foster, ed., *New Men*, 51–70, and Michelle LeMaster, *Brothers Born of One Mother: British–Native American Relations in the Colonial Southeast* (Charlottesville: University of Virginia Press, 2012).
7. Bryan C. Rindfleisch, *Brothers of Coweta: Kinship, Empire, and Revolution in the Eighteenth-Century Muscogee World* (Columbia: University of South Carolina Press, 2021); Natalie R. Inman, *Brothers and Friends: Kinship in*

Early America (Athens: University of Georgia Press, 2017). Inman's study is cross-cultural, but her discussions about Cherokee networks include Dragging Canoe and others mentioned herein. Inman argued that kinship networks directed the political actions of members. Rather than just recognizing that kinship was an important component of Native politics, I interrogate how networks functioned through a gendered lens to highlight ways in which women influenced major political decisions, and how masculine ideals were constructed in response to the desires of clan women.

8. "Kana'ti and Selu: The Origin of Corn and Game," in *History, Myths, and Sacred Formulas of the Cherokees,* ed. James Mooney (Asheville, NC: Bright Mountain Books, 1992), 242–49; Fogelson, "On the 'Petticoat Government.'"
9. "Kana'ti and Selu," 242–49; Fogelson, "On the 'Petticoat Government.'"
10. For separate spheres historiography, see Linda K. Kerber, "Separate Spheres, Female Worlds, Woman's Place: The Rhetoric of Women's History," *Journal of American History* 75, no. 1 (June 1988): 9–39.
11. Sheidley, "Hunting and the Politics of Masculinity," 167–85. Jon W. Parmenter discussed the generational discord created by land sales in "Dragging Canoe (Tsi'yu-gunsi'ni)." Tom Hatley offered a different interpretation from the perspective of elders like Attakullakulla; see Hatley, *The Dividing Paths: Cherokees and South Carolinians Through the Revolution* (New York: Oxford University Press, 1993), 205–8. According to Hatley, Cherokees ceded lands to traders, including Alexander Cameron and Richard Pearis, who lived in Cherokee towns with their Cherokee wives. Cherokee headmen made such cessions to create a buffer zone between their towns and encroaching White settlers.
12. "The Deputy Superintendent Mr. Henry Stuart's Account of His Proceedings with the Cherokee Indians About Going Against the Whites," 25 August 1776, in *Colonial Records of North Carolina,* ed. William Saunders, 26 vols. (Raleigh, NC: P. M. Hale, 1890), 10:764, 777–79.
13. Tyler Boulware, *Deconstructing the Cherokee Nation: Town, Region, and Nation Among Eighteenth-Century Cherokees* (Gainesville: University of Florida Press, 2011), 161–62; John Boggs to William Blount, report, 23 September 1792, in *American State Papers: Indian Affairs,* 4:293.
14. Boulware, *Deconstructing the Cherokee Nation,* 162–63. Jon W. Parmenter claimed that Dragging Canoe and others relocated to the five Lower Towns in 1782 rather than 1779; see Parmenter, "Dragging Canoe (Tsi'yu-gunsi'ni)," 128–29.
15. "The Deputy Superintendent Mr. Henry Stuart's Account of His Proceedings," 10:764.
16. Parmenter, "Dragging Canoe (Tsi'yu-gunsi'ni)," 124–25.

17. Raymond D. Fogelson, "Cherokee Notions of Power," in *The Anthropology of Power: Ethnographic Studies from Asia, Oceania, and the New World*, ed. Raymond D. Fogelson and Richard N. Adams (New York: Academic Press, 1977), 193; Perdue, *Cherokee Women*, 54.
18. John Christian to Governor Blount, Knoxville, 5 October 1792, in *American State Papers: Indian Affairs*, 4:294; Boulware, *Deconstructing the Cherokee Nation*, 159–68; Parmenter, "Dragging Canoe (Tsi'yu-gunsi'ni)," 130; Fogelson, "On the 'Petticoat Government,'" 177–78.
19. "The Memorial of Bennett Ballew to the President of the United States," 22 August 1789, in *American State Papers: Indian Affairs*, 4:56. Toqua, located in present-day Monroe County in southeastern Tennessee, was ninety-six miles west of present-day Cherokee, North Carolina. Tassel's town affiliation is listed as Toqua next to his signature on the Treaty of Hopewell, signed in 1785.
20. Boulware, *Deconstructing the Cherokee Nation*, 165; Stanley Hoig, *The Cherokees and Their Chiefs: In the Wake of Empire* (Fayetteville: University of Arkansas Press, 1998), 71–72.
21. Wurteh's sons were Bob Benge (often called Bench) and The Tail; see John P. Brown, *Old Frontiers: The Story of the Cherokee Indians from Earliest Times to the Date of Their Removal to the West, 1838* (Kingsport, TN: Southern, 1938), 278, 353; Hoig, *The Cherokees and Their Chiefs*, 72, 79; and "Information by James Carey, One of the Interpreters of the United States in the Cherokee Nation, to Governor Blount," 20 March 1793, in *American State Papers: Indian Affairs*, 4:438.
22. Fred Gearing, "Priests and Warriors: Social Structures for Cherokee Politics in the 18th Century," *American Anthropologist* 64, no. 5 (October 1962): 21; Perdue, *Cherokee Women*, 52–53.
23. Nancy Badger to Colonel Return J. Meigs, 14 September 1805, Records of the Cherokee Indian Agency in Tennessee, 1801–1835, microfilm, M208, roll 3 (Washington, DC: National Archives and Records Administration, 1952). The Badger identified Black Fox as his nephew and their clan as "Paint"; see "Journal of the Grand Cherokee National Council," 29 June 1792, in *American State Papers: Indian Affairs*, 4:273. For other family connections, see Brown, *Old Frontiers*, 169, 270.
24. John Reid, deposition, n.d., in *The Papers of Thomas Jefferson*, vol. 2, *1777 to 18 June 1779*, ed. Julian P. Boyd (Princeton, NJ: Princeton University Press, 1950), 86.
25. "Talk of Tuskegetchee Delivered to Colonel Joseph Martin," 25 March 1787, Penelope Johnson Allen Collection, Tennessee State Archives, Nashville; Emmet Starr, *History of the Cherokee Indians and Their Legends and Folk Lore* (Oklahoma City, OK: Warden, 1922), 350, 468–69.

Missionary Models of Evangelical Manhood and Womanhood

ASHLEY E. MORESHEAD

IN 1812, after two decades of supporting British missions in India, American Protestants sent their first missionaries overseas to help spread Anglo-American evangelical beliefs and values. Soon, Americans had their own missionary heroes and martyrs to venerate alongside the British pioneers they celebrated in transatlantic evangelical print culture. Promoters of missions in the early nineteenth century published missionary writings and biographies to provide role models for American men and women, as well as to recruit volunteers and financial support for evangelistic enterprises abroad. Producers of missionary literature—mostly White evangelicals in the Northeast and mid-Atlantic states—tried to reconcile competing ideals of masculinity and femininity in their depictions of missionary life and character. Historians have shown how, despite the evangelical movement's relatively egalitarian roots, White evangelicals of the early republic largely adapted to the patriarchal culture around them and replicated conservative social norms in their church hierarchies.[1]

But the culture and economy of the early republic presented challenges to traditional values and prompted new debates about gender roles. Evangelical Protestant conceptions of manhood and womanhood changed in response to American nation-building efforts, the country's educational and economic opportunities, and the growing Protestant missionary enterprise. Consequently, missionary biographers promoted paradoxical and conflicting characteristics of manhood and womanhood in efforts to help the evangelical movement spread Anglo-American Protestant beliefs and practices.

Published accounts of missionaries' lives, usually titled "memoirs" because they quoted at length from their subjects' letters and journals, were published posthumously and edited heavily by ministers or missionaries who added information and commentary. The blending of biography and memoir became common within evangelical print culture, where the two genres served a similar function. Editors essentially operated as biographers who crafted models of Christian character for readers to emulate.[2]

Male missionary memoirs presented subjects who climbed from humble backgrounds to join a new cultural elite, showing how mission work offered a prime career option for young religious men exploring new opportunities amid the commercial and religious transformations of the early republic. In the eighteenth century, the clergy had been dominated by well-connected men whose families could afford to send them to Harvard or Yale. By the early nineteenth century, clergy ranks expanded to serve the growing nation. New provincial colleges and theological seminaries offered more affordable training, and charitable organizations supplemented incomes of men lacking family support. Such institutions transformed ministry from the purview of the genteel class into a profession any man could join. Some clergy embraced the competitive spirit of the era and advanced their careers by continually moving to larger and wealthier churches. Beginning with periodicals in the first decades of the nineteenth century, however, evangelical publications elevated missionary work—either overseas or in the West—as the most significant job a minister could undertake.[3] Missionary memoirs, then, provided examples of self-made men who reached the pinnacles of professional and spiritual success.

Missionary memoirs demonstrated one avenue for navigating tensions between individual ambition and public spirit that had emerged in the early years of the republic. In the eighteenth century, ambition was associated with selfish desires considered incompatible with communal and familial welfare. In the nineteenth century, national leaders cultivated more positive connotations for personal ambition as they tried to reconcile self-interest with republican ideals. As historian J. M. Opal argued, "The self and the nation rose or fell together." New academies and colleges aimed to broaden young people's awareness of the world beyond their hometowns. Liberal reformers and teachers encouraged emulation of peers and public figures with expectations that striving for excellence rewarded both the individual and the nation. But many Protestant leaders still associated youthful enterprise with pride and rebellion and feared the implications of ambition.[4] Promoters of foreign missions hoped to channel individual ambition toward their cause, presenting missionaries as models for young men seeking broader horizons.

An 1820 memoir told the story of Samuel Mills Jr., son of a rural Connecticut clergyman. Mills entered Williams College, one of New England's new provincial institutions for higher education, to prepare for the ministry in 1806. The editor of his memoir warned students against preparing only for the future if "it does not come within the scope of their plans to do good, but only to obtain it." Mills maintained his piety by finding a group of like-minded friends. They encouraged each other's ambitions, but instead of success in commerce or politics, they sought an intensification of the "missionary spirit." In 1810, they urged New England's Congregationalist church leaders to establish the American Board of Commissioners for Foreign Missions, the first organization in the United States devoted to sponsoring overseas missionaries. Mills never became a missionary but he helped to organize evangelical enterprises, including the American Bible Society. He died in 1818 after touring Sierra Leone, where he had hoped to establish a colony of Black Americans to spread Protestant Christianity. Evangelicals venerated him as a missionary martyr because of his achievements as well as his death in devotion to the cause of missions.[5]

Subsequent memoirs depicted relatively poor men pursuing higher education to join the ministry and missionize as a vocation. For example, William Crocker, a Baptist missionary to Africa, was a son of a shoemaker in Newburyport, Massachusetts. He worked several jobs and obtained financial support from the Northern Baptist Education Society before entering the Newton Theological Institution at age twenty-six.[6] Mission promoters used such memoirs to demonstrate that heroes of the mission field could rise from humble backgrounds to become members of a new cultural elite. The keystone was education. In the 1820s, local fundraising societies coalesced into the American Education Society, which supported young men such as Henry Lobdell, whose Connecticut father worked in manufacturing. The American Education Society supplemented his teaching salary while he worked his way through Amherst College and then trained to become a missionary physician. Samuel Munson, orphaned at age ten, taught school while receiving support from the American Education Society to attend Bowdoin College. Munson "did not complain, though compelled to make a thanksgiving dinner on bread and milk," as his memoirist explained, because his goal was worth "any measure of privation which would ensure ultimate success."[7]

Higher education not only prepared young men for ministry in a distant parish but also inspired them to look beyond the United States. The editor of George Dana Boardman's memoir described the transformation of Waterville Seminary in Maine into a college that equipped young men to serve rural New England and "whose religious influence should be felt on other continents." Boardman, one of the seminary's "first and ablest sons," went on to India, while another "of her most meek and godly pupils" evangelized in Africa. Such institutions proudly advertised graduates who left farms, villages, and even the United States because they channeled their ambitions into spreading evangelical Protestantism.[8]

Young men's ambitions sometimes included desires to learn more about the world. Levi Parsons's biographer claimed that few men were "more anxious to store their minds with useful knowledge" than Parsons, but he was not motivated by "a worldly ambition." Samuel Munson studied a variety of subjects to achieve "the highest possible usefulness as an ambassador of Christ to the heathen." His goal of becoming a missionary motivated him to explore "the sacred text" as well as "the field of physical science" according to his biographer: "It was his firm belief, that the minister and the missionary should be the last men to grow remiss in stated efforts to invigorate and enrich their minds." The editor of Pliny Fisk's memoir described him as an avid student of mathematics and philosophy who "became more and more deeply interested in this department of science, the farther he pursued it." At one point, Fisk turned his focus away from liberal education because "he feared the influence which intense application to the sciences might have on his piety." Fisk later decided it was a "mistaken notion that vigorous and persevering application to the sciences was necessarily unfavorable to the cultivation of the religious affections."[9] Ultimately, missions offered opportunities to advance both intellectual and spiritual ambitions. Memoirs showed readers that they could achieve individual success—even fame as a missionary—and simultaneously pursue the personal piety promoted by the evangelical movement.

Yet, by the 1830s, the nation's economic and physical boundaries had expanded, and many evangelicals believed the United States faced a crisis of masculinity. Urban reformers linked problems of crime, poverty, and vice to the perceived crisis. As they had since the late eighteenth century, women filled the ranks of voluntary associations and reform societies, and continued to outnumber men in church membership—a "feminization" of Protestant Christianity that increased concerns about the spiritual state of American men. Reformers urged young men to join reform societies and adopt visions of masculinity as compassionate, temperate, and disciplined. Some missionary memoirs in the 1840s and 1850s crafted a new image of evangelical manhood to appeal to a broader audience and compete with changing visions of successful manhood proliferating in American print culture. Missionaries embodied aspects of "restrained manhood" with its emphasis on family, temperance, work, morality, and discipline to which middle-class northern men typically aspired. Memoir writers and editors began to emphasize characteristics of "martial manhood" associated with White southern and working-class northern men—physical strength, aggression, and adventurousness—to show how such traits might fit into evangelical manhood.[10]

Increasingly, memoirs presented missionaries engaging in reckless and risky behaviors that occasionally hastened their deaths. Martyrdom had always been on the table for American missionaries overseas, and some reveled in the possibility.[11] In 1839, the first book to depict martyrdom through violence—in contrast to earlier stories that attributed missionaries' deaths to illness—appeared: a dual biography of Samuel Munson and Henry Lyman. Its author and editor, William Thompson, combined the memoir of each man with the story of their partnership and deaths at the hands of Native people in the East Indies.

Henry Lyman had been a troublemaker in college until he experienced conversion and developed an interest in overseas missions. "My duty, my happiness, my all depend upon my laying down my life among untutored savages," he declared. He studied theology diligently while preparing for the mission field by depriving himself of sleep and physical comforts. Thompson emphasized Lyman's eagerness for adventure: "Endowed with almost Herculean strength, and dauntless courage, united with glowing benevolence, he longed to enter the region of toil, of danger, and wretchedness."[12]

The American Board indulged Lyman's ambition by assigning him and Samuel Munson to investigate the potential for a mission in the East Indies. Munson and Lyman went first to the Dutch colony of Batavia, where they left their wives and children, before exploring neighboring islands. With the bravado typical of martial manhood, Lyman boasted that the expedition was far more daring than those undertaken by most missionaries: "To separate from one's family in the midst of a heathen country, and to plunge still further into the depths of heathenism, is quite another thing from leaving home to enter upon a foreign mission." Both Dutch and Indigenous leaders warned the Americans not to venture too far from colonial outposts, partly because the Dutch slave trade had worsened conflict on the islands. The two men ignored the advice, although they did agree to carry weapons. As Lyman, Munson, and a few assistants traveled inland, five armed men warned them to retreat. They refused to heed the warnings. Rather, they gave the scouts some tobacco and a message for their chief that the missionaries "came to visit them as friends and not as enemies." Soon, Native peoples ambushed and murdered Lyman, Munson, and one of their servants. The rest of their companions fled, taking word to Dutch colonial authorities of the Americans' fate.[13]

One Dutch official blamed Lyman and Munson for endangering themselves by refusing to "give ear to any one's warning or good counsel." Others, including a British missionary in Batavia, claimed they had taken only necessary risks. Thompson, editor of their memoir, insisted that Munson and Lyman had made a perfect missionary team: "Munson was placid, deliberate, and firm," and "Lyman was ardent, fearless and active," characteristics that together made an ideal missionary.[14]

Other missionaries exposed themselves to danger in different ways. In the 1840s, Walter Lowrie, brother of a Presbyterian missionary to India and son of an executive on the Presbyterian Board of Foreign Missions (established in 1837), sailed to China during the First Opium War. Between Macao and Singapore, he survived a shipwreck. In 1843, he and a colleague explored some of the cities opened to Westerners by the 1842 Treaty of Nanjing. They ventured upriver from the treaty port of Amoy (now Xiamen) to a city that remained off-limits, and a British official censured them. Lowrie remained in Macao for several years to study language and perform administrative tasks. In 1847, he sailed to Ningpo (now Ningbo) to meet with other missionaries. Pirates captured his ship, attacked its crew, plundered its cargo, and threw Lowrie overboard. The missionary who reported Lowrie's death claimed that the pirates did not steal his personal belongings or assault him as they did the sailors. When the pirates seized Lowrie, he was reading his pocket Bible, which had survived the earlier shipwreck. As they were "casting him into the sea, he turned himself partially around, and threw his Bible upon the deck." The scene intimated that Lowrie experienced divine protection even in death, and that he faced death with courage—evidence that he was a true martyr. The memoir featured letters from other colleagues highlighting Lowrie's reputation "as a faithful ambassador for Christ, in perils often." Lowrie never viewed the early death of a missionary as tragic but as a reminder that "God's children are employed in services infinitely more glorious ... in the sanctuary above, than any employments entrusted to them on earth." Lowrie's memoir thus justified his penchant for adventure and his eagerness to risk his life for the church.[15]

Another adventurer, Asahel Grant, died from disease like so many other missionaries, but only after he faced a multitude of other dangers. In 1835, the American Board sent him to Persia to work as a missionary physician among Assyrian Christians known as Nestorians. He opened a clinic in Oroomiah (now Urmia in western Iran), but he decided to explore the Nestorian villages in the mountains of Kurdistan, where Europeans seemingly had yet to venture. As he traversed the Ottoman Empire, he encountered snow, wind, rain, rivers, and political unrest. Grant's colleague at the mission, Thomas Laurie, editor of Grant's 1853 memoir, claimed that Grant's "spirit of reliance on God" undergirded decisions to take risks that others found "inexplicable" because "he was assured that the mountains formed a part of 'all the world' into which the disciples were to go and preach the gospel." Grant believed "that a readiness to face danger, and even death, is implied in the command to take up the cross, and fear not them who can kill the body." Laurie highlighted the dangers of Grant's travels by describing his strategies for avoiding attention: Grant carried only medicine, collected no minerals or plants, took no notes in public, and checked his compass discreetly. He spent several years working largely alone in a mountain village, making annual tours of the mountains, even as hostilities brewed among the Nestorians, Kurds, and Ottoman Turks. Grant anticipated war but trusted that "it is not by might or by power, but by the Spirit of God that the world is to be converted; and if missionaries, even by their death, only awaken more prayer for the Holy Spirit, they will not have toiled in vain." In 1844, he died in Mosul (on the edge of Kurdistan in modern-day Iraq) from a disease he had been fighting among Nestorian war refugees.[16]

Laurie occasionally reminded readers that Grant had a family. He fathered two sons with his first wife, who had died four years into their marriage, and he left their boys with relatives in the United States. His second wife, Judith Campbell Grant, was essentially chosen for him by the American Board—she had already applied and been accepted as a candidate for the mission field when she agreed to marry Grant. She gave birth to three children in Persia before dying in 1839. Grant left those children with other missionaries in Oroomiah while he made his first journey through the mountains. He returned in time to see his two daughters fall ill and die. He then took his youngest son to the United States before returning to the field and dying. For Grant, fatherhood was secondary to his work on the mission field.

Publications about Munson, Lyman, Lowrie, Grant, and others provided models of a heroic Christian manhood, increasingly considered necessary as evangelicalism drew more women than men into churches and missionary societies. Whereas early promoters of foreign missions engaged with the ideal of the self-made man and an expansive definition of ambition, by the 1840s and 1850s debates over the state of masculinity intensified. Missionaries' piety and temperate habits reinforced the values of religious reformers, but their pioneering impulses and adventurous travels situated them in more violent and escapist models of masculinity. Just as American literature filled with the myth of the frontiersman who opened the American continent to "civilization" by fighting wilderness and racialized Others, missionary memoirs presented courageous men exploring dangerous lands and encountering exotic Others. Missionaries became both evangelical saints and American heroes. In the words of one memoirist, they were the "heroes of modern history, who contend against fearful odds, win bloodless battles, plant the standard of the cross on distant shores, and annex the farthest East with the remotest West to the dominions of the Prince of Peace."[17]

CRAFTING MODELS of evangelical womanhood through missionary memoirs proved more difficult. Women's roles in foreign missions—and the evangelical movement generally—were controversial. They comprised a substantial portion of readers, contributors, and financial supporters for the evangelical press, and missionary societies depended on the support of female donors.[18] After three New England women left for India with the first American missionaries in 1812, foreign missions became an avenue for evangelical women's activism, and through missionary literature, some women became transatlantic celebrities. White evangelical women found opportunities in missions to use their educations, exercise spiritual authority, and become Protestant martyrs alongside men.[19] But stories of particularly accomplished women, such as the martyr Harriet Newell and the heroine Ann Judson, became contentious as evangelicals disagreed over the extent to which women should share in the spiritual and practical achievements of missions.[20]

A member of the American Board's first cohort, Harriet Atwood Newell died just months after reaching India with her husband in 1813. Andover Theological Seminary professor Leonard Woods edited her memoir for publication the following year. Although she had not lived long enough to work in the mission field, Woods argued that Newell's commitment exemplified self-sacrifice. While not a true missionary like her husband, her sacrifice was "more remarkable, because for her to forsake friends and country is an instance of greater self-denial," and "her mind is more delicate in its construction; more sensible to the tenderness of natural relations, and to the delights of domestic life." Woods compared Newell to the first Christian martyrs, claiming that God had favored her by "permitting her to be the first martyr to the Missionary cause from the American world." Woods demonstrated that women could be martyrs, even if they were not technically missionaries. The American Board and other evangelical Protestant organizations relegated women to specific roles as missionary wives, assistants, and evangelists to women and children. But Woods's interpretation of Harriet Newell's spiritual and physical journey inspired many to join and support foreign missions. New Englanders published poems in her honor, sold engravings of her, christened ships after her, and even named their daughters for her.[21]

As women followed Newell to the mission field, promoters of foreign missions used her legacy as a martyr to justify their early deaths. In 1833, Louisa Wilson married Presbyterian missionary John C. Lowrie, brother of Walter Lowrie, and she died just weeks after reaching India. The clergyman who edited her memoir claimed, "Like Harriet Newell . . . the same sainted missionary (whom in many respects she much resembled) it has been her lot to seal, by an early death, her testimony to the unspeakable importance of the enterprise for the conversion of the world." Elisha P. Swift, leader of a Presbyterian foreign missions society, wrote an introduction to Lowrie's memoir in which he argued that a woman's commitment to missions furthered the cause in three ways: by providing an illustration of the "practical influence of real piety," by aiding the spread of the gospel, and by exerting a direct influence on the unconverted. He asserted that Louisa Lowrie and Harriet Newell contributed to missions through two of these means, so their deaths were not in vain.²²

Promoters affirmed the significance of martyred women in part to deflect criticism of high mortality rates among White women in foreign climates. Given that women formed the majority of supporters for mission organizations, missionary publications celebrated women's martyrdom to energize their supporters—ultimately inspiring women readers to channel more ambition and spiritual authority than some evangelicals found comfortable.²³

Even more empowering was the example of Harriet Newell's friend Ann Hasseltine Judson, who spent almost fifteen years in foreign missions. In contrast to the martyr who experienced premature death, Judson was, in the words of historian Dana L. Robert, an "activist heroine." Her memoir, first published in 1829, became the most popular antebellum missionary memoir—either male or female. She assisted her husband, Adoniram, in his work in Burma (now Myanmar) as well as pursuing her own goals for the Baptist mission. Her memoir recounted efforts to cultivate connections with the wives of Burmese elites, conduct evangelistic meetings with other women, start a boarding school for Native children, and translate religious literature into Burmese and Thai languages. When authorities jailed Adoniram, suspecting him of spying for the British during the first Anglo-Burmese War, Ann bribed them for better conditions, brought him food and medicine, and concealed his translation work to prevent it from being destroyed. By the time she died in 1826, Ann Judson had become a transatlantic celebrity. She published letters from the mission field in evangelical periodicals, made a speaking tour of the United States and Great Britain (during a health-related furlough), and published a book about the first years of the Burmese mission in 1823. In editing her memoir, Baptist minister James D. Knowles highlighted Judson's work as a teacher and advocate for women's education. Many of the women who followed her to Asia expected to conduct their own ministries, separate from their husbands' work, mainly by administering schools for women and children.²⁴

Despite—or perhaps because of—Judson's legacy, missionary memoirs of the 1830s increasingly emphasized the domesticity of their subjects. Most women failed to achieve the ideal of evangelical motherhood due to competing commitments, health challenges, and cultural differences they faced on the mission field, but memoirs still emphasized that women's first duty was to husbands and children. In 1835, Miron Winslow, one of the American Board's first missionaries to Ceylon (now Sri Lanka), published a memoir of his late wife, Harriet Lathrop Winslow. Her letters described her domestic duties and the support she provided her husband. She assured friends in the United States that still "there is time to do much for the female sex," but her husband interjected that "the employment of a female missionary, if married, will centre very much in her family . . . that she may relieve her husband, and enable him with less interruption to pursue his appropriate work." Harriet Winslow had in fact administered schools for girls and prayer meetings for women, and her husband affirmed that wives were crucial contributors to the mission. But he worried about "the romance of missions" among readers back home. Ambitious and educated young women were applying to missions boards or seeking to marry missionaries so they could participate in the fame, adventure, and spiritual achievement they associated with foreign missions. Winslow argued that the duties of a missionary wife reduced, rather than expanded, opportunities for a young woman who might work as a teacher or reformer in the United States.[25]

Rufus Anderson, a formative leader of the American Board, defended sending White women overseas but emphasized their importance as wives rather than as martyrs or teachers. In an introduction to a memoir of Mary Ellis, wife of a British missionary in the Pacific, Anderson compared a missionary's wife to a minister's wife: both provided companionship, rendered practical assistance, and preserved their husbands from fleshly temptations. He argued that missionary wives should model Christian family life, exemplifying "domestic order, neatness, comfort, and whatever else sheds beauty and sweetness over domestic life" in places where "the wife is a degraded slave." Ellis did this with her husband in Tahiti, and then she traveled to Hawaii where she encouraged overworked American women to worry less about teaching or missionizing and focus strictly on household management and childrearing as forms of evangelism.[26]

Other memoirs also promoted the idea that missionary wives should focus on family life, both to model evangelical domesticity and to protect their children from unchristian influences. For example, H. G. O. Dwight, a widowed missionary to Constantinople (now Istanbul), argued that a missionary's wife might do some teaching and "exert an influence on the people around her, in whatever way the providence of God may direct" but should expect "that her principal, direct efforts will be made in her own household."²⁷ Still, women continued to push beyond domestic roles into other mission work, provoking varying responses.

Some editors justified women's mission work. Emily Chubbock Judson tried to finesse contradictions in the life of her subject, Sarah Hall Boardman Judson. Sarah initially joined the Baptist mission in Burma with her first husband, George Boardman. After he died, she spent several years preaching as an itinerant evangelist in the Burmese jungle. She later married Adoniram Judson following the death of his first, famous wife, Ann Hasseltine Judson. After Sarah died, Adoniram solicited Emily Chubbock, a published author under the name Fanny Forester, to compose Sarah's biography, and Emily later became Judson's third wife. Chubbock took pains to emphasize how "Mrs. Boardman had always been peculiarly domestic in her character and habits," finding satisfaction in "administering to her husband's happiness, or unfolding the budding intellects of her children." Sarah Boardman preached but in a way that was "meek, and sometimes tearful, speaking in low, gentle accents, and with a manner sweetly persuasive." Chubbock claimed that Boardman resembled the biblical female heroes Miriam and Anna, not "the wild-eyed priestess of Apollo." Sarah Boardman Judson was one of many Baptist women working in Burma, where male missionaries were relatively scarce and women translated, preached, and assumed roles typically reserved for men. Emily Chubbock Judson rendered Sarah Judson's work acceptable by depicting her preaching in a feminine manner.²⁸

Other evangelicals rejected the idea that women could do anything other than be wives and homemakers. In the 1850s, William Dean, a Baptist missionary in China, criticized martyrdom and mission work among women. In an introduction to Lucy Lyon Lord's 1854 memoir, he presented a list of American and European women who had served and died in Protestant missions in China. Rather than celebrate their martyrdom, Dean complained that at least twenty-four women had died prematurely in less than five decades, including his first and second wives. He did not blame foreign climates or diseases but women's ambitions to be missionaries as well as wives and mothers. Dean bemoaned how many women went abroad "to attempt what is called a missionary's work, instead of attending to the duties of a missionary's wife. Thus, attempting to do what they can not perform, they sacrifice health and life in the vain endeavor, and what is more, neglect the duties of their sacred calling and domestic relations." He blamed "public sentiment" for women who expected to work in a "high and romantic sphere," making them think that to "come down to the common duties of the wife, was lowering the dignity of their calling, and that these domestic services would not be called 'missionary work.'" The true calling of a missionary wife, Dean argued, was to support her husband and raise their children.[29]

In fact, William Dean's second wife, Theodosia Barker, had traveled to East Asia with the goal of teaching Chinese women, sponsored as a single British woman by the Society for the Promotion of Female Education in the East. She met Dean in China and sacrificed her sponsorship to marry him and join the American Baptist mission. Boston minister Pharcellus Church published her memoir following her death from smallpox. He praised her intellect and educational efforts, calling her an "active and zealous participant" of the mission and comparing her to the early Christian martyrs.[30] But Theodosia Barker Dean's widower lashed out at such ambitions and used the life and death of Lucy Lord, a niece of Mary Lyon, the founder of Mount Holyoke Female Seminary, to make his case. Lord spent several years teaching at Mount Holyoke before marrying a missionary and sailing for China in 1847. Her husband, William Lord, encouraged her to study the Chinese language and pursue her own "benevolent purposes." She worked on translation projects while suffering ill health and giving birth to two children, both of whom died as babies. She succumbed to illness herself in 1853.[31] William Dean hoped to discourage readers from emulating Lucy Lord and repeating her tragedies.

The published lives of women were always about more than just their accomplishments. When editors such as Miron Winslow and Emily Chubbock Judson emphasized women's domesticity, they adopted a strategy resembling that of female urban reformers who feigned prioritizing domestic roles to head off controversy over their public activism. Efforts to curb American women's enthusiasm for the "romance of missions" and emphasize traditional roles for missionary wives partly reflected concerns about women's ambitions in their churches at home. By the 1830s, a backlash arose against female believers who asserted spiritual authority and spoke or prayed publicly during revivals.[32] At the same time, missionary literature highlighted the importance of missionary wives, recognized the importance of maintaining female support, and encouraged women's contributions. The intertextual debate reflected how evangelicalism potentially empowered women, as well as how male leaders and missionaries differed in their responses—some trying to capitalize on it and others trying to control it.

Portrayals of unmarried women in missions reveal additional concerns about the meanings of Protestant womanhood. The first full-length memoir of an unmarried woman in foreign missions comparable to the popular memoirs of missionary wives was not published until 1868.[33] Although the subject of missionary marriage produced much debate in the early 1800s, very little was said about what role unmarried women might have in the mission field, despite single women expressing interest. As early as 1816, the Baptist Board of Foreign Missions for the United States published an application letter submitted by Charlotte H. White, a widow who described her conversion experience, baptism, and longstanding interest in "missionary endeavours." She requested permission to accompany a Mr. and Mrs. George Hough on their journey to reinforce the new American Baptist mission in Burma. White hoped to "reside in their family in the character of a sister to Mrs. Hough and a sister in the Lord," to support the missionaries and to manage a school or meet with Native women.[34]

The Baptist Board of Foreign Missions agreed to support White "as a member of Brother Hough's family," although they later reported that she had paid her own way and donated three hundred dollars to the mission fund.[35] In 1817, the Baptist Board announced her marriage to a British missionary in India. American and British missionaries celebrated her marriage as a "providential circumstance" that resulted in her taking over a large school and being "introduced into a sphere of respectability, usefulness, and comfort" as part of the British Baptist mission.[36] She never reached the American mission in Burma.

Many women tried to follow in Charlotte White's footsteps and join missions as single women, but most found that marrying a missionary offered the surest way to enter the foreign mission field. Privately, Adoniram Judson (founder of the Baptist mission in Burma) discouraged the Baptist Board of Foreign Missions from sending any more unmarried women. He expressed concerns about their safety and social status, and he feared that if unmarried women lived with married couples, the people of Burma might assume that the missionaries practiced polygamy even as they preached against it.[37]

The Congregationalist American Board also received applications from many single women but preferred to send only married couples abroad.

In 1836, when American Board leader Rufus Anderson published an essay supporting missionary wives—to assist missionaries, model American Christian family life, and teach Native women and children—he discouraged employing unmarried women because of "the difficulties in the way of placing the single female in circumstances to live and labor happily in pagan lands." He suggested another reason, though: that the "blessed enterprise of protestant missions must not be spoiled by introducing into it the monastic principles of the Romish church." Anderson believed that marriage was "the natural state of man" and helped to distinguish Protestantism from Catholicism with its celibate ministry.[38] Yet mission organizations ultimately had to accept the labor of single women if they wanted to accomplish their many goals.

As early as the 1820s, missionary societies sent single women to teach in schools at missions among Native Americans.[39] Sometimes women's names appeared in published reports, but not always. When the *Missionary Herald* published an overview of the American Board's missions in 1823, it listed seventy-one male missionaries, Native preachers, and assistant missionaries employed throughout Asia, the Pacific, and North America. Then it noted that "besides these, there are 54 female helpers, a few of whom are single women, but most are wives of the missionaries." When Congregationalist minister Joseph Tracy published a history of the American Board in 1840, he named many of the women who had accompanied missionary couples among the Cherokees, Choctaws, Osages, and Senecas, although he said little about their actual labors. When two new women—Lucy Ames and Delight Sargeant—joined the Cherokee mission in 1828, Tracy explained that their contracts were for a limited time because the board believed that "such temporary engagements were better, when practicable, in the case of assistants, than engagements for life." The desire to classify single women as temporary assistant missionaries reflected cultural assumptions that women who worked as teachers did so as precedent to, rather than a replacement for, marriage. Some women, such as Charlotte White, did marry missionaries after reaching the field. By the 1840s, such framing rendered teaching an acceptable role for Protestant women, contrasting them to Catholic nuns who taught in convent schools and were viewed with suspicion by many Protestants.[40]

Before 1840, the idea that unmarried women could serve as teachers, if only temporarily, became sufficient justification for sending them overseas, even as reformers worked to feminize the teaching profession in the United States.[41] The first woman to serve officially as an overseas assistant missionary for the American Board was Cynthia Farrar, a teacher who sailed for India with two missionary couples in 1827. She ultimately served the American Board's Bombay mission for thirty-four years. She received brief mentions in the *Missionary Herald,* usually when missionaries reported on the progress of schools for girls. By 1833, the Bombay mission boasted of twelve schools exclusively for girls, listing Farrar as "Superintendent of Female Schools." Several times over the years, published mission reports praised her "for the zeal and perseverance she has manifested in this difficult and discouraging department of missionary labor."[42]

Yet Farrar was not held up as a model of piety or self-sacrifice. When she died, the *Missionary Herald* published a brief obituary describing her as a "faithful and useful laborer" devoted to the "education of native females." When Myra Allen, one of the married women with whom Farrar had traveled to India, died after only a few years of mission work, a full-length memoir celebrated Allen's "religious character" and depicted her as an inspiration for young New Englanders. Like memoirs of other missionary wives, the Allen memoir quoted her letters and journals, which occasionally mentioned Farrar and the challenge of filling in for her when she fell ill.[43] Despite Farrar's position as a superintendent of up to twelve schools, as a single woman she remained in the background.

Baptist periodicals, in contrast, celebrated several single women for evangelizing in Burma. Eleanor Macomber initially worked in schools for Native Americans in Michigan Territory, but in 1836 she became the third single woman to join Baptist missions in Burma. Macomber ventured beyond the established missions to villages the missionaries had not yet reached. The *Baptist Missionary Magazine* published several letters in which she described proselytizing among men and women, young and old. She started a school, trained Native teachers, and supervised several Burmese "assistants" who preached throughout neighboring villages. Macomber described one man as "my principal preacher" who "certainly does admirably," but she asserted that "I find it necessary to see him, look over every subject, and give him all the ideas I wish to have advanced." She reported numerous baptisms, all performed by male missionaries, but she and her non-White male assistants were responsible for the actual conversions.[44]

After Macomber's death from illness in 1840, the *Baptist Missionary Magazine* published several tributes from missionaries who credited her with building a "little flock" of "Christian disciples." She was the only unmarried woman whom Baptist clergy Daniel Eddy included in his *Heroines of the Missionary Enterprise,* dedicated to women who died prematurely in the mission field. Eddy praised Macomber's piety while facing "a thousand perplexities" and "a thousand cares" as a "weak, defenceless woman" without a husband "for support and protection." In 1856, a Virginia Baptist magazine published a three-page memorial emphasizing how Macomber, despite her "womanly weakness," demonstrated "strength, irresistible energy in that calm determination which burned in her heart."[45] While Baptist publications celebrated her efforts, Macomber was never the subject of a full-length memoir.

Similarly, Sarah Cummings received some publicity in Baptist literature. She joined the Baptists in Burma as a teacher in 1832 but moved into a jungle village to evangelize and start a new school. She died from illness in 1834. At least one of her letters was published in the *Baptist Missionary Magazine,* and other missionaries referenced her. After her death, one missionary described her as "truly a *godly* woman" who was "uniformly calm and patient, self-denying, and heavenly-minded."[46]

Baptists allowed women to travel and preach among men as well as women and children because they lacked enough men to staff the missions, and because men and women did not live segregated in Burma as they did in India. Baptists also had a stronger tradition of spiritual egalitarianism than New England Congregationalists and Presbyterians. That some Baptist publications celebrated women's missionary work contrasted with the approach of the American Board, which ultimately sent more single women overseas than the Baptists but did little to publicize their activities.[47]

The American Board's inclination to downplay the role of single women in its missions, and the fact that Baptist women's missionary work received little attention outside of denominational publications, reflect the broader purposes that many evangelicals hoped missionary literature would fulfill. Missionary memoirs provided models of piety and service for readers to emulate, and figures such as Harriet Newell and Ann Judson appealed to audiences across denominational lines. But the backlash to Newell's and Judson's legacies grew in the 1830s. Even as education reformers pushed for women to become teachers, and the American Board quietly sent unmarried women to teach in mission schools, many clergy worried about the spread of female evangelism during the Second Great Awakening and the potential for more radical activism. Many Americans expressed concern about the growth of Catholicism, particularly in New England, and the challenge that convents presented to Protestant gender roles and domestic ideals.[48]

The intertextual debate over women's roles in missions involved justifying early deaths of American women and giving future missionaries realistic expectations. It also reflected the need to motivate female supporters—and assuage the concerns of clergy whose flocks might feel empowered by the spiritual authority granted to women such as Harriet Newell and Ann Judson. Designing memoirs to have broad appeal became a growing challenge. Hence Emily Chubbock Judson, when memorializing Sarah Boardman Judson in the 1840s, emphasized the great hesitancy and "singular modesty" with which she had engaged in her late husband's evangelistic work until his male replacement was ready.[49]

Yet increasing cultural acceptance of teaching as a premarital career for women helped render such activism less threatening. Sarah Boardman's eventual marriage to the widowed Adoniram Judson meant that her stint as an unmarried female preacher was temporary, and Theodosia Barker's tenure as a teacher in China ended when she married William Dean, making their lives less controversial than those of Eleanor Macomber or even Cynthia Farrar. In 1860, a memoir titled *The Missionary Sisters* presented a dual biography of two women, Harriet Lovell Hamlin and Seraphina Haynes Everett, who were colleagues at the American Board's mission in Constantinople. Much of the book documented Hamlin's years as an unmarried teacher.[50] A publication devoting unprecedented space to the character and career of an unmarried woman evidenced the respectability their contributions had gained by 1860. Because Hamlin eventually married a widowed missionary and stopped teaching to raise his children, her story still reinforced the ideal of teaching as a temporary phase for women.

ADAPTING EVANGELICALISM to mainstream American culture was an ongoing and contested process throughout the early republic. Memoirs of both male and female missionaries gave evangelicals a way to address concerns about gender in American culture while promoting the global spread of Protestant Christianity. Their engagement with cultural debates regarding gender also helps to explain why foreign missions became a popular cause among young Americans. Foreign missions, with their potential for fame, adventure, and martyrdom, sanctified individual ambitions and justified pushing the boundaries of respectable manhood and submissive womanhood. The "romance of missions" continually drew more support from women than men as the feminization of Protestant Christianity progressed throughout the nineteenth century.[51] The publicity surrounding women's achievements as martyrs, teachers, and evangelists challenged mainstream patriarchal ideals, and the backlash it provoked demonstrated the heterogeneity of evangelical views regarding women's spiritual authority. Protestant efforts to exploit the ambitions of educated young Americans successfully expanded the foreign missions movement but simultaneously exacerbated divisions and accelerated cultural trends that many evangelicals had hoped to control.

Questions to Consider

1. To what extent does missionary literature illustrate gaps between ideals of manhood and womanhood and the realities of gender roles?
2. How did men and women use evangelical beliefs and goals to broaden their own definitions of manhood and womanhood?

Notes

1. Christine Leigh Heyrman, *Southern Cross: The Beginnings of the Bible Belt* (New York: Knopf, 1997); Susan Juster, *Disorderly Women: Sexual Politics and Evangelicalism in Revolutionary New England* (Ithaca, NY: Cornell University Press, 1994); Janet Moore Lindman, *Bodies of Belief: Baptist Community in Early America* (Philadelphia: University of Pennsylvania Press, 2008).
2. Candy Gunther Brown, *The Word in the World: Evangelical Writing, Publishing, and Reading in America, 1789–1880* (Chapel Hill: University of North Carolina Press, 2004), 88.
3. Joyce Appleby, *Inheriting the Revolution: The First Generation of Americans* (Cambridge, MA: Harvard University Press, 2000), 117–21; E. Anthony Rotundo, *American Manhood: Transformations in Masculinity from the Revolution to the Modern Era* (New York: Basic Books, 1993), 19; Donald M.

Scott, *From Office to Profession: The New England Ministry, 1750–1850* (Philadelphia: University of Pennsylvania Press, 1978), 54–73.

4. J. M. Opal, *Beyond the Farm: National Ambitions in Rural New England* (Philadelphia: University of Pennsylvania Press, 2008), 75–76, 97–110 (quote on 75).

5. Gardiner Spring, *Memoirs of the Rev. Samuel J. Mills, Late Missionary to the South Western Section of the United States, and Agent of the American Colonization Society, Deputed to Explore the Coast of Africa* (London: Francis Westley, 1820), 20, 26, 29; Christine Leigh Heyrman, *American Apostles: When Evangelicals Entered the World of Islam* (New York: Hill and Wang, 2015), 20–22, 41–42; Opal, *Beyond the Farm*, 130; David W. Kling, "The New Divinity and the Origins of the American Board of Commissioners for Foreign Missions," in *North American Foreign Missions, 1810–1914: Theology, Theory, and Policy*, ed. Wilbert R. Shenk (Grand Rapids, MI: Eerdmans, 2004), 33.

6. R. B. Medbery, *Memoir of William G. Crocker, Late Missionary in West Africa Among the Bassas*, 2nd ed. (1848; Boston: Gould and Lincoln, 1860). Congregationalist examples of similar stories include Horatio Bardwell, *Memoir of Rev. Gordon Hall, A.M., One of the First Missionaries of the Amer. Board of Comm. for Foreign Missions, at Bombay* (New York: Dayton and Saxton, 1841), and Alvan Bond, *Memoir of the Rev. Pliny Fisk, A. M., Late Missionary to Palestine* (Boston: Crocker and Brewster, 1828).

7. Scott, *From Office to Profession*, 55; W. S. Tyler, *Memoir of Rev. Henry Lobdell, D. D., Late Missionary of the American Board at Mosul* (Boston: American Tract Society, 1859); William Thompson, *Memoirs of the Rev. Samuel Munson, and the Rev. Henry Lyman, Late Missionaries to the Indian Archipelago, with the Journal of Their Exploring Tour* (New York: Appleton, 1839), 18.

8. Alonzo King, *Memoir of George Dana Boardman, Late Missionary to Burmah* (Boston: Gould, Kendall, and Lincoln, 1835), 28.

9. Daniel O. Morton, *Memoir of Rev. Levi Parsons, Late Missionary to Palestine* (Poultney, VT: Smith and Shute, 1824), 43; Thompson, *Memoirs of the Rev. Samuel Munson, and the Rev. Henry Lyman*, 25; Bond, *Memoir of the Rev. Pliny Fisk*, 21–22.

10. Bruce Dorsey, *Reforming Men and Women: Gender in the Antebellum City* (Ithaca, NY: Cornell University Press, 2002), 104–8; Heyrman, *American Apostles*, 200–203, 226–31; Scott E. Casper, *Constructing American Lives: Biography and Culture in Nineteenth-Century America* (Chapel Hill: University of North Carolina Press, 1999), 81; Amy S. Greenberg, *Manifest*

Manhood and the Antebellum American Empire (New York: Cambridge University Press, 2005), 11–13.
11. On the embrace of martyrdom, see Heyrman, *American Apostles,* 214–16.
12. Thompson, *Memoirs of the Rev. Samuel Munson, and the Rev. Henry Lyman,* 38, 52–53, 61.
13. Thompson, *Memoirs of the Rev. Samuel Munson, and the Rev. Henry Lyman,* 88, 116–17, 182.
14. Thompson, *Memoirs of the Rev. Samuel Munson, and the Rev. Henry Lyman,* 183, 188–92, 194.
15. Walter Lowrie, *Memoirs of the Rev. Walter M. Lowrie, Missionary to China* (Philadelphia: Presbyterian Board of Publication, 1854), 98, 165, 380–82, 391, 385.
16. Thomas Laurie, *Dr. Grant and the Mountain Nestorians,* 2nd ed. (1853; Edinburgh: Johnstone and Hunter, 1855), 89, 93, 114, 116, 266–67.
17. Michael Kimmel, *Manhood in America: A Cultural History,* 2nd ed. (1996; New York: Oxford University Press, 2006); Richard Slotkin, *The Fatal Environment: The Myth of the Frontier in the Age of Industrialization, 1800–1890* (New York: Atheneum, 1985); Slotkin, *Regeneration through Violence: The Mythology of the American Frontier, 1600–1860* (Middletown, CT: Wesleyan University Press, 1973); Tyler, *Memoir of Rev. Henry Lobdell,* 11.
18. Mary Kupiec Cayton, "Canonizing Harriet Newell: Women, the Evangelical Press, and the Foreign Mission Movement in New England, 1800–1840," in *Competing Kingdoms: Women, Mission, Nation, and the American Protestant Empire, 1812–1960,* ed. Barbara Reeves-Ellington, Kathryn Kish Sklar, and Connie A. Shemo (Durham, NC: Duke University Press, 2010), 70–74, 76–79.
19. Christine Leigh Heyrman, *Doomed Romance: Broken Hearts, Lost Souls, and Sexual Tumult in Nineteenth-Century America* (New York: Knopf, 2021), 16. On limited opportunities for Black women in foreign missions, see Alice T. Ott, "The 'Peculiar Case' of Betsey Stockton: Gender, Race and the Role of an Assistant Missionary to the Sandwich Islands (1822–1825)," *Studies in World Christianity* 21, no. 1 (2015): 4–19, and Gregory Nobles, *The Education of Betsey Stockton: An Odyssey of Slavery and Freedom* (Chicago: University of Chicago Press, 2022).
20. Emily Conroy-Krutz, "The Forgotten Wife: Roxana Knott and Missionary Marriage in Bombay," *Early American Studies* 16, no. 1 (Winter 2018): 64–90; Heyrman, *Doomed Romance;* Dana L. Robert, "Evangelist or Homemaker? Mission Strategies of Early Nineteenth-Century Missionary Wives in Burma and Hawaii," in Shenk, ed., *North American Foreign Missions,* 116–32.

21. Leonard Woods, *Memoirs of Mrs. Harriet Newell, Wife of the Rev. S. Newell, American Missionary to India. Also, a Sermon on Occasion of Her Death*, rev. ed. (1814; London: John Mason, 1833), 215, 217, 229; Clare Midgley, *Feminism and Empire: Women Activists in Imperial Britain, 1790–1865* (New York: Routledge, 2007), 100; Dana L. Robert, *American Women in Mission: A Social History of Their Thought and Practice* (Macon, GA: Mercer University Press, 1997), 32–36; Cayton, "Canonizing Harriet Newell," 85–87; Heyrman, *American Apostles*, 30–31, 78, 230; Robert, *American Women in Mission*, 42, 50.
22. Ashbel G. Fairchild, *Memoir of Mrs. Louisa A. Lowrie, of the Northern India Mission*, 2nd ed. (1836; Philadelphia: William S. Martien, 1837), 219, viii, x.
23. Cayton, "Canonizing Harriet Newell," 85; Heyrman; *Doomed Romance*.
24. Robert, *American Women in Mission*, 48, 83; Joan Jacobs Brumberg, *Mission for Life: The Story of the Family of Adoniram Judson, the Dramatic Events of the First American Foreign Mission, and the Course of Evangelical Religion in the Nineteenth Century* (New York: Free Press, 1980), 13–19; James D. Knowles, *Memoir of Ann H. Judson, Late Missionary to Burmah; Including a History of the American Baptist Mission in the Burman Empire*, rev. ed. (1829; Boston: Gould, Kendall, and Lincoln, 1845), 72.
25. Cassandra N. Berman, "Motherhood on a Mission: Missionaries, 'Heathens,' and the Maternal Ideal in the Early American Republic," *Early American Studies* 17, no. 4 (Fall 2019): 474–97; Miron Winslow, *Memoir of Mrs. Harriet L. Winslow, Thirteen Years a Member of the American Mission in Ceylon*, rev. ed. (1835; New York: American Tract Society, 1840), 67–69, 274, 382–84. On the appeal of missions to educated young women, see Heyrman, *Doomed Romance*; Ashley E. Moreshead, "'Beyond All Ambitious Motives': Missionary Memoirs and the Cultivation of Early American Evangelical Heroines," *Journal of the Early Republic* 38, no. 1 (Spring 2018): 37–60; and Robert, *American Women in Mission*, 10–23.
26. Rufus Anderson, "Introductory Essay," in William Ellis, *Memoir of Mrs. Mary Mercy Ellis, Wife of Rev. William Ellis, Missionary in the South Seas, and Foreign Secretary of the London Missionary Society* (Boston: Crocker and Brewster, 1836), x–xi; Robert, "Evangelist or Homemaker?" 128–29.
27. H. G. O. Dwight, *Memoir of Mrs. Elizabeth B. Dwight, Including an Account of the Plague of 1837. With a Sketch of the Life of Mrs. Judith S. Grant, Missionary to Persia* (New York: M. W. Dodd, 1840), 157.
28. Fanny Forester, *Memoir of Sarah B. Judson, Member of the American Mission to Burmah* (New York: L. Colby, 1848), 167–71; Robert, *American Women in Mission*, 51–56.

29. William Dean, "Introduction," in Edward Lord, *Memoir of Lucy T. Lord, of the Chinese Baptist Mission. With an Introduction by William Dean, D. D.* (Philadelphia: American Baptist Publication Society, 1854), 5, 8–11.
30. Pharcellus Church, *Notices of the Life of Theodosia Ann Barker Dean, Wife of Rev. William Dean, Missionary to China* (Boston: New England Sabbath School Depository, 1851), 250.
31. Lord, *Memoir of Lucy T. Lord,* 172, 236.
32. Robert, "Evangelist or Homemaker?" 117; Anne M. Boylan, *The Origins of Women's Activism: New York and Boston, 1797–1840* (Chapel Hill: University of North Carolina Press, 2002), 75–76. For clergy worried about female evangelism and preaching, see Catherine A. Brekus, *Strangers and Pilgrims: Female Preaching in America, 1740–1845* (Chapel Hill: University of North Carolina Press, 1998), 275–78.
33. D. T. Fiske, *Faith Working by Love: As Exemplified in the Life of Fidelia Fiske* (Boston: Congregational Sabbath School and Publishing Society, 1868).
34. *The Second Annual Report of the Baptist Board of Foreign Missions for the United States* (Philadelphia: Anderson and Meehan, 1816).
35. *Second Annual Report of the Baptist Board of Foreign Missions.*
36. *Third Annual Report of the Baptist Board of Foreign Missions,* quoted in *Christian Herald* 3, no. 16 (July 1817): 241–46.
37. Adoniram Judson to Lucius Bolles, 9 November 1916, quoted in R. Pierce Beaver, *All Loves Excelling: American Protestant Women in World Mission* (Eugene, OR: Wipf and Stock, 1968), 66–67. Dana L. Robert found that many women "consented to, in effect, arranged marriages" to become missionaries; see Robert, *American Women in Mission,* 23.
38. Emily Conroy-Krutz, "'The Greatest Blessing or the Greatest Hindrance': British and American Perspectives on Missionary Marriage," paper presented at the Nineteenth Annual Conference of the Omohundro Institute of Early American History and Culture, Baltimore, MD, June 2013; Anderson, "Introductory Essay," viii–ix, xii.
39. Beaver, *All Loves Excelling,* 60; Robert, *American Women in Mission,* 108.
40. "Survey of Missionary Stations," *Missionary Herald* 19, no. 1 (January 1823): 4; Joseph Tracy, *History of the American Board of Commissioners for Foreign Missions* (Worcester, MA: Spoon and Howland, 1840), 180; Beaver, *All Loves Excelling,* 60, 81–82; Cassandra L. Yacovazzi, *Escaped Nuns: True Womanhood and the Campaign Against Convents in Antebellum America* (New York: Oxford University Press, 2018), chap. 4.
41. Jo Anne Preston demonstrated that teaching was not truly "feminized" in New England until the 1860s; see Preston, "Domestic Ideology, School Reformers, and Female Teachers: Schoolteaching Becomes Women's Work

in Nineteenth-Century New England," *New England Quarterly* 66, no. 4 (December 1993): 531–51.
42. "Embarkation of Missionaries Destined for Bombay," *Missionary Herald* 23, no. 7 (July 1827): 29–30; "Bombay Mission," *Missionary Herald* 29, no. 12 (December 1833): 444–45; "Report of the Ahmednuggur Station for 1849," *Missionary Herald* 46, no. 8 (August 1850): 271; "Report of the Ahmednuggur Station for 1850," *Missionary Herald* 47, no. 8 (August 1851): 269. See also "Ahmednuggur Annual Report," *Missionary Herald* 50, no. 7 (July 1854): 214, and "Labors Among Women at Ahmednuggur," *Missionary Herald* 66, no. 2 (February 1870): 61.
43. "Deaths," *Missionary Herald* 58, no. 4 (April 1862): 133; Cyrus Mann, *Memoir of Mrs. Myra W. Allen,* 2nd ed. (1832; Boston: Massachusetts Sabbath School Society, 1834), vi, 196.
44. Beaver, *All Loves Excelling,* 72; "Extracts from a Letter of Miss Macomber," *Baptist Missionary Magazine* 18, no. 2 (February 1838): 36–37; "Letter of Miss Macomber," *Baptist Missionary Magazine* 18, no. 10 (October 1838): 256. See also "Extract from a Letter of Miss Macomber, Dated Maulmain, July 30, 1838," *Baptist Missionary Magazine* 19, no. 3 (March 1839): 62–63.
45. "Extract from a Letter of Mr. Mason, Tribute to the Memory of Miss Eleanor Macomber," *Baptist Missionary Magazine* 23, no. 11 (November 1843): 285; "Obituary Notices of Miss Eleanor Macomber," *Baptist Missionary Magazine* 21, no. 2 (February 1841): 34; Robert, *American Women in Mission,* 49; Daniel C. Eddy, *Heroines of the Missionary Enterprise; or, Sketches of Prominent Female Missionaries* (Boston: Ticknor, Reed, and Fields, 1850), 142–53; "Miss Eleanor Macomber," *American Baptist Memorial, a Statistical, Biographical, and Historical Magazine* 15 (1856): 7, 10, American Baptist Historical Society, Atlanta, GA.
46. Moung Shway Goon, *Mission to Burma: A Memoir of Miss Sarah Cummings; Together with Some Related Matters Set in Order by Ephraim Chamberlain Cummings* (Privately printed, 1892), P.B. 122, no. 28, American Baptist Historical Society; "Death of Miss Cummings. Mr. Brown to Messrs. Kincaid and Cutter (1834)," *American Baptist Magazine* 15, no. 5 (May 1835): 202.
47. Robert, *American Women in Mission,* 51–56; Lindman, *Bodies of Belief,* 7; Beaver, *All Loves Excelling,* 71.
48. Yacovazzi, *Escaped Nuns,* chap. 3; Stephanie Kermes, *Creating an American Identity: New England, 1789–1825* (New York: Palgrave Macmillan, 2008), chap. 6.
49. Forester, *Memoir of Sarah B. Judson,* 167–71.
50. Mrs. M. G. Benjamin, *The Missionary Sisters: A Memorial of Mrs. Seraphina Haynes Everett, and Mrs. Harriet Martha Hamlin, Late Missionaries*

of the A. B. C. F. M. at Constantinople (Boston: American Tract Society, 1860).
51. Gail Bederman, *Manliness and Civilization: A Cultural History of Gender and Race in the United States, 1880–1917* (Chicago: University of Chicago Press, 1995); Patricia R. Hill, *The World Their Household: The American Woman's Foreign Mission Movement and Cultural Transformation, 1870–1920* (Ann Arbor: University of Michigan Press, 1985).

"First White Man Sets Hisself Inside That Rail Fence Gets It from the Gun"

FIREARMS, FATHERHOOD, AND SLAVERY IN THE SOUTH

Antwain K. Hunter

In 1849, fugitive-turned-abolitionist Frederick Douglass blasted enslavers' hypocrisy in promoting an idealized version of the family while simultaneously shattering Black ones, "sundering husbands and wives, parents and children, sisters and brothers,—leaving the hut vacant, and the hearth desolate."[1] The Black family—and Black fatherhood—were under constant threat from both slavery and the anti-Black sociopolitical culture that dominated the nineteenth-century United States. Enslaved people pragmatically developed family relationships to counter this assault on their families, and although Black men were not monolithic in their gender constructions, many of them strove to provide for and defend their families and communities. They rejected the limitations that White supremacy forced on Black fatherhood and manhood and charted their own courses.

Earlier historiographical trends asserted women's nearly solitary parental positions within slavery. As historian Jürgen Martschukat explained, enslaved men's "unfreedom meant subjugation under a sovereign power, severe constraints on their ability to fulfill the role as provider and protector of their families or to act autonomously." Libra R. Hilde, in contrast, demonstrated that enslaved families existed along a diverse and practical spectrum—"egalitarian, matriarchal, or patriarchal, depending on local conditions, the constituent members, and the personalities involved."[2] Like enslaved mothers, many fathers loved and took great interest in their partners and children, and they employed an array of coping mechanisms as they struggled against enslavers' and states' restrictions on their family lives, including by constructing alternative kinship and community dynamics. At times, they turned to firearms to aid their resistance. This essay shows how despite the heavy legal restrictions on Black people's firearm access, some enslaved men constructed their masculine identities partly via gun use, which helped them to defy outsiders and take care of their families. These constructions were salient during slavery's existence and in its afterlife, as racist structures and social conditions persisted into freedom.

Many Black men understood resistance as part of their responsibility to their families and broader communities. In 1829, Boston-based abolitionist David Walker passionately argued that Black men's defensive violence against slavery's oppression was a natural response to brutality and one that his readers should embrace. He asked his fellow Black men, "Do you suppose one man of good sense and learning would submit himself, his father, mother, wife and children, to be slaves to a wretched man like himself, who, instead of compensating him for his labours, chains, handcuffs and beats him and family almost to death, leaving life enough in them, however, to work for, and call him master? No! no! he would cut his devilish throat from ear to ear, and well do slave-holders know it."[3]

Walker's family-centered statement about Black masculinity was assertive, as it needed to be in the context of that anti-Black society. The very act of expressing a Black manhood rooted in defense of the family was radical but also difficult to maintain because, as Hilde explained, "the power and sexual dynamics of slavery put all slaves in an excruciating position. If they tried to protect one another, they risked physical punishment or sale, separating them from loved ones." Alternatively, if an enslaved person lacked the ability or will to act, they might be subjected to watching a family member being beaten, assaulted, stolen, or sold. Free people of color with enslaved relatives often found themselves in similar situations. Walker believed that men, at least those of "good sense and learning," resisted enslavers' brutalization of their families.[4] This masculine ideal resonated with some Black people despite how hard it could be for most of them to express, which highlights the noteworthiness of instances wherein they did violently defend their families.

Firearms were unique among the myriad tools of resistance that enslaved people deployed because of the heavy cultural weight with which White southern men imbued them. Guns' cultural symbolism was arguably more important than their practical use—historian Nicholas Proctor described the gun as the "decisive symbol of white masculinity" in the

South.⁵ Still, White southerners understood armed Black people differently than themselves. In an era of few general gun restrictions, legislators controlled enslaved people's gun use via law and expectation, to the end of allowing enslavers to arm their workers for labor. Ultimately, states would back away from this practice after Nat Turner's 1831 rebellion in Virginia.⁶ Essentially, White southerners believed armed Black people required supervision and regulation. Armed Black men who provided for or defended their families and communities claimed a particular masculine identity and challenged enslavement's constraints on their gender constructions and family lives.

During Reconstruction, many White people continued to scrutinize and target armed Black men as threats. Charlie Harvey related how the Ku Klux Klan in Union County, South Carolina, murdered Black militiamen and, in the process, illustrated the important symbolic aspects of their guns. Although the state ostensibly sanctioned the militiamen's firearm use, Klansmen rejected the Republican government and its auxiliaries. Even some moderate Republicans shied away from Black militias.⁷ The Union County Klansmen took the Black men out on a boat and drowned them. As Harvey described it, they took "the negroes' own guns, most of them had two guns, and tie the guns around their necks in the following manner: The barrel of one gun was tied with wire around the negro's neck, and the stock of the other gun was fastened with wire around the negro's neck." Harvey recounted that once the terrorists lashed a militiaman's guns to him, "over the side the negro went, with his guns and bullets taking him to a watery grave." For some time after, old gunstocks occasionally washed up on the riverbank and White supremacists picked them up "as mementoes."⁸

Of course, firearms' powerful symbolism did not negate their tactical importance. While an enslaved person might offer deadly resistance with knives, sticks, tools, farming implements, or even bare knuckles, a gun provided a clear advantage. In Ida B. Wells's scathing critique of America's lack of justice for lynching victims in the late nineteenth century, she pointed out a Black man often escaped threats only "when he had a gun and used it in self-defense." Although her advice was not specific to fathers—and Black women wielded arms as well—she framed such defense as masculine. Wells saw firearms as crucial for protecting Black families and famously argued that this defensive gun use demonstrated how "a Winchester rifle should have a place of honor in every black home, and it should be used for that protection which the law refuses to give. When the White man who is always the aggressor knows he runs as great risk of biting the dust every time his Afro-American victim does, he will have greater respect for Afro-American life." Long after the Thirteenth Amendment abolished slavery, with the glaring exception of "as a punishment for crime," Black people in the United States continued to face a range of challenges, as *de jure* and *de facto* White supremacy were often the law of the land.[9]

In American memory, armed White men became celebrated symbols of the national past, but with the limited exception of rebellion, armed enslaved people are seldom represented in popular depictions of the eighteenth and nineteenth centuries. Nonetheless, firearms, when accessible, were part of many Black men's quotidian experiences, shaping how some understood themselves as men and as fathers. For example, firearms provided the means to feed and defend families. Not every enslaved father took up arms or understood his manliness in this way. Men's identities were multidimensional and could shift to different masculine expressions at various life stages or in response to changing conditions. Individuals might embrace armed defense at various points in their lives but not others. In addition, many enslaved people had a difficult time acquiring firearms. In some areas, guns were so rare that some Black people saw them as wholly out of reach. When a Works Progress Administration (WPA) interviewer asked Cal Woods what he remembered of resistance while enslaved in South Carolina, he replied that he "never knowed bout no slave uprisings" and that "the black man couldn't shoot. He had no guns."[10]

While this perhaps reflected Woods's local situation, some enslaved people did have guns, though how many and under what circumstances is difficult to determine. Some stole weapons or purchased them through illegal channels. Others had far more permissive enslavers who allowed them access, albeit typically for very specific reasons. Some enslavers "would not know" and "did not care nuther" about enslaved men "huntin' game," even if they took their oppressors' firearms without permission to do so.[11] State legislatures and county courts were less lenient, looking to balance the dangers they believed armed Black people represented with the labor they could be forced to perform. Legislatures regulated Black people's access to and use of guns and set guidelines for enslavers, county courts adjudicated their violations, and individual enslavers made a range of decisions to maximize the potential but minimize the autonomy of armed bondsmen.[12]

Enslaved people performed a wide range of labor across the South and relied on different tools. Firearms were just one of these, but they were symbolically significant and made many tasks easier. Enslaved and free Black people labored with guns. Hunting provided some people with leisure, but enslavers also stood to benefit. Ned and Hannibal, two enslaved North Carolinians, used guns to guard their enslavers' store. An unnamed enslaved man in Virginia shot and killed a robber who broke into his enslaver's house. North Carolinian Charles Eaton used an enslaved man named David to kill wolves, for which the enslaver collected a bounty. Other enslavers armed bondsmen to protect their fields and livestock from vermin and hawks.[13] This armed labor was a small but significant part of enslavement.

Some Black men engaged in commerce or hired out their labor to provide for their families, but others needed to hunt, which could be done through a variety of means, including firearms. Alabamian Josh Horn proudly remembered how he used his hunting prowess to provide for his family without resorting to theft. He declared to a WPA interviewer: "I's telling you de troof, ef I was took 'fore God, I'd say jes' lak I's saying now, ef my chillun ever et a moufful dat wasn't honest, dey et it somewhar else, 'ca'se I ain't ever stole a moufful of somepin' t'eat for 'em in all my life." Of course, some enslaved men did steal food for their families and communities, and as historian Sergio A. Lussana illustrated, they "earned respect accordingly" and bonded with each other through the process. Nonetheless, Horn took pride in how he provided for his family, feeding his wife and sixteen children from the "varmints" he shot in the woods. Horn worked hard, and he noted that "soon's I found out dat I could help feed 'em dat way, I done a heap of hunting. And everybody knows I's a good hunter."[14]

Horn kept his incredibly large family well-fed, and his community knew it. He hunted throughout the week, but his wife, Alice, made sure he hunted for their Sunday dinner on Fridays. She was "a good Christian woman" and did not want their neighbors to see him sullying the Sabbath by "coming in Sunday morning" with his dogs and gun. He provided and was seen as a morally upright man too. By hunting, Horn avoided indebtedness and never owed anything to anyone, "not a nickel." His hunting saved money, which he could apply to other needs. For instance, he revealed that a doctor had always "come clear out here to see us" from about nine miles away "'ca'se I always pay him."¹⁵

Horn's hunting took place at least in part during freedom and might have been completely so, as he was at least fifteen when slavery ended. Many WPA *Slave Narratives* are chronologically unclear. During these interviews—conducted by the federal government in the 1930s, decades after emancipation—formerly enslaved people and their interviewers discussed events without consistently referencing *when* they transpired. Additionally, as historian Sharon Ann Musher explained, "the climate of race relations in the South, the rules of racial etiquette, and the financial constraints of an elderly poor population" impacted those interviews. Some interviewees were forthcoming, but others responded pragmatically or covered up larger truths. Much rested on their rapport with the interviewer, most of whom were White people. Zora Neale Hurston argued that some Black people were politely evasive in such situations. She explained, "We do not say to our questioner, 'Get out of here!' We smile and tell him or her something that satisfies the White person because, knowing so little about us, he doesn't know what he is missing."[16] Nonetheless, the WPA narratives are a treasure trove of Black people's self-described experiences during enslavement—many of the more forthcoming interviewees shared memories of significant people and events. They are ultimately the richest source for some questions, including what enslaved children thought of their fathers' gun use, or how enslaved fathers understood their own manly proficiency with firearms.

Horn's hunting spanned the gap between slavery and freedom, but other people explicitly defined hunting within the confines of the institution of slavery. Some enslavers provided rations that were insufficient in variety, quality, or quantity. Some formerly enslaved people remembered that "us had all us could eat," but others recalled being so hungry that they considered stealing food from dogs. When they supplemented their diets themselves, with or without enslavers' consent, those enslavers also benefited. Millie Ann Smith, a woman enslaved in East Texas, recounted her grandfather Josh Chiles regaling her with stories about hunting for his enslaver back when their county "was jus' a big woods." As a girl, she had listened to Chiles's stories about staying "in the woods all the time, killing deer and wild hawgs and turkeys and coons and the like for the white folks to eat." Chiles "made money sellin' wild turkey and hawgs to the poor white folks. He used to go huntin' at night or jus' when he could." Smith's grandfather might have supplied his community as well and likely continued in this work for years, as Smith noted that she was a "strappin' big girl" when he died.[17] By turning his hunting skills into cash, Chiles imbued his armed labor with a deeper meaning that resonated within his family for multiple generations.

Other formerly enslaved people recalled contributing to their communities via hunting. Charlie Davenport, who grew up near Natchez, Mississippi, explained that, in addition to enslaved people gardening, "mos' ever plantation kep' a man busy huntin' an' fishin' all de time. (If dey shot a big buck, us had deer meat roasted on a spit.)" Alex Woods remembered his own father, Major Woods, as such a man. He recalled how his father's enslaver in Orange County, North Carolina, "'lowed my father to hunt wid a gun. He wus a good hunter an' he brought a lot o' game to de plantation. Dey cooked it at de great house and divided it up. My father killed deer and turkey. All had plenty o' rabbits, possums, coons, an' squirrels." Major Woods's skill allowed him to assume what Proctor called the "patriarchal mantle of provider," affirming Woods's manhood, which his enslaver had undercut by selling away the Black hunter's first wife. (Alex's mother was Major's second wife.)[18]

Even though such firearm use came at enslavers' pleasure, subsistence hunting was masculinity-affirming for Black hunters and therefore subversive, because the outcome differed from what enslavers intended. Enslavers simply extracted a particular type of labor from armed bondsmen, and by having an enslaved person take wild game, saved themselves money. These instances when children and grandchildren fondly recounted fathers' and grandfathers' hunting reveal how they remembered enslaved hunters not as captive laborers but as Black *men* who provided for their families and communities.

Hunting empowered a certain type of manhood, one that enslavers sometimes tolerated because they could directly benefit from it. Some armed Black men took a different approach. They deployed a "heroic masculinity" to protect their family and community from enslavement's encroachment, despite the potential for White retaliation. The United States' slave system normalized brutality against Black people, regardless of sex or age, and enslaved people constantly resisted physical abuse and tried to protect others as well. In his *Appeal* of 1829, David Walker declared that White people have "made us so wretched, by subjecting us to slavery" and abusing our wives, parents, and "dear little children." He added that White people "know well, if we are *men*—and there is a secret monitor in their hearts which tells them we are—they know, I say, if we *are* men, and see them treating us in the manner they do, that there can be nothing in our hearts but death alone." Granny Cain, who grew up in Newberry County, South Carolina, remembered her father, Joseph Gilliam, resisting harassing slave patrols. Cain was enslaved on a different plantation in the neighborhood, but she recalled a story about how patrollers "come to my pa's house and want to come in, but pa had an old musket gun and tole them if dey come in dey wouldn't get out alive." Gilliam's boldness deterred the patrollers, and they left him alone.[19] Although he was not defending his daughter directly, his armed resistance stood out in her memory as a strong part of who he was—it was one of the few comments that she made about him in her short interview.

Biological fathers were not the only people who engaged in armed defensive posturing. In historian Brenda E. Stevenson's examination of enslaved families in Loudoun County, Virginia, she demonstrated that, while many families were matrifocal, the absence of husbands and fathers was not "inherently problematic, structurally or functionally" because there were often "other males available to take on some, if not all, of the socializing responsibilities, nurture, discipline, emotional commitment, and even protective stances that slave fathers ideally provided." Mattie Lee spoke with a WPA interviewer about her mother, Caroline Head, who was enslaved in Louisiana. Head "separated" from one partner twice and "married three times" altogether, but she remained part of a supportive community. While she was pregnant with one of her eight children and seemingly living without a partner, her overseer physically assaulted her. This brutal attack left her with lifelong health complications. Lee suggested that her mother's enslaver would have killed the overseer himself, but he was away at the time. A "colored man," probably enslaved, told the overseer that he would "kneck his brains out" with a hoe if he struck Head again. He was not the only community member to respond, however. Lee recounted that three men, likely also enslaved, "came up to kill de overseer with guns for beatin'" her mother. Their threat apparently drove the overseer away.[20]

Enslavers, overseers, and their anti-Black state apparatus were not the only threats facing enslaved southerners. Sarah Woods Burke remembered that during her childhood in western Virginia wild animals posed a constant problem, and that "after it got dark we children would have to stay indoors for fear of them." Her father and other men in the community guarded the children's safety. Burke recalled how her father sat on top of their house "with a old flint lock across his legs awaiting for one of them critters to come along close enough" for him to shoot them. He carried a weapon with the enslaver's permission because he had been raised by a poor White man whom their enslaver hired, which inculcated a sense of trust.[21] Burke remembered her father as a man who, though armed with an outdated firearm, protected her and other children in their community from danger.

These armed protective actions became easier for enslaved people to undertake when oversight by enslavers or the state was limited. Consider William Moore's recollections of his childhood growing up with his mother, Jane, on Tom Waller's plantation in Mexia, Texas. William's earliest memory involved sitting on Jane's lap as his father, Ray, told her that he had been hired out to work on a dam near Houston. Like many hired-out enslaved laborers who were sometimes purchased by employers or, free from their enslavers' surveillance, ran away, Ray never returned home. His circumstance was more tragic—he was killed when he fell out of a wagon that he was driving, and it rolled over him.[22]

Without his father's presence, Moore and his mother probably felt more exposed. He remembered their enslaver as a "fitty man for meanness" who "jus' 'bout had to beat somebody every day to satisfy his cravin." Tom once beat Jane with the toothed edge of a handsaw because he was dissatisfied with a meal she prepared, leaving her badly injured and scarred. Later, when Waller was giving her another severe whipping, William pleaded for mercy. Failing to sway Waller, William threw a rock at him, which struck him in the head and dropped him "like a poled ox." William and Jane escaped and laid out for nearly three months, returning only after Sam and Billie, two men Waller enslaved, told them that it was safe to do so. The Civil War had erupted, and the two men, whom Moore remembered as "the two biggest niggers on the place," told the fugitive mother and son that the nation was at war over slavery and that the enslaved people on the Waller plantation had "'clared to Marse Tom they ain't gwinebeno more beatin's." They invited Jane and William to return, promising that "they'd see Marse Tom didn't do nothing." This was not idle talk. Sam and Billie had, as Moore remembered, "done got the shotguns out the house some way or 'tother." Thus empowered, they planned to dictate the terms under which their community worked.[23]

In response, Tom Waller hired five White neighbors at three dollars apiece to help him whip Sam, Billie, and the other unmanageable enslaved individuals into submission. When Waller's reinforcements arrived, however, Sam and Billie were undaunted. They stood in the fenced-in front yard with their newly acquired shotguns, and Sam turned and told Waller that the "first white man sets hisself inside that rail fence gits it from the gun." The undoubtedly embarrassed enslaver heeded their threat. Despite the White men's enthusiasm to try and carry out their task, Waller convinced them to stay out of the yard. They left after he paid them.[24] Sam and Billie prepared to use violence against their enslaver—and any other White men to whom he turned—to protect their community, specifically a young widow and her child. Their heroic masculinity proved instrumental in shielding the community from an abusive enslaver and the oppressive system that enabled him.

Enslavers were not the only people who threatened Black families or their ability to chart their own courses. At times, non-slaveholding White people and even other Black people interfered. Historian Jeff Forret's work on violence within communities of enslaved people illustrates these dynamics. Black men had extremely limited recourse to courts of law, necessitating they solve conflict through other means, including gun violence. Sam, a man enslaved by a Dr. Ewing in Louisville, Kentucky, provides an example. His family life was complicated, as were those of many other enslaved people. Sam's wife and son were free people, and the boy was apprenticed to Lewis Williams, a free Black barber who "treated him cruelly." Frustrated and angry, Sam contacted his former enslaver, who, apparently thinking that the court would protect the child and respect Sam's paternal claims, advised him to take his son back and let Williams sue him. The plan failed miserably, however—Sam took his son home, but Williams called on a policeman who promptly "put the little boy in jail."[25]

At his wit's end, Sam tried to shoot Lewis Williams in front of his barbershop, but "from excitement, and little knowledge of the use of firearms, Sam's nerves were unsteady, and his ball missed the target." The police arrested Sam, but Ewing bailed him and his son out of jail, bonding him for two hundred dollars to assure the frustrated father's "peaceable behavior" for three months.[26] Although we cannot definitively know what price Sam was willing to pay to break his son's indenture, his decision to shoot Lewis Williams could have had much graver consequences. If Sam had been successful, his son might have been free from the mistreatment, but the state might very well have executed Sam. Further, Sam's poor marksmanship and unfamiliarity with the weapon, which he likely borrowed or had recently purchased, put bystanders on that Louisville street at great risk. In his desperation to save his son from an abusive employer, he saw the pistol as a viable solution.

Much like enslaved fathers, free Black fathers sometimes took up firearms to defend their families or create masculine identities. A few months after Nat Turner's bloody rebellion in 1831, Virginia's legislators constrained Black people's access to firearms, stripping justices of the peace of their ability to permit enslavers to arm enslaved people and barring the county courts from licensing free Black people to carry guns. The regulations essentially disarmed the state's Black population, and some free Black men responded by petitioning the legislature. Bedford County's Joseph Ruff wrote that he "humbly represents that he is one of that unfortunate class in Virginia, who neither possesses the common privileges of a free man, nor has the protection and security of a slave." He added that he was a "peaceable industrious citizen" whom the local court allowed to carry a gun before the law changed. Ruff also framed his father's armed service in the Revolutionary War as proof of his own fitness to carry arms. He explained that "his own character for honesty and quiet industry aided by the services of his Father in the war of the Revolution were sure guarantees" for these privileges, relating gun ownership to political rights and manliness. The assembly was unpersuaded, however, and rejected his appeal.[27]

Around 1824, Malachi Hagins, a mixed-race man in Jefferson County, Mississippi, successfully petitioned the state legislature for permission to "enjoy all the rights privileges and immunities of a free white person" under state law. He explained that both in Mississippi and in his previous home of South Carolina he had "so conducted himself as to acquire the good will and respect of the most respectable Citizens of the neighborhood in which he resides." He was a trustworthy member of the community. Like Ruff, Hagins pointed to his father's armed service in the Revolutionary War as added proof of his own fitness for inclusion in the body politic. Hagins's father "entered the service of the Revolted Colonies" and was killed in action along the Coosawhatchie River while serving under Colonel John Laurens's inept command. Hagins moved to Mississippi around the turn of the century where he purchased land, became an enslaver, and married a White woman with whom he had nine children.²⁸ His father's firearm use and sacrifice in the name of American independence helped him to blaze his own path to citizenship, and that of his children, though at the expense of other people of color.

Both Ruff and Hagins relied on their fathers' military service to claim masculine citizenship for themselves and their children, but some free Black men based their appeals on their own armed service. Samuel McCulloch Jr., another mixed-race man, fought in the Texas Revolution. He petitioned the Texas legislature in 1857 to get access to bounty lands and "the privileges of citizenship" that had previously been denied him because of his "unfortunate admixture of African blood." He told the lawmakers that his African ancestry came through a maternal ancestor "without any fault" of his own. He had settled in Texas when it was still a part of Mexico and had "by marriage become the head of a family." He petitioned the legislature to grant him "the quantum of land that is allowed to other persons who were citizens of the Country before the [Texan] declaration of Independence." McCulloch further requested that "he *and his children* may be allowed to enjoy the privileges of Citizenship in this Republic." He based his petition and this bold claim of citizenship for himself and his posterity on his meritorious service for Texas. Two of his comrades testified that McCulloch was the first man to enter the Mexican defenses during the Texans' assault on Goliad. He was also shot through the shoulder during the battle, which left him "permanently disabled" and provided a constant and public reminder of his military service.²⁹

From the Revolutionary War to the War for Texas Independence, military service buttressed armed Black men's claims to manliness. When the Civil War erupted, they found further opportunities to assert masculine and paternal prerogatives. In 1864, formerly enslaved Missourian Spotswood Rice used his position as a Union soldier to claim his daughter, Mary, which he understood to be his "God given rite." He chastised his daughter's enslaver, Kittey Diggs, on moral grounds, and he threatened her that "we are now makeing up a bout one thoughsand blacke troops to Come up tharough and wont to come through Glasgow and when we come wo be to Copperhood rabbels and to the Slaveholding rebbels." Rice boldly proclaimed, "My Children is my own and I expect to get them and when I get ready to come after mary I will have bout a powrer and authority to bring hear away and to exacute vengencens on them that holds my Child[.] you will then know how to talke to me[.] I will assure that and you will know how to talk rite too."³⁰ Rice's armed service provided a means to enforce his fatherhood claims, regardless of what Diggs believed. He might have argued solely on moral grounds, but as an enlisted man, he saw his service in the US Army, and that of his "one thoughsand blacke" compatriots, as a lever to pry his daughter from Diggs's hands. Mary greatly appreciated his efforts. In her mid-eighties, she still remembered him quite fondly. She explained that "I love army men, my father, brother, husband, and son were all army men. I love a man who will fight for his rights, and any person that wants to be something."[31]

Armed service became a powerful legacy that sustained some Black people's views of masculinity and fatherhood. J. F. Boone, born after the Civil War to formerly enslaved parents, gushed over his father's service as a Union soldier. His recorded comments to the WPA interviewer began with an adamant declaration: "My father's name was Arthur Boone. My mother's name was Eliza Boone. I am goin' to tell you about my father. Now, be sure you put down there that this is Arthur Boone's son." He recounted how his father fought in a "hard battle down in Mississippi" and returned home with his martial trappings. For years, J. F.'s oldest brother "kept that gun and them old blue uniforms with big brass buttons," and kept them "as particular as you would keep victuals." One can sense the pride that Arthur Boone's sons took in his service, evidenced by their attention to these heirlooms—his gun remained important to them. J. F. Boone also recalled his father's physical strength. He had been a "first-class rating as a good healthy Negro" and a "mighty fine man" who once sold for more than $1,000. The Boone brothers remembered their father as a warrior who fought his oppressors as equals on the battlefield. J. F. Boone ended his interview with the same fatherly pride that he started it: he asked his interviewer, "Now whose story are you saying this is? You say this is the story of Arthur Boone, father of J. F. Boone? Well, that's alright; but you better mention that J. F. Boone is Arthur Boone's son."[32]

In some regards, Black people's firearm use became more challenging in slavery's aftermath, as terrorists tried to disrupt the revolutionary advances that Black people theoretically gained through the Thirteenth, Fourteenth, and Fifteenth Amendments. Throughout the South, White supremacists sought to disarm Black people through both legislative and extralegal actions. In Mississippi, for example, during the latter months of 1865, state legislators moved to make gun ownership illegal among Black Mississippians, whom legislators alleged to be "well equipped with fire arms, muskets, double barrel shot guns & pistols." As legal scholar

Stephen P. Halbrook demonstrated, some White people intent on maintaining the antebellum status quo believed that Black Mississippians needed to "prove themselves to be good citizens in their altered state" before being permitted to carry arms. It was ultimately a flimsy justification to keep the Black population unarmed, which limited their ability to resist political terror or independently provide for themselves. When state legislatures did not act so aggressively, the Klan and other terrorists extralegally stripped Black people of their firearms to make it easier to intimidate, attack, or murder them.[33] On the postwar South's violent landscape, freedpeople's access to firearms sometimes made the difference between life and death.

White terrorists employed murders, political assassinations, rapes, arsons, and incessant surveillance to disrupt Black people's families and deny them their place in a free society. Black fathers rose to protect their households through numerous means, including defensively using firearms. Willis Johnson of Newberry County, South Carolina, testified before a US Congress joint select committee about a raid on his home by fifteen or twenty Ku Klux Klansmen. They came in the middle of the night while he, his wife, and their three children were in bed. The Klansmen broke down the cabin's front and back doors, and a pair rushed in through the front. Johnson was ready, however, revolver in hand. As the two Klansmen ran into his house, they were "within arm's length," and he put his pistol "right up to one's back, and shot." Johnson fired again as the other man dragged his badly wounded comrade out of the front door and into the yard. Johnson then charged the door and fired a third shot at the assembled Klansmen before turning and escaping through the house's back door. Such attacks evidenced historian Hannah Rosen's argument that Klansmen's "consistent pattern of attacking freedpeople in their homes, or dragging them from their homes" held "enormous symbolic significance." It upended the site of Black men's domestic authority and order, which they "widely represented as justifying their claim to citizenship and political power." Some White people used violence against Black households as a political weapon, and Black fathers answered in kind.[34]

Johnson was fortunate to escape the assault on his house, but such bold resistance proved impossible for many others. A "band of men" attacked the home of James Alston, a Black Alabamian and member of the state legislature, in the spring of 1870 for his Republican politics. With the house shuttered up in the middle of the night, Alston could not see if his assailants were dressed as Klansmen, but the group opened fire on his house and riddled it with bullets. At least 265 shots hit his exterior walls and another 60 passed through the windows, striking furniture and hitting the state representative in his back and hip, his wife in her foot, and one of their children.[35] During his testimony, Alston did not state whether he owned a gun, but even if he had, he was essentially powerless to protect his family against the overwhelming firepower that the attackers mustered.

Throughout the southern states, Black men's defensive violence against the Klan, or their inability to respond to it, understandably influenced how their children remembered their fathers. For the rest of their lives, Alston's children undoubtedly remembered the night that a "band of men" rained bullets into their home, injuring both of their parents and a sibling. Additionally, Henry Blake recalled the Klan coming through and harassing his community in Little Rock, Arkansas. His father, Doc Blake, had a horse that was too fast for the Klansmen, and "they never did catch him. They caught many another one and whipped him." The horse was a great asset, but Blake's father did more than simply evade these terrorists. "My daddy was a pretty mean man," Blake recalled, "he carried a gun and he had shot two or three men. Those were bad times. I got scared to go out with him. I hated that business. But directly it got over with. It got over with when a lot of the Ku Klux was killed up." Blake recounted how the Klansmen "kept up that business for about ten years after the war" until "folks began to kill up a lot of 'em." Blake's father was active in the fight. He explained that this violence was "the only thing that stopped them. My daddy used to make his own bullets." Blake remembered his father as "mean," but this partly stemmed from Doc Blake's defensive violence. Henry was unsettled by it but recognized that his father protected him. He recounted that "my father had nine children and took care of them."[36]

For a fuller understanding of Black southerners' experiences in enslavement and emancipation, we must, as Libra R. Hilde warned, "avoid normative, presentist definitions of household, family, and fatherhood." Despite nineteenth-century gendered expectations, free and enslaved Black women also relied on firearms to resist harsh treatment and terror, often in the same manner as their male counterparts. Mothers did not necessarily assume masculine identities, but they did use firearms to engage in behaviors that nineteenth-century Americans coded as masculine. Their decisions were pragmatic. Consequently, as Brenda Stevenson concluded, "neither 'fathering' nor 'mothering,' therefore were embodied in one person in a slave family."[37] Black women boldly and practically turned to armed defense to protect their households too.

Ellen Cragin remembered how Tom Polk, who enslaved her family in Mississippi, severely whipped her mother for failing to work at a pace that suited him. Although still young, Cragin was furious. She told her interviewer that she "went out one day and got a gun" in response. She explained, "I don't know whose gun it was. I said to myself, 'If you whip my mother today, I am goin' to shoot you.' I didn't know where the gun belonged. My oldest sister told me to take it and set it by the door, and I did it." Interpreting this event is challenging because of Cragin's succinct retelling, but she likely acquired the weapon because it had been left unattended, either by another enslaved person or a member of the Polk family. Antebellum newspapers listed numerous examples of people, even enslavers, carelessly storing their firearms. Cragin's older sister intervened and told her to put the weapon "by the door," likely indicating that it came from their enslaver's house. Returning it would prevent Cragin from bringing the full weight of either the law or plantation justice onto her young head.[38]

In Craven County, North Carolina, Harriet Jacobs's grandmother Molly Horniblow, who was known locally as a "woman of a high spirit," chased off a White man with a loaded pistol after he "insulted" one of Horniblow's daughters, probably by making unwanted sexual advances toward her. Laura Ramsey Parker remembered how she relied on her own defensive firearm use to protect her household from anti-Black violence during Reconstruction. She could not remember much about the Klan's activities in her neighborhood around Nashville, Tennessee, but one event stood out. She recollected "dat one nite dey passed our home en I grab'ed a shotgun en said dat I wuz gwine ter shoot dem if dey kum on de place." Parker was probably no older than her mid-twenties when she, like the youthful Cragin or the maternal Horniblow, picked up a firearm to protect herself and her family from outside threats.[39]

Firearms bolstered opportunities for Black people to resist oppression both during and after enslavement, but they could also be destructive. Mary Gladdy remembered that a "colored foreman" on Hines Holt's plantation in Muscogee County, Georgia, tried to whip her father, who successfully resisted first him and then the five "big buck Negroes" whom the foreman later enlisted to help. The embarrassed foreman turned to his shotgun to unequivocally reassert his authority, shooting Gladdy's father and "inflicting wounds from which he never fully recovered." This episode was not only a test of enslaved versus enslaver (as embodied in Holt's Black surrogates) but between men.[40] The armed threat against Black families was not only external. Some enslaved men turned their firearms against their own families, as Sam did in North Carolina in 1849. He tried to shoot both his wife and mother-in-law and wounded the latter. Afterward, Sam fatally shot himself. Domestic abuse was upsetting but sometimes firearms helped the victims resist. After emancipation, Ellen Cragin's husband slapped her for running late preparing dinner. She responded by grabbing her pistol and running him off.[41]

Enslavers, aided by their laws and customs, relentlessly undercut Black families as they pursued control and profits. As Frederick Douglass explained, "Slavery does away with fathers, as it does with families," because it had no use for either. He added, however, that "when they *do* exist, they are not the outgrowths of slavery, but are antagonistic to that system." Their very existence was resistance, and many enslaved fathers strived to fulfill their fatherly duties, illustrating how deeply they cared for their families. David Walker charged that any impartial observer could see that Black men "feel for our fathers, mothers, wives and children, as well as the whites do for theirs." Claims to the contrary were lies. By seizing their roles as fathers, these men pushed back against enslavement's pernicious reach. They were sometimes better able to do so when armed, and gun use challenged systems of power. Firearms were not merely the "talisman of white manhood" but tools that some enslaved people used to forge and maintain their positions as fathers and men. Thus equipped, they were better able to feed, defend, and care for their families, who recognized these labors of love. For a man like Arthur Boone, his gun was a significant part of what made him the kind of father whose children so proudly remembered him as "quite a young man in his day."[42]

Questions to Consider

1. What are the similarities and differences between the armed experiences of free and enslaved Black fathers in the antebellum era?
2. What do armed enslaved fathers teach us about the system of enslavement, relationships within enslaved families and communities, and the aftermath of enslavement during Reconstruction?

Notes

1. Frederick Douglass, *Narrative of the Life of Frederick Douglass, an American Slave* (Boston: Anti-Slavery Office, 1849), 119. The assault on Black families was backed by law. As abolitionist William Goodell wrote, an enslaved man was "unable to contract marriage . . . he can bring no action at law against the violator of his bed. Having no marital or parental rights, he has none for the Government to protect"; see Goodell, *The American Slave Code in Theory and Practice* (London, UK: Clarke, Beeton, 1853), 270.
2. Jürgen Martschukat, *American Fatherhood: A History*, trans. Petra Goedde (2013; New York: New York University Press, 2019), 51; Libra R. Hilde, *Slavery, Fatherhood, and Paternal Duty in African American Communities over the Long Nineteenth Century* (Chapel Hill: University of North Carolina Press, 2020), 11.
3. David Walker, *Walker's Appeal in Four Articles; Together with a Preamble, to the Coloured Citizens of the World* (Boston: David Walker, 1830), 37.
4. Hilde, *Slavery, Fatherhood, and Paternal Duty*, 50; Walker, *Walker's Appeal in Four Articles*, 37.
5. Nicholas Proctor, *Bathed in Blood: Hunting and Mastery in the Old South* (Charlottesville: University of Virginia Press, 2002), 44.
6. Antwain K. Hunter, "'A Nuisance Requiring Correction': Firearm Laws, Black Mobility, and White Property in Antebellum Eastern North Carolina," *North Carolina Historical Review* 93, no. 4 (October 2016): 388–89.
7. Charlie Harvey, interview, in *Slave Narratives: A Folk History of Slavery in the United States from Interviews with Former Slaves*, vol. 14, *South Carolina Narratives, Part 2* (Washington, DC: Works Progress Administration, 1941), 250–51, Library of Congress, Washington, DC; Eric Foner, *Reconstruction: America's Unfinished Revolution, 1863–1877* (New York: HarperCollins, 1988), 438–39.

8. Harvey, interview, 250–51. Harvey aligned with the Klan and helped several hundred of them break into a jail to kill eight Black militiamen—Sylvanus Wright, Andy Thomson, Ellison Scott, Bill Fincher, Aaron Thomson, Amos McKissick, Barrett Edwards, and Tom Byars—after they shot an illegal whiskey-dealing Confederate veteran when he fled; see Edmund L. Drago, *Hurrah for Hampton! Black Red Shirts in South Carolina During Reconstruction* (Fayetteville: University of Arkansas Press, 1998), 35; Bradley David Proctor, "Whip, Pistol, and Hood: Ku Klux Klan Violence in the Carolinas During Reconstruction" (PhD diss., University of North Carolina at Chapel Hill, 2013), 176–77, 259, 261, 262; *Yorkville Inquirer* (York, SC), 23 February 1871; and *Charleston [SC] Daily News*, 20 March 1872.
9. Ida B. Wells, *Southern Horrors and Other Writings: The Anti-Lynching Campaign of Ida B. Wells, 1892–1900*, ed. Jacqueline Jones Royster (Boston: Bedford/St. Martin's, 1997), 69–71; Amendment 13, section 1, US Constitution. During a 1972 interview with Swedish journalist Bo Holmström, political activist Angela Davis perfectly summed up how crucial armed defense was for Black families well into the twentieth century. She pushed back against his question of whether she approved of violence, exasperatedly declaring, "You ask me . . . you know . . . whether I approve of violence. I mean, that just doesn't make any sense at all. Whether I approve of guns. I grew up in Birmingham, Alabama. Some very, very good friends of mine were killed by bombs. Bombs that were planted by racists. . . . I remember from the time I was very small . . . I remember our father having to have guns at his disposal at all times, because of the fact that at any moment we might expect to be attacked." See Göran Hugo Olsson, dir., *The Black Power Mixtape, 1967–1975: A Documentary in 9 Chapters* (Stockholm: Sveriges Television, 2011).
10. Hilde, *Slavery, Fatherhood, and Paternal Duty*, 34; Cal Woods, interview, in *Slave Narratives*, vol. 2, *Arkansas Narratives, Part 7*, 231.
11. *State v. Pompey*, jury presentment, December Term 1816, "1816, Criminal Actions Concerning Slaves, 1767–1829," Chowan County Records, State Archives of North Carolina, Raleigh; *Massachusetts Spy* (Worcester), 24 February 1858; George Rogers, interview, in *Slave Narratives*, vol. 11, *North Carolina Narratives, Part 2*, 231 (quotes). On the illegal trade between enslaved and poor White people, see Jeff Forret, *Race Relations at the Margins: Slaves and Poor Whites in the Antebellum Countryside* (Baton Rouge: Louisiana State University Press, 2006).
12. For more on such legislative balancing acts, see Hunter, "'A Nuisance Requiring Correction,'" 386–404.
13. John F. Burgwin and Thomas F. Davis, bond, March 1805, "Permission for Slaves to Carry Guns," 1795–1841, New Hanover County Records, State

Archives of North Carolina; Alex Woods, interview, in *Slave Narratives*, vol. 11, *North Carolina Narratives, Part 2*, 418; *State v. Hannibal and Ned, Slaves*, in Hamilton C. Jones, *Reports of Cases at Law Argued and Determined in the Supreme Court of North Carolina: From December Term, 1853, to June Term, 1862, Both Inclusive*, 8 vols. (Raleigh, NC: S. Gales, 1854–62), 4:57–58; *Alexandria [VA] Gazette*, 25 May 1844; Charles Eaton, bounty, May 1771, "Bounties for Scalps of Wolves and Wild Cats," n.d., 1762–86 (broken series), Miscellaneous Records, 1722, 1747–1920, Granville County Records, State Archives of North Carolina; William Calvin, petition, n.d., "Records of Slaves and Free Persons of Color, Crime Act," 1788–1869, Misc.: C-S, 1825–87, Randolph County Records, State Archives of North Carolina.

14. Josh Horn, interview, in *Slave Narratives*, vol. 1, *Alabama*, 201–2; Sergio A. Lussana, *My Brother Slaves: Friendship, Masculinity, and Resistance in the Antebellum South* (Lexington: University Press of Kentucky, 2016), 97.
15. Horn, interview, 201–2.
16. Horn, interview, 205; Sharon Ann Musher, "The Other Slave Narratives: The Works Progress Administration Interviews," in *The Oxford Handbook of the African American Slave Narrative*, ed. John Ernest (New York: Oxford University Press, 2014), 101; Zora Neale Hurston, *I Love Myself When I Am Laughing . . . and Then Again When I Am Looking Mean and Impressive*, ed. Alice Walker (New York: Feminist Press, 1979), 83.
17. Henry Barnes, interview, in *Slave Narratives*, vol. 1, *Alabama*, 21; Alex and Elizabeth Smith, interview, in *Slave Narratives*, vol. 5, *Indiana Narratives*, 182–83; Millie Anne Smith, interview, in *Slave Narratives*, vol. 16, *Texas Narratives, Part 4*, 41, 43.
18. Charlie Davenport, interview, in *Slave Narratives*, vol. 9, *Mississippi Narratives*, 37–38; Alex Woods, interview, 418; Proctor, *Bathed in Blood*, 157.
19. Rebecca Fraser, "Negotiating Their Manhood: Masculinity Amongst the Enslaved in the Upper South, 1830–1861," in *Black and White Masculinity in the American South, 1800–2000*, ed. Lydia Plath and Sergio Lussana (Newcastle, UK: Cambridge Scholars, 2009), 76, 79; Walker, *Walker's Appeal in Four Articles*, 68–69; Granny Cain, interview, in *Slave Narratives*, vol. 14, *South Carolina Narratives, Part 1*, 166. Fraser challenged us to think about the breadth of masculinities that enslaved men took up and to not see violent resistance as the only legitimate masculine expression; see Fraser, "Negotiating Their Manhood," 78–80.
20. Brenda E. Stevenson, *Life in Black and White: Family and Community in the Slave South* (New York: Oxford University Press, 1996), 222; Mattie Lee, interview, in *Slave Narratives*, vol. 10, *Missouri Narratives*, 224.

21. Sarah Woods Burke, interview, in *Slave Narratives*, vol. 12, *Ohio Narratives*, 16–17.
22. William Moore, interview, in *Slave Narratives*, vol. 16, *Texas Narratives, Part 3*, 134.
23. Moore, interview, 134–35.
24. Moore, interview, 134–36.
25. Jeff Forret, *Slave Against Slave: Plantation Violence in the Old South* (Baton Rouge: Louisiana State University Press, 2015), 259–61, 360–61; *Louisville [KY] Daily Journal*, 27 May 1859.
26. *Louisville Daily Journal*, 26, 27 May 1859. One newspaper article listed the barber's name as Cowan, but Lewis Williams appeared in multiple reports; see *Louisville [KY] Daily Courier*, 26 May 1859.
27. "An Act to Amend an Act Entitled, 'An Act Reducing into One the Several Acts Concerning Slaves, Free Negroes and Mulattos, and for Other Purposes,'" chap. 22, sec. 4, in *Session Laws of Virginia, 1831* (Richmond, VA: Thomas Ritchie, 1832), 21; Joseph Ruff, petition, 9 December 1833, Legislative Petitions Digital Collection, Library of Virginia, Richmond, https://lva.primo.exlibrisgroup.com/permalink/01LVA_INST/altrmk/alma9917813221805756; Committee for Courts of Justice, resolution, 11 December 1833, in *Journal of the House of Delegates of the Commonwealth of Virginia, Begun and Held at the Capitol, in the City of Richmond, on Monday, the Second Day of December, One Thousand Eight Hundred and Thirty-Three* (Richmond, VA: Thomas Ritchie, 1833), 42.
28. Loren Schweninger, ed., *The Southern Debate over Slavery*, vol. 1, *Petitions to Southern Legislatures, 1778–1864* (Urbana: University of Illinois Press, 2001), 88–89, 89n1; Gregory D. Massey, *John Laurens and the American Revolution* (Columbia: University of South Carolina Press, 2000), 135, 136, 267n38.
29. Schweninger, ed., *The Southern Debate over Slavery*, 229–31. The 1850 US Census listed McCulloch and the other residents of his household as "mulattoes"; see 1850 US Census, Jackson County, TX.
30. Spotswood Rice to Kittey Diggs, 3 September 1864, in *Letters of a Nation: A Collection of Extraordinary American Letters*, ed. Andrew Carroll (New York: Broadway Books, 1997), 126–27.
31. Mary A. Bell, interview, in *Slave Narratives*, vol. 10, *Missouri Narratives*, 31.
32. J. F. Boone, interview, in *Slave Narratives*, vol. 2, *Arkansas Narratives, Part 1*, 210, 211–13. For analysis of how strong bodies inspired self-respect and community admiration, see Sergio Lussana, "To See Who Was Best on the Plantation: Enslaved Fighting Contests and Masculinity in the

Antebellum Plantation South," *Journal of Southern History* 76, no. 4 (November 2010): 913–14.
33. Douglas R. Egerton, *The Wars of Reconstruction: The Brief, Violent History of America's Most Progressive Era* (New York: Bloomsbury Press, 2014), 178–81; Lee Guidon, interview, in *Slave Narratives*, vol. 2, *Arkansas Narratives, Part 3*, 123; Stephen P. Halbrook, *Freedmen, the Fourteenth Amendment, and the Right to Bear Arms, 1866–1876* (Westport: Praeger, 1998), 2–3, 148.
34. Shawn Leigh Alexander, ed., *Reconstruction Violence and the Ku Klux Klan Hearings* (Boston: Bedford/St. Martin's, 2015), 9–10; Willis Johnson, testimony before the US Congress's Ku Klux Klan hearings, in Alexander, ed., *Reconstruction Violence and the Ku Klux Klan Hearings*, 93–96; Hannah Rosen, *Terror in the Heart of Freedom: Citizenship, Sexual Violence, and the Meaning of Race in the Postemancipation South* (Chapel Hill: University of North Carolina Press, 2009), 189–90. Action against Klansmen could have negative consequences. Marilda Pethy, previously enslaved in Missouri, recounted during Reconstruction how a "colored man, named McPherson" warned the Klan against "pesterin' round his cabin." They showed up anyway, so he shot and killed one of them with his double-barreled shotgun. Pethy added, however, that McPherson "had to leave his home. He went to Illinois and I ain't never seen him since"; see Marilda Pethy, interview, in *Slave Narratives*, vol. 10, *Missouri Narratives*, 281–82.
35. James H. Alston, testimony before the US Congress's Ku Klux Klan hearings, in Alexander, ed., *Reconstruction Violence and the Ku Klux Klan Hearings*, 61–62.
36. Henry Blake, interview, in *Slave Narratives*, vol. 2, *Arkansas Narratives, Part 1*, 176, 177, 179.
37. Hilde, *Slavery, Fatherhood, and Paternal Duty*, 7; Stevenson, *Life in Black and White*, 256.
38. Ellen Cragin, interview, in *Slave Narratives*, vol. 2, *Arkansas Narratives, Part 2*, 45. Carelessly stored firearms could lead to deadly consequences, often for children. A few examples illustrate this. Three Black boys, all under ten years of age, found a loaded shotgun on their enslaver's porch in North Carolina. They were playing with the gun when it went off, badly injuring two of them; see *Democratic Press* (Raleigh, NC), 28 May 1859. This was not exclusive to Black children. In Baltimore, Maryland, an eight-year-old White boy picked up his father's pistol and accidentally shot himself; see *Richmond [VA] Dispatch*, 29 January 1858. The deaths from poorly stored guns were not always accidental. An enslaver in North Carolina left his shotgun unsecured and someone got into his house and

used it to kill a woman he enslaved; see *Fayetteville [NC] Observer,* 4 June 1850.
39. Harriet Jacobs, *Incidents in the Life of a Slave Girl, Written by Herself,* ed. J. Maria Child (1861; rpt., New York: Signet Classic, 2000), 7–8; Laura Ramsey Parker, interview, in *Slave Narratives,* vol. 15, *Tennessee Narratives,* 62.
40. Mary Gladdy, interview, in *Slave Narratives,* vol. 15, *Georgia Narratives, Part 4,* 17. The six Black men were disciplining Holt's enslaved people on the planters' behalf, highlighting the divisions within enslaved communities. For more on this complexity, see Forret, *Slave Against Slave.* Similarly, David Steven Doddington suggested that the Black foreman shot Gladdy's father because "enslaved men who faced resistance when imposing discipline were aware that their reputation was at stake"; see Doddington, *Contesting Slave Masculinity in the American South* (New York: Cambridge University Press, 2018), 85.
41. *Fayetteville Observer,* 24 July 1849; Cragin, interview, 48.
42. Frederick Douglass, *My Bondage and My Freedom* (New York: Miller, Orton, and Mulligan, 1855), 51; Walker, *Walker's Appeal in Four Articles,* 7; Proctor, *Bathed in Blood,* 44; Boone, interview, 212.

REIMAGINING CITIZENSHIP

In 1787, John Jay wrote in Federalist no. 2: "To all general purposes we have uniformly been one people each individual citizen everywhere enjoying the same national rights, privileges, and protection."[1] Of course, not all people living in the early United States enjoyed equal rights, similar privileges, or uniform protection under the law. A minority of residents—White men mostly—had voting rights that situated them to define the citizenship of others, from orphans and widows to the enslaved, homeless, and migratory. In the early years of the republic, as the nation and states worked out who deserved citizenship, some White women and Black men had moments in which they achieved comparable citizenship to White men before it was swept away. Who gets to enjoy rights, privileges, and protection has remained a question at the heart of the American experiment for over two centuries.

In this section, authors articulate the complexities of some early Americans' citizenship. Jacqueline Beatty examines representations of non-Western women in magazines, revealing how female readers, while finding commonality with other women across the globe, also received the message that they were, in comparison, "free enough" in their rights and privileges. Kenneth E. Marshall relates the story of Silvia Dubois, an enslaved New Jersey woman whose use of aggression, assumed to be a masculine trait, elevated her as a "self-possessed" adult woman, a status often denied enslaved people. Consequently, she acquired some privileges and protections usually reserved for White men. Steven Peach follows Presbyterian missionaries into the trans-Mississippi Indian Territory to explore how Indigenous women perceived missions, part of the United States' "plan of civilization," as disruptive to their citizenship in their own nations.

As you read these essays, consider what it meant to be a citizen, why some people were excluded from citizenship, and how exclusion reinforced norms and hierarchies in the United States and in various Native American nations. Since these essays all center women, consider how the inclusion of women threatened traditional notions about rights, privileges, and protections. Beyond delineating citizenship, what reasons did men likely have for representing women from across the globe, in enslaved status, or in Native nations in ways that "Othered" them?

Note

1. John Jay, "Concerning Dangers from Foreign Force and Influence," in *The Federalist Papers*, ed. Clinton Rossiter (New York: Penguin, 2003), 33.

The Slave, the Concubine, and the Unnatural Beauty

DEPICTIONS OF THE OTHER AND THE CONSTRICTION OF
WOMEN'S RIGHTS IN AMERICAN MAGAZINES, 1790-1800

JACQUELINE BEATTY

THE JANUARY 1790 edition of Matthew Carey's *American Museum* featured a "Short Account of the Women of Egypt." Just over one page in length, the piece delineated stark differences between the lives of the magazine's White female readers and those in the North African country. The unnamed author argued that European women "appear as sovereigns on the theatre of the world. They preside over manners; and decide on the most important events. The fate of nations is often in their hands." In Egypt, however, "what difference! They are there only to be seen loaded with the chains of slavery." In their "servitude," Egyptian women exerted "not the smallest influence on public affairs." Instead, "their empire is limited to the walls of the haram." The article left American women who read this purportedly nonfiction screed to contemplate their own status relative to the sexual enslavement of the women of Egypt, whose only power lay in their "charms."[1]

The *American Museum* fixated on a common trope within magazines in the early republic, juxtaposing the status of European and White American women to that of enslaved peoples, drawing a clear and unfavorable contrast to what their own largely White middling to elite female readership experienced.[2] Ironically and much to their surprise, many American women who read the piece decided that their Egyptian counterparts lived much as they did: "Confined within the bosom of their family, the circle of their life does not extend beyond domestic employments." Especially familiar to wealthy White American women of the early republic was that the "first duty" of Egyptian women centered on "the education of their children." A similarly titled piece published five months later opined further on the subject: "Such is the ordinary life of the Egyptian women. To bring up their children, to employ themselves solely in the affairs of house-keeping, to live retired in the interior of their family, constitute their duties."[3] What difference indeed!

American magazines in the 1790s published numerous, allegedly nonfiction accounts of non-Western women's lives.[4] Some magazines unwittingly printed narratives that demonstrated commonalities among women's experiences around the world. The majority focused on distinctions in treatment among women, including in the United States. The content was didactic, demonstrating to American magazine readers ways in which the supposedly unnatural execution of gender roles had real-world consequences for foreign cultures and states.

Yet such pieces also served as warnings. In the early years of the republic, some elite leaders attempted to rein in democratic impulses unleashed by the American Revolution. Although some women agitated for expanded rights, the tone of early American magazines sent the subtle—or at times rather overt—message that White American women were, essentially, free enough. In other words, they already possessed rights sufficient for their proper participation in the American experiment. To agitate for more rights threatened to not only make their own lives (and the lives of family members) worse but also endanger the fragile American republic. Magazines that printed negative depictions of "Othered" women ultimately buttressed the claim that White American women possessed sufficient rights. In so doing, these pieces cultivated patriotic sentiment among magazine readership and bolstered the claims of traditional patriarchal power in the broader service of the young nation. Gender was thus the lens through which Americans viewed and defined themselves in relation to the Other.

Scholars have long investigated the founding generation's purposeful and painstaking efforts to craft a new culture, a political society, and a national identity that would win the allegiances of a new body of citizens and ensure their investment in the success of the United States.[5] Magazines played an important role in constructing a new national identity, providing vehicles for editors to set forth their visions for the republic.[6] As devoted federalists, many American magazine editors, including lexicographer Noah Webster and publisher Matthew Carey, promoted what historian Jared Gardner termed "literary nationalism." Their words focused on fostering national unity, republicanism, and "fellow feeling" among likeminded citizens. Because of their commitment to these principles, editors persisted in producing periodicals despite the reality that such ventures seldom lasted long, often lost money, and they, like historians today, found it challenging to discern the uses to which readers put their intended messages.[7]

The project of nation-building, of course, included women whom the state considered political beings only insofar as their gender allowed. The early republic's ever-expanding print culture provided spaces in which women actively participated in public and political realms. Still, magazine content geared toward female audiences remained deeply prescriptive, demarcating the proper boundaries of feminine comportment.[8]

Historians of the early republic have explored the ways in which magazines and other print media highlighted and reinforced clear distinctions between the gendered roles of American men and women.[9] Under-analyzed, however, are ways in which magazine articles about non-Western and subaltern women proved essential to delineating and reinforcing those republican gender norms.[10] In the critical decade of the 1790s, magazines exploited and purposefully Othered foreign values and social practices in order to promote cultural and national unity in the United States.[11]

Focusing on non-Western and subaltern women's depictions in print culture exposes the need for a broadened scope of what scholars have previously considered "prescriptive literature." Pieces promising true accounts of women's lives across the globe often appeared alongside traditional conduct literature. In one issue of the *Weekly Museum,* for example, readers found excerpts from the missives of French botanist and explorer Abbé Jean Louis Marie Poiret's travels among Arabic cultures in which he detailed the appalling lack of liberty afforded to women. Turning the page, they read a brief, nine-line poem urging "Caution to the Fair-Sex," which suggested that women use "reason" in courtship to avoid being entrapped by "faithless men." Most conduct literature was overtly didactic, such as the essay exhorting the "good wife" to be "virtuous, constant, and faithful to her husband."[12] Pieces about non-Western and subaltern women, however, used elements of narrativity and the alleged authority of nonfiction writing to teach lessons, much like the vast array of early American literature that depicted women in the Western world.

American magazine editors and contributors thus employed an imagined conception of the Other to indirectly prescribe behavior to their readership. Pieces that described treatment of women in non-Christian, non-republican societies painted horrifying portraits of what American women might experience if they lost the patriarchal protections inherent to the new nation's power structures. Should the American experiment fail, elite White women would find themselves confined to their homes, shrouded in clothing that obscured their identities, and sexually enslaved by tyrants. If they rejected republican virtue, they would become vapid prima donnas, caring more about their appearances and raiment than the freedoms for which the founding generation so valiantly fought. This body of conduct literature made clear to American women, particularly those inclined to agitate for more expansive legal, educational, and political rights, that their lives could be much worse. The message of rebuke simultaneously highlighted the fact that some American women were advocating for such rights.[13]

Pieces in early American magazines exploited xenophobic tropes to convince women readers of the superiority of their status in the United States. In an essay distilled from his *Travels Through Syria and Egypt* (1787), the Comte de Volney, a French philosopher and traveler, argued that in those countries, "the women are rigorously secluded from the society of men." Syrian and Egyptian women allegedly spoke only to men in their immediate families and when permitted. When they left home, they were "carefully veiled in the streets." Volney blamed the "facility of divorces"—the ease with which divorces could be obtained—for women's forced seclusion. He identified the underlying cause for Syrian and Egyptian misogyny as "the laws and government," insisting that "the Orientals . . . entertain a general sentiment of contempt for that sex." The same government that allegedly instituted forced social isolation of women "denies them the possession of any landed property, and so completely deprives them of every kind of personal liberty, as to leave them dependent all their lives on a husband, a father, or a relation," equating their situation to "the state of slavery." But the piece demonstrated Volney's myopia. Customary laws of coverture prohibited married women in the United States from owning property, contracting in their own names, and possessing legal identities distinct from that of their husbands. In countless ways, most American women, much like the women whom Volney described, depended on men.[14]

Such blunders by male authors often appeared in magazine essays and excerpts from books. Several essayists, intent on describing the horrors facing women in non-Western and subaltern countries, described experiences quite like that of elite White American women. While it is difficult to chart women reader's reactions to and uses of these didactic depictions of the Other, the intentions were clear and represent an understudied counterpart to republican motherhood and companionate marriage: gendered ideas pressed on women in print media and popular culture that women sometimes embraced, sometimes rejected, and sometimes turned to their own purposes. One wonders, then, how women readers interpreted such narratives, carefully crafted to convince them of their superiority over non-Western and subaltern women, even as the messages inadvertently reinforced the disturbing nature of their own inequality.

Early American magazine editors routinely compensated for American women's inequality by overemphasizing the minimal rights they did enjoy under law. One area in which women's rights expanded (in a limited capacity) in the early American republic was in education. The founding generation believed that to ensure that the nation's rising generation would be virtuous and dedicated to republican principles, mothers of future citizens needed to be educated to cultivate civic values in their children: to prepare sons to become leaders and voters, and daughters to become mothers who in turn would inculcate republican ideology in successive generations. In an address to the Philadelphia Young Ladies' Academy in 1787, physician and social reformer Benjamin Rush, an ardent advocate for women's education, argued that "a principle share of the instruction of children naturally devolves upon the women. It becomes us therefore to prepare them by a suitable education, for the discharge of this most important duty of mothers." Early American magazines warned that a frivolous education for women would "waste their younger years in learning merely shewy and nugatory accomplishments, which give them a relish only for splendour and amusement."[15] Women's education—particularly that of elite, White women responsible for raising future generations of citizens—was of the utmost import.

Essays on non-Western and subaltern women, therefore, often focused on their lack of access to even minimal education. In an excerpt from his 1797 *Constantinople, Ancient and Modern, with Excursions to the Shores and Islands of the Archipelago and to the Troad,* the English topographer and writer Reverend James Dalloway assumed Muslim women's ignorance foundational to Islamic faith: "It was ordained by Mahommed that women should not be treated as intellectual beings, lest they should aspire to equality with men." Dalloway argued that women's education in Islamic cultures, including in the Ottoman Empire, was not intellectual but aesthetic. "They are taught to dance with more luxuriance than grace," implying value and attention to sensuality rather than refinement.[16] Greek women, living under the Ottoman Empire, similarly studied dance, embroidery, and music because, according to English scholar Richard Chandler, "improvement of the mind and morals is not considered as a momentous part of female education at Athens." Another author argued that in Indian culture, men believed it "injurious to that simplicity of manners and decorum of behaviour" to educate women, concluding that "by too much engaging the mind, they would lead their attention away from their children and husband." Evidently, an exception was made for the "dancing women." Those who served as "the votaries of pleasure" received educations suited to their occupation: they were "taught every qualification which they imagine may tend to captivate and entertain the other sex."[17] Such excerpts deemed Ottoman and Indian women as either frivolous or sexual objects, requiring education only insofar as it guaranteed men's pleasure and entertainment—a stark distinction to the movement to educate White women in the early American republic.

The single greatest focus directed at the lives of non-Western and subaltern women in the pages of early American magazines centered on experiences surrounding marriage. Writers routinely depicted these women as enslaved to their husbands. William Francklin, a scholar and officer in the British Army stationed in Bengal, determined that Persian wives, along with married women "in all Mahomedan nations," Korea, Indonesia, and other non-Western and subaltern cultures, were "little better than slaves."[18] Turkish and Chinese men allegedly kept wives imprisoned in their homes. Horrified American readers learned of the "Suttee," the Indian custom in which widows of Brahman or elite castes ceremonially threw themselves on their deceased husbands' funeral pyres.[19] No matter how difficult their marriages, women readers in the United States knew there was no equivalent social custom in their lives. Throughout the states, widows enjoyed legal protections that provided a measure of support, the expectation they could remarry, and even, at least in the case of New Jersey, potential for the voting franchise.[20]

Magazine articles on courtship rituals across non-Western and subaltern cultures reinforced American women's freedom relative to their non-Western and subaltern counterparts. Magazines embraced the emerging ideal of companionate marriage in which young men and women, rather than fulfilling parents' aspirations through arranged marriages, sought out loving relationships with likeminded republican partners. The Comte de Volney insisted that the "great contrast" between Syrian "manners and ours" was that Syrians were "absolutely ignorant of love, in *our* sense of the word." In other cultures, "little apparent courtship precedes . . . marriages."[21] Instead, parents chose spouses for their children, and the two met only on the day of their wedding.

Authors specifically contrasted American courtship practices with those to which non-Western and subaltern women were subject. "With *us*," one writer boasted, "courtship includes the idea of humble intreaty on the man's side, and favour and condescension on the part of the woman, who bestows person and property for love." In contrast to the common American expectation that women had some agency in choosing a partner, these other cultures forced the wife "to be the slave, and not the companion, of her husband." Under such circumstances, "neither are possessed of the feelings necessary for that delicately sentimental prelude of the social state of wedlock."[22] It was a troubling notion for American readers who, through the vehicle of print culture, came to believe that republican unions in the home were essential to bolstering the broader republican experiment.

Other essayists deployed tales of marital customs abroad to scold American women for being insufficiently committed to their own unions. One author argued that the women of Suriname "voluntarily enter into . . . connections" with White men and "exult in the circumstance of living with an European, whom in general they serve with the utmost tenderness and fidelity." Surinamese women were not formally or legally married to their European partners, Dutch-born Scottish soldier and essayist John Stedman observed, yet nonetheless served them devotedly. In their loyalty and exaltation, such Surinamers "reprove those numerous fair ones who break through ties more sacred and solemn." The essayist then urged those "numerous fair ones"—White women readers—to consider themselves fortunate to be married to White men, shunning thoughts of breaking the "sacred and solemn" bonds of matrimony.[23]

The rhetoric of the American Revolution and republicanism influenced how prescriptive literature portrayed marriage and divorce. While legal in most states in the early republic, divorce remained uncommon, liberalized in only a few places such as Pennsylvania. Prescriptive literature generally discouraged divorce, providing a plethora of examples from non-Western and subaltern cultures that permitted it.[24] Generally, magazines depicted the practice in foreign nations as granted on rather arbitrary or frivolous grounds, seeking to demonstrate how greater access to divorce ultimately hurt women. In Persia, a husband could divorce his wife if he was "discontented" with her. The men of Tonkin—in present-day Vietnam—could "divorce their wives for a very slight offence; but the woman has not the same priviledge." The wives of Tonkin could only seek marital separations if husbands were found "guilty of some very notorious crime." Women on the island of Celebes (in present-day Indonesia) were "remarkably chaste and reserved" because any casual look or gesture at a man other than her husband provided grounds for divorce. Siamese women could not divorce their husbands; only men held that right.[25] Notably, such examples indicated few opportunities for women to divorce, and far more protections for their husbands. The subtle hint of this corpus was that American divorce law, which granted women more rights than in Tonkin, Celebes, and Siam, had gone far enough.

Magazine writers also depicted the harsh punishments inflicted on women in non-Western and subaltern cultures accused of adultery. Certainly, American women who were unfaithful to their husbands faced public scorn, social ostracism, and even divorce and financial ruin. Pieces in American magazines, however, insisted that such consequences paled in comparison to what non-Western and subaltern women experienced. French diplomat Pierre-Joseph de Beauchamp asserted that while Turkish law permitted divorce, the Ottomans punished adultery with death, which was—to be sure—"a great restraint to the infidelities of wives." Even worse, in Korea "it is lawful for a man to kill his wife for adultery." In Tonkin, a woman found guilty of adultery faced execution in dramatic fashion: she would be "exposed to an elephant" who was literally "bred up for these executions; and he having tossed her up in the air, she no sooner falls than he tramples her to death."[26] Such horrifying practices, regardless of their factual accuracy, effectively made American women grateful that they lived in a civil society. Tales of executions of unfaithful wives implicitly argued that less severe consequences meted out to women in the United States were just and measured.

Discussions about adultery often depicted supposed sexual deviance in non-Western and subaltern cultures. The sexuality and sexual expression of such women became a fixation in these purported nonfiction accounts. In Western writings, the *seraglio,* the women's apartment in Ottoman palaces, was a rhetorical space of European voyeurism. Certainly, essays replete with sensuous tales of licentiousness and debauchery tantalized readers. Swedish naturalist Frederik Hasselquist wrote that "Egyptian dancers," for example, expressed "movements and gestures . . . calculated entirely to excite sensual desires." The dancers, almost exclusively young women, "were little better than naked," so exposed that "the face was the only part they seemed solicitous to hide."[27] Such vivid descriptions conjured explicit images in the minds of magazine readers.

Such allegedly true accounts reminded Western White women of their obligations to be pure, chaste, and refined, outlining the dangers that would befall them if they were not. Hasselquist suggested that Egyptian dancers "make no scruple of exposing those parts, which European ladies never suffer to be seen in public." American women readers understood how such immodest behavior left them vulnerable to men seeking only sexual gratification. When French naturalist François le Vaillant encountered a "female half-savage of the Cape of Good Hope," he wrote, "The scantiness of her attire left great part of her charms exposed to view; but she thought no more of indelicacy in exhibiting, than of modesty in concealing them. A man of less temperance would have had no favour to ask, and no denial to fear."[28] The woman's purported lack of rational capacity left her ignorant of the message that the "scantiness" of her clothing sent to voyeurs. American women readers were to make no mistake in interpreting this piece: only "savage," ignorant women physically exposed themselves to men, and in so doing invited the wanton, lustful desires of rakes.

Authors of these pieces drew a direct line between non-Western and subaltern cultures' hypersexualization of women to the widespread practice of concubinage. Dalloway described the seraglio in Constantinople as a "woman market" wherein women from "Egypt, Abyssinia, Georgia, and Circassia" were "exposed to public sale every Friday morning." Essays about Muslim culture frequently described the inner workings of the seraglio, paying special attention to the place and purpose of women. "The Turks," claimed de Beauchamp, "know no other pleasure but the physical enjoyment of their wives, whom they treat as slaves." Stories of women held captive in the seraglio were replete with "cabals, intrigues, animosities, and tragic scenes."[29] Authors hatefully blamed the Islamic faith for permitting and even encouraging such treatment. Magazines depicted Ottoman women's bodies as marketable objects to be exploited for the sexual gratification of men. Of course, all women, including White women in the United States, understood the threat of sexual use and abuse to varying degrees. Yet authors exploited extreme narratives to argue that without the protections of republican patriarchs, White American women faced similar dangers.

Depictions of the seraglio also demonstrated the absence of republican values in non-Western and subaltern societies. The sultan's treatment of favored concubines provided them with material comforts of which some American women might have been envious, but ultimately such preferential treatment led to decadence and effeteness among women in his seraglio. With the sultan's favor, women spent their days engaged in "a series of sedentary amusements," including donning the "most sumptuous" clothing, which they "changed frequently in the course of the day," and occupying the most "magnificent apartments" while enjoying the "incessant homage of their subordinate companions." They often "recline[d] on the sofa for hours, whilst dancing, comedy, and buffoonery, as indelicate as our vulgar puppet show, are exhibited before them." Favored treatment led to idleness and excess, values leaders in the new republic dissuaded American men and women from emulating. Dalloway particularly lamented that the status of favored concubine was "all that most Turkish women aspire to, or are qualified to experience."[30] Any American woman who might be jealous of the luxurious lifestyle of women in the seraglio was to understand that their behavior was the inevitable consequence of concubinage.

Authors routinely described the experiences of Turkish or Arabic women by noting that they dressed in a way that covered their bodies and concealed their true identities, rendering them undesirable. "They look like walking mummies," English author and playwright Lady Elizabeth Craven opined. Abbé Poiret argued that Islamic women "entirely conceal[ed] all their graces." The only gap in the apparel, complained yet another observer, was around the eyes, "admitting space enough for sight." Readers intuited that those facial coverings obscured people's true identities, "confound[ing] all shape or air so much that men or women, princesses and slaves, may be concealed under them." Authors argued that such dress made it "impossible to discern if they be young or old, handsome or ugly."[31] Magazine pieces crafted an image for their readers that was troubling both because this clothing concealed its wearer and erased visible distinctions of gender and class in public spaces.

Writers wanted American women to be particularly disturbed by how Muslim women's dress restricted their freedom. Essayists presented Muslim women as completely covered in public, effectively depicting Arabic spheres as exclusively masculine and obliterating women's power in these spaces. Even in Muslim homes, Francklin contended, no one outside the family saw women uncovered for "it would be deemed an insult." If a woman appeared in public uncovered, Volney claimed, she would be assumed a "prostitute" or providing "a signal for a love adventure."[32] Although women's political rights and access to the public sphere in the early American republic were unequal to men's, the language and imagery of such narratives rendered only one interpretation possible for readers: American women fared better than their Muslim counterparts.

Yet, while American women reading such accounts might appreciate the liberation they experienced, they were not the only audiences for such pieces. Men who read descriptions of Muslim women's clothing would feel a different—and highly gendered—sympathy. Inundated with messages of confinement, restriction, and concealment, a male American readership likely intuited that Muslim women cried out for liberation both from their burqas and from the culture that compelled them to move about always covered. One piece provided alleged evidence of such yearning: "In their houses they lay aside part of their dress, and in the evening, when their husbands are at the mosque, it is not uncommon to see them enjoying the cool air on their terraces; but they instantly disappear at the sight of a man—I mean a Musselman—for they are very fond of the Christians, and when they perceive them, they readily expose to their view everything that the jealousy of their husbands obliges them to hide."[33]

Freed from the controls of their tyrannical husbands, Muslim women in such narratives abandoned the most restrictive clothing until, frightened at the sight of men from their own culture, they quickly covered themselves. But if they saw a Western man, they remained as they were:

open, free, and unrestricted by their clothes and their culture. Such descriptions provided tantalizing, voyeuristic fantasies for the American patriarchal archetype. The lesson was clear: Muslim women needed Western, Christian male influence to free them from the confines of their own society and faith.[34]

Comparisons between American and European women on one side and non-Western and subaltern women on the other underscored the value of patriarchal protections in Western societies. Even men sympathetic to expanding access to divorce, educating young girls, and enshrining women's property rights under law balked at measures that undermined their own patriarchal powers and those of the state. American men, then, could read the essays that highlighted insidious, nonconforming, and "unnatural" gender comportment across the globe as a warning. Certain cultures seemed to flout the purportedly divinely ordained roles of men and women embedded in Anglo-American, republican ideals. Consequences for repudiating nature and (the Christian) God would be grave. Male readers were to understand that they had an important role in protecting prescribed gender roles, the patriarchal power structure that reinforced these roles, and, by extension, the American republic.

Natural protections—those afforded to the weaker, subordinate, and dependent sex—were part of the language of natural rights that became central to the American lexicon in the early republic, enshrined in the young nation's laws of coverture as well as social, cultural, and economic practice.[35] Reciprocal friendship and love became tenets of an emerging ideal of companionate marriage, a critical social paradigm bolstering republican values in marital relationships. Magazine authors made their positions clear: in societies that permitted polygamy, women's natural chastity and modesty fell victim to husbands' rapacious lust, undermining friendship, love, and companionship. Such consequences amounted to tyranny raged against society's most helpless and violated the laws of nature.

Anxiety over breaches in the natural gendered order also shaped how writers interpreted women's appearance.[36] Magazines routinely detailed physical appearances, describing the beauty of women across the globe.[37] In some instances, cosmetic applications enhanced non-Western and subaltern women's allure. Francklin described a "very striking beauty" whose pleasing visage was "in a great measure owing to art, as they rub their eye brows and eye lids with the black powder of antimony which adds an incomparable brilliancy to their natural lustre." In a way, however, such "artificial beauty" amounted to a form of deceit, according to William Lemprière, a medical writer in the British military. As many magazine writers suggested, non-Western and subaltern women concealed or impeded their natural beauty with cosmetics, ornaments, and dress. Cosmetics could even conceal the race of its wearer. One author described Chinese women as "not content" with the "fair skins" they had been given "by nature," and instead sought to "whiten them with cosmetics." Women used makeup to create artificial appearances, deceive people about the true nature of their beauty, and, perhaps most troublingly to late eighteenth-century White American readers, cross otherwise rigid racial boundaries.[38]

Early American women were not strangers to cosmetic products and at-home recipes for altering their appearances. Yet magazine authors emphasized how use of cosmetics rendered women "rather disgusting than handsome," paying particular attention to the practice among non-Western and subaltern women. Lady Craven argued that Turkish women's leisure activities—lounging on chaises for most of the day—combined with their unflattering use of makeup made "women at nineteen look older than I am at this moment." She was thirty-six years old, nearly twice the age of the women she scorned in her exposé.[39] Her epistolary travelogue provided a moralistic warning to "the rising generation" of Western women seeking to emulate Turkish women's beautification practices: "They will always fade as fast as the roses they are so justly fond of."[40]

Lest female readers be tempted by the lavish ornamentation of non-Western and subaltern women described in magazines, writers pointed out the dangers posed by excessive physical adornment. The Turkish woman described by Lady Craven lounged "at home bedecked with jewels," while her "wretched husband" labored for a "subsistence." Her idleness and desire for ornamentation meant that "the fruits of his labour are appropriated to her use." Craven was not the only essayist to link family indigence to women's idleness and insidious obsession with jewelry. "All these trinkets," warned one writer, "which the women are exceedingly desirous to obtain, were originally signs of slavery." To "render [slavery's] yoke more sufferable," men reconstituted the meaning of such objects. Here too the author provided a lesson in the civilizing influence of Western culture. Europeans, he claimed, successfully altered "tokens of dependence" and "embellished them with all the riches of nature" until they transformed into "the paraphernalia of the empire of beauty."[41] Superior Western culture, in writers' depictions, colonized material goods such as jewelry, liberating ornamentation so that, instead of acting as symbols of enslavement, they bestowed beauty.

Accounts of the physical appearances of non-Western and subaltern women presented shocking narratives, depicting practices that diminished women's beauty and, in some cases, were cruel and violent. Authors occasionally and explicitly linked beautification practices to barbarity. One essayist listed myriad global beauty regimens that seemed quite strange to American readers. Japanese women "gild their teeth," while "those of the Indies paint them red." "Indian" women "smeared" themselves "with bear fat," while "the female Hottentot" received as a gift from an admirer "warm guts and reeking tripe, to dress herself with enviable ornaments." Some beauty practices also caused pain. In Peru, women pierced their septums "as our ladies do their ears." Chinese women bound their feet to make them "diminutive as those of the she goats." The author contended that in some countries "the mothers break the noses of their children."[42] In no cases did the author describe any of the women as beautiful. The reader was left to feel horrified at the disturbing lengths to which women of other cultures went to disfigure their natural bodies and visages.

Women's deviations from natural beauty hinted at something more insidious: a challenge to political, social, and legal order. A favorite topic among magazine editors was the fierce, gender-defying Amazons. The notorious and militant all-female society of legend provided a cautionary tale to American women who might defy the supposed natural constraints of their sex.[43] According to these tales, they outlawed both marriage and monogamous relationships and encouraged sexual promiscuity, including with a semi-annual ritual where they exploited men for sex and afterward banished their paramours. Any emotional attachment stemming from sexual intimacy was discouraged. The Amazons practiced a form of heathenism that permitted infanticide specifically on male babies, keeping daughters to be educated in the ways of the Amazons. One author described the Amazons' matriarchal system: an "opulent queen, who maintains a splendid court, consisting entirely of ladies," ruled over her people, displaying excess and governing in the style of "the most perfect despotism that exists, perhaps, on the face of the earth."[44] Images of such a society upended the ideals of the patriarchal American republic.

Other pieces warned of a society with laws that favored women over men. In Metelin (or Mitilini, the present-day capital city of the Greek island of Lesbos), women "arrogated to themselves the department and privileges of the men." Irish statesman James Caulfeild, Earl of Charlemont, described a system of inheritance in which oldest daughters inherited family properties while sons received "small dowers, or which is still worse, turned out penniless to seek their fortune." Metelin, then part of the Ottoman Empire, operated on a system of primogeniture that prioritized women, rather than the more familiar Anglo-American custom which favored men. The city's gender hierarchy followed from those principles. The eldest daughter occupied the most favorable position: "Her husband is her obsequious servant—her father and mother are dependent upon her." Her privileged status situated her to dress "in the most magnificent manner . . . with pearls and with pieces of gold . . . thus continually carrying about her the enviable marks of affluence and superiority." When sons came of age, households banished them, often "without any thing to support them." Caulfeild concluded that most young men turned to labor as sailors or servants until they gained enough "competency" to return home, marry, and "be hen pecked."[45]

Caulfeild cast women of Metelin as not only vain and excessive but also exhibiting masculine traits. "In all their customs," he noted, "these manly ladies seem to have changed sexes with the men." They "*wear the breeches.*" They "shewed so little attention to that decent modesty, which is or ought to be, the true characteristick of the sex" that their clothing was "thin and transparent . . . through which every thing is visible, their breasts only excepted, which they cover with a sort of handkerchief." They rode horses astride, while their husbands rode side-saddle. Husbands took the last names of their wives. Women owned the family homes, "in the management of which the husband never dares to interfere." A husband was, for all intents and purposes, "his wife's first domestick, perpetually bound to her service, and slave to her caprice." Caulfeild shifted the focus on husbands' enslavement to their wives, emphasizing the tyrannical and deviant nature of marriages in Metelin: "[Women] look down upon all mankind as creatures of an inferiour nature, born for their service and doomed to be their slaves." Suggesting the source of such a deviant culture, Caulfeild noted that the island "was formerly inhabited by Amazons" but certain practices may have resulted from "Turkish tyranny."[46]

In Caulfeild's telling, the men of Metelin experienced a system at least akin (if not identical) to coverture and primogeniture as it existed under Anglo-American common law. Of course, American readers would have recognized such an arrangement through its gendered mirror image: Metelin's was a hierarchical system in which men were subservient to women. In the eighteenth-century American worldview, such a power dynamic defied legally and socially prescribed gender roles as well as the laws of nature. To avoid such a similar fate, Caulfeild subtly encouraged male readers to bolster, rather than chip away at, coverture.

In the 1790s, essays such as Caulfeild's, which depicted the purported lives of people very different from those of Western societies, filled the pages of American magazines. Authors discussed at length the supposed oddities of non-Western and subaltern women and the troubling treatment of women in these societies. Effectively didactic in nature, purported nonfiction stories of non-Western and subaltern women's experiences demonstrated to White American women the benefits and superiority of living in the United States. Such tales implied that women should refrain from agitating for more rights lest they upset supposed natural gendered order and thus undermine the minimal rights they enjoyed. Yet, despite authors' best attempts to draw distinctions between the experiences of their female readers and subjects, American women could recognize that they shared some kinship with non-Western and subaltern women about whom they read.

Moreover, the essays were replete with contradictions, both within themselves and among the larger corpus. Were Turkish women, for example, confined both in their homes and by their clothing, as some articles suggested? Or were they scantily clad, adorned with jewels and makeup, exercising a shameless vanity that disrupted the socioeconomic system? Were they legally repressed and desirous of an education that their male counterparts refused to provide? Or were they rationally incapable of such an education? Authors tied themselves up in knots, presenting paradoxical pieces to justify their patriarchal pursuits.

Nonfictional narratives of the Other were critical to Americans' conception of the gendered self in the early republic, particularly as the nation's leaders sought to cultivate patriotic sentiment and a new national culture. Magazines in the 1790s printed moralizing materials that prescribed women's proper comportment through the medium of supposed nonfiction narratives of non-Western and subaltern women. Alongside promoting republican motherhood and companionate marriage, early American magazine publishers and writers used constructs of non-Western and subaltern womanhood to try and suppress the democratic and egalitarian impulses of the American Revolution, shore up patriarchal power in the early republic, and curb any revolution in women's rights before it could begin.

Questions to Consider

1. How did early American magazines depict non-Western and subaltern womanhood?
2. In what ways did conceptualization of the gendered Other help to define American identity in the early republic?

Notes

1. "Short Account of the Women of Egypt," *American Museum; or, Universal Magazine* 7, no. 1 (January 1790): 56.
2. Some elite White female magazine readers were enslavers, yet the piece on Egyptian women (and others employing similar tropes) did not acknowledge chattel slavery in the United States. Surprisingly, magazines reached an audience of middling economic status, though content tilted toward elite readership. Literary scholar Jared Gardner concluded that editors at the *New-York Magazine,* among the cheapest of its contemporaries, "were at least partially successfully getting across their message that magazine reading was a vital form of participatory democracy, a tool of citizenship and self-improvement"; see Gardner, *The Rise and Fall of Early American Magazine Culture* (Urbana: University of Illinois Press, 2012), 104.
3. "Short Account of the Women of Egypt," 56; "Short Account of the Women of Egypt," *American Museum; or, Universal Magazine* 7, no. 6 (June 1790): 312. For republican motherhood, see Linda K. Kerber, "The Republican Mother: Women and the Enlightenment—An American Perspective," *American Quarterly* 28, no. 2 (Summer 1976): 187–205, and Kerber, *Women of the Republic: Intellect and Ideology in Revolutionary America* (Chapel Hill: University of North Carolina Press, 1980).

4. On the 1790s and magazine culture, see Gardner, *Rise and Fall*; Mark L. Kamrath, "An 'Inconceivable Pleasure' and the *Philadelphia Minerva*: Erotic Liberalism, Oriental Tales, and the Female Subject in Periodicals of the Early Republic," *American Periodicals* 14, no. 1 (2004): 3–34; and Kamrath, "'Eyes Wide Shut' and the Cultural Poetics of Eighteenth-Century American Periodical Literature," *Early American Literature* 37, no. 3 (2002): 497–536. When analyzing depictions of Othered women in American magazines throughout the 1790s, I utilize the phrase "non-Western and subaltern" to denote cultural divisions of the late eighteenth and early nineteenth centuries between White American and European cultures and those beyond that sphere, namely in Asia, Africa, and the Middle East. The phrasing leaves space to recognize the marginalization and oppression of colonized peoples. Neither term precisely represents all women living outside of the United States and Western Europe in the 1790s, so I employ both to provide a more capacious characterization of their experiences.
5. See, for example, Benjamin H. Irvin, *Clothed in Robes of Sovereignty: The Continental Congress and the People Out of Doors* (New York: Oxford University Press, 2011); Kerber, *Women of the Republic*; and David Waldstreicher, *In the Midst of Perpetual Fetes: The Making of American Nationalism, 1776–1820* (Chapel Hill: University of North Carolina Press, 1997).
6. See, for example, Robb K. Haberman, "Magazines, Presentation Networks, and the Cultivation of Authorship in Post-Revolutionary America," *American Periodicals* 18, no. 2 (2008): 141–62; Mark L. Kamrath and Sharon M. Harris, eds., *Periodical Literature in Eighteenth-Century America* (Knoxville: University of Tennessee Press, 2005); Christine A. Modey, "Newspapers and Magazines," in *The Oxford Handbook of Early American Literature*, ed. Kevin J. Hayes (New York: Oxford University Press, 2008), 311–20; Frank Luther Mott, *A History of American Magazines*, vol. 1, *1741–1850* (Cambridge, MA: Harvard University Press, 1957); Lyon N. Richardson, *A History of Early American Magazines, 1741–1789* (1931; rpt. New York: Octagon Books, 1966); John Tebbel and Mary Ellen Zuckerman, *The Magazine in America, 1741–1990* (New York: Oxford University Press, 1991), 3–56; and Mary Ellen Zuckerman, *A History of Popular Women's Magazines in the United States, 1792–1995* (Westport, CT: Greenwood Press, 1998).
7. Gardner, *Rise and Fall*, 70, 74–75, 78. For context, see Nicole Eustace, *Passion Is the Gale: Emotion, Power, and the Coming of the American Revolution* (Chapel Hill: University of North Carolina Press, 2008), esp. 241, 253–84; G. J. Barker-Benfield, *The Culture of Sensibility: Sex and Society in*

Eighteenth-Century Britain (Chicago: University of Chicago Press, 1992); and Sarah Knott, *Sensibility and the American Revolution* (Chapel Hill: University of North Carolina Press, 2009).

8. On women's political roles in the early republic, see Catherine Allgor, *Parlor Politics: In Which the Ladies of Washington Help Build a City and a Government* (Charlottesville: University Press of Virginia, 2000); Susan Branson, *These Fiery Frenchified Dames: Women and Political Culture in Early National Philadelphia* (Philadelphia: University of Pennsylvania Press, 2001); and Rosemarie Zagarri, *Revolutionary Backlash: Women and Politics in the Early American Republic* (Philadelphia: University of Pennsylvania Press, 2007).

9. See, for example, Lisa M. Logan, "'The Ladies in Particular': Constructions of Femininity in the *Gentlemen and Ladies Town and Country Magazine* and *The Lady's Magazine; and Repository of Entertaining Knowledge*," in Kamrath and Harris, eds., *Periodical Literature in Eighteenth-Century America*, 277–306. On gendered expectations in marriage in conduct literature, see Margaret Beetham, *A Magazine of Her Own? Domesticity and Desire in the Woman's Magazine, 1800–1914* (New York: Routledge, 1996); Cathy N. Davidson, *Revolution and the Word: The Rise of the Novel in America* (New York: Oxford University Press, 1987); Kevin J. Hayes, *A Colonial Woman's Bookshelf* (Knoxville: University of Tennessee Press, 1996); Catherine Kerrison, *Claiming the Pen: Women and Intellectual Life in the Early American South* (Ithaca, NY: Cornell University Press, 2005); E. Jennifer Monaghan, *Learning to Read and Write in Colonial America* (Amherst: University of Massachusetts Press, 2007); Mott, *A History of American Magazines*; and Kathryn Shevelow, *Women and Print Culture: The Construction of Femininity in the Early Periodical* (New York: Routledge, 1989).

10. Studies of non-Western content in American magazines often focus on the "Oriental Tale," didactic fiction that taught moral lessons through fables from Eastern cultures; see Mukhtar Ali Isani, "The Oriental Tale in America Through 1865: A Study in American Fiction" (PhD diss., Princeton University, 1962); Kamrath, "An 'Inconceivable Pleasure' and the *Philadelphia Minerva*," and Matthew H. Pangborn, *Enlightenment Orientalism in the American Mind, 1770–1807* (New York: Routledge, 2019). For broader studies of the Other in early American literature, see Anupama Arora and Rajender Kaur, "Writing India in Early American Women's Fiction," *Early American Literature* 52, no. 2 (June 2017): 363–88; Robert Battistini, "Glimpses of the Other before Orientalism: The Muslim World in Early American Periodicals, 1785–1800," *Early American Studies* 8, no. 2

(Spring 2010): 446–74; and Jim Egan, *Oriental Shadows: The Presence of the East in Early American Literature* (Columbus: Ohio State University Press, 2011).

11. Arora and Kaur, "Writing India," 379; Pangborn, *Enlightenment Orientalism*, 24. Much of this content revolved around the behavior and treatment of the Othered woman; see Kamrath, "An 'Inconceivable Pleasure' and the *Philadelphia Minerva*," 3–4.

12. "Arabian Women. From Abbé Poiret's Letters Respecting Barbary," *Weekly Museum* 4, no. 164 (2 July 1791): 1; N. Rowe, "A Caution to the Fair-Sex," *Weekly Museum* 4, no. 164 (2 July 1791): 2; M., "The Character of a Good Husband, and a Good Wife," *American Universal Magazine* 1, no. 6 (20 February 1797): 283.

13. For a similar conclusion, see Rosemarie Zagarri, "The Significance of the 'Global Turn' for the Early American Republic: Globalization in the Age of Nation-Building," *Journal of the Early Republic* 31, no. 1 (Spring 2011): 19–25.

14. "Manners and Character of the Inhabitants of Syria [Extracted from the Second Volume of Volney's Travels through Syria and Egypt]," *Massachusetts Magazine; or, Monthly Museum* 2, no. 4 (April 1790): 211–12. On the complicated legal, social, and economic distinctions between coverture and enslavement, see Kirsten Sword, *Wives Not Slaves: Patriarchy and Modernity in the Age of Revolutions* (Chicago: University of Chicago Press, 2021). On coverture, see Kerber, *Women of the Republic*, 120–21. On the complex nature of women's dependence, see Jacqueline Beatty, *In Dependence: Women and the Patriarchal State in Revolutionary America* (New York: New York University Press, 2023).

15. "Review 4," *American Monthly Review; or, Literary Journal* 2, no. 2 (June 1795): 128; Benjamin Rush, "Thoughts upon Female Education, Accommodated to the Present State of Society, Manners, and Government, in the United States of America: Addressed to the Visitors of the Young Ladies' Academy in Philadelphia, July 28, 1787, at the Close of the Quarterly Examination" (Philadelphia: Prichard and Hall, 1787), 6; Mary Kelley, *Learning to Stand and Speak: Women, Education, and Public Life in America's Republic* (Chapel Hill: University of North Carolina Press, 2006); Kerber, *Women of the Republic*; Kerrison, *Claiming the Pen*; Lucia McMahon, *Mere Equals: The Paradox of Educated Women in the Early American Republic* (Ithaca, NY: Cornell University Press, 2012).

16. "SELECTIONS. Condition of the Female Sex at Constantinople [from Dalloway's Description of Constantinople]," *Monthly Magazine, and American Review* 1, no. 5 (August 1799): 381–82. On refinement, see Richard L. Bushman, *The Refinement of America: Persons, Houses, Cities*

(New York: Knopf, 1992), and Catherine E. Kelly, *Republic of Taste: Art, Politics, and Everyday Life in Early America* (Philadelphia: University of Pennsylvania Press, 2016).

17. "Account of the Turkish, Greek, and Albanian Women [from Dr. Chandler's Travels]," *Time Piece; and Literary Companion* 2, no. 31 (24 November 1797): 1; "Manners and Customs of the Hindoos," *American Museum; or, Universal Magazine* 11, no. 6 (June 1792): 266.

18. See, for example, "Some Account of the Persian Ladies. [From W. Franklin's Tour from Bengal to Persia, in 1786]," *Massachusetts Magazine; or, Monthly Museum* 3, no. 12 (December 1791): 738, and "Brief Account of Women of Different Nations, Asia. Women of China," *Time Piece; and Literary Companion* 2, no. 45 (27 December 1797): 1. William Francklin's surname is alternately spelled "Franklin" in some publications, including in the *Massachusetts Magazine* piece referenced here.

19. Accounts of the practice of *suttee* (or *sati*) are detailed in "Singular Customs of the Hindoos," *New York Weekly Magazine; or, Miscellaneous Repository* 2, no. 101 (7 June 1797): 388–90; "An East-Indian Custom," *Massachusetts Magazine; or, Monthly Museum* 8, no. 7 (July 1796): 396–98; and "Description of the Ceremony of a Gentoo Woman, Being Burned Alive on the Same Pile with Her Husband [from Campbell's Journey over Land to India]," *Weekly Magazine of Original Essays, Fugitive Pieces, and Interesting Intelligence* 2, no. 23 (7 July 1798): 303–5.

20. On widowhood, see Kristin A. Collins, "'Petitions without Number': Widows' Petitions and the Early Nineteenth-Century Origins of Public Marriage-Based Entitlements," *Law and History Review* 31, no. 1 (February 2013): 1–60; Vivian Bruce Conger, *The Widows' Might: Widowhood and Gender in Early British America* (New York: New York University Press, 2009); Lisa Wilson, *Life After Death: Widows in Pennsylvania, 1750–1850* (Philadelphia: Temple University Press, 1992); and Kirsten E. Wood, *Masterful Women: Slaveholding Widows from the American Revolution Through the Civil War* (Chapel Hill: University of North Carolina Press, 2004). On New Jersey women and the franchise, see Zagarri, *Revolutionary Backlash*, 31–34.

21. "Manners and Character of the Inhabitants of Syria [Concluded from Page 212]," *Massachusetts Magazine; or, Monthly Museum* 2, no. 5 (May 1790): 265, emphasis added; "Curious Particulars of the Inhabitants of Sumatra," *Weekly Magazine; or, Monthly Museum* 1, no. 5 (3 March 1798): 144; Jan Lewis, "The Republican Wife: Virtue and Seduction in the Early Republic," *William and Mary Quarterly*, 3rd series, 44, no. 4 (October 1987): 689–721; Anya Jabour, *Marriage in the Early Republic* (Baltimore: Johns Hopkins University Press, 1998).

22. "Curious Particulars of the Inhabitants of Sumatra," 144, emphasis added; "A Historical Dissertation on Courtship," *Christian's, Scholar's, and Farmer's Magazine* 2, no. 4 (October–November 1790): 472.
23. "Anecdotes Illustrating the Manners and Civilization of the Colony of Surinam [from Stedman's Narrative, &c]," *Philadelphia Magazine; or, Universal Repository of Knowledge and Entertainment* 2, no. 9 (September 1798): 131. The source utilizes the spelling "Surinam."
24. On divorce, see Norma Basch, *In the Eyes of the Law: Women, Marriage, and Property in Nineteenth-Century New York* (Ithaca, NY: Cornell University Press, 1982); Basch, *Framing American Divorce: From the Revolutionary Generation to the Victorians* (Berkeley: University of California Press, 1999); Thomas E. Buckley, *The Great Catastrophe of My Life: Divorce in the Old Dominion* (Chapel Hill: University of North Carolina Press, 2002); Richard H. Chused, *Private Acts in Public Places: A Social History of Divorce in the Formative Era of American Family Law* (Philadelphia: University of Pennsylvania Press, 1994); Nancy F. Cott, *Public Vows: A History of Marriage and the Nation* (Cambridge, MA: Harvard University Press, 2002); and Kerber, *Women of the Republic*, 157–84.
25. "Ceremony of a Persian Marriage," *Massachusetts Magazine; or, Monthly Museum* 4, no. 2 (February 1792): 92; "Brief Account of Women of Different Nations. Ceylon," *Time Piece; and Literary Companion* 2, no. 46 (29 December 1797): 1; "Brief Account of Women of Different Nations, Asia. Women of China," *Time Piece; and Literary Companion* 2, no. 45 (27 December 1797): 1.
26. M. de Beauchamp, "Account of a Tour Made in Persia in the Year 1787, with Reflections on the Manners of the East," *New York Magazine, or Literary Repository* 3, no. 8 (August 1792): 494; "Brief Account of Women of Different Nations, Asia. Women of China," 1; "Brief Account of Women of Different Nations. Ceylon," 1.
27. "Manners and Customs of the Egyptians, &c [from the Travels of Dr. Hasselquist]," *The Lady's Magazine, and Repository of Entertaining Knowledge* 1, no. 1 (November 1792): 267; Battistini, "Glimpses of the Other before Orientalism," 466.
28. "Manners and Customs of the Egyptians," 267; "Character and Deportment of a Female Half-Savage of the Cape of Good Hope [from Vaillant's Travels in Africa]," *New York Magazine, or Literary Repository* 8, no. 10 (October 1797): 548.
29. "SELECTIONS. Condition of the Female Sex at Constantinople," 381; Beauchamp, "Account of a Tour Made in Persia," 494.
30. "SELECTIONS. Condition of the Female Sex at Constantinople," 382.

31. "On the Turkish Women, &c. [from Lady Craven's 'Journey to Constantinople']," *Massachusetts Magazine; or, Monthly Museum* 3, no. 6 (June 1791): 362–63; "Arabian Women. From Abbé Poiret's Letters Respecting Barbary," 1; "SELECTIONS. Condition of the Female Sex at Constantinople," 381–85; "Account of the Turkish, Greek, and Albanian Women," 1.
32. "Some Account of the Persian Ladies," 738; "Manners and Character of the Inhabitants of Syria [Concluded from Page 212]," 265.
33. "Arabian Women. From Abbé Poiret's Letters Respecting Barbary," 1.
34. "Arabian Women. From Abbé Poiret's Letters Respecting Barbary," 1.
35. Rosemarie Zagarri, "The Rights of Man and Woman in Post-Revolutionary America," *William and Mary Quarterly*, 3rd series, 55, no. 2 (April 1998): 203–30.
36. Kate Haulman, *The Politics of Fashion in Eighteenth-Century America* (Chapel Hill: University of North Carolina Press, 2011); Rachel E. Walker, "A Beautiful Mind: Faces, Beauty, and the Brain in the Anglo-Atlantic World, 1780–1860" (PhD diss., University of Maryland, 2018), 80–123.
37. Persian women, for instance, were "tall and well shaped; but their bright and sparking eyes was a very striking beauty," and Turkish women's "faces were remarkable for their symmetry and brilliant complexion, with the nose straight and small, the eyes vivacious, either black or dark blue, having the eye-brows partly from nature, and as much from art, very full and joining over the nose." See, respectively, "Some Account of the Persian Ladies," 738, and "SELECTIONS. Condition of the Female Sex at Constantinople," 383.
38. "Some Account of the Persian Ladies," 738; "Dress of the Moorish Women [from Lempriere's Tour to Morocco]," *Massachusetts Magazine; or, Monthly Museum* 4, no. 8 (August 1792): 491. In the late eighteenth century, these remedies were used both as health care and beautification; see Kathy Peiss, *Hope in a Jar: The Making of America's Beauty Culture* (New York: Metropolitan Books, 1998), 9–36.
39. "Customs and Manners of the Chinese, with an Account of the City of Pekin," *Rural Magazine; or, Vermont Repository* 2, no 16 (May 1, 1796): 230; "A Visit to a Turkish Lady of Quality [from Lady Craven's Journey Through the Crimea to Constantinople]," *New York Magazine* 2, no. 11 (November 1791): 659; Elizabeth Craven, *A Journey Through the Crimea to Constantinople* (1786; rpt. Ann Arbor, MI: Text Creation Partnership, 2011).
40. "A Visit to a Turkish Lady of Quality," 659.
41. "On the Turkish Women, &c.," 362; "Description of the Moorish Women," *Massachusetts Magazine; or, Monthly Museum* 7, no. 7 (October 1795): 421.

42. "Female Beauty and Ornaments, in Various Parts of the World," *New York Weekly Magazine; or, Miscellaneous Repository* 1, no. 18 (November 4, 1795): 142. It is unclear in the text whether "Indian" refers to South Asian or Native American women.
43. Throughout the 1790s, alleged "Amazons" were traced to societies in South America, Africa, and ancient Greece. Some writers denied their existence and some questioned narratives detailing the inner workings of Amazonian society. Regardless, magazine editors continued to publish stories alleging lurid details; see "The Modern Amazons," *Weekly Magazine of Original Essays, Fugitive Pieces, and Interesting Intelligence* 3, no. 35 (March 9, 1799): 274, and "Account of the Amazons," *Massachusetts Magazine; or, Monthly Museum* 8, no. 2 (February 1796): 107.
44. "Account of the Amazons," 107; "Review 6" (of Archibald Dalzel's *The History of Dahomy, an Inland Kingdom of Africa*), in *American Monthly Review; or, Literary Journal* 3, no. 5 (December 1795): 458–59; "The Modern Amazons," 275.
45. "Singular Custom at Metelin [by the Right Hon. James Earl of Charlemont, P.R.I.A.]," *Massachusetts Magazine; or, Monthly Museum* 4, no. 6 (June 1792): 368–69.
46. "Singular Custom at Metelin," 369, 370. See also Professor Pallas, "A New and Authentic Account of the Circassians," *The Lady's Magazine, and Repository of Entertaining Knowledge* 1, no. 5 (October 1792): 201–6.

Squaring for a Fight in the Early Republic

SILVIA DUBOIS, A BIOGRAFY OF THE SLAV WHO WHIPT HER MISTRES AND GAND HER FREDOM

Kenneth E. Marshall

African Americans left few firsthand accounts of their enslaved lives in New Jersey. We also know little from the Black perspective about the interior day-to-day experiences of free Black persons in the Garden State. For the most part, free and enslaved Black residents in late eighteenth- and nineteenth-century New Jersey lived and died in the shadows of society, rendered faceless and mute.[1]

Yet, a powerful Black voice appeared in *Silvia Dubois, a Biografy of the Slav Who Whipt Her Mistres and Gand Her Fredom*, written and published in 1883 by Cornelius Wilson Larison (1837–1910). A New Jersey physician, educator, publisher, amateur historian, and devoted advocate of spelling reform, Larison developed "a deep interest" in the history of his native Hunterdon County and its inhabitants.[2] Among his subjects was the poor, elderly, and once notorious Silvia Dubois (ca. 1788/89–1888), whom Larison documented in his own phonetic alphabet with diacritical marks after an extended interview with the local legend.[3] Larison acquainted his readership with a Black woman who, in slavery and freedom, resisted White patriarchal oppression. To be sure, the local historian, who racialized Dubois as a Black exotic subject, was the rare White man in post–Civil War America to show interest in a lowly Black woman who aggressively defied the status quo.[4] This essay uses his pathbreaking interview to make a unique contribution to gender studies, delineating the ways in which Dubois incorporated elements of masculine authority into her arsenal of resistance. A gendered analysis of Dubois allows readers to learn a great deal about the world in which she lived and the oppressions she ultimately overcame through her use of aggression not commonly associated with women.

And yet, historians face a challenge in telling Dubois's remarkable story of dogged self-determination: the odd spelling of words in the narrative and the title, a reflection of Larison's learning issues as a youth.[5] The 1980s saw efforts to normalize the spelling of the narrative that rendered it much more readable and accessible as a historical document. As a result, Dubois's life and *Biografy* received a range of penetrating scholarly analysis. For example, American literature scholar Michael C. Berthold described Dubois as a self-defined Black woman whose "transgender combat," "independent maternity," and "public notoriety (her fighting, drinking, and vernacular outspokenness)" defied "her culture's tyrannies of decorum, station, and femininity." As Berthold viewed it, the *Biografy* or, more properly, colloquy stages what he deemed "the great hegemonic divide between an unlettered black woman and a professional white man" who sought to maintain superintendence throughout their discourse. Building on such important insights, gender and race scholars DoVeanna S. Fulton Minor and Reginald H. Pitts convincingly demonstrated how the *Biografy* illustrates the fascinating oral tradition of Black women's resistance. By contrast, historians Susan E. Klepp, Kenneth E. Marshall, Shaun Armstead, Brenann Sutter, Pamela Walker, and Caitlin Wiesner utilized the *Biografy* to illuminate, with different points of emphasis, the harsh realities of northern Black life in the late eighteenth- and nineteenth-century United States.[6]

What does the *Biografy* offer in yet another critical scholarly context, as a narrative of self-possession and alternative citizenship? With a hint of envy, Larison described Dubois this way: "Her love of freedom is boundless. To be free is the all-important thing with Sylvia. Bondage, or even restraint, is near akin to death for Sylvia. Freedom is the goal—freedom of speech, freedom of labor, freedom of the passions, freedom of the appetite—unrestrained in all things."[7] Larison waxed on about Dubois's relentless pursuit of self-possession as a free Black woman who controlled her person, including her sexuality. To be sure, this was no small feat in early nineteenth-century New Jersey, where free Black people ran up against deeply entrenched and ideologically driven racism and discrimination.

As historian Gregory Evans Dowd has shown, republican thought in New Jersey was influenced not only by racism but also by the bloody

Revolutionary War that traversed the small state whose close proximity to the British base in New York City rendered it vulnerable. In the aftermath of the Revolution, the ideal republican citizen, Dowd explained, was imagined as "a freeholding citizen-soldier, possessed of an unwavering concern for the public good, shunning luxury and self-indulgence." Measured against this ideal of land-owning, independent, and virtuous (White) manhood were Black folk, women, and Indigenous peoples, groups traditionally excluded from the political nation. Many White male Americans who put their thoughts about the new nation's political economy into letters, books, and speeches characterized Black Americans as outcasts and treacherous mercenaries who had sided with British tyranny, women as lacking the strength and character to protect themselves, and Indigenous peoples as slovenly savages. All three groups, according to the revolutionaries and their heirs of the early nineteenth century, lacked the virtue required to participate as citizens. As a correlation, in 1807 the New Jersey legislature stripped women and free Black residents of the vote, a privilege both groups had held since 1776. The franchise became limited to free, White, adult males worth fifty pounds. In the view of the state legislature, the appearance of women and free Black voters at the polls threatened "the safety, quiet, good order and dignity of the state."[8]

Living in a society designed for White men, Silvia Dubois boldly constructed her own version of citizenship by assuming control of her mobility, labor, sexuality, and grandfather's tavern, where her strength and aggression assumed centerstage, enhancing her "public notoriety." In Susan E. Klepp's discussion of how revolutionary rhetoric enabled American women to assert their political stances to authority, she remarked that "independence and citizenship could be claimed even by those legally excluded from those categories." Historians Elizabeth Stordeur Pryor and Kirsten E. Wood pointed out that citizenship in the early republic was not solely about political power and participation (e.g., voting) but also involved a host of activities, including independent mobility, travel, and tavern-going. Even so, Black mobility and Black use of tavern spaces incurred a major risk. "Most white Americans," Wood indicated, saw these two acts of Black self-determination "as a threat to the early republic's racial hierarchy." By possessing herself in various ways, Dubois defied the notion that, as a Black person, or "nigger" (a term that she consciously evoked in her narrative), she lacked independent adulthood—the mark of a citizen. As historian Susan M. Ryan observed, "Nineteenth-century Americans admitted of a range of notions of the self as property apart from the practice of chattel slavery. Independent adulthood was often figured as self-possession, a state to which African Americans . . . were thought to have little access."[9] As we shall see, Dubois forcefully opposed this presumption in her daily life as a self-defined free Black woman in the Somerset-Middlesex-Hunterdon Counties of central New Jersey.

TO BETTER understand Silvia Dubois's remarkable life in freedom, it is important to briefly consider how she *became* free. Our heroine was born into slavery under Richard Compton, the proprietor of a hotel and tavern on Sourland Mountain in Hillsborough Township, Somerset County, New Jersey. She inherited her enslaved status from her mother, Dorcas Compton, whom Silvia emphasized "was ambitious to be free." When Silvia was around two years old, Dorcas purchased her own and her children's freedom with a loan from Hillsborough resident Dominicus "Minna" Dubois (whom Silvia called Minical). Unable to repay the loan, Dorcas and the children became Minical's property. Angered by this arrangement, Minical physically tortured Dorcas, who fought back. "Under the laws of New Jersey," Silvia averred, "when the slave thought the master too severe, and the slave and the master did not get along harmoniously, the slave had the right to hunt a new master." Dorcas courageously quit Minical and asked William Baird to purchase her, and he agreed. Her act of resistance came at a high price as infant Silvia remained with Minical.[10]

Without her mother's protection, Silvia endured years of physical abuse at the hands of Minical's wife, Elizabeth Scudder Dubois, whom Silvia acidly referred to as the "devil himself." The abuse began in Silvia's youth in Flagtown, a hamlet in Hillsborough. The terrorizing continued as Silvia became a young adult in Great Bend, Pennsylvania, along the Susquehanna River where the Dubois family had relocated around 1803 (teenage Silvia walked the entire journey, over 150 miles). Around 1808, when Silvia was about twenty years old, the situation between her and Elizabeth came to a head. Displeased with the way Silvia cleaned the family barroom, her enslaver scolded the bondwoman, who "sauced her," or talked back. Elizabeth struck Silvia with her hand.[11]

In her prime, Silvia stood five feet ten inches tall, weighed over two hundred pounds, and possessed great physical strength. That is to say, the once-defenseless Black child had become a physically powerful Black woman who could fight back. Although the barroom "was full of folks," including vacationers, wagon drivers, hunters, and boatmen, Silvia struck Elizabeth with such force and pent-up rage that Elizabeth fell through the door panels. The fracas startled the patrons—all White—who, after seeing Elizabeth sprawled out on the floor, headed toward Silvia to subdue the bondwoman. Undaunted, Silvia squared for a fight, threatening to "trash every devil of 'em" as she smacked her fists. The threat worked for they all backed away. Still, Silvia understood that she had to leave the scene at once, and she bolted to Chenago Point across the state line in Binghamton, New York, and found a job.[12]

Away on business, Minical was not pleased by what had transpired between his wife and Silvia. Minical sent for the enslaved woman to return home immediately. He accepted that the two women would never get along, but that was partially his fault. It seems that Minical and Silvia had a sexual relationship that fueled Elizabeth's animosity toward the bondwoman. Upon Silvia's return to the Dubois household, Minical made his reputed sex partner a late-night deal, namely, "if I would take my child and go to New Jersey and stay there, he would give me free," as Silvia disclosed. She took the deal. Minical wrote her a pass to travel, and early the next morning she set out for Flagtown where she believed Dorcas remained in bondage.[13]

On the face of it, the beleaguered Minical had freed Silvia. Yet, such an interpretation ignores the critical role of Silvia's aggressive personality. Historians James Oliver Horton and Lois E. Horton posited that, owing to how "slavery attempted to dehumanize [Black people] without regard to gender," it comes as no surprise that "for black women no less than black men, freedom and dignity were tied to assertiveness, even to the point of violence." Rather than waiting for Minical to perhaps free her one day, as northern states gradually abolished slavery, Silvia took matters into her own hands. To reiterate, she chose to assault Elizabeth while Minical was away from home, performing his duty as "a grand jury man" at Wilkes-Barre, Pennsylvania. With Minical gone, she could freely vent her pent-up rage. After the slap, Silvia retorted, "Thinks I, it's a good time now to dress you out, and damned if I won't do it." Silvia seemingly had been thinking about publicly humiliating Elizabeth for quite a while. She chose this incident to finally act, engaging Elizabeth "in a barroom brawl" that undermined "her claim to ladyhood as manifested in the respectable appearance of the tavern."[14] In short, Silvia's violence was more calculating than spontaneous. It added to the toxicity of Minical's household, forcing his hand to send Silvia far away. Likened to a declaration of war, the assault brought Silvia's relationship with Minical and Elizabeth to the precipice, a risky move that paid off.

The assault served as a critical turning point in Silvia's life. Elizabeth could no longer abuse young Silvia with impunity: things would never be the same between them. Silvia's very public thrashing of Elizabeth, whereby Silvia took command over her life, guided her going forward. As the newly freed woman trekked back to New Jersey, carrying her infant, Judith, through desolate Pennsylvania woods inhabited by bears, wolves, and howling panthers, Silvia determined to live life on her own terms.[15]

After arriving in Flagtown, Silvia Dubois discovered that her mother, Dorcas Compton, had been relocated to New Brunswick, New Jersey, so Silvia continued her trek to find her. On the way, an anonymous White man confronted Silvia, inquiring, "Whose nigger are you?" Outraged, Silvia sharply replied, "I'm no man's nigger—I belong to God—I belong to no man." Dissatisfied, the man persisted in interrogating Silvia, demanding that she reveal her intended destination. "That's none of your business," Silvia retorted. "I'm free. I go where I please." As the man approached her, the physically imposing Black woman sat down her infant child and squared for another fight. Assessing his opponent, the man departed but threatened to have Silvia "arrested as soon as he could find a magistrate."[16]

Luckily for Silvia, a magistrate never came: "He didn't arrest me—not a bit," she triumphed. Still, she admitted how disastrous the situation could have turned out, explaining that "in those days the negroes were *all* slaves, and they were sent nowhere, nor allowed to go anywhere without a pass." She added, matter of factly, "anybody had authority to arrest vagrant negroes. They got paid for arresting them and charges for their keeping till their master redeemed them." The 1798 New Jersey slave law not only called for the arrest of mobile captives found without written permission of their enslavers but also prohibited free Black travelers from crossing state lines without a certificate verifying their status.[17] Yet despite the harrowing encounter, henceforth, mobility formed a core component of Silvia's self-possession.

When Silvia's antagonist essentialized her as someone's "nigger," he steeled her resolve that she was her own woman, the property of a much higher power in God. It mattered not that her former enslaver wrote her a pass to travel to New Jersey for carrying a pass did not affirm self-possession. The episode required Silvia to stand her ground. And so, in that all-important moment, she challenged her antagonist's hegemonic White gaze with a gaze of defiance: "I sat down my young one, showed him my fist, and looked at him." Eschewing racial protocol by directly looking back, she gazed at him as if she might win this battle, and incredibly she did: "He moseyed off." In the astute analysis of philosopher George Yancy, "The concept of resistance is inextricably linked to the concept of identity. As one resists, one affirms a reconfigured identity; for in the act of resistance, the Black subject has already achieved a level of separation from the Black imago bounded by the white imaginary."[18] Through the harrowing confrontation, Silvia Dubois affirmed her self-possession and reconfigured her identity as a "free" woman. The confrontation (like striking Elizabeth) was psychologically liberating and transformed Silvia's self-perception. She repudiated the notion of her person as a confiscated (Black) body in form and in White people's imaginations.

The significance—and sheer boldness—of Silvia's mobility must be understood in light of the perils inherent in moving about as a Black person in early nineteenth-century New Jersey, a danger that stemmed in part from slavery's lingering importance in the state. By 1800, New Jersey boasted the second largest enslaved population in the North. After much planning and political debate, state legislators passed a gradual emancipation law in 1804, making New Jersey the last northern state to commit to the immediate or gradual elimination of slavery. The law conferred freedom to enslaved children (born after 4 July 1804) following the completion of their apprenticeships, women at age twenty-one, and men at age twenty-five. A law passed in 1846 freed children born thereafter but made lifelong "apprentices" of those persons already in bondage, "yet another form of bondage," remarked historian James J. Gigantino II. In effect, the 1846 law allowed racial bondage to continue its conservatively gradual demise. Involuntary servitude of African Americans in New Jersey persisted until passage of the Thirteenth Amendment to the US Constitution in 1865. Small wonder, then, that Black mobility was a dangerous undertaking in New Jersey, where treatment of African Americans often was compared to their treatment in the South.[19]

To be sure, law enforcement—sheriffs, magistrates, constables, and jailors—manifested as a bane to Black peoples, filling the mobile with dread. Recounting his childhood in Burlington County, New Jersey, James Still (1812–1882) remembered seeing a constable for the first time: "His name was Israel Small. He was riding on horseback in pursuit of some one of the Milligan family, who lived opposite to us, and so impressed was I by the terror of the law, that I did not know at that time but that in the constable was invested all power on the earth." The terrifying image remained with Still as a young Black man. Upon his release from indentured servitude in 1833, Still decided to leave Burlington County for Philadelphia, traveling "by-roads and through woods." He recalled that "with not more than ten dollars' worth of clothing, and nine dollars and fifty cents in money, and without home or friends, my condition was a sad one." As such, "I suspected I might be taken for a runaway." Eventually, Still reasoned, "as I had my indentures, I thought that to show them would be sufficient proof of my honesty."[20] But as a mobile Black person, he could never be completely sure that law enforcement would interpret him as honest.

For all of James Still's worries as a mobile free Black man, it was infinitely more dangerous for Silvia Dubois as a free Black woman to exercise mobility. Enslaved men in New Jersey often worked as stage drivers, sailors, and stablemen, so it was common for White people to encounter Black males away from farms or plantations in the service of their enslavers. Relegated to domestic and farm work, enslaved women had relatively little access to the outside world.[21] In her analysis of how the "geography of containment" involved southern enslavers' efforts to confine captives and regiment their motion, historian Stephanie M. H. Camp stressed that it "was somewhat more elastic for men than it was for women, in large measure because the work that provided opportunities to leave the plantation was generally reserved for men." Similarly, historian Elizabeth Stordeur Pryor posited, "It was much easier for [enslaved] men to make their escape on public conveyances than it was for women," a reality rooted in the gendered "division of enslaved labor."[22] Living within the shadow of slavery's regimentation of Black people's mobility along gender lines, Silvia Dubois risked all to be mobile as a Black woman, a risk that she took over and over again.

For many African Americans, to be mobile was not only practical but also political. In her excellent study *Colored Travelers,* Pryor showed that in their quest for citizenship, "free people of color negotiated white hostility" while traveling in antebellum America. Traveling on steamships, stagecoaches, and railroads, elite and middle-class African Americans such as Frederick Douglass and Paul Cuffee resisted the structural restrictions, or racist ideologies, that made Black mobility a crime. They contested the notion that travel in America "was meant to be a free white masculine domain." Although a relatively obscure, nonelite Black woman, Silvia Dubois exemplified the African American freedom struggle for mobility. Through her dogged mobility in New Jersey, she spurned the "tyrannies of decorum, station, and femininity." She refused to remain at home, or stay in her proper place, but persisted in staying on the move and arriving on the public scene.[23]

For example, Silvia "used to walk a good way to [prayer] meeting—to Pennington, to Princeton, to Hopewell, and to Harlingen, and to camp meeting." She developed an affinity for camp meetings, outdoor evangelical spectacles that attracted throngs of "blacks and whites" from miles around. "That was the best kind of meeting for me. I'd walk ten miles to a camp meeting—further, too," she insisted.[24] In stressing her mobility, Silvia Dubois laid claim to her self-possession. Attending religious events was not only about serving God but also about asserting control over her life and body.

Silvia recalled a camp meeting near Trenton around 1819 that "I and some more of our color" attended, referring to it as the biggest and nicest camp meeting she experienced. Besides the fact that there were no fights or incidents of drunkenness, she heard preaching and hollering that she considered unprecedented. She explained that at the meeting, "there were four pulpits, a good way apart, and four preachers were preaching all the time. And they hollered, and the folks hollered—good God, how they hollered: I never saw such a time—I guess nobody did."[25]

Camp meetings provided Silvia and her "color" with a critical psychic release that confirmed their humanity and provided them with a temporary sanctuary from racial oppression. So it is hardly surprising that after getting a "bellyful" of the best camp meeting ever (which she attended for about three days before returning home), the next year when she heard rumor of another camp meeting, she "wanted to go just as bad as ever."[26] The religious, communal excitement of camp meetings fed Silvia's spirit and kept her in motion, fueling her self-possession.

To that end, Silvia attended General Training and other "big days" in Flemington (the seat of Hunterdon County). General Training was a one-day interracial affair usually held in June that celebrated the troops of a county militia as they assembled and went through their drills. Silvia recollected that during the grand occasion Black celebrants drank whiskey, became merry, and engaged in brawls that led to constables going "after the niggers," who, if caught, endured merciless whippings while tied to a post. Despite how General Training elicited racial violence, it provided valued opportunities for Black people to drink, share in each other's company, and display physical prowess. Like religious revivals, General Training and other communal events allowed Black peoples to be "seen." Silvia Dubois became a local celebrity as much from her ability to arrive on the scene as for her physical prowess. To put it differently, her legendary status derived in part from her attendance at community functions that defied her circumscribed mobility as a Black person and woman. She militated against her public erasure by White people who, as she declared, believed "that niggers ain't no account." Indirectly, she indicated that most White people did not view African Americans as actual or legitimate US citizens. Recall how she bluntly declared that "in those days the negroes were *all* slaves." Like free Black activists who, as Pryor pointed out, "used the term nigger in their lectures and literary productions" as "a verbal symbol of U.S. racial repression," Silvia Dubois evoked it throughout her reminiscence to highlight the marginalized citizenship that she fought against when appearing at local happenings.[27]

Interestingly, Silvia Dubois's persistent mobility owed in part to her former enslaver Minical Dubois. Despite Minical's abuse, she admired how "he was away from home a great deal" doing business with other "great men," and she retained the surname Dubois as an apparent show of respect to the man who freed her.[28] Minical's constant travels modeled how independent mobility served as a crucial component of citizenship. Silvia thus made it a point to perform this aspect of White male privilege, giving her life definition and meaning.

Silvia Dubois's independent mobility intersected with her desire to exercise control over her labor and time. After 1776, averred historian Seth Rockman, common American men and women equated personal freedom with the ability "to work when and where they wanted, to pursue their own interests free from government interference, to succeed or fail as the impartial forces of the market dictated, and to control their own destinies in a society of boundless opportunity." Free Black persons experienced great difficulty putting such personal freedom into action in postrevolutionary rural New Jersey. As historian Graham Russell Hodges described it, "Lacking political power and credit and with tiny incomes, unable to buy land, free blacks combined hiring out their backs to white farmers with part-time labor on their own miniscule plots of land." In search of economic opportunities and a more satisfying cultural life, hundreds of newly freed Black New Jerseyans abandoned the countryside for the city in the 1780s. Yet life in the urban North was no panacea either. As historian Ira Berlin explained, many free Black people were largely but not exclusively "confined to the unskilled and service sectors of the economy, laboring as cooks, washerwomen, seamstresses, coachmen, gardeners, and valets."[29]

So, when Silvia Dubois mentioned that shortly after finding her mother in New Brunswick, "I went to work," we may assume that she found work as a domestic laborer. Although it is impossible to determine where she lived, scholars have shown that late eighteenth- and early nineteenth-century free Black residences in New Brunswick were somewhat scattered, located mainly on the outskirts of the city. Wherever they lived, free Black residents on the move could not avoid the looming presence of the New Brunswick jail located near the center of the city, which served as the city's most potent symbol of enslaved and free Black residents' shared precariousness. Indeed, like the enslaved, free Black residents of New Brunswick faced incarceration for violating curfew, selling alcohol, vagrancy, or simply suspicion of crime. It would have been nearly impossible for Silvia Dubois to transform her circumstances in New Brunswick, so not surprisingly, in the early 1800s she left New Brunswick for Princeton where she worked "a long while" for the family of Victor Tulane.[30]

Despite how Silvia described the Tulane family as good people who treated their servants well, she lacked control over her body and time, not to mention that she worked under White surveillance. The most effective way that she could control her labor was to become an independent landowner like her maternal grandfather, Harry Compton, also known as Harry Put (d. ca. 1814).[31]

A legend in his own right, Compton endured slavery on Sourland Mountain in Hillsborough Township. According to Silvia, "He was short, but very stout, and very strong. He was considered the strongest man on the mountain, and they used to say he was the strongest Negro that ever lived, and he was very active. He could put any man upon the ground, white or black." After the mighty bondman reportedly served as a fifer in the Revolutionary War, he purchased his freedom by making and selling charcoal, which was in high demand as a heating and cooking fuel. While living in New Brunswick in 1803, Compton purchased the freedom of his daughter Kate and her three children enslaved in Amwell Township, Hunterdon County. He later moved to Amwell, where he built Put's Tavern (established between 1803 and 1812), an interracial social world of sex, hard drinking, gambling, and physical combat. For roughly a decade, Compton operated his unlicensed establishment on Sourland Mountain, "surrounded by a virgin forest that extended for miles in every direction," as Cornelius Larison described it. In this "virgin forest," Compton "managed his business, accumulated wealth, and became renowned," making his own rules and answering to no one. Compton fully possessed himself in America's exclusive and racist republic.[32]

Was it a coincidence, then, that following a prolonged absence from Compton's life, Silvia Dubois went to visit the "old man," who later asked her to stay and take care of him? Dubois claimed that "at his death I inherited his property." Her recollection, however, does not square with her grandfather's will that first mentions his "loving wife," Jude, and daughter Rachel as the rightful heirs of his estate.[33] How did Dubois (who is not mentioned in his will) come to inherit the property?

It may be a case of the property literally falling into her hands. Apparently, no one mentioned in Compton's will was physically able to handle the rough-and-tumble types who frequented the tavern: lewd and intellectual White men, White women dressed in expensive and gaudy attire, mountain and city bandits, ragged Black guests, the farmer-gambler donning his linsey-woolsey, the mechanic who sported satinet, the dandy, the drab. Such a motley crew of characters came from all around: Trenton, Princeton, New Brunswick, New York, Philadelphia, and cities farther away. A visitor at the tavern recalled witnessing a vulgar interracial social scene where people placed bets on and formed a ring "around two bullies, one a white man, the other black, fighting for no other reason than to see which could whip." Combat, the visitor maintained, also took place between "white women and wenches." In addition, the outcasts and renegades drank, gambled, conversed, used profane language, sang indecent songs, witnessed cock fights, and had illicit sex on relative terms of equality that, on the one hand, rejected the mores of the local officialdom (proponents of the early republic's racial hierarchy) and, on the other hand, emulated the defiant spirit of the Revolutionary War, leveling racial and class distinctions. The boisterous sporting scene required the authority of someone such as Silvia Dubois, a common laborer with no other prospects of becoming a landowner, who was more than happy to assume responsibility for what she termed "the old homestead." In doing so, she joined the ranks of other northern women—typically single, widowed, and White—who kept taverns, commonly called houses, to earn a living. Most of these women kept taverns in urban areas under the surveillance of White male hegemony.[34]

Significantly, Dubois laid claim to an institution associated with American independence and citizenship. Historian Benjamin L. Carp argued that taverns took on particular importance during the revolutionary era, transforming into staging grounds of cross-class political mobilization vital to coordinated resistance to British policy. In the taverns of New York City and throughout the eastern American seaboard, mobs gathered to resist imperial encroachment, thereby setting the Revolution in motion. Historian Kirsten E. Wood stressed that from the 1780s through the 1820s, formal tavern political meetings "embodied the distinctive privileges of manly and especially white men's citizenship." Tavern politicking, she observed, typically excluded White and Black women and Black men, all of whom collectively gathered and organized elsewhere. In her grandfather's stead, Dubois presided over a space symbolically linked to the Revolution's beginnings and where the uprising could, in a sense, be continued, bringing together people to engage in civic and political work toward the building of a better (republican) society.[35] More practically, the tavern enabled her to own land, gain a livelihood, and publicly wield (masculine) authority.

Among their many functions, taverns in early America operated as gendered spaces that enabled men to socialize and drink with each other as well as demonstrate masculine prowess. In 1700, for example, Lewis Morris, an American colonial official and future royal governor of New Jersey, complained to the bishop of London about the uncivilized sporting culture in rural Middletown, Monmouth County. These "most ignorant and wicked people," Morris lamented, held their Sunday church meetings "at a Publick house, where they get their fill of Rum, and go to fighting and running of [horse] races which are Practices much in use that day all the Province over." One New Jersey writer described "training-day fights" as "a mixture of tests of strength and personal antagonisms . . . held in the stable yards of taverns, when eye-gouging and chewing of ears were allowable under rough and ready 'rules' governing such affairs."[36]

Interestingly, Larison described Silvia Dubois as "decidedly a peacemaker," noting that "some of her most noteworthy feats were accomplished when suppressing a row, or, parting combatants; indeed, her presence often prevented a fight. Because, if the fight began contrary to her will, oftentimes she, to make them more obedient in the future, and to terrify others of a quarrelsome or pugilistic nature, would severely whip both combatants." She was known to break up a brawl of five to ten men by throwing "one negro in one direction, and another in another direction, until the last fellow was hurled from the arena of [the] fight."[37] Larison's provocative comments appear to reflect the rowdy scene at Put's Tavern where Dubois responded to brawls with diplomacy or, if need be, even greater violence. Her word became law at the tavern, and anyone failing to recognize it paid a price. Like her once mighty grandfather, she stood at the center of visibility and power at the tavern—the master of men who got out of line. As she bested men physically, she subverted her subordination to male authority. Put's Tavern was her republic, where a Black woman reigned supreme over a rowdy citizenry. In her world, Silvia Dubois more fully realized "freedom from labor." She used her body to not merely survive but to accentuate her authority over an egalitarian social scene.

No doubt Put's Tavern also promoted Silvia Dubois's "independent maternity," as Michael Berthold put it. Larison's remark that she experienced "freedom of the passions" intimates an unrestricted sex life whereby she "belong[ed] to no man." This was not always the case. Regarding her relationship with Minical Dubois, our heroine said, "I tried to please him and he tried to please me and we got along together pretty well—except sometimes I would be a little refractory, and then he would give me a severe flogging." It is difficult to read this comment without sexual innuendo. It also arouses curiosity about baby Judith, who, as historian Marc Mappen observed, suddenly appeared in the *Biografy* upon Silvia's (forced) emancipation.[38] Was Judith Minical's child? Did she fuel his wife Elizabeth Dubois's animosity toward Silvia?

As an enslaved woman, Silvia would have had great difficulty refusing a sexual relationship with Minical for enslavers claimed patriarchal rights to Black women's bodies. In other words, her young and powerful body belonged to Minical.³⁹ Yet, as part of their apparent sexual arrangement, Minical allowed Silvia certain privileges, such as keeping the money she earned from ferrying passengers across the Susquehanna River and attending "frolics and balls" away from home with other "black folks" in the Great Bend area. For her part, Silvia played the role of the "good negress," as she put it. In the end, Minical dictated the terms of their sexual relationship, held together by his violence, which Silvia conveniently excused: "He never whipped me unless he was sure that I deserved it," she stated unconvincingly. At best, Silvia, also an apparent victim of psychological abuse, tolerated the terms of their sexual relationship as opposed to accepting them. That is, sex with Minical on the Pennsylvania frontier would have been a matter of survival for Silvia, and not of fondness or consent.⁴⁰

Once freed, Silvia Dubois no longer had to make bargains regarding her sexuality: it was *hers*. In Susan Klepp's words, "Procreation is power," for it "helps define adulthood and shapes images of femininity and masculinity." Dubois wielded power in this regard, another important marker of her self-possession. Hence, she refused to reveal the paternity of her six children to Cornelius Larison, who documented their names: "Moses, Judith, Charlotte, Dorcas, Elizabeth, and Rachel." The matter of who fathered her children was solely her business. US Census records offer a glimpse into Dubois's private life. According to the 1830 census, six persons lived in her household, including a free Black man between the ages of fifty-five and ninety-nine. Author Jared C. Lobdell posited that this man was Silvia Dubois's grandfather Harry Compton, but his will indicates that he died around 1814. Perhaps this anonymous man was Dubois's husband or lover, especially when considering that three girls also lived in the household. Such an analysis, however, is complicated by the 1840 census, which lists only one male (under age ten) and three females living in the household of "Precilla Debois." The 1850 census lists no adult male and only two other persons, Elizabeth Dubois and Rachel Dubois, living in "Savilla" (Silvia) Dubois's household. Significantly, Elizabeth (b. ca. 1824) and Rachel (b. ca. 1827) had Dubois's surname, and not that of the man (or men) who sired them. Conversely, the 1880 census indicates that "Silvey De Bois"—age one hundred—was "widowed," suggesting that she married at some point in her life (perhaps in 1830?). When and if Dubois was ever legally married, we will probably never learn. At Put's

Tavern, Dubois set up what amounted to a domestic female household that perhaps paid tribute to her enslaved mother, Dorcas Compton, the one who originally was "ambitious to be free" but died in bondage around 1838.[41]

How did Silvia Dubois engage the social scene at the tavern, a space where, as Larison lamented, people's "passions could be unbridled"? We may assume that Silvia, like her patrons, sometimes casually indulged in sexual activity. Indeed, the tavern allowed women to openly express sexuality as well as display public drunkenness without real scrutiny. After the mid-eighteenth century and into the nineteenth century, evangelical religions and republican ideals emphasized self-control and monogamous behavior, particularly for women. Put's Tavern eschewed those rigid standards of decorum, echoing heterodox sects in eighteenth-century rural Pennsylvania that encouraged sexual experimentation among women. Was Silvia Dubois any less empowered than the other women at Put's Tavern, a sexually liberated environment in which she physically dominated belligerent men? If anything, the tavern's culture reinforced her self-possession with regards to procreation, or "the passions." According to Larison, Dubois lived "a life of dissoluteness," a moral projection that suggests she had little use for monogamous relationships.[42]

In a way, such an approach to her sexuality situated Dubois with women beyond the world of Put's Tavern. According to Klepp, in women's desires to limit childbearing and thereby gain more control over their own bodies between the 1760s and 1820s, they embraced the revolutionary ideals of restraint, virtue, and rationality. The dangers they faced during the Revolutionary War, when their bodies came under attack by a barbarous enemy, inspired women to reject their maternal roles of lifelong childbearing for self-controlled, sensible, and rational womanhood that shunned luxury and extravagance. In doing so, they found opportunity to both assert their relative liberty and promote republican civic virtue.[43]

While Put's Tavern, as a place of recreation, eschewed sexual restraint and female modesty, it seems unlikely that Silvia Dubois engaged the scene with reckless abandon. She was purposeful. As the person in charge of the tavern, she needed to exhibit power and authority. She may have limited her childbearing due to practical concerns that included her ability to remain mobile. She may have consciously decided not to have more than six children, a rejection of the abundant fertility of eighteenth-century America that sustained the patriarchal family.[44] At the same time, as a formerly enslaved person who likely had to bargain with her sexuality, Dubois took her pleasure as it suited her, with no consideration of how it aligned with the body politic, which had excluded her. Owning the tavern came with responsibilities that called for sexual restraint, while at the same time allowing her to indulge freely as a Black woman in a White man's world.

A lifetime later, when asked by Larison if her Black and White neighbors on Sourland Mountain ever married, Dubois asserted, "When they want to, but they don't do much marrying up here—they don't have to—and then it's no use. It's too much trouble." One senses that Dubois was talking as much about her younger years at Put's Tavern as about neighbors who lived together without "distinction of color."[45] One senses her comfort with not being tied down by marriage, with being her own woman in all facets of life, including her sexuality.

A Black woman who possessed herself in several critical ways, in open defiance against male authority, would have attracted attention and enemies. Indeed, Dubois was eventually arrested and taken to Flemington, apparently for operating an unlicensed and notorious tavern. Even for Larison, as Michael Berthold pointed out, "the idea of a propertied Dubois, presiding over an American Sodom [was] insupportable." Larison showed no sympathy that persons unknown burned down Put's Tavern in 1840 while Dubois was away. He concluded that "such is the history of the house that was the arena, tradition says, of the vilest deeds that were ever perpetrated in Hunterdon County." Dubois lost many important items during the conflagration, including "a bible containing the family record." Undeterred, she erected another home built of cedar and became a successful hog breeder. Farmers often traveled long distances to purchase from her herd. Then, around 1880, "those damned Democrats"—as Dubois fumed about the political party that during Reconstruction became the party of White supremacy and racial violence—burned down her home. Homeless and penniless, the discouraged elderly woman went to live with her daughter Elizabeth Alexander in a rustic home on Sourland Mountain, losing much of the self-possession that had made Silvia Dubois a local legend.[46]

A RARE first-person account of the life of a northern Black woman in slavery and freedom, *Silvia Dubois, a Biografy of the Slav Who Whipt Her Mistres and Gand Her Fredom* reveals the complex interactions of race, class, gender, and sexuality in the life of a rural early nineteenth-century

Black woman, despite Cornelius Larison's superintendence. As this essay shows, the narrative demonstrates how Silvia Dubois constructed a complex gendered identity that drew from a variety of sources: her mother, father, maternal grandfather, and even her abusive enslaver. More importantly, it makes an important contribution to gender studies, suggesting how the pursuit of masculine aggression and authority was not the exclusive preserve of men in early American society. Some women too valued the masculine ideals of assertiveness, independence, and self-reliance in a society that restricted their lives. In defiance of a society that tried to render her as a noncitizen, as "no-account," Dubois defined self-possession through her mobility, labor, sexuality, and grandfather's tavern, which fell under her control. Through the sheer force of her will, and by using Put's Tavern to undermine male authority in public acts of violence and aggression, Dubois constructed an alternative version of citizenship that repudiated her marginality. As a glimpse into her fury, she wanted to trash "every damned lawyer, the judge, and the jury" in Flemington for denying her justice as certain people tried to fleece her of her property. She thundered to Larison, "You can't get anything there without money. Nobody is considered anything unless he has money." Flemington was a microcosm for how she saw *his* America: unjust, corrupt, and hegemonic. She pursued every possible challenge to those norms to build *her* America. In doing so, she became a legend, so much so that someone like Larison—"imperious," "Victorian," and "quirky"—wanted to document her story.[47] Even he could appreciate how Silvia Dubois claimed agency over her life and body at a time when self-possession proved an impossibility for many African Americans. Although an outsider in the republic of Larison's forefathers, she exhibited self-possession as forcefully as any White, male patriot.

Questions to Consider

1. In what ways does the life of Silvia Dubois suggest how masculine ideals of assertion, independence, and self-reliance held great appeal for some women?
2. What does Dubois's biography reveal about early Americans' ideas about gender and citizenship?

Notes

1. On the importance of New Jersey slavery and the "muteness" of Black life in the early historical record, see Kenneth E. Marshall, *Manhood Enslaved: Bondmen in Eighteenth- and Early Nineteenth-Century New Jersey* (Rochester, NY: University of Rochester Press, 2011), 1–5, 7–11.
2. C. W. Larison, *Silvia Dubois, a Biografy of the Slav Who Whipt Her Mistres and Gand Her Fredom*, ed. and trans. Jared C. Lobdell (1883; rpt. New York: Oxford University Press, 1988), 26–27 (quote on 26). Lobdell normalized the phonetic spelling of Larison's 1883 version of the *Biografy* but reprinted the original in its entirety at the end of his translation. Although both the phonetic and translated versions of the biography are in the same book, references to Lobdell's translated version are cited as Lobdell, ed., *Silvia Dubois, a Biografy,* and references to Larison's original version are cited as Larison, *Silvia Dubois*.

    For the standard account of Larison's life, see Harry B. Weiss, *Country Doctor: Cornelius Wilson Larison of Ringoes, Hunterdon County, New Jersey, 1837–1910; Physician, Farmer, Educator, Author, Editor, Publisher and Exponent of Phonetic Spelling* (Trenton: New Jersey Agricultural Society, 1953). See also Lobdell, "Introduction," in Lobdell, ed., *Silvia Dubois, a Biografy,* 16–20; Michael C. Berthold, "'The Peals of Her Terrific Language': The Control of Representation in *Silvia Dubois, a Biografy of the Slav Who Whipt Her Mistres and Gand Her Fredom,*" *MELUS* 20, no. 2 (Summer 1995): 3–14; T. J. Luce, *New Jersey's Sourland Mountain* (Neshanic Station, NJ: Sourland Planning Council, 2001), chap. 20; and "Silvia Dubois, Slave of the Sourlands, Related Life Story to Larison," *Princeton Recollector* 5, no. 4 (Winter 1980): 1–24.
3. Jared Lobdell made a solid case that Dubois was born around 1788–89; see Lobdell, "Introduction," 4–12. For Dubois's death date of 1 May 1888, see Will of Sylvia Dubois, no. 9013, New Jersey Department of State, Division of Archives and Records Management, Archives Section, Trenton (hereafter NJSA). Dubois's first name had various spellings, although I strictly use "Silvia."
4. On Dubois as a Black exotic subject, see Marshall, *Manhood Enslaved,* 33–34.
5. On Larison's learning issues, see Weiss, *Country Doctor,* 27–30, 155–56; Berthold, "'The Peals of Her Terrific Language,'" 4, 5; and Lobdell, "Introduction," 16–18.
6. Berthold, "'The Peals of Her Terrific Language,'" 3, 4; DoVeanna S. Fulton, *Speaking Power: Black Feminist Orality in Women's Narratives of Slavery* (Albany: State University of New York Press, 2006), 49–54; DoVeanna S.

Fulton Minor and Reginald H. Pitts, "Introduction," in *Speaking Lives, Authoring Texts: Three African American Women's Oral Slave Narratives*, ed. DoVeanna S. Fulton Minor and Reginald H. Pitts (Albany: State University of New York Press, 2009), 23–30; Susan E. Klepp, "Seasoning and Society: Racial Differences in Mortality in Eighteenth-Century Philadelphia," *William and Mary Quarterly*, 3rd series, 51, no. 3 (July 1994): 483–86; Marshall, *Manhood Enslaved*, 14, 68, 77, 87–89, 93, 125–26; Kenneth E. Marshall, "Work, Family and Day-to-Day Survival on an Old Farm: Nance Melick, a Rural Late Eighteenth- and Early Nineteenth-Century New Jersey Slave Woman," *Slavery and Abolition* 19, no. 3 (December 1998): 33–34; Shaun Armstead et al., "'And I Poor Slave Yet': The Precarity of Black Life in New Brunswick, 1766–1835," in *Scarlet and Black: Slavery and Dispossession in Rutgers History*, ed. Marisa J. Fuentes and Deborah Gray White (New Brunswick, NJ: Rutgers University Press, 2016), 92–93, 95, 97, 111–12.

7. Lobdell, ed., *Silvia Dubois, a Biografy*, 45.
8. Gregory Evans Dowd, "Declarations of Dependence: War and Inequality in Revolutionary New Jersey, 1776–1815," *New Jersey History* 103, nos. 1–2 (Spring–Summer 1985): 47–65 (quote on 49); legislature quoted in Susan E. Klepp, *Revolutionary Conceptions: Women, Fertility, and Family Limitation in America, 1760–1820* (Chapel Hill: University of North Carolina Press, 2009), 249.
9. Klepp, *Revolutionary Conceptions*, 92; Elizabeth Stordeur Pryor, *Colored Travelers: Mobility and the Fight for Citizenship Before the Civil War* (Chapel Hill: University of North Carolina Press, 2016), chap. 2; Kirsten E. Wood, *Accommodating the Republic: Taverns in the Early United States* (Chapel Hill: University of North Carolina Press, 2023), 39–45 (quote on 44); Susan M. Ryan, *The Moral Economies of American Authorship: Reputation, Scandal, and the Nineteenth-Century Literary Marketplace* (New York: Oxford University Press, 2016), 91.
10. Lobdell, ed., *Silvia Dubois, a Biografy*, 53–55 (quotes on 54). It remains unclear what happened to Dorcas's other children. In Tax Ratables, Hillsborough Township, Somerset County, September 1779, book 1731, NJSA, Richard Cumpton (Compton) is listed as the owner of one enslaved person who undoubtedly was Dorcas. Dominicus Duboys (Dubois) is also listed in the tax ratables. New Jersey State Census, 1875, East Amwell, Hunterdon, indicates that Silvia was born in Somerset County. On the practice of slave quitting, see Billy G. Smith, "Black Women Who Stole Themselves in Eighteenth-Century America," in *Inequality in Early America*, ed. Carla Gardina Pestana and Sharon V. Salinger (Hanover, NH: Dartmouth College, 1999), 144.

11. Lobdell, ed., *Silvia Dubois, a Biografy,* 55, 56–57, 63–65 (quotes on 64–65).
12. Lobdell, ed., *Silvia Dubois, a Biografy,* 44, 65–66 (quotes on 65–66).
13. Lobdell, ed., *Silvia Dubois, a Biografy,* 66.
14. Lobdell, ed., *Silvia Dubois, a Biografy,* 65, 66; James Oliver Horton and Lois E. Horton, "Violence, Protest, and Identity: Black Manhood in Antebellum America," in *A Question of Manhood: A Reader in U.S. Black Men's History and Masculinity,* vol. 1, *"Manhood Rights": The Construction of Black Male History and Manhood, 1750–1870,* ed. Darlene Clark Hine and Earnestine Jenkins (Bloomington: Indiana University Press, 1999), 394; Edgar J. McManus, *Black Bondage in the North* (Syracuse, NY: Syracuse University Press, 1973), chap. 10, esp. 161–62; Fulton, *Speaking Power,* 53.
15. Lobdell, ed., *Silvia Dubois, a Biografy,* 69. Minor and Pitts, "Introduction," 25n22, established that the baby in question was Judith.
16. Lobdell, ed., *Silvia Dubois, a Biografy,* 69. Armstead et al., "'And I Poor Slave Yet,'" 95, located the altercation "just outside of New Brunswick."
17. Lobdell, ed., *Silvia Dubois, a Biografy,* 69–70, emphasis added; Paul Axel-Lute, comp., "The Law of Slavery in New Jersey: An Annotated Bibliography," The Law of Slavery in New Jersey, 2013, A75 (sections 6–7 and 27–28), https://njlaw.rutgers.edu/collections/slavery/bibliog.php.
18. Lobdell, ed., *Silvia Dubois, a Biografy,* 69; George Yancy, *Black Bodies, White Gazes: The Continuing Significance of Race* (Lanham, MD: Rowman and Littlefield, 2008), 3, 10, 111–14 (quote on 114).
19. *Second Census of the United States: 1800* (New York: Norman Ross, 1990), 1; James J. Gigantino II, *Ragged Road to Abolition: Slavery and Freedom in New Jersey, 1775–1865* (Philadelphia: University of Pennsylvania Press, 2015), 9, 65, 92–94, 97, 106–10, 214–15, 232–38 (quote on 9). See also Hendrik Hartog, *The Trouble with Minna: A Case of Slavery and Emancipation in the Antebellum North* (Chapel Hill: University of North Carolina Press, 2018), 50–52; Graham Russell Hodges, *Slavery and Freedom in the Rural North: African Americans in Monmouth County, New Jersey, 1665–1865* (Madison, WI: Madison House, 1997), 135–36; and Giles R. Wright, *Afro-Americans in New Jersey: A Short History* (Trenton: New Jersey Historical Commission, Department of State, 1988), 13, 25, 27.
20. James Still, *Early Recollections and Life of Dr. James Still* (Philadelphia: J. B. Lippincott, 1877), 14–15, 40–42 (quote on 41).
21. Henry Scofield Cooley, *A Study of Slavery in New Jersey* (Baltimore: Johns Hopkins University Press, 1896), 55.
22. Stephanie M. H. Camp, *Closer to Freedom: Enslaved Women and Everyday Resistance in the Plantation South* (Chapel Hill: University of North Carolina Press, 2004), 6, 16–17, 24–25, 27–34, 65, 128–30, 137–38 (quotes on 28); Pryor, *Colored Travelers,* 57.

23. Pryor, *Colored Travelers*, 2, 32, 47.
24. Lobdell, ed., *Silvia Dubois, a Biografy*, 96.
25. Lobdell, ed., *Silvia Dubois, a Biografy*, 97n5.
26. Lobdell, ed., *Silvia Dubois, a Biografy*, 97.
27. Lobdell, ed., *Silvia Dubois, a Biografy*, 51, 74–75; Francis Bazley Lee, *New Jersey as a Colony and as a State: One of the Original Thirteen*, 4 vols. (New York: Lewis Historical, 1902), 2:454; Andrew D. Mellick Jr., *The Story of an Old Farm; or, Life in New Jersey in the Eighteenth Century* (Somerville, NJ: Unionist Gazette, 1889), 577–78, 607; Pryor, *Colored Travelers*, 11.
28. Lobdell, ed., *Silvia Dubois, a Biografy*, 66. The point about Silvia's retention of the surname Dubois draws on Venture Smith, *A Narrative of the Life and Adventures of Venture, a Native of Africa: But Resident Above Sixty Years in the United States of America. Related by Himself* (New London, CT: C. Holt, 1798), 30.
29. Seth Rockman, "The Unfree Origins of American Capitalism," in *The Economy of Early America: Historical Perspectives and New Directions*, ed. Cathy Matson (University Park: Pennsylvania State University Press, 2005), 336; Graham Russell Hodges, *Root and Branch: African Americans in New York and East Jersey, 1613–1863* (Chapel Hill: University of North Carolina Press, 1999), 175–76 (quote on 175); Ira Berlin, *Many Thousands Gone: The First Two Centuries of Slavery in North America* (Cambridge, MA: Harvard University Press, 1998), 245 (quote). See also Hodges, *Root and Branch*, 178.
30. Lobdell, ed., *Silvia Dubois, a Biografy*, 70; Gigantino, *Ragged Road*, 153, 198–99; Armstead et al., "'And I Poor Slave Yet,'" 91; Debra L. Newman, "Black Women in the Era of the American Revolution in Pennsylvania," *Journal of Negro History* 61, no. 3 (July 1976): 96–101 (quote on 97–98), 282–84.
31. Lobdell, ed., *Silvia Dubois, a Biografy*, 70. For Compton's life, see Kenneth E. Marshall, "Tough, Rugged, and Evolving Masculinity: Harry Compton, an Enslaved and Free Black Man in Eighteenth- and Early Nineteenth-Century New Jersey," *New Jersey Studies* 7, no. 1 (Winter 2021): 107–44.
32. Lobdell, ed., *Silvia Dubois, a Biografy*, 28–32, 94 (quotes on 28, 30, and 94); Marshall, "Tough, Rugged, and Evolving Masculinity," 122–28, 131–35. According to Larison, to highlight Compton's elevated status on Sourland Mountain as a tavern owner, certain people shortened his adopted name of Harry Putnam to Harry Put, and his house became commonly known as Put's Tavern. The names drew inspiration from General Rufus Putnam, a military officer during the Revolutionary War. Larison contended that

Rufus Putnam was one of Compton's three former enslavers. Larison, *Silvia Dubois*, 28.
33. Lobdell, ed., *Silvia Dubois, a Biografy*, 70; will quoted in Marshall, "Tough, Rugged, and Evolving Masculinity," 139.
34. Lobdell, ed., *Silvia Dubois, a Biografy*, 28–32 (quotes on 32), 70; Sharon V. Salinger, *Taverns and Drinking in Early America* (Baltimore: Johns Hopkins University Press, 2002), 161–64, 170–71; Peter Thompson, *Rum Punch and Revolution: Taverngoing and Public Life in Eighteenth-Century Philadelphia* (Philadelphia: University of Pennsylvania Press, 1998), 40–41, 46; David W. Conroy, *In Public Houses: Drink and the Revolution of Authority in Colonial Massachusetts* (Chapel Hill: University of North Carolina Press, 1995), 103–4, 131–39, 318.
35. Benjamin L. Carp, *Rebels Rising: Cities and the American Revolution* (New York: Oxford University Press, 2007), chap. 2; Wood, *Accommodating the Republic*, 175–87 (quote on 177).
36. Lewis Morris, "Introductory Memoir," in *The Papers of Lewis Morris, Governor of the Province of New Jersey, from 1738 to 1746*, ed. William A. Whitehead (New York: George P. Putnam, 1852), 8–9; Lee, *New Jersey as a Colony and as a State*, 2:454.
37. Lobdell, ed., *Silvia Dubois, a Biografy*, 61–62 (quote on 62).
38. Lobdell, ed., *Silvia Dubois, a Biografy*, 55; Marc Mappen, *Jerseyana: The Underside of New Jersey History* (New Brunswick, NJ: Rutgers University Press, 1992), 51.
39. For the sexual exploitation of enslaved women, see, for example, Daina Ramey Berry, *The Price for Their Pound of Flesh: The Value of the Enslaved, from Womb to Grave, in the Building of a Nation* (Boston: Beacon Press, 2017), 78–85; Wilma King, "'Prematurely Knowing of Evil Things': The Sexual Abuse of African American Girls and Young Women in Slavery and Freedom," *Journal of African American History* 99, no. 3 (Summer 2014): 174–79; Thelma Jennings, "'Us Colored Women Had to Go Through a Plenty': Sexual Exploitation of African-American Slave Women," *Journal of Women's History* 1, no. 3 (Winter 1990): 60–65; Elizabeth Fox-Genovese, *Within the Plantation Household: Black and White Women of the Old South* (Chapel Hill: University of North Carolina Press, 1988), 34–35, 44–45, 242–43, 290–91, 292, 356–59; and Deborah Gray White, *Ar'n't I a Woman? Female Slaves in the Plantation South*, rev. ed. (1985; New York: Norton, 1999), 102–3, 152–53, 164–65, 174–75.
40. Lobdell, ed., *Silvia Dubois, a Biografy*, 67. This analysis draws on Agatha Rowe-Crowder, "Authority and Identity in Sylvia Dubois: A Biografy of the Slav Who Whipt Her Mistres and Gand Her Fredom by C. W. Larison,"

Liberated Arts: A Journal for Undergraduate Research 5, no. 1 (2018): 7–8, https://ojs.lib.uwo.ca/index.php/lajur.

41. Klepp, *Revolutionary Conceptions*, 3; Lobdell, ed. *Silvia Dubois, a Biografy*, 54–55; Larison, *Silvia Dubois*, 85; Lobdell, "Introduction," 11; US Census, 1830, Amwell, Hunterdon, NJ; US Census, 1840, Amwell, Hunterdon, NJ; US Census, 1850, East and West Amwell, Hunterdon, NJ; US Census, 1880, East Amwell, Hunterdon, NJ.
42. Lobdell, ed., *Silvia Dubois, a Biografy*, 27, 31; Klepp, *Revolutionary Conceptions*, 243–46 (quote on 246). On the drunkenness of women, see Salinger, *Taverns and Drinking*, 223–24.
43. Klepp, *Revolutionary Conceptions*, 3–4, 6, 54–55, 94–98, 106–14.
44. Klepp, *Revolutionary Conceptions*, 8.
45. Lobdell, ed., *Silvia Dubois, a Biografy*, 52.
46. Lobdell, ed., *Silvia Dubois, a Biografy*, 34–35, 38, 70 (quote on 70); Berthold, "'The Peals of Her Terrific Language,'" 12. On the hostile proslavery sentiment of White New Jerseyans, see Marion Thompson Wright, "New Jersey Laws and the Negro," *Journal of Negro History* 28, no. 2 (April 1943): 182–84.
47. Lobdell, ed., *Silvia Dubois, a Biografy*, 73–74 (quotes on 73); Lobdell, "Introduction," 16.

Gender, Race, and Missionization in Antebellum Indian Territory

STEVEN PEACH

IN MARCH 1850, a Presbyterian missionary named Hamilton Balentine reported about the Kowetah Mission School, one of three Presbyterian missions located in the Creek and Seminole nations in Indian Territory. Like its counterparts, the school offered courses in English composition and other subjects to children and young adults. Balentine remarked that a mission education was "by no means offensive to their parents who take no small pains to let their neighbors know what their children can do." Women especially gloated about their children's educational achievements. One member of Balentine's church told him "that she had shown her little daughter's letter to our town Chief who is a notorious opposer of the Gospel." She "demanded" that the headman abandon his opinion "that the children learn nothing at Mission School."[1]

Following her cue, this essay traces the impact of missionization on women of color in the antebellum Creek and Seminole nations. Drawing on a voluminous Presbyterian correspondence, it reveals that women shaped the missionary enterprise to accommodate individual, familial, community, and national interests. While some earned wages from the missions, others experimented with new religious beliefs, practices, and spaces. Still others found ways to recreate and strengthen bonds of kinship. Altogether, women of color advanced a strategy of cautious engagement with missionaries who furthered US imperial expansion in the trans-Mississippi West.[2]

Study of women of color in the Creek and Seminole nations, like the proud mother and talented daughter at Kowetah, raises new questions about gender, religion, and colonialism in the area designated by Congress as Indian Territory in 1834 and the state of Oklahoma in 1907. Historians have demonstrated that nineteenth-century southern Indian men, especially the leadership, opposed missionization because it undermined religious practices, siphoned tribal monies for mission budgets, and challenged the political leadership for influence over local communities. To these men, missionization was an extension of colonialism. Yet, this scholarly conversation overlooks ways in which women addressed missionaries' presence in Indian Territory. What did Native women think of the missionaries, and how did they respond to missionary assaults on Native autonomy? How did these women respond to missionaries' goals to disrupt gender roles and advance the US government's "plan of civilization"?[3]

Furthermore, women of African descent shaped this line of inquiry. Historians have shown that southern Indian men and women enslaved Black people beginning in the late eighteenth century and sculpted a racial hierarchy premised on the elevation of Native over Black. Native enslavers endorsed anti-Black racism in legal codes and social encounters with Black people, enslaved or free. Racism and Native sovereignty, then, went hand in hand. Still, Black women were central to the histories and cultures of the southern Indians. We must ask, accordingly, how they shaped missionaries' gendered project of conversion. In what ways did Black women seek to control their own lives, define religion, care for children, and, most importantly, pursue avenues toward freedom?[4]

Surviving records make it challenging to answer these questions. Missionaries identified some women as Creek or Seminole, others as African or "colored," and still others as a mixture of Native, Black, and White. Presbyterian missionary Mary Price understood that people living in Indian Territory defied easy racial categorization. Sounding like an anthropologist more than a missionary, she wrote in 1855 about "a motley looking group" that attended a religious gathering and commented that "the African & and the Indian are so confounded that it [cannot] be told when one Race ends, or the other begins." Price's observations underscore not only the malleability of race but also the abundance of interracial relationships among Indigenous nations of Indian Territory. While the problem of race in southern Indian history is extraordinarily complex, racial categories had real meaning for women of color. Black women were more subject to enslavement, experienced more racism, and exercised less mobility than did Native women of the Creek and Seminole nations. Still, the same records indicate that Native and Black women frequently associated with one another and sought to transcend the racial structures of nineteenth-century Indian Territory and, more broadly, the United States. Women asserted agency as laborers and teachers, translators and churchgoers, and healers and mothers. Consequently, gendered meanings of work, spirituality, and community offered a bypass around the entrenchment of scientific racism and the hardening of social relations based on race in the antebellum era.[5]

Presbyterian ministers and teachers arrived in Indian Territory on the heels of Indians' forcible expulsion from the Southeast in the 1830s. Accompanied by soldiers, merchants, and settlers, the Presbyterians came at the behest of the American Board of Commissioners for Foreign Missions. Founded in 1810 in Boston, the organization set up missions across North America with money from the federal government's Civilization Fund, middle-class donors on the East Coast, and tribal money from host Native nations. The Second Great Awakening set the context for missionaries' zeal to convert so-called heathen Native Americans. By transforming Native peoples into American Christians, the Presbyterians hoped to instill Christian values, teach biblical literacy, and usher in the new millennium. Yet they clashed with other denominations, including the Methodists and Baptists who founded missions in Indian Territory and seemingly attracted more interest among Native peoples. Whereas Presbyterians preferred careful instruction in the classroom and prayer inside the walls of a church, Baptists and Methodists preached at out-of-doors camp meetings beneath brush arbors that resembled the square grounds of southern Indian towns of the previous century.[6]

All missionaries pursued the cultural as well as spiritual transformation of the continent's Indigenous peoples. Particularly alarmed by Native women's traditional influence in southern Indian societies, missionaries attempted to supplant the flexibility of Native kin networks with the rigidity of the nuclear family. They promoted middle-class practices such as domestic work and consumption in the private household, obedience to male authorities, and lay piety. To advance these goals, the Presbyterians founded Kowetah (1843) and Tullahassee (1848) in the Creek nation and Oak Ridge (1848) in the Seminole nation.[7] Each was a mission and manual labor boarding school designed to administer theological instruction and educate children in White American gendered customs. William Robertson, who taught at Tullahassee, wanted to equip children with "a good English education" and "industrious habits." Superintendent of Oak Ridge John Lilley waxed eloquent about gender-based instruction, boasting that "Boys & Girls . . . work in their appropriate spheres." As he wrote one of his superiors in the East, J. Leighton Wilson, boys "are engaged in the different labors of the farm" while "girls [perform] the various household duties," such as spinning, weaving, quilting, and cooking. Hannah Greene, caretaker for Kowetah's female students, strove for "order, neatness, punctuality, industry" among her charges and encouraged them to be "respectful and obedient" toward superiors.[8]

Presbyterians welcomed Black families into the mission fold as readily as Indigenous ones. James R. Ramsay, a missionary and teacher at Kowetah, wrote about the "very large" number of "African" parents who "make every effort to get their children educated." Despite objections from the Creek government, he could not "easily refuse taking in some of them especially as many of their children are very promising." Creek headmen worried that the Presbyterians would take tribal money for less-than-deserving Black souls. As they sought to compete with other denominations' missionaries, Ramsay and other Presbyterians defied the headmen. Aside from interdenominational competition, many Presbyterians, including Ramsay, thought that Black Americans made better Christians than Native Americans. Historians note that enslaved and free Black people espoused Christian revivalism in the era before removal and continued to practice a form of Black Christianity in Indian Territory. Because many Black men spoke and read English, they served as translators and other go-betweens for southern Indian headmen who refused to treat directly with missionaries and government agents in the 1840s and 1850s. Presbyterians and other missionaries heaped praise on educated Black converts, ensuring that people of African descent could access mission resources in Indian Territory.[9]

To build and run missions in the Creek and Seminole nations, the Presbyterians inserted themselves into an economy of local, regional, and national scale. Each of their three missions relied on farming wheat and keeping livestock, especially cows and hogs. When drought wilted crops or disease killed animals, missionaries bought food and other supplies from merchants around the United States. Fort Gibson on the Arkansas River was a popular source of goods, as was Cincinnati, Ohio, otherwise known as Porkopolis. On occasion, the Presbyterians purchased bacon and other pork products from the city. Labor kept the missions afloat, and Presbyterians depended heavily on the paid and enslaved work of women of color. Native and Black women prepared meals for faculty and students, cleaned and organized classrooms and sleeping quarters, washed and mended clothing, raised money, served as cross-cultural translators, and secured lucrative teaching positions.[10]

Culinary skills and cleaning services were in high demand. Superintendent of the Tullahassee mission R. M. Loughridge wrote to a superior in April 1850 that "in the kitchen & house work we have an Indian woman hired & black woman" on loan from her enslaver. "We also hire an *Indian* woman one day in the week to wash" the mission's laundry, Loughridge noted a few months later. Superintendent Lilley hired a female Seminole cook at Oak Ridge because there was no available "white woman within 60 miles." She earned cash too. "Our Cook gets $5 pr month," Lilley reported, "which is as low as we can get one," suggesting that she haggled with Lilley for better wages. "Her pay," he explained, "is half cash & half in trade."[11]

Mission labor provided enslaved women with opportunities to win freedom from enslavement. In fall 1852, Loughridge devised a plan to buy an enslaved woman from her enslaver, compensate her for her labor, and eventually manumit her. He "concluded to purchase a *black woman,* who is the wife of *Robin,* the interpreter of Kowetah" for six hundred dollars. Loughridge claimed that his actions would keep wife and husband together by preventing her enslaver from selling her to another White man far from the missions. She was skilled, being "a good seamstress," and "understands cooking pretty well." He pledged to pay her "fair wages" for her labor so that presumably she might buy herself out of enslavement. But no evidence confirms that she earned sufficient money, let alone the full six hundred dollars, to clear her debt to him. In another example, Loughridge paid an enslaved woman named Cealia to serve as Tullahassee's "cook." Before attempting to purchase her freedom, however, she died. Although freedom remained elusive for the Presbyterians' enslaved women (and men), they nonetheless pursued it in carefully circumscribed situations.[12]

Other women of color looked to the missions to weave a safety net for themselves and their families. In 1855, William Templeton, a teacher at Kowetah, profiled a Creek woman known only as Mrs. Jones. A "pious widow," she served Kowetah as a cook but earned too little money to enroll her three children in the mission. She "being poor needs assistance in educating her children." Templeton pled with his superior on her behalf, indicating that Jones was a church member and "a very economical woman" who could benefit the mission immensely. In Templeton, Jones found an ally as she reeled from impoverishment and isolation in Indian Territory. Other women struggled to find work at all. One "colored womman who lives here has been indulgeing a hope for some work," wrote Mary Price, a Tullahassee teacher. According to Price, the free Black woman sought odd jobs and attempted to enmesh herself in the mission economy. Like Jones, this woman joined the church to find both community and money.[13]

Mission students also wished to earn money and build social ties. On a Saturday afternoon in January 1855, Elizabeth Diament penned a letter from the caretakers' bedroom. She summarized the goings-on during Tullahassee's winter session, explaining that the students had been clamoring for money all week, and that specifically "two little girls came to our room, saying they had no money & wished us to let them" work. Diament and other teachers subsequently "employed them to do some little work & paid them for it." The pupils earned up to twenty dollars for their labor. Whether they saved the money for themselves or someone else is unclear, but they expressed a desire to earn cash. One year later, Price paid several female students to sew and mend clothing, compensating their labor with "bits" of picayune, a Spanish coin that circulated in the nineteenth-century economy. Some students donated earnings to support mission activities. According to Anna Turner, a Tullahassee faculty member, the school decided to cancel classes on New Year's Day in 1859 so that "the pupils might earn money to [support] our Monthly Concert." Twenty-eight girls ended up making money from an unknown task, and each of them donated $1.50 for the concert. Praising the mission's success, Turner gloated, "I know of no place like Tallahassee for dispatching work."[14]

Women labored beyond the mission walls as well, drawing on their knowledge of cultures, languages, and foodstuffs. While it is well-known that missionaries and headmen hired Native and Black men as translators, women also served in that capacity. In August 1855, for example, John Lilley touted the accomplishments of one Seminole student who "could not speak any English" when she first arrived at Oak Ridge. Lately, however, "she reads well & speaks quite plainly." She had become so literate in English that a Seminole headman "with evident satisfaction used [her] as an interpreter," although he may have paid the mission for her services rather than the student. Literate, bilingual, and comfortable in multiple worlds, the young Seminole woman made an impact on mission life and Native-missionary relations. Lilley reported four years later that "both Boys & Girls [from Oak Ridge] are sometimes used as interpreters" by Seminole headmen. Many, he averred, labor "for the Glory of God, & the good of the Seminole people."[15] The Presbyterians' Native neighbors also transacted with missionaries on occasion. When Oak Ridge's steel mill gave out in 1855, Lilley hired "some women to beat some corn in the common Indian way." He thought it was a "poor way" to make food, but the women's efforts filled hungry bellies and confirmed the quotidian interactions between Native people and missionaries.[16]

Moreover, career-driven women who graduated from the missions accepted faculty positions in Indian Territory, earning prosperous incomes and applying skills nurtured in mission classrooms and other educational spaces. Whether the women considered themselves Christians is difficult to gauge, but evidence suggests that they and other Native Americans in the nineteenth century preferred secular to spiritual education.[17] One of them was Kizziah Lewis, an exemplary student by all accounts. In fall 1850, at roughly fourteen years of age, she began her schooling at Tullahassee and soon excelled in the curriculum. She took algebra in spring 1853 and wrote one of her first letters in 1855.[18] Following her graduation, Lewis moved to Arkansas where she enrolled at Cane Hill Female Seminary. She then returned to the Creek nation to work at Tullahassee.[19] By early 1858, she and several other female graduates were serving the mission as teachers, earning $250 each per annum. While missionaries celebrated the women as model converts, Lewis and her colleagues masterfully negotiated educational and financial opportunities to benefit themselves and their nation.[20]

Women of color encountered a world of spirits as they labored at the Presbyterian missions and otherwise involved themselves in missionary affairs. That spirit world was the product of centuries of settler colonialism, Christian missionization, Black and Indian enslavement, and an amalgam of religions drawn from the Americas, Europe, and Africa. The women cannot therefore be pigeonholed into Christian, animistic, or syncretic affiliations. Rather, Native and Black women created relationships and community by borrowing from and experimenting with whatever spiritual tools were available or needed in the moment.

A woman whom the Presbyterians called "Aunt Lacy" exemplified Indian Territory's dynamic spiritual landscape. Known also as "Old Aunt Lacy," she ran a popular healing business in the 1840s and 1850s. She treated the ill in an environment rife with disease, including trachoma or "sore eyes," an illness that plagued mission students; rheumatism and various fevers; and other maladies the missionaries called "sickness."[21] From Kowetah, James Ramsay reported in April 1850 that this "Doctoress" treated her patients by "'blowing' in medicine" for a small fee. This had been "her principal means of support" for many years. Like female and male medicine makers (*hilis-haya*) in the pre-removal Native Southeast, Lacy learned how to diagnose and treat illnesses attributed to the spiritual realm. Like medicine makers before her too, she devised cures by using the pharmacopeia around her. Being "very old" with gray hair, she possessed esoteric knowledge and commanded respect from her many patients in Indian Territory. Aunt Lacy became so popular as to draw the ire of missionaries and doctors, such as Dr. James Junkin, who complained about "the preeminence of . . . old conjurors" undermining his medical practice at Tullahassee.[22]

As a healer, Lacy sought fresh spiritual knowledge and power from the missions. While she annoyed Tullahassee's doctor, she befriended other missionaries and attended church gatherings. According to Ramsay, Lacy "has constantly come to church" at Kowetah accompanied by a young woman. They "are full Creeks, I believe[.] They are neighbours to us, & for a long time have been steady attendents" of prayer meetings where Ramsay "preached Gospel at the mission." By spring 1850, Lacy "expressed a desire to be Baptized." When Ramsay asked for assurance that she would quit her "superstitious" healing practice, "she said she believed" that Christ would provide for her and pledged to "quit 'blowing' in medicine." Before the rite of baptism, Lacy and her young friend united with the church on "Examination" and "profession of their faith in Christ." Presbyterians normally bestowed a "Certificate" on those who pledged to follow Christ, but whether the two of them received it in this case is uncertain. The rituals culminated in the baptism of both women. Thus, Lacy cemented her access to the Presbyterians and further captured spiritual powers.[23]

Lacy appeared in the archives once more, in January 1859, when Hamilton Balentine "baptized 'Aunt Lacy's' black baby and called it Samuel." Hamilton's use of "black" to describe the child indicates that Lacy had formed a sexual relationship with a man of African descent, thereby offering more evidence of the dynamic interracial climate of Indian Territory. What became of her partner is unclear, but Lacy chose baptism for herself and her newborn. Her knowledge of medicine, healing, and Christianity point to a woman who understood baptism and other rituals as transformative and regenerative. The space in which those rituals unfolded mattered too, as Kowetah's church was sacred, the pure water used in baptism was sacred, and the people surrounding the baptized child lent a community ethos to the sacred practice. By having Samuel baptized, moreover, Lacy may have looked to protect him from otherworldly dangers. Baptism was spiritual insurance for women of color and their children.[24]

Other women in the Creek nation believed baptism to be important. Superintendent Loughridge reported from Tullahassee in 1857 that "an aged coloured woman was baptized & admitted to all the privileges of the Church on the profession of her faith." Drawing from the conviction of her beliefs, she united with a diverse community of churchgoers. Even women skeptical of Christianity accepted baptism as they lay dying. In spring 1855, Lilley traveled from Oak Ridge to the homes of "two sick women to baptize them." They were unable "to come to the Station & desired to be received into the church." The following winter, Lilley baptized a woman in her home because chronic rheumatism kept her from attending the mission's weekly prayer meetings. She passed away soon thereafter. Ramsay related a similar account of a dying woman in the nearby Creek nation.[25]

Family and neighbors participated in such rituals that reflected and reinforced community belonging in Indian Territory, pulling missionaries beyond the confines of church walls. During the baptism of one sick woman near Oak Ridge, Lilley reported that "she talked with her friends about leaving them to go to be with her Savior." He baptized another dying woman during a prayer meeting that was "well attended" at her home. Indeed, the busy gathering continued several days after her death. Near Kowetah, one ill woman received a visit from Ramsay only because her community "requested" that he "go & hold a prayer meeting" for her. She passed away the same day of his visit. Afterward, he and the community buried her in a makeshift coffin. Missionaries held prayer meetings beyond the walls of the mission in other contexts. Lilley revealed to a superior that the "people enjoy prayer & praise the meetings [which] are well attended at the [Oak Ridge] Mission & neighborhood too." Kowetah's William Templeton preached throughout the Creek and Seminole nations in the 1850s, including in the neighborhood around

Little River and once "at a colored woman's [home] in another neighborhood." Local demand forced missionaries to abandon the Presbyterian custom of preaching indoors and remain open and flexible to community preferences.[26]

In other cases, missionaries preached to community members on terms set by women. In February 1857, Lilley wrote J. Leighton Wilson about two "married men" who were steadfast churchgoers and recently received into the church on profession of their faith. "Both their wives opposed" these developments and "used every means to get their husbands to quit praying & turn again to heathenism." Relations between one husband and wife deteriorated so much that "she would not speak to" him. The marital row generated a "warm interest" among the community, inspiring neighbors and missionaries alike to intervene. After Lilley's persistent entreaties, the wife "said she would not oppose her husband again" on the sole condition that prayer meetings "continued at her house." She and other women who weighed in on missionization surely experienced pressure from multiple quarters, but they controlled the community spaces and households in which church members gathered to pray and discuss religion. Lilley recognized that Oak Ridge's success rested in part on women who called the shots from time to time.[27]

Inside the missions, daily life fostered relationship-building among female students and faculty alike. Elizabeth Diament reported in 1855 that she and other female caretakers at Tullahassee led a "female prayer meeting" with their charges each evening. Here and elsewhere, the female students practiced a lived, emotive style of worship that complemented formal instruction in biblical literacy and mandatory church attendance on the Sabbath. Diament opined that religious gatherings among female pupils were "very important" in developing "character." The talented Kizziah Lewis offered a student's perspective on the impact of Tullahassee's ritual schedule. Speaking for the other "girls" in a letter penned to Wilson, she lamented "the death of one of the girls" who was "a good christian" and stated, "We have very kind missionaries but we love Miss Price best." The female students liked Price "because," Lewis wrote, "she looks something like an Indian [with her] dark hair. We have a great taste for beauty as well as goodness and we consider her both good and pretty." Lewis stood at the center of a spiritual support network that encouraged connections between student and teacher.[28]

Cultivation of community and the production of labor in and around the Presbyterian missions gave women of color time to shore up family ties. Southern Indians arrived in Indian Territory as heirs to a rich matrilineal kinship system that told them who belonged to a specific clan, lineage, and household (*huti*). Gender and matrilineality in the eighteenth and early nineteenth centuries have been well-researched, but less evident are ways in which southern Indians practiced kinship in the 1840s and 1850s, following the catastrophe of ethnic expulsion from the Southeast. Presbyterian records paint a grim picture of shattered families and orphaned children to be sure, but they also underscore the resiliency of southern Indian peoples and kinship patterns. Among antebellum Creeks and Seminoles, women assumed numerous familial responsibilities that normally fell to other relatives in previous generations. They adapted ancient kin traditions to meet present needs in Indian Territory.[29]

Mothers taking pains to supervise children litter the records on Indian Territory. Shortly after Tullahassee's opening, William Robertson described a Sunday School event attended by "mothers and their children" of "all colors from White to red, & from red to black." Some families became church members and attended weekly meetings, including one "mother and one daughter, members" of the Kowetah church.[30] Over time, missionaries simultaneously welcomed parents and children into church life not only because they sought converts but also because they recognized that parents, mothers especially, wished to protect little ones. James Ramsay baptized three students along with the "mother of one of them" at Kowetah in spring 1851.[31] On another occasion, he described a promising young male student whose "mother has long been, & at present is a member of the church." Although her Christian devotion apparently lapsed, she raised no objections when her son participated in church life. A few years later, Loughridge reported from Tullahassee that "a man & a woman, both Colored persons" were received into the church. The woman "& her little son who is about two years old," he elucidated, "were baptized at the same time." Teachers and administrators recognized, then, that mothers were never far from any ritual, meeting, or activity that put their children and missionaries in the same space.[32]

In the Seminole nation too missionaries received whole families into the church so long as women consented. In November 1856, Lilley accepted four people into the church at Oak Ridge, including an "old woman," her "Daughter" and "Son," and the son's "wife." Although the siblings were "exemplary" Christians according to Lilley, the elder mother had been "serious a long time" about Christianity but never joined the church. She finally evinced a "change of heart" and decided to unite with the Presbyterians. Whether her children or Lilley wore her down is unclear, but Lilley's report confirms that her decision constituted approval for the remainder of the family to join the church and take communion at Oak Ridge. Lilley suggested, moreover, that a woman like her reinterpreted an important matrilineal custom. Historically, a mother's brother cared for her son (his nephew), but Lilley did not mention an avuncular figure. Nor did it appear that her son moved into his wife's household, as matrilineal culture had once dictated. Thus, the shock of removal may have prompted such changes and spurred people to reconstitute and redefine family ties. The "old woman" and her kin at Oak Ridge embraced innovation to survive in a new world.[33]

Like the missionaries, headmen needed women's support in religious affairs. Seminole headman John Jumper could not have his child baptized by Lilley until Jumper's wife agreed to it. Ramsay, who labored at Oak Ridge beside Lilley in the late 1850s, observed that Jumper "& some of his relatives" had been baptized and attended church regularly. Ramsay noted that the baptism of the headman's "little son," however, was "postponed until we would see whether his mother would soon become a christian." She took her time. "The Chief's wife held back a good while," he wrote, exposing the opposition that some women in the Seminole nation exercised toward Christian missionaries. Nevertheless, "she came forward as Inquirer has been very attentive to meeting & last night met the session was examined & received into the church." Later reports suggest that she and her son were baptized at Oak Ridge, although the young boy soon passed away from a likely bout of whooping cough.[34]

Jumper's wife as well as many other women of color contended with new social circumstances in Indian Territory. The death of loved ones from forcible removal, disease, and other misfortunes scythed kin networks and put enormous pressure on women to raise children. In addition, missionaries aggressively encouraged patriarchy, pushing husbands to commandeer households, oversee wives, and control children. The tension in the Jumper family exemplified these changes. Still, women refused to concede ground to their male counterparts. Jumper's wife, for one, attended church with her son, approved her son's baptism, and received baptism alongside her son. Without an apparent brother to raise her son, as per matrilineal customs, she stepped up, forcing her husband and missionaries to respect the familial power that Native women continued to exercise.

Following removal, moreover, orphanage became an alarming trend in Indian Territory. Some women responded by adopting and caring for orphans. William Templeton generated a roster of Kowetah's student body in fall 1852 and wrote brief biographies of each student. According to Templeton, ten-year-old Susan Vann had lost her mother or father (or both) in recent years but was "an adopted child of a woman who clothed her." By the 1850s, some of Tullahassee's students, including Mary Penn, had been orphaned. Like the gifted Kizziah Lewis, Penn quickly advanced in the school's curriculum and learned to read and write in English. In a letter to a Presbyterian benefactor, she wrote in legible prose: "This is the first letter I have ever tried to write," and "I think we are learning fast in school." After describing her daily schedule, she revealed, "I have neither father nor mother," adding that "I have two little sisters in school." The orphaned family of three may have lived with the missionaries, for Loughridge later acknowledged that "two little orphan girls . . . stay with us" during summer break. And at Kowetah, Ramsay's wife decided to take in "a girl . . . until she is grown."[35]

Despite missionaries' occasional support, orphaned pupils adopted their own solutions to isolation from kin networks. To do so, they harkened back to the seventeenth and eighteenth centuries when Indigenous women adopted outsiders as fictive kin, thereby turning strangers into allies. Penn exemplified this centuries-old tradition: she and her younger sisters "look up to the missionaries as our dearest relations," especially "Mrs [Mary Junkin and] Dr. Junkin." Mary Junkin "is a very kind lady. We like to visit her." Penn added that "all missionaries are good to us." Although students' letters were monitored and probably censored by the mission faculty, Penn's words speak volumes about the shaping of kinship and intimacy in nineteenth-century mission spaces. Just as Kizziah Lewis "love[d]" Mary Price, so Penn and her sisters forged a meaningful connection with Mary Junkin. As orphans, the Penn siblings drew on the past to meet present needs, associating with specific faculty and writing boldly about attempts to create kin.[36]

If the Presbyterian missions fostered new avenues for kinship, they also cemented existing kin lines between children and parents. Recurring disease in Indian Territory exposed families' priorities and helped to strengthen family ties. In May 1851, for instance, William Templeton reported from Kowetah that student Eliza Thomas had been absent for several weeks. She had been sick "part of the time," but for the "rest of the time she was absent on acct. of her mother's sickness." Thomas decided that caring for her mother outweighed attending class and completing homework. Templeton sided with her, telling superiors that she was less a truant than a concerned daughter who ought to be permitted to care for her "sick mother." Generally, he added, students should "be encouraged to [a]ttend to their parents when sick, & in need of their help." One year later, two male students from Kowetah returned home for over two weeks "because there mother was sick." The faculty had heard nothing from the students and wondered whether they would return.[37]

The frequency with which students skipped class to tend to ill parents, especially mothers, forced school administrators to develop an absentee policy in the 1850s. Loughridge informed his superior that students could not go home "on any account, except in case of . . . sickness of some of the relatives." Administrators like Loughridge viewed most students who skipped class as aberrant "runaways" who ought to return to school or surrender their seat to another, more promising pupil. Throughout the 1840s and 1850s, students ran away from the missions to be sure, as missionary documents are littered with references to student rebelliousness. Yet missionaries noted the exceptions when students returned home to care for mothers in need. Those absentee students were not rebels; rather, they were attentive family members.[38]

Just as students worried about their mothers' health and safety, mothers took swift action when their children fell ill in the missions. In October 1851, Lilley drafted a lengthy report about a Seminole student who "took sick & died" despite his mother's efforts to save him. His English name was Gilbert Combs, and he had a sister named Mable. According to Lilley, Gilbert's "mother took him off some distance to an Indian doctor, but with all his powwowing he failed to benifit the child." She later returned to Oak Ridge to enlist Lilley's assistance. She told him that the Native healer had "tried all he could & that he could do the boy no good." Despite lacking medical expertise, Lilley visited the dying child but believed that "he was in no condition to take medicine. His eye was glazed his voice gone. he knew no one, all hope of recovery was past." Gilbert soon passed away and left a grief-stricken mother and sister behind.[39] The death of Gilbert Combs evidenced the tragedies that accompanied the missionization on southern Indian nations in nineteenth-century Indian Territory.

THE HISTORY of missionization and colonialism continues to haunt Native North America as the 2021 news coverage of unmarked and mass student graves at former Canadian boarding schools highlights. Christian missionaries in Indian Territory accelerated long-existing vectors of disease, cultural disruption, and settler expansion in Native North America. In the Creek and Seminole nations, Presbyterians commented on the regularity of sickness in and beyond the missions; the loss of kin following expulsion from the Southeast; the intense pressure on women as well as men to conform to Anglo-American, middle-class Christian practices; and the variety of labor regimes, including chattel slavery, tying Native and Black people to mission economies on the southern Plains and the entire United States.[40]

Letters among Presbyterian ministers, teachers, administrators, and benefactors testify to these horrific trends, but they also unearth moments when women of color in the Creek and Seminole nations seized opportunities to empower themselves, loved ones, neighbors, and the larger Indigenous community. These women vetted White American newcomers, deciding that a careful engagement with Presbyterian missions could generate economic, spiritual, and familial sustenance in the post-removal era. In a word, gender trumped race as these women made their impact felt in southern Indian societies. In return for money and goods, the women cooked food, cleaned laundry, served as translators and teachers, and carried out other services that eased daily life in the missions. Some women toiled under slavery but clamored for freedom. Moreover, Native and Black women participated in a vibrant spiritual world that produced cures for the ill, spaces for worship, and ways to build community and togetherness. Women guided these developments, doing everything possible to ensure the physical and spiritual well-being of kin.

In the generation before the American Civil War, then, women of color shaped the missionary encounter in Indian Territory. If headmen bristled at Christian missionaries, Native and Black women beyond officialdom devised their own understandings of and approaches to missionization. From missions, women generated cash, goods, secular and spiritual knowledge, new ties of kinship, and numerous other assets unforeseen by the newcomers. Despite missionaries' concerted efforts to replace southern Indian gender norms with White American patriarchy, Native and Black women remained influential agents in the financial, spiritual, and familial affairs of their nations.

Questions to Consider

1. In what ways did Native and Black women advance individual and collective interests in response to missionary assaults on Native autonomy?
2. How did the US government's "plan of civilization" and attempts at missionization impact gender roles and expectations in Indian Territory?

Notes

1. Hamilton Balentine to Walter Lowrie, 13 March 1850, box 12, volume 2, letter 7, American Indian Correspondence: The Presbyterian Historical Society Collection of Missionaries' Letters, 1833–93, RG 224, Presbyterian Historical Society, Philadelphia. I thank Theda Perdue for lending me the late Michael D. Green's microfilm of the American Indian Correspondence.
2. My idea of "cautious engagement" is inspired by Theda Perdue, "Catharine Brown: Cherokee Convert to Christianity," in *Sifters: Native American Women's Lives*, ed. Theda Perdue (New York: Oxford University Press, 2001), 77–91, esp. 85–89, and conversations at the American Indian Center at the University of North Carolina at Chapel Hill. For religion as a dynamic rather than static practice, see Thomas A. Tweed, *Crossing and Dwelling: A Theory of Religion* (Cambridge, MA: Harvard University Press, 2006), esp. 8–10, 54–55, 167–71.
3. Kathryn E. Holland Braund, "Guardians of Tradition and Handmaidens to Change: Women's Roles in Creek Economic and Social Life During the Eighteenth Century," *American Indian Quarterly* 14, no. 3 (Summer 1990): 239–58; Theda Perdue, *Cherokee Women: Gender and Culture Change, 1700–1835* (Lincoln: University of Nebraska Press, 1998); Mary Jane Warde, *George Washington Grayson and the Creek Nation, 1843–1920* (Norman: University of Oklahoma Press, 1999); Perdue, "Catharine Brown," 77–91; Carolyn Ross Johnston, *Cherokee Women in Crisis: Trail of Tears, Civil*

War, and Allotment, 1838–1907 (Tuscaloosa: University of Alabama Press, 2003); Julie Reed, *Serving the Nation: Cherokee Sovereignty and Social Welfare, 1800–1907* (Norman: University of Oklahoma Press, 2016); Rowan Faye Steineker, "'Fully Equal to That of Any Children': Experimental Creek Education in the Antebellum Era," *History of Education Quarterly* 56, no. 2 (May 2016): 273–300.

4. Claudio Saunt, *Black, White, and Indian: Race and the Unmaking of an American Family* (New York: Oxford University Press, 2005); Kevin Mulroy, *The Seminole Freedmen: A History* (Norman: University of Oklahoma Press, 2007); Gary Zellar, *African Creeks: Estelvste and the Creek Nation* (Norman: University of Oklahoma Press, 2007); David A. Chang, *The Color of the Land: Race, Nation, and the Politics of Land Ownership in Oklahoma, 1832–1929* (Chapel Hill: University of North Carolina Press, 2010); Barbara Krauthamer, *Black Slaves, Indian Masters: Slavery, Emancipation, and Citizenship in the Native American South* (Chapel Hill: University of North Carolina Press, 2013); Alaina E. Roberts, *I've Been Here All the While: Black Freedom on Native Land* (Philadelphia: University of Pennsylvania Press, 2021).

5. Price used the term "creolization" to interpret the cultural and racial hybridity she witnessed; see Mary S. Price to J. Leighton Wilson, 12 November 1855, American Indian Correspondence, box 6, volume 1, letter 42. See also Sydney W. Mintz and Richard Price, *The Birth of African-American Culture: An Anthropological Perspective* (1976; rpt. Boston: Beacon Press, 1992).

6. No wonder missionary and teacher William Robertson groused about his competitors' attempt to "discredit . . . the whole" Presbyterian agenda; see Robertson to Walter Lowrie, 31 March 1851, American Indian Correspondence, box 12, volume 2, letter 54. See also Rowena McClinton, "Cherokee and Christian Expressions of Spirituality Through First Parents," in *The Native South: New Histories and Enduring Legacies*, ed. Tim Alan Garrison and Greg O'Brien (Lincoln: University of Nebraska Press, 2017), 70–83; John Demos, *The Heathen School: A Story of Hope and Betrayal in the Age of the Early Republic* (New York: Vintage Books, 2014); and John Lilley to J. Leighton Wilson, 10 August 1858, American Indian Correspondence, box 6, volume 1, letter 169. On square grounds, see "Observations on the Creek and Cherokee Indians, 1789," in *William Bartram on the Southeastern Indians*, ed. Gregory A. Waselkov and Kathryn E. Holland Braund (Lincoln: University of Nebraska Press, 1995), 180–83.

7. Presbyterians also founded missions and boarding schools among the Choctaw and Chickasaw nations. I have focused on the Creeks and Seminoles because they shared (and share) ethnic and kin ties dating to the

early to mid-eighteenth century when peoples known as Lower Creeks migrated to Florida to dodge British expansion. Migrants developed a separate, Seminole identity over time, but they remained in contact with their Creek forbears. For context, see Jack M. Schultz, *The Seminole Baptist Churches of Oklahoma: Maintaining a Traditional Community* (Norman: University of Oklahoma Press, 1999), 36–38; Steven C. Hahn, *The Invention of the Creek Nation, 1670–1763* (Lincoln: University of Nebraska Press, 2004), 235; John T. Ellisor, *The Second Creek War: Interethnic Conflict and Collusion on a Collapsing Frontier* (Lincoln: University of Nebraska Press, 2010), 335–416; and Steven J. Peach, "The Failure of Political Centralization: Mad Dog, the Creek Indians, and the Politics of Claiming Power in the American Revolutionary Era," *Native South* 11 (2018): 81–116, esp. 98–105.

8. Robertson to Lowrie, 31 March 1851; John Lilley to J. Leighton Wilson, 7 January 1857; Lilley to Colonel Samuel Rutherford [US agent to the Seminoles], 25 August 1859, American Indian Correspondence, box 6, volume 1, letters 97, 217; Hannah Greene to Walter Lowrie, 16 July 1851, American Indian Correspondence, box 12, volume 2, letter 68.

9. James Ross Ramsay to Walter Lowrie, 13 November 1851, American Indian Correspondence, box 12, volume 2, letter 98; Krauthamer, *Black Slaves, Indian Masters*, 53–57; Saunt, *Black, White, and Indian*, 10–26; Zellar, *African Creeks*, 1–10.

10. John Lilley to Walter Lowrie, 6 December 1851, American Indian Correspondence, box 12, volume 2, letter 105.

11. R. M. Loughridge to Walter Lowrie (?), 16 April 1850; Loughridge to Lowrie, 16 August 1850; John Lilley to Lowrie, 18 June 1851, American Indian Correspondence, box 12, volume 2, letters 12, 20, 66. Lilley and other missionaries normally identified someone they believed to be Black as "African" or "colored." Since he did not in this case and since no White women aside from faculty lived near Oak Ridge, it is safe to assume that the cook was Seminole.

12. R. M. Loughridge to Walter Lowrie, 4 October 1852, American Indian Correspondence, box 12, volume 2, letter 153; Loughridge to Lowrie, 16 April 1855, American Indian Correspondence, box 6, volume 1, letter 17.

13. William H. Templeton to J. Leighton Wilson, 19 May 1855, American Indian Correspondence, box 6, volume 1, letter 21; Price to Wilson, 12 November 1855. On Jones's late husband, see Hamilton Balentine to Wilson, 14 January 1859, American Indian Correspondence, box 6, volume 1, letter 196.

14. Elizabeth ("E.") Diament to J. Leighton Wilson, 6 January 1855; Mary S. Price to Wilson, 14 January 1856; Anna M. Turner ("A. M. Turner") to

Wilson, 7 January 1859, American Indian Correspondence, box 6, volume 1, letters 6, 49, 195.
15. John Lilley to "Mr. Washburn," 20 August 1855, American Indian Correspondence, box 6, volume 1, letter 34; Lilley to Rutherford, 25 August 1859. Lilley recognized that Native students used their educations to promote what is today called tribal sovereignty. I could locate no information on Washburn; he was perhaps a benefactor like Walter Lowrie or J. Leighton Wilson.
16. John Lilley to J. Leighton Wilson, 31 December 1855, American Indian Correspondence, box 6, volume 1, letter 4. For another example, see James Ross Ramsay to Walter Lowrie, 1 January 1850, American Indian Correspondence, box 12, volume 2, letter 1. These documents suggest traditional female farming remained widely practiced among southern Indians in Indian Territory.
17. Christina Snyder, *Great Crossings: Indians, Settlers, and Slaves in the Age of Jackson* (New York: Oxford University Press, 2017), 13–14, 71, 82–98.
18. R. M. Loughridge to Walter Lowrie (?), 30 September 1850; Loughridge to "Mr. Sharpe," 3 January 1851; William Robertson to Lowrie (?), November 1851, American Indian Correspondence, box 12, volume 2, letters 28, 43, 90; Kizziah Lewis to J. Leighton Wilson, 18 January 1855; Loughridge to Lowrie, 1 July 1855, American Indian Correspondence, box 6, volume 1, letters 9, 28. In her letter to Wilson, Lewis referred to herself as an "Indian girl."
19. William Robertson to J. Leighton Wilson, 9 April 1855; Elizabeth Diament to Wilson, 16 May 1855, American Indian Correspondence, box 6, volume 1, letters 16, 20.
20. William Robertson to J. Leighton Wilson, 31 January 1858, American Indian Correspondence, box 6, volume 1, letter 150.
21. James Ross Ramsay to Walter Lowrie, 8 April 1850, American Indian Correspondence, box 12, volume 2, letter 11; Mary S. Price to J. Leighton Wilson, 18 December 1856; John Lilley to Wilson, 31 January 1856, American Indian Correspondence, box 6, volume 1, letters 91, 54; William Templeton to "Colonel Rankin," 19 December 1850, American Indian Correspondence, box 12, volume 2, letter 37; William Robertson to Wilson, 1 October 1857, American Indian Correspondence, box 6, volume 1, letter 127. I could locate no information about Rankin.
22. Ramsay to Lowrie, 8 April 1850; Dr. James G. Junkin to Walter Lowrie, 14 June 1851, American Indian Correspondence, box 12, volume 2, letter 65; Caleb Swan, "Position and State of Manners and Arts in the Creek, or Muscogee Nation in 1791," quoted in *Information Respecting the History, Condition and Prospects of the Indian Tribes of the United States*, ed. Henry

Rowe Schoolcraft, 6 vols. (Philadelphia: J. B. Lippincott, 1855), 5:270–71. See also John R. Swanton, *Creek Religion and Medicine* (1928; rpt. Lincoln: University of Nebraska Press, 2000), 614–15. Swanton explained that those who mixed "medical and priestly functions" were known as "knowers" (*kilas*); Europeans called them "prophets." There were also "doctors proper" (*alektca*) and, in Lacy's case, "medicine makers" (*hilishaya*). Angela Pulley Hudson noted that a nineteenth-century "Doctress" also provided abortion care; see Hudson, "The Indian Doctress in the Nineteenth-Century United States: Race, Medicine, and Labor," *Journal of Social History* 54, no. 4 (2021): 1160–87, specifically 1160–65.

23. Ramsay to Lowrie, 8 April 1850; Lilley to Wilson, 31 January 1856.
24. Balentine to Wilson, 14 January 1859. On religious studies theory that privileges space, place, and fluidity over the hegemonic term "syncretism," see Tweed, *Crossing and Dwelling*, 5–7.
25. R. M. Loughridge to J. Leighton Wilson, 9 July 1857; John Lilley to J Wilson, 23 April 1855, American Indian Correspondence, box 6, volume 1, letters 117, 18; Lilley to Wilson, 31 January 1856; Ramsay to Lowrie, 1 January 1850.
26. Indeed, an Indigenized Presbyterianism took shape in these years. See Lilley to Wilson, 23 April 1855; Lilley to Wilson, 31 January 1856; Lilley to Wilson, 10 August 1858; Ramsay to Lowrie, 1 January 1850; John Lilley to J. Leighton Wilson, 25 March 1856, American Indian Correspondence, box 6, volume 1, letter 62; and William Templeton to Walter Lowrie, 8 September 1852, American Indian Correspondence, box 12, volume 2, letter 148. Works Progress Administration records discuss funerary rites among mid-nineteenth-century Creeks and Seminoles; see L. W. Wilson, transcript of interview of A. J. Kennedy, 27 July 1937, interview 6988, volume 50, Indian-Pioneer Papers Collection, Western History Collections, University of Oklahoma, Norman. Kennedy, a "White" man, lived in Vian, Oklahoma.
27. John Lilley to J. Leighton Wilson, 16 February 1857, American Indian Correspondence, box 6, volume 1, letter 101.
28. Diament to Wilson, 6 January 1855; Lewis to Wilson, 18 January 1855.
29. Braund, "Guardians of Tradition," 239–58; Natalie R. Inman, *Brothers and Friends: Kinship in Early America* (Athens: University of Georgia Press, 2017), 2–9; Bryan C. Rindfleisch, *Brothers of Coweta: Kinship, Empire, and Revolution in the Eighteenth-Century Muscogee World* (Columbia: University of South Carolina Press, 2021), 29–30, 40–41; Steven Peach, *Rivers of Power: Creek Political Culture in the Native South, 1750–1815* (Norman: University of Oklahoma Press, 2024), 8–10. On Cherokee kinship in the long nineteenth century, see Reed, *Serving the Nation*, 23–59.

30. William Robertson to Walter Lowrie, 20 August 1850, American Indian Correspondence, box 12, volume 2, letter 22; Balentine to Wilson, 14 January 1859.
31. James Ross Ramsay to Walter Lowrie (?), 26 March 1851, American Indian Correspondence, box 12, volume 2, letter 55. See also Ramsay to Lowrie, 15 July 1851, American Indian Correspondence, box 12, volume 2, letter 67.
32. James Ross Ramsay to Walter Lowrie, 12 February 1851, American Indian Correspondence, box 12, volume 2, letter 49; R. M. Loughridge to J. Leighton Wilson, 1 April 1856, American Indian Correspondence, box 6, volume 1, letter 63.
33. John Lilley to J. Leighton Wilson, 15 November 1856, American Indian Correspondence, box 6, volume 1, letter 87; Charles M. Hudson, *The Southeastern Indians* (Knoxville: University of Tennessee Press, 1976), 190–202.
34. James Ross Ramsay to J. Leighton Wilson, 11 May, 28 July 1857, 5 October 1858, American Indian Correspondence, box 6, volume 1, letters 111, 119, 180. The Seminole boy, named after Wilson, died in late 1858; see Ramsay to Wilson, 16 November 1858, American Indian Correspondence, box 6, volume 1, letter 1851, which reported cases of whooping cough that perhaps claimed the boy's life.
35. William Templeton to Walter Lowrie (?), September 1852; Mary Penn to Lowrie, 24 December 1852, American Indian Correspondence, box 12, volume 2, letters 150, 172; R. M. Loughridge to J. Leighton Wilson, 16 July 1856, American Indian Correspondence, box 6, volume 1, letter 74; Templeton to Lowrie, 19 November 1850, American Indian Correspondence, box 12, volume 2, letter 36.
36. Penn to Lowrie, 24 December 1852; Lewis to Wilson, 18 January 1855.
37. William Templeton to Walter Lowrie, 29 May 1851; Daniel Porter to Walter Lowrie, 16 July 1852, American Indian Correspondence, box 12, volume 2, letters 62, 142.
38. R. M. Loughridge to Walter Lowrie, 3 April 1851, American Indian Correspondence, box 12, volume 2, letter 58; William Templeton to Lowrie (?), 1 January, 4 January 1855; William Robertson to J. Leighton Wilson, 7 June 1858, American Indian Correspondence, box 6, volume 1, letters 1, 3, 161.
39. John Lilley to Walter Lowrie, 7 October 1851, American Indian Correspondence, box 12, volume 2, letter 86.
40. Ian Austen, "How Thousands of Indigenous Children Vanished in Canada," *New York Times*, 7 June 2021.

THINKING ABOUT INTERSECTIONALITY

WHAT DID it mean to be a woman or a man in the early American republic? What did it mean to be Black or White or Indigenous? What about heteronormative or queer, categories that did not exist at the time but applied to many people who lived in the early republic? For a long time, historians generally considered these questions separately, siloing race from gender, assuming the normalcy of White experiences and the prevalence of heterosexuality, and thus creating only partial portraits of how early Americans understood themselves. Then in the 1990s, feminist scholars of color formulated new ideas about expanding the late twentieth-century's women's rights movement beyond middle- and upper-class heterosexual White women. Among them was Kimberlé Crenshaw, whose theory of *intersectionality* centered how people are defined by multiple rights and inequalities simultaneously. Crenshaw argued that "focus on the most privileged group members marginalizes those who are multiply-burdened and obscures claims that cannot be understood as resulting from discrete forms of discrimination."[1] The most privileged group in the early republic was White men of some wealth and status, and historians certainly studied them to understand the era for a long time. Only since the late twentieth century have scholars begun to pursue more complex understandings of the diversity of people living in the early republic and how they faced oppression, lacked privilege, and lived on the margins.

For example, a Black woman and a White man both working in a New England factory in the 1840s experienced different levels of discrimination, even though both may have been considered working or lower class. Her femaleness made her susceptible to misogyny, and her Blackness made her a target of racism. His work fit more neatly into what privileged early Americans (and many historians) assumed was the "proper" role for men, whereas her work may have categorized her as "unruly," "uppity," or "mannish." Still, he may have faced discrimination for his poverty, immigrant status, religion, or sexuality.

In this section, three authors provide readers with opportunities to consider intersectionality—those overlapping systems of privilege and oppression. Lynn Kennedy presents the story of divorce between a wealthy, White, native-born man and an immigrant woman of mysterious family background. Shannon C. Eaves introduces us to an enslaved women who, having born a child by an affluent White man, was dissatisfied with the future that her daughter faced. Joshua A. Lynn explores the ways in which two prominent men—one Black, the other White—saw themselves and were perceived by others as embodying national politics. Collectively, these three essays suggest important questions about intersectionality in the early American republic. How were White men situated at the center of categorizing Others? What discriminations did immigrant women, enslaved children, and Black men face? How were individuals defined by more than one identity? What means did people use to move beyond the marginalized status ascribed to them?

Note

1. Kimberlé Crenshaw, "Demarginalizing the Intersection of Race and Sex," *University of Chicago Legal Forum* 1989, no. 1 (1989): 139–67 (quote on 140); Crenshaw, "Mapping the Margins: Intersectionality, Identity Politics, and Violence Against Women of Color," *Stanford Law Review* 43, no. 6 (June 1991): 1241–99.

"Scorned by Every Man of Honour"
THE MIDDLETON FAMILY, DIVORCE, AND
MASCULINE RESPECTABILITY

Lynn Kennedy

Edward Middleton met and married Edwardina de Normann in Naples, Italy, in 1845. After settling his new bride, known familiarly as Edda, with his extended family in Philadelphia, Edward resumed his career as a naval officer. Only a few years later, perhaps due to the separations that such a life entailed, the marriage began to fall apart. Accusations of improper flirtations led to charges that Edda had been unfaithful, and ultimately Edward sued for divorce. The Middletons undoubtedly felt both their happiness and unhappiness as uniquely their own, yet their relationship sat at the nexus of significant changes occurring around marriage, divorce, and gender relations in the mid-nineteenth century. Their narrative, told almost exclusively from the perspective of Edward and his relations, is particularly suggestive of the ways that competing conceptions of manhood and masculinity provided a distinct means of understanding the shifting patterns of interpersonal relationships.

That Edward Middleton married a woman unknown to his family made the couple's relationship stand out from the beginning. Edwardina de Normann's family background was shadowy at best. Gossip at the time suggested that her mother might have been a secret daughter of the Duke of Kent, making her Queen Victoria's half-sister, but the truth of such rumors, and Edda's own paternity, remain unclear. In contrast, Edward Middleton belonged to a well-established South Carolina family. His grandfather Arthur Middleton had signed the Declaration of Independence, and his father, Henry, had served as both governor and a congressman. For generations, the Middletons had used marriage to forge connections to other prominent South Carolina families. His relatives would have expected Edward to choose his bride from the social circles

143

that comprised the antebellum southern elite as most of his ancestors, siblings, and cousins had done.[1]

The Middleton family—parents, siblings, and extended kin—seemed to feel entitled to comment on Edward's life choices, including his selection of Edwardina as a spouse. Most expressed displeasure. Although Edward was a naval officer in his mid-thirties, serving half a world away when he met and fell in love with Edda, he still felt obligated to seek his father's permission to wed. At first, his request met with significant resistance and required much pleading to gain even limited parental approval. His mother, Mary, outlined the situation, writing to her daughter Eliza Fisher:

> But you will be surprised when you learn that your Father after reading the last letter & finding how devoted E^d was to the young girl, that he consented to his marrying her, observing that he had always been a good son. He however desired me to tell him that he could give him no money, & that as his pay was profitable, it must be sufficient to support him & his wife. This consent astonished me, because he had before so peremptorily refused it, but he seemed to feel for the poor fellow & I think *you* my dear Eliza would too, were you to read his letter.[2]

Eliza may indeed have been astonished by her father's capitulation, but she expressed no similar softening of opinion toward the marriage. While she evinced some pity for Edward's despondence at being initially denied approval for his marriage, she also expressed hope that her father's change of heart would not reach Edward until it was too late, "as it seems impossible that such a match should turn out well—and far better that he should grieve at a temporary disappointment than suffer from a permanent evil for so I should consider matrimony for him under the circumstances."[3] Thus, although she concluded that "he must now decide for himself," Eliza forthrightly expressed her thoughts on the matter, viewing it as fully in her purview as Edward's sister.

Edward's brother John, like Eliza, acknowledged that it was "no doubt Edward's affair," but he too expressed serious reservations. He suggested precisely why he believed the choice of a marriage partner should involve not merely the couple alone, observing that "a silly marriage involves in its consequences, not only the parties themselves, but all of their relat[ions]."[4] Edward and Edwardina's marriage, and its subsequent dissolution, sat amid the changing and competing interests—a juxtaposing of individual and family desires, and a balancing of emotional connections and practical concerns. For Edward Middleton's family, it also became a site of debate around shifting conceptions of manhood, and the limits and expectations of proper masculine behavior in the mid-nineteenth century. While the Middleton family's wealth and status set them apart from most Americans in this era, they were insulated from neither the emotional nor behavioral expectations of this society around proper gender relations.

ONE OF the first issues faced by Edward and Edwardina was that they married with limited input from the Middleton family. Historians have long debated the balance between personal desires and social expectations, between emotional connections and patriarchal and property concerns, in contracting marriage. Although scholars share a broad consensus of a gradual shift toward what has been termed *companionate* or *affective* marriage, they continue to debate what such a match entailed, and, equally contentiously, when and why the "new" form of marriage emerged.[5] In the context of nineteenth-century America, historian Ellen K. Rothman has suggested both the individual and the social importance of choosing marriage partners in nineteenth-century America, calling it "an amalgam of expectation, experience and convention" that has been "both a private journey and public rite of passage."[6] This description mirrors many of Edward's and Edda's experiences as they navigated between social and familial expectations and their own desires.

The changing views of marriage apparent by the mid-nineteenth century generally reflected larger social shifts. The establishment of the North American colonies coincided with evolving ideologies and understandings about the individual's place within society. Enlightenment philosophies that contributed so essentially to the revolutionary ethos in North America also, on a more personal level, raised questions that challenged the traditional model of patriarchal marriage. Historians have posited that the revolutionary era ushered in a more "participant-run system" of marriage with affection as an important part of mate selection, and with parental control over the choice of a partner all but disappearing by the beginning of the nineteenth century. Still, historian Ruth H. Bloch offered a caution that historians should not understand romance and economic interests as a dichotomy in which one consideration gained prominence over the other.[7]

The Middleton family's reaction to the marriage of Edward and Edwardina demonstrates a lingering desire to balance emotional attachment with familial imperatives and economic interests. Edward was a grown and apparently independent man when he met and fell in love with Edwardina, but before he could act on his feelings, he felt compelled to seek parental consent. His father, Henry Middleton, seemed to expect at least consultation, and ultimately the right to withhold approval. Yet the senior Middleton appeared torn in his perception of what a marriage should be. Initially, he rejected out of hand a match with someone of unknown character and family, but he eventually rescinded his objections, according to his wife, because of evidence of the strong emotional attachment of the couple. But at the same time, Henry continued to assert that Edward, in pursuing this path, should be cut off and forced to live on his naval salary alone. Clearly economic considerations had not entirely given way to emotional claims for this family.

Henry Middleton was a southerner, an enslaver, and a plantation owner, and Edward and his siblings had been raised to view themselves as southerners despite several family members taking up long-term residency in Philadelphia.[8] Scholars debate how southern attitudes toward marriage, particularly those of elite White southerners, might have been shaped by the presence of slavery and the patriarchal social system it engendered. Some historians, including Jane Turner Censer and Joshua Rothman, argued that the move toward companionate marriages mirrored trends in the rest of the nation, with Rothman writing that in the South, as in the North, "men and women increasingly married because they loved one another and because they believed marriage would bring the couple a lifetime of happiness and mutual affection."[9] In contrast, Bertram Wyatt-Brown, who viewed southern culture as distinctive from northern patterns, found an adherence to traditional patriarchal marriage lingering much longer among southerners, particularly those considered to be elite. "For all the talk of romance, undying passion and self-fulfilling independence," Wyatt-Brown wrote, "sons and daughters no less than parents expected elders to have a strong, even final voice on marital choices."[10] The experience of Edward Middleton in choosing a partner seems to have fallen somewhere between these two historiographical interpretations.

While he both followed his own romantic inclinations and sought parental permission, it would eventually be his siblings and extended family who assessed his marriage to Edwardina, and when they found her wanting, it was they who pressed for an end to the marriage. This narrative thus most closely aligns with Steven M. Stowe's work highlighting the importance of both emotive expressions of romantic love and the expectation that couples would seek parental approval. Central to such decisions was the role of family—not just the patriarch—in influencing the choice and ultimate acceptance of a mate into the family circle.[11]

Distinct southern views on marriage, as suggested in Wyatt-Brown's interpretation, reflected the centrality of patriarchal structures in this region. For White men throughout the United States, particularly of the growing middle class, gender expectations required an independence in decision-making so as not to have to rely on parental support and thus undermine a sense of self-reliance that was foundational to constructions of nineteenth-century masculinity. On the surface, familial interference into Edward's personal romantic affairs seems to contradict the autonomy required of this manhood. Yet historian Michael P. Johnson's study of Charleston elites, which included the Middleton family, illuminated the paradoxes of a southern patriarchal social structure that demanded independence of action while at the same time expecting sons of elite planters to be both subordinate and obedient to the family patriarchs in return for material resources and prestige.[12] Edward Middleton's marital experience placed him between these two versions of manhood, between independence and family responsibilities.

Courtship and marriage necessarily bring together the experiences of men and women since the interests of both genders combined in forming heterosexual marriage bonds. The interests of women, however, have attracted more scholarly attention, perhaps because historians of women have taken the lead in writing it, and perhaps just as importantly because the moment of a marriage proposal was one of the pivotal points when women made a choice and exercised control of their own fates—at least in theory. In practice, broader social concerns undoubtedly constrained any real sense of control. The development of companionate marriage may have provided more status for women, both in the negotiations involved in choosing a partner and potentially within the marriage itself, but a focus on affective relations did not eliminate gender ideals and expectations for either men or women. Edward Middleton's experiences in gaining approval for his marriage and his subsequent marital struggles suggest that many men found these decisions and events equally consequential.

Edward and Edwardina may have believed they were embarking on a companionate marriage, but his family's views of proper behavior, shaped by gender expectations, soon challenged the couple's emotional bond.[13] Edward Middleton's semi-independence likely underlay the troubles that emerged only a few years into the marriage. A deposition of his brother-in-law, taken as part of the divorce proceedings, indicated that Edward received a salary from the US Navy of $1,500 a year, and despite the threats made prior to his marriage of being cut off, he also received approximately $2,000 a year from his father's estate. Neither was an inconsiderable sum, but Edward did not set up an independent household for his young family. Rather, Edda lived with his relatives in Philadelphia while he returned to a naval career that kept him away from her and their child for long periods of time. The circumstances strained the marriage, challenging the emotional connections that had originally brought them together.[14]

Perhaps ironically, the rise of companionate marriage contributed to a concomitant rise in divorce rates. Individuals who had come to believe that marriage partners should provide emotional sustenance to each other discovered that the romance often did not last.[15] Left alone with her husband's family in Philadelphia, Edda found herself frequently criticized for her behaviors, particularly by Edward's sister Eliza Fisher and Eliza's husband, Joshua, who had expressed great skepticism of the match from its beginnings. Now, they turned their attention to what they believed were Edda's too friendly flirtations with the men she met at social events. In 1848, Joshua felt compelled to write to his brother-in-law Williams Middleton to deny that he had ever called Edda's behavior "shameful," although the tone of his letter and other comments regarding her conduct suggest that was exactly what he thought. Such flirtation did not align with patriarchal ideals of a virtuous wife, creating questions about both Edda's and Edward's gender roles.[16]

Criticisms turned to outrage when a maidservant employed by the family reported that she witnessed Edda entertaining late-night visits with a man named Harry McCall. Predisposed to think the worst of their young sister-in-law, Edward's relatives jumped to the belief that she had committed adultery despite her adamant protestations to the contrary. To justify their presumptions, the Middletons returned to their original objections to Edward marrying an unknown woman without reputable family ties. After hearing rumors of the alleged affair, for example, Edward's brother John remarked that "if a man will take a wife from the Stews [slang for a district of brothels], he must expect the natural consequences."[17] Edda's opaque origins and the hints at illicit royal linkages became the basis for condemning her as an inherently immoral woman.

Although denigrating Edda's worth as a woman appeared to occur quite easily, the route to defending Edward's manhood as the victim of this alleged cuckolding was more complicated. Some of his kinsmen advocated challenging McCall to a duel. Avenging adultery was not socially proscribed in the mid-nineteenth century. In the late 1850s, New York politician Daniel Sickles successfully pled temporary insanity, claiming it was a crime of passion when he murdered Philip Barton Key for having an affair with his wife.[18] In May 1849, John Middleton advised that Edward must "call out McCall without delay and sue for divorce." In December of the same year, Sidney Fisher, Joshua's cousin who would later represent Edward in his divorce suit, wrote somewhat facetiously in his diary of Edward's "conscientious scruples," noting that "already many severe things have been said here & in Carolina about Middleton's forbearance, and people seeming to think he should have sought his revenge ere this, regardless of consequences." He concluded that Edward might still issue a challenge after he secured a divorce.[19]

Interestingly, and contrary to stereotypes, it was Edward's family and friends in Philadelphia who most vocally advocated for dueling as an option. In contrast, his southern relatives, led by his brother Williams, focused their counsel on divorce, despite South Carolina being the only state that completely banned divorce regardless of cause. When Edward proved reluctant to take even the less violent approach to ending his marriage, his brother-in-law Joshua Fisher angrily pushed the matter, warning Edward that if he refused to move forward with divorce, he would lose "the confidence, even the intercourse of this family, & of all his friends. By no one connected with you could you ever again be recognized as a kinsman." As for Edward's naval career, Fisher further warned, "you would be pointed at & scorned by every man of honour." The stakes could hardly get higher: "A change of country & of *name* would be the only & last advice that I should give you."[20] Amid rumors of Edda's infidelity, Edward was thus counseled toward both dueling and divorce. He refused to pursue the duel but eventually he was persuaded to take the legal course toward ending his marriage. Divorce was still relatively rare in the mid-nineteenth century, although over the next decades the rate would greatly increase as both justifications and means for being granted a divorce shifted.

Much of the explanation for these changes may be found in the legal system, although as sociologist Martin Schultz warned, that system "involves a bewildering array of statutes, provisions, and changes in jurisdiction" because each state set their own laws, and these laws underwent considerable alterations over the course of the nineteenth century.[21] The two central questions for understanding the changing history of divorce law during the early republic era, and the legal course taken by Edward Middleton, involve justification and jurisdiction: What were the allowable reasons for granting divorce? And who was tasked with making this decision? First, there was a general expansion of the grounds for divorce. States that had limited allowable reasons for divorce to adultery, bigamy, impotence, and desertion increasingly included cruelty, and then recognized expansive definitions of what cruelty entailed. Second, in many states, responsibility for granting divorce shifted from the legislature to the judiciary.[22]

Such developments occurred to differing degrees and at different times in each state. In most states, including in the South, there was a growing allowance of marital cruelty as a justification for divorce, arising alongside the growing prevalence of companionate marriage. Historian Robert L. Griswold found that by 1866, only six states failed to include cruelty as the basis for a divorce suit.[23] In many states there was also a gradual transition of divorce from a legislative to a judicial responsibility. Further, these changing grounds allowed one to successfully sue for full divorce, as opposed to more limited separations from bed and board. National studies of shifting nineteenth-century divorce laws indicate that southern states, excepting South Carolina, did not significantly differ from other states in accepting divorce.[24]

Understanding these shifts in divorce law provides context for comprehending the actions taken by Edward Middleton and his family, both in terms of justification and jurisdiction. Joshua Fisher's deposition, which later became front-page news, discussed at length the financial burden that he believed Edda's spending had created for Edward, and potentially for the entire family. Private family letters expressed outrage at her financial demands for alimony.[25] Perceived extravagances, however, were not legally recognized reasons for divorce, but adultery clearly was. So, the great emphasis on Edwardina's misbehavior with Harry McCall, to the extent of taking sworn statements from those alleged to have witnessed the behavior, made strategic sense. Historian Merril D. Smith, in her 1991 study of marital discord in Pennsylvania, where Edward Middleton filed for divorce, noted that men "overwhelmingly cited adultery as grounds" in their early nineteenth-century divorce suits.[26] Thus, a likely source of personal anguish for Edward became a legal strategy for ending his marriage. His attempts to reconcile with Edda conversely endangered any future appeal to the legal system, leading the author of a pamphlet titled "Middleton Divorce Case" to despair: "A Divorce, on any existing ground, has now become hopeless."[27]

The pamphlet, printed by the Middleton family, reflected a concern not only for Edward's manly reputation but also for the potential impact on the family honor. Alongside trying to control Edward's behavior, the Middletons and their extended kin network sought to control the narrative of events, saving the family name if not the doomed marriage. The Middletons' attempts to control the gossip may have reflected a familiarity with the Butler divorce case that had occurred only a few years before in the same jurisdiction. Fanny Kemble Butler was an acquaintance of the Fishers in Philadelphia, and her husband, Pierce, was a large slaveholder in Georgia. In late 1843, Eliza Fisher wrote of the "tittle tattle" surrounding the Butlers' marital "squabbles." Eventually, the warring couple published competing accounts of their failed marriage to gain public favor.[28]

The Middletons and their allies took a roughly similar path. First, they gossiped in ways intended to paint Edda as the guilty party and an unrepentant harlot. Sidney Fisher, the family's lawyer, shared the claims of Thomas Huger, another South Carolinian and naval officer, that Edda had "from the time of their marriage flirted desperately & most imprudently in all directions."[29] Repeating such reports amplified the more current accusations against her.

The family eventually printed two different pamphlets detailing Edwardina's alleged misbehaviors and the divorce proceedings: one to present their case to the legislature and another to address "the subject of so much discussion in the society of Philadelphia and elsewhere." The latter tract revisited some of the family's original doubts about a match based solely on mutual affection, noting how "it is true that the family were at first opposed to the connexion. They had never heard of the lady." The pamphlet questioned Edda's intrinsic morality "as a foreigner educated at Naples where the standard of female virtue is lower than in any part of the world," and contended that Edward's entry into such a match was "a perilous venture."[30]

Publication of pamphlets detailing other scandalous divorce cases became increasingly common in the 1840s and 1850s, although they were generally published by third parties, usually newspapers, hoping to profit from the entertainment value. Notably, such pamphlets tended to present the women as sympathetic victims—the opposite of the Middletons' intent.[31] At the same time that Edward and Edda's divorce went before the Pennsylvania legislature, the body was hearing another divorce case that sparked publication of the other sort of pamphlets. Edwin Forrest was a dramatic actor who in 1849 had been implicated in the so-called Astor Place theater riots that left nearly two dozen people dead. Two years later, he accused his wife, Catherine, of adultery and sued for divorce. Newspapers recounted the case in lurid detail, amplified by a widely circulated pamphlet sympathetic to Catherine. Although Edwin failed to attain a divorce, he continued to appeal for eighteen years. The two divorce cases, the Middletons and the Forrests, appeared together in an 1850 newspaper article in which the author lamented both the choices of venue and the charges of adultery made against the wives: "If a husband can leave his home, go into a state convenient for his purpose, and there, before a strange tribunal, and without having to pass the ordeal of a jury, blast his wife's character by a divorce on the charge of adultery, what female is safe?" Although apparently more disturbed by Edwin Forrest's deeds, the writer expressed little sympathy for Edward Middleton. Undoubtedly to the relief of the Middleton family, the Forrest divorce garnered much of the spotlight and the Middleton divorce remained generally confined to a much smaller gossip network.[32]

While clearly intending to publicly frame Edwardina as the guilty party in the marriage's failure, the author of one of the Middleton pamphlets contended that "the foregoing pages, when prepared, were intended for a very limited circulation." The author claimed that the document had been meant solely for the family's "own use," threatening legal action against any reprinting and wider distribution. All of this seemed entirely disingenuous. Indeed, such efforts primarily sought to sway public opinion when other remedies appeared in doubt or out of reach. The Middletons sought to shape the narrative in ways that, as much as possible, preserved their name and reputation while destroying Edwardina's.[33]

The Middletons' pursuit of a legal divorce reflected changing patterns across jurisdictions, both in terms of geographic and legal venues. Edward engaged in an early version of venue shopping in seeking his divorce, a frequent approach given the diversity of legal qualifications from state to state. He wanted to pursue his complaint in his home state of South Carolina, which remained his legal domicile despite a lengthy absence due to naval service. Legal counsel, however, informed Edward "that in South Carolina there was no hope of relief." South Carolina barred divorce for any reason. The complete ban (which persisted until the 1870s) ostensibly represented a principled moral objection to the dissolution of marriage, particularly among White social elites who controlled the state's legal system. Yet, the avidity with which the South Carolina–based Middleton siblings pushed him toward divorce suggests that laws did not reflect universal attitudes.[34] Alongside the legal frameworks, the Middleton divorce must be situated in a broader understanding of the personal, emotional, and gender implications embedded in the decision to end a marriage. In particular, the decisions made by Edward shaped, and were shaped by, masculine identity and ideals.

Thwarted by the laws of South Carolina, Edward tried his luck in Pennsylvania, where he had left Edda with his Philadelphia family and where the alleged adultery occurred. Pennsylvania's increasingly liberal divorce laws certainly offered a better chance for ending his marriage, but applying for divorce in Pennsylvania gave rise to another set of issues. Edward sought a legislative divorce, a necessary tactic because he was not technically a resident of the state. His own petition to the state legislature admitted "as the act of Assembly expressly requires citizenship and one year's residence in the state previous to filing a petition or libel for a divorce and as Mr. Middleton has only resided in the State since September last, it is obvious that the courts now have no jurisdiction over the case and it would seem to follow, as a necessary consequence that the Legislature has." The petition further asserted that "the peculiar circumstance of this case are, that injury was suffered within the State by means of a violation of its laws, and that the petitioner has no remedy in his own State." Nor would waiting until Edward met the residency requirement necessarily be a solution since the "crime" had already occurred.

Pennsylvania legislators did not amend the state constitution to prohibit legislative divorce until 1875, but long prior to 1850 it had become increasingly common for Pennsylvanians to expect divorce through the courts rather than the legislative branch. Again, Edward's petition recognized this pattern: "It is said that legislative divorces are contrary to the sound maxims of public policy, injurious to public morals and if granted too easily and for light causes, subversive of the best interests of society."[35] Nevertheless, he sought such a solution for his marital woes.

When the Pennsylvania senate "rejected, by a large majority" Edward's divorce petition in March 1850, the *Philadelphia Bulletin* applauded the decision and denounced legislative divorces, remarking that "Mr. Middleton must now go to the courts if he wishes a divorce, where his wife will have an equal chance to be heard, and where the application will be granted or refused by twelve impartial men, sworn to give a true verdict according to the evidence."[36] Despite pursuing multiple legal paths, Edward Middleton failed to secure the divorce he, or at least his family, sought as a remedy to his marital troubles. Perhaps Edward's heart was never really in the effort. A newspaper that made the divorce case a front-page story in 1850 reported a year later on the couple's reunion, suggesting Edda had "convinced her husband that the whole accusation is a conspiracy of officious mischief-makers." The report announced that "a reconciliation has taken place between the husband and wife, and the twain romantic ones promise to be happy again."[37]

Although the press celebrated love reborn, behind the scenes Edward's family seethed. Writing long, angry letters to Edward and to each other, they questioned his sense, his honor, and his manliness. They continued to try to convince Edward to set aside any romantic feelings that lingered, end his marriage, and negotiate through lawyers for an alimony settlement that would convince Edda to permanently leave the country and return to Europe.[38]

Edward's repeated failures reveal the great difficulties and uncertain outcomes facing unhappy couples when they sought to legally end their marriages. Many thwarted by legal obstacles undertook what historian Beverly Schwarzberg termed "self-divorce"—separating partially or permanently without legal sanction but as befit their emotional, social, and economic needs.[39] Even for those who did formally divorce (and who thus left more complete records for historians), the legal intricacies were perhaps the least personally significant part of their experiences. Focusing on individual experiences may provide more complex understandings of the emotional expectations and disappointments, the physical and economic interactions, and the roles of families and communities in shaping a marriage or its ultimate dissolution through divorce, and how these became intertwined with the couples' gender identities.

Newspapers and popular fiction contributed to varied discussions around the growing prevalence of divorce, offering "disparate and competing narratives," as historian Norma Basch described them, on one hand to sell salacious scandals to an eager public and on the other to present the dire consequences of the social declension created when individuals failed to fulfill their duties and appropriate gender roles.[40] When Edward and Edda tried to untangle their marital difficulties, they encountered these many competing messages about divorces, and the powerful community and cultural pressures the messages engendered. As historian Thomas E. Buckley explained, "In every divorce the presence of family members, neighbors, and friends during domestic altercations brings a communal aspect to the conflict."[41]

Gender expectations mattered deeply to individual, family, and community perceptions of divorce. Seeking an end to a marriage, like accepting the proposal that began a marriage, was a liminal moment—one in which individuals made a choice that would radically alter their lives and places in society. For women who took active roles in suing for divorce and in the ensuing trials, divorce became, in the words of historian Leslie Harris, "a lens through which gender was performed, contested, and regulated," as divorce challenged the "cultural expectations of proper womanhood."[42] Despite the pitfalls, women whose situations had become untenable might seek to protect their economic and familial interests through a legal divorce. While an unhappy husband could, if he chose, simply leave, continuing to support himself, most unhappily married women did not have this option. In some cases, an estranged husband continued to exert control over all marital assets including any wages or inheritances, even after the couple physically separated.

Thus, in many jurisdictions, women were as likely or more so than men to petition for divorce and to have their requests granted. Even if denied complete divorces, wives often received a separation that allowed them to operate as *femes sole*.[43] Once engaged with the judicial system, women frequently encountered what historian Michael Grossberg termed "judicial patriarchy," in which the presiding judge stepped into the masculine role vacated by the erring husband to protect her interests. These patterns reflected larger societal views about women, and how the expansion of definitions of cruelty often became remedies for "wronged wives," especially of the middle class, who had been thrust from the protection of the domestic ideal through no fault of their own.[44]

Yet the story of the Middleton divorce, viewed from Edward's perspective, evidences how divorce proved a pivotal moment for men as well. If expectations of companionate marriage challenged the ideal of the male-controlled household, divorce introduced an even greater threat to the ideals of patriarchal authority, even when a husband initiated divorce proceedings. Accusations of adultery against one's wife, necessary for success in most divorce suits, called into question not only a wife's virtue but also a husband's manliness. Seeking divorce on the grounds of infidelity, as Edward did, raised fears of community judgment and personal humiliation. Further, according to historian Robert L. Griswold, the legal system generally set up these matters to critique male behavior, and even men who won their suits might not escape remonstrance for their failures in leading their families.[45] The Middleton family's emphasis on reputation evinced concerns about how Edward's divorce would affect his position as an honorable man, and perhaps more importantly, how it would impact the family name.[46]

Even before his marital troubles, Edward had seemingly stretched the boundaries of appropriate behavior for a man in his social circle, particularly among his own kinship network. Although a nineteenth-century naval officer might seem like the epitome of masculinity to many, and Edward's divorce petition emphasized his dedication to duty, his chosen career meant that Edward relied on a salary and obeyed the orders of others.[47] Edward was not the master of his own household either, as he left his young bride with relatives when he returned to active duty. Further, even when his father's complicated will left Edward technically a partial owner of the family plantations, and of the enslaved population contained therein, his South Carolina siblings managed the assets. He was master in name but not in practice, both of this patrimony and of a household. So, when his relatives counseled Edward to act decisively in seeking a divorce, they clearly framed it as a requirement for retaining whatever mastery, manhood, and honor he still possessed.

The Middleton family's efforts to bring about a divorce worked eventually. Although details of the final settlement remain murky (as does what became of Edda), the ill-fated couple parted. In 1865, Edward married Ellida Davison with whom he remained until his death in 1883.[48] Still, Edward never lived up to most of his family's understanding of honorable manhood, even after his marriage to Edda ended, and even as he became a navy captain and then a rear admiral. Indeed, remaining in the US Navy during the Civil War created yet more conflict with many in his family. The honor and loyalty expected of a southern man always seemed to lead to complicated choices for Edward Middleton.[49]

IN *ANNA KARENINA*, Leo Tolstoy opined, "All happy families resemble one another; every unhappy family is unhappy in its own way."[50] Edward and Edwardina Middleton were not a unique or extraordinary pair when it came to either their romance or its dissolution. Although some of the details of their lives may have set them apart, in broad strokes they were like many other nineteenth-century couples who met, fell in love, and married. And, despite growing expectations that marriage should create an intensely emotional bond, as with many other couples circumstances created tensions and disappointments. Like other couples too the Middletons were part of a larger family and community, with members who held strong opinions about the pair, their relationship, and how they ought to behave—often looking after their own interests as much as the interests of the young couple.

Edward and Edwardina married and divorced in a time of significant attitudinal changes: individuals increasingly sought companionate marriages to fulfill emotional as well as practical needs, unhappy couples found growing acceptance of divorce as a solution to their unhappiness, and shifting gender roles and expectations undergirded all these ideas about marriage and divorce. Understandings about masculinity shaped how Edward chose a mate to marry, his conflicted feelings about if and how his marriage should end, and how he saw himself as a member of his extended family. Perhaps just as profoundly, masculine ideals and male gender expectations shaped how his family members viewed him and his predicament. While we can never know exactly what happened within Edward and Edda's marriage, their story provides a revealing portal for examining and understanding fundamental shifts occurring in nineteenth-century marital relations, and particularly how these developments must be understood through the lens of gender ideals.

Questions to Consider

1. How was the experience of the Middletons typical of larger changes in marriage and divorce happening in the nineteenth century? How was their experience atypical?
2. Many different forces acted on the marriage and divorce of Edward and Edwardina Middleton—individual emotions, familial expectations, economic concerns, gender ideals, shifting legal structures. Which of these forces do you think most shaped their experiences and why?

Notes

1. By the time of the divorce suit, a pamphlet produced by the Middleton family asserted that "whatever portion of Royal blood might mingle through an adulterous connexion in her veins, they thought was rather a subject of shame rather than of pride." "Middleton Divorce Case," ca. 1851, 3, Middleton Place Manuscripts, box 5, sleeve 37, microfiche, South Caroliniana Library, Columbia. For the Middleton family, see Judith Lee Hunt, "'Beyond the Power of Fortune': The Middleton Family of South Carolina, 1784 to 1877" (PhD diss., University of Florida, 2005), and Eliza Cope Harrison, ed., *Best Companions: Letters of Eliza Middleton Fisher and Her Mother, Mary Hering Middleton, from Charleston, Philadelphia, and Newport, 1839–1846* (Columbia: University of South Carolina Press, 2001), xxxix–xlii.
2. Mary Middleton to Eliza Fisher, 14 December 1844, in Harrison, ed., *Best Companions*, 413–14.
3. Eliza Fisher to Mary Middleton, 19 December 1844, in Harrison, ed., *Best Companions*, 415.
4. John I. Middleton to Eliza Fisher, 7 March 1845, in Harrison, ed., *Best Companions*, 412.
5. For debates, see, for example, Mary Beth Sievens, "Divorce, Patriarchal Authority, and Masculinity: A Case from Early National Vermont," *Journal of Social History* 37, no. 3 (Spring 2004): 658, and Steven M. Stowe, *Intimacy and Power in the Old South: Ritual in the Lives of the Planters* (Baltimore: Johns Hopkins University Press, 1987), 10. For a different early twentieth-century movement toward "companionate marriage," see Rebecca L. Davis, "'Not Marriage at All, but Simple Harlotry': The

Companionate Marriage Controversy," *Journal of American History* 94, no. 4 (March 2008): 1137–63.
6. Ellen K. Rothman, *Hands and Hearts: A History of Courtship in America* (New York: Basic Books, 1984), 3.
7. Daniel Scott Smith, "Parental Power and Marriage Patterns: An Analysis of Historical Trends in Hingham, Massachusetts," *Journal of Marriage and Family* 35, no. 3 (August 1973): 421, 426; Carl N. Degler, *At Odds: Women and the Family in America from the Revolution to the Present* (New York: Oxford University Press, 1980), 11, 76; Rothman, *Hands and Hearts,* 26; Sara T. Damiano, "Writing Women's History Through the Revolution: Family Finances, Letter.Writing, and Conceptions of Marriage," *William and Mary Quarterly,* 3rd series, 74, no. 4 (October 2017): 700; Ruth H. Bloch, "Changing Conceptions of Sexuality and Romance in Eighteenth-Century America," *William and Mary Quarterly,* 3rd series, 60, no. 1 (January 2003): 14. For one couple's experiences, see Anya Jabour, *Marriage in the Early Republic: Elizabeth and William Wirt and the Companionate Ideal* (Baltimore: Johns Hopkins University Press, 1998).
8. For southern elites in Philadelphia, see Daniel Kilbride, *An American Aristocracy: Southern Planters in Antebellum Philadelphia* (Columbia: University of South Carolina Press, 2006).
9. Joshua Rothman, "'To Be Freed from Thate Curs and Let at Liberty': Interracial Adultery and Divorce in Antebellum Virginia," *Virginia Magazine of History and Biography* 106, no. 4 (Autumn 1998): 451; Jane Turner Censer, *North Carolina Planters and Their Children, 1800–1860* (Baton Rouge: Louisiana State University Press, 1984), 72. See also Joan E. Cashin, *A Family Venture: Men and Women on the Southern Frontier* (New York: Oxford University Press, 1991); Mary P. Ryan, *Cradle of the Middle Class: The Family in Oneida County, New York, 1790–1865* (New York: Cambridge University Press, 1981), 33; and Cynthia Culver Prescott, "'Why She Didn't Marry Him': Love, Power, and Marital Choice on the Far Western Frontier," *Western Historical Quarterly* 38, no. 1 (Spring 2007): 29.
10. Bertram Wyatt-Brown, *Southern Honor: Ethics and Behavior in the Old South* (New York: Oxford University Press, 1982), 207.
11. Stowe, *Intimacy and Power in the Old South,* 50–51, 61, 97–99, 154.
12. Michael P. Johnson, "Planters and Patriarchy: Charleston, 1800–1860," *Journal of Southern History* 46, no. 1 (February 1980): 45–72; Craig Thompson Friend and Lorri Glover, "Rethinking Southern Masculinity: An Introduction," in *Southern Manhood: Perspectives on Masculinity in the Old South,* ed. Craig Thompson Friend and Lorri Glover (Athens: University of Georgia Press, 2004), xi–xiii. For honor, reputation, and southern men's sensitivity to perceived slights, see Kenneth S. Greenberg,

Honor and Slavery: Lies, Duels, Noses, Masks, Dressing as a Woman, Gifts, Strangers, Humanitarianism, Death, Slave Rebellions, the Proslavery Argument, Baseball, Hunting, and Gambling in the Old South (Princeton, NJ: Princeton University Press, 1996).

13. Karen Lystra, *Searching the Heart: Women, Men, and Romantic Love in Nineteenth-Century America* (New York: Oxford University Press, 1989), 230–31.
14. "Extract of Joshua F. Fisher's Deposition," in "Revelations in High Life," *Star of the North* (Bloomsburg, PA), 7 March 1850. The fate of their child remains a mystery. See Harrison, ed., *Best Companions*, xl, and Eliza Fisher to Williams Middleton, 4 January 1851, folder 4, Middleton Family Papers, South Caroliniana Library.
15. See, for example, Adam Tuchinsky, "'Woman and Her Needs': Elizabeth Oakes Smith and the Divorce Question," *Journal of Women's History* 28, no. 1 (Spring 2016): 39.
16. Joshua Fisher to Williams Middleton, 8 December 1848, box 4, folder 9, Middleton Family Papers.
17. John Izard Middleton to Williams Middleton, 8 May 1849, box 4, folder 12, Middleton Family Papers. A version of Edward Middleton's case for divorce, including depositions, is in "In the Matter of the Petition of Edward Middleton to the General Assembly of the Commonwealth of Pennsylvania, for Divorce from His Wife," n.d., Charleston Library Society, Charleston, SC.
18. Robert M. Ireland, "The Libertine Must Die: Sexual Dishonor and the Unwritten Law in the Nineteenth-Century United States," *Journal of Social History* 23, no. 1 (Autumn 1989): 27–44; Hendrik Hartog, "Lawyering, Husbands' Rights, and 'the Unwritten Law' in Nineteenth-Century America," *Journal of American History* 84, no. 1 (June 1997): 67–96.
19. John Izard Middleton to Williams Middleton, 8 May 1849; Sidney Fisher, "The Diaries of Sidney George Fisher, 1849–1852," *Pennsylvania Magazine of History and Biography* 86, no. 2 (April 1962): 184; Kilbride, *An American Aristocracy*, 45–46.
20. J. F. Fisher to Edward Middleton, 14 January 1851, box 5, folder 4, Middleton Family Papers.
21. Martin Schultz, "Divorce in the South Atlantic States: Origins, Historical Patterns, and Recent Trends," *International Journal of Sociology of the Family* 16, no. 2 (Autumn 1986): 233.
22. Roderick Phillips, *Putting Asunder: A History of Divorce in Western Society* (New York: Cambridge University Press, 1988).
23. Robert L. Griswold, "Law, Sex, Cruelty, and Divorce in Victorian America, 1840–1900," *American Quarterly* 38, no. 5 (Winter 1986): 722–23.

24. Griswold, "Law, Sex, Cruelty, and Divorce in Victorian America," 722–23; Jane Turner Censer, "'Smiling Through Her Tears': Ante-Bellum Southern Women and Divorce," *American Journal of Legal History* 25, no. 1 (January 1981): 34; Glenda Riley, "Legislative Divorce in Virginia, 1803–1850," *Journal of the Early Republic* 11, no. 1 (Spring 1991): 51–67; Rothman, "'To Be Freed from Thate Curs and Let at Liberty,'" 445n3. Bed and board divorces, also called *a mensa et thoro*, were legal separation agreements in which the couple lived separately, and maintenance might be paid, but remarriage was proscribed. The legal parameters of divorce did not always reflect gender roles or how couples ended relationships; see, for example, Honor R. Sachs, "The Myth of the Abandoned Wife: Married Women's Agency and the Legal Narrative of Gender in Eighteenth-Century Kentucky," *Ohio Valley History* 3, no. 4 (Winter 2003): 3–20.
25. "Extract of Joshua F. Fisher's Deposition"; Eliza Fisher to Williams Middleton, 4 January 1851.
26. Merril D. Smith, *Breaking the Bonds: Marital Discord in Pennsylvania, 1730–1830* (New York: New York University Press, 1991), 29.
27. "Middleton Divorce Case," 18. A copy of the pamphlet is in the Middleton Family Papers, box 5, folder 3.
28. Eliza Fisher to Mary Middleton, 14 December 1843, in Harrison, ed., *Best Companions*, 339. Thomas E. Buckley, in *The Great Catastrophe of My Life: Divorce in the Old Dominion* (Chapel Hill: University of North Carolina Press, 2002), suggests divorce sometimes became "a vehicle for vindicating personal innocence and family reputation" (41).
29. Fisher, quoted in Kilbride, *An American Aristocracy*, 45.
30. "In the Matter of the Petition of Edward Middleton," 4; "Middleton Divorce Case," 1–2.
31. Norma Basch, *Framing American Divorce: From the Revolutionary Generation to the Victorians* (Berkeley: University of California Press, 1999), 147–55.
32. Basch, *Framing American Divorce*, 172–76; "The Divorce Cases," *The Republic* (Washington, DC), 25 March 1850, reprinted from the *Philadelphia Bulletin*, 21 March 1851. An exception to the relative inattention was a front-page story in the *Star of the North*, 7 March 1850, entitled "Revelations in High Life." Although gossip spread among the Middleton social network, the family generally received sympathy. See, for example, Louisa Porcher to Adele Allston, 16 October 1849, Allston Family Papers, South Carolina Historical Society, Charleston.
33. "Middleton Divorce Case," 19.
34. "In the Matter of the Petition of Edward Middleton," 4. For growing acceptance of ending troubled marriages, see Loren Schweninger, *Families*

in Crisis in the Old South: Divorce, Slavery, and the Law (Chapel Hill: University of North Carolina Press, 2012), 77; Buckley, *The Great Catastrophe of My Life*, 7; and Censer, "'Smiling Through Her Tears,'" 24. For shifts in South Carolina divorce laws, see Kellen Funk, "'Let No Man Put Asunder': South Carolina's Law of Divorce, 1895–1950," *South Carolina Historical Magazine* 110, nos. 3–4 (July–October 2009): 134–53.

35. "In the Matter of the Petition of Edward Middleton," 8, 10; Smith, *Breaking the Bonds*, 35, 38.
36. "The Divorce Cases."
37. *Star of the North*, 3 April 1851.
38. Eliza Fisher to Williams Middleton, 4 January 1851; Eliza Fisher to Williams Middleton, 29 January 1851; Joshua Fisher to Edward Middleton, 14 January 1851, box 5, folder 4, Middleton Family Papers. The first of these letters also mentions a custody demand, but the outcome is unclear.
39. Smith, *Breaking the Bonds*, 29, 38; Beverly Schwarzberg, "'Lots of Them Did That': Desertion, Bigamy, and Marital Fluidity in Late-Nineteenth-Century America," *Journal of Social History* 37, no. 3 (Spring 2004): 582.
40. Basch, *Framing American Divorce*, 187.
41. Buckley, *The Great Catastrophe of My Life*, 3.
42. Leslie Harris, *State of the Marital Union: Rhetoric, Identity, and Nineteenth-Century Marriage Controversies* (Waco, TX: Baylor University Press, 2014), 31, 37.
43. Schultz, "Divorce in the South Atlantic States," 228, 246; Riley, "Legislative Divorce in Virginia," 52; Smith, *Breaking the Bonds*, 42.
44. Michael Grossberg, *Governing the Hearth: Law and the Family in Nineteenth-Century America* (Chapel Hill: University of North Carolina Press, 1985), 301; Censer, "'Smiling Through Her Tears,'" 25, 27. See also Griswold, "Law, Sex, Cruelty, and Divorce in Victorian America," 738.
45. Wyatt-Brown, *Southern Honor*, 52; Robert L. Griswold, "Divorce and the Legal Redefinition of Victorian Manhood," in *Meanings for Manhood: Constructions of Masculinity in Victorian America*, ed. Mark C. Carnes and Clyde Griffen (Chicago: University of Chicago Press, 1990), 96–99.
46. Joshua Rothman concluded that divorce revealed "a chink in the armor" of southern men; see Rothman, "'To Be Freed from Thate Curs and Let at Liberty,'" 454.
47. "In the Matter of the Petition of Edward Middleton," 3.
48. "Middleton of South Carolina," *South Carolina Historical and Genealogical Magazine* 1, no. 3 (July 1900): 252.
49. Hunt, "'Beyond the Power of Fortune,'" 57.
50. Leo Tolstoy, *Anna Karenina*, trans. Nathan Haskell Dole (1878; rpt. New York: Thomas Y. Crowell, 1899), 1.

"It's Possible That He Is the Author of the Poor Thing's Being"

INTERRACIAL SEX AND THE BATTLE WITH HONOR

Shannon C. Eaves

In November 1859, Julia Alexander, an enslaved woman from Chester, South Carolina, sparked a firestorm of emotion—fear, shame, and frustration—among a group of White men who moved within South Carolina's most elite social and professional circles. Dr. James Moultrie Jr., a well-respected physician in Charleston who contributed to the founding of the state's first medical college, became the nexus around which this cadre of men and the controversy formed. Moultrie's troubles started when Alexander identified him as the father of her child. Although Moultrie was White, affluent, and free, Alexander and her child were enslaved. After naming Moultrie as her child's father, Alexander demanded that he not only provide financial support but also publicly acknowledge their daughter by giving her his last name.[1]

At first, Moultrie most likely rejected Alexander's demands. Enslavers assumed absolute power over the enslaved, and her requests threatened this power dynamic. Black subjugation, along with patriarchal authority, were hallmarks of southern life. In rare instances, in their last wills and testaments White men openly acknowledged their enslaved children, legally emancipated them, and bequeathed land and money for their educations and long-term care. Such actions were exceptional and far from the rule. Most White men looked on enslaved progeny like other children born to enslaved women—as extensions of their wealth rather than themselves. Alexander intended for Moultrie to make her daughter the exception, whether through choice or coercion.[2]

Moultrie had innumerable reasons to resist Alexander's threats, all of which would have been clear and reasonable to the small group of friends and associates to whom he turned for assistance. Southern men like Moultrie placed tremendous value on honor, one of the pillars on which they cultivated reputations and status, and through which they asserted authority within the public and private spheres. Moultrie was not just a prominent physician but an institution builder. In addition to cofounding the Medical College of South Carolina, Moultrie helped create the American Medical Association, the South Carolina Medical Association, and the South Carolina Historical Society. As a landed enslaver, he was, to himself and his associates, inherently honorable and aligned with the tenants of southern manhood.

Ideally, an honorable southern gentleman refrained from engaging in interracial sex. Former South Carolina governor and US senator James Henry Hammond was an ardent defender of slavery, and in response to northern criticism he claimed that "this intercourse is regarded in our society as highly disreputable," and "if carried on habitually, it seriously affects a man's standing." However, southern men, including Hammond, frequently had sex with enslaved women—by force and other coercive means—and fathered enslaved children with impunity. In fact, men considered it a privilege of mastery. Their sexual relations with Black women—free or enslaved—might have been labeled illicit but White southerners accepted, or at least overlooked, them if the relationships were discreet and avoided bringing shame on White men and their families. White southerners generally carried on with their day-to-day activities, blocking out the visual and auditory evidence of the sexualized violence and reproductive exploitation perpetrated on enslaved females *and* males.[3]

Fearful of the damage that Alexander's claims could do to Moultrie's reputation, he and his associates moved quickly to protect his honorable status. They believed strongly that his reputation should not be scathed by something as ubiquitous as sexual relations with an enslaved woman. James Petigru, a highly sought attorney in Charleston, was one of Moultrie's key allies. Intent on preserving his friend's honor, Petigru utilized his legal acumen to initiate a letter-writing campaign on Moultrie's behalf. Throughout his communications with Alexander and other associates of Moultrie, Petigru was careful to neither deny nor confirm Moultrie's paternity of Alexander's child. Due to what Petigru called the "possibility" that Moultrie could have fathered the girl, however, he promised Moultrie's cooperation in aiding the child in exchange for everyone's discretion and a promise from Alexander that she would stop demanding a formal acknowledgment of paternity.

Petigru's negotiations shed light on the reality that for southern White men, being perceived as honorable was far more important than behaving honorably. This was especially true for men of the elite, slave-owning class like Moultrie and Petigru, who understood the extent to which their power rested in their performance of honor. As a result, they took exhaustive measures to preserve it.[4]

Although Alexander's enslaved daughter, because of her race, gender, and enslaved status, would never be untethered from the gendered prescriptions of White supremacy and southern patriarchy that subjugated her, Alexander understood the power of connecting her daughter to Moultrie's Whiteness and social standing. She insisted Moultrie acknowledge her child and give the child his last name because she knew that a respectable name carried power. As an enslaved Black woman, Alexander seemed at first an improbable opponent for the esteemed Charleston physician. But she was able to use her knowledge of southern honor and its correlation to White southern manhood, freedom, economic security, and status to leverage influence over Moultrie and his associates. Effectively, she turned Moultrie's status and investment in southern honor into a weapon, drawing Moultrie and his friends into a battle to defend his honor. Alexander's campaign and the response of Moultrie's team demonstrate how fragile the constructs of southern honor and respectability were for White men and the lengths they would go to maintain, at the very least, a facade of honor to remain in southern society's good graces. Moultrie was not simply in a battle to defend his honor but in a battle with honor itself. No matter what choice he made, there would be consequences, especially considering Alexander's tenacity. Whether Moultrie denied or acknowledged his daughter, he risked jeopardizing his public reputation, shaking the foundation of his marriage and household, and losing the privileges afforded an honorable White southern gentleman.

FROM ALL accounts, Julia Alexander was a formidable woman. Although the law forbade it, she knew how to read and write, skills that she did not hide. She openly corresponded with White people such as James Moultrie to express her needs. Many of the details of Alexander's life are lost to the archive. Her owner, Charles, was identified only by his first name in the letters among Moultrie, James Petigru, and their associates. The extent of his landholdings and number of people he enslaved are unknown. He had enough means, however, to pay a doctor to treat his enslaved laborers when they became ill. Dr. Alexander P. Wylie, a graduate of the Medical College of South Carolina who became a noted botanist, told Petigru that Charles had called on him numerous times to treat Alexander for "several spells of sickness & recently with a violent attack of hemorrhage of the lungs."[5]

Nor does the archive reveal the circumstances that led to Alexander's pregnancy. We can only speculate on where and when Alexander and Moultrie first met and engaged in sexual relations, and whether they had one sexual encounter or a long-term sexual liaison. Many enslaved women did not travel beyond plantation boundaries. They commonly performed agricultural or household work, including skilled labor, occupations that kept them close to the plantation. Their mandate to birth and rear children also kept them nearby.

Possibly, Alexander was less tethered to Charles's plantation than most enslaved women. Had Charles lent out her services as a dressmaker, she would have traveled from her home in the Upcountry to the Charleston District where Moultrie lived. Had she been the personal maid to Charles's wife, Alexander would have joined her enslavers on annual pilgrimages to Charleston, the state's economic and social epicenter, where they shopped, engaged with various civic organizations, and mingled with the state's elite, including James Moultrie and his wife, Sarah Louisa Shrewsbury Moultrie, who went by Louisa. Perhaps Alexander accompanied her enslavers on a social call to the Moultries' home, or James might have crossed paths with Alexander on Market Street—Charleston's historic business district—on his way home, just a few blocks away. Enslaved women were routinely in urban marketplaces, shopping for their enslavers, selling produce and other goods, or managing businesses, including boardinghouses and brothels.[6] Moultrie may have propositioned Alexander while she was shopping for her enslavers or buying a small trinket for herself. There were so many opportunities for a White man, particularly one of wealth and status, to find a sexual partner or target, particularly an enslaved Black woman. With great probability, Moultrie coerced Alexander, even resorting to bribery, threats, or violence.[7]

By 1859, James and Louisa Moultrie had been married forty-one years. Louisa descended from a prominent family. Her grandfather had proudly served in the Continental Army during the American Revolutionary

War, and her father, Stephen Shrewsbury, was a savvy businessman. The Shrewsburys lived among the Charleston elite on East Bay Street. Upon her father's death in 1815, Louisa and her sister inherited a sizable bequest of federal, state, and bank stocks. According to Louisa's father's will, upon her own death, her fortune was to pass to any children she bore. But the Moultries did not have children, a blemish on their otherwise picture-perfect lives of honor and virtue.[8]

Moultrie also hailed from American revolutionaries, most notably his great uncle Major General William Moultrie, for whom Fort Moultrie in South Carolina was named. Like his father and grandfather, Moultrie studied medicine, receiving his training at the country's oldest and preeminent medical college in Philadelphia. Moultrie's involvement in building prestigious institutions in Charleston and the larger nation meant that it would not have been easy to damage his reputation. James and Louisa's childlessness, however, created a vulnerability, opening the door to gossip of interracial sex and an illegitimate child with an enslaved woman, the perfect fodder for scandal.[9]

When Alexander confronted Moultrie with his paternity of her daughter, she did not do so alone. She drew on support from a small group of people who, though unidentified, were likely White people of enough status to position them to confront Moultrie. According to Petigru, Alexander had appealed to her "friends," as he called them, to be "witnesses" to "the way with which the child first saw the light."[10] Her "friends" demanded that Moultrie take responsibility for fathering Alexander's child, clearly giving credence to her accusation. Despite his deep entrenchment in Charleston society, Moultrie believed that Alexander's friends' testimonies could generate the kind of scandal he wanted to avoid.[11]

How Alexander formed an alliance with this group and why they took such an interest in ensuring that Moultrie supported her child remains unclear. In an undated memorandum to Alexander, Petigru asked her to "see the persons who have a feeling for your child, and consult them to know how your child is to be brought up." If they had been providing aid for the child, their motives were likely financial, expecting Moultrie to pay money toward the child's expenses. Importantly, the alliance illustrates Alexander's ability to navigate different spaces and people—Black, White, enslaved, and free. With her enslaver's permission, she maneuvered unpaved highways from Chester to the streets of Charleston, holding private meetings where she revealed secrets and rallied support.

She did so where free, pseudo-free, and enslaved Black and mixed-race people of all hues were constantly surveilled, under the watchful eye of White citizens and slave patrollers, who were always suspicious of insurrection and other forms of resistance.[12]

Alexander's strategizing, along with pressure from her allies, captured Moultrie's attention. He saw no choice but to seek allies of his own if he wished to walk away with his reputation intact. By the time Moultrie confided his troubles in Petigru, a friend and trusted legal counsel, he had already paid Alexander two lump sums of money, with at least one in the amount of three hundred dollars, and had pledged a third. Although Moultrie adamantly denied being the father of Alexander's child, he hoped the payments would induce her and her friends to end their campaign against him and remain silent about his paternity. In a letter to James Petigru dated 15 November 1858, Moultrie signaled that he had failed to neutralize Alexander's threats, enclosing the latest letter that Alexander had written to him. Although the letter likely has been lost to the passage of time, possibly destroyed to cover up Moultrie's indiscretions, subsequent correspondence from Petigru reveals that it contained details about the affair. It could have wreaked havoc on Moultrie's life had it fallen into the wrong hands. And yet, Moultrie risked exposure by mailing it to Petigru.[13]

An early graduate of South Carolina College, Petigru came from more humble means than Moultrie. His grandfather James Pettigrew died with three hundred acres of land and two enslaved people to his name, but his father, William Pettigrew, lost it all because of his alcoholism. After college, James changed the spelling of his surname from Pettigrew to Petigru to distance himself from the shame brought on by his father's drinking. He studied law and gained a law partnership in Charleston in 1819. By 1822, he had become the state's attorney general, cementing his place in South Carolina politics and among Charleston's elites. Like Moultrie, he was well versed in the principles of southern honor and counseled Moultrie accordingly.[14]

In addition to providing emotional support and legal advice, Petigru served as an intermediary, creating both physical and figurative distance between Moultrie and Alexander. When Moultrie sent Alexander's letter to Petigru, he enclosed a third undisclosed sum of money that Petigru needed to pass along to Alexander to induce her silence. After receiving Moultrie's letter, Petigru sat down to write the first of several letters he drafted on Moultrie's behalf. He sent the first, dated 17 November 1859, to Robert A. Pagan, sheriff of Chester District. Before Petigru's involvement, Moultrie had relied on Pagan to serve as his intermediary, and it was Pagan who placed Moultrie's first two payments in Alexander's hands. In addition to serving as sheriff, the thirty-eight-year-old Pagan was a lawyer and a small-scale enslaver. Although not among South Carolina's elite, he was an officer of the law, as much invested in White supremacy as the wealthiest of enslavers.[15]

Petigru thanked Pagan for the "friendly aid" he had provided Moultrie and emphasized the importance of trust among men when it came to complex matters such as interracial sex. Since Moultrie had requested that Petigru forward Alexander's letter to Pagan, Petigru hoped that Pagan would "have the good will to put it in the fire" after reading it, due to its incriminating nature, unless he knew of someone "who takes an interest on behalf of the individual to which it relates." Petigru sealed the envelope to Pagan with two curt messages: At the top he wrote, "Trusted Intermediary," and below quite larger than those words, he added, "To be Burned." His calls for discretion and the destruction of Alexander's letter from the archive underscore men's commitment to preserving southern honor not just for their individual selves but also for one another.[16]

While Moultrie insisted to Alexander and her allies that he did not father Alexander's child, he confided in the members of his inner circle that he had in fact had sex with her, making his paternity a possibility. In subsequent correspondence, Moultrie's intermediaries, quite performatively, proclaimed him a man of honor and restated his public position that he was not the father of Alexander's child. Only then would they speak frankly about Moultrie's probable paternity. "Doctor Moultrie whose word and honor will be disputed by no gentleman that knows him is undoubtedly persuaded that the paternity of the child does not belong to him," Petigru explained, before adding, "But unfortunately it cannot be denied that it's *possible* that he is the author of the poor thing's being." Petigru told Pagan that, in his opinion, the monetary "concessions" that Moultrie had been forced to make exceeded "what might be deemed as satisfaction of a duty" based on "a mere possibility."[17]

According to James Petigru, his friend James Moultrie was "suffering far beyond the common lot for a common fault." Although not every powerful White man had sex with enslaved women, behavior that people of means and status considered to be "illicit" or "faulty," it was ubiquitous enough to be declared common. The rules were simple. If men of honor (or the boys preparing to become men of honor) were discreet, fulfilled their household and civic duties, and avoided public scandal, their family members and neighbors looked the other way. Interracial sex was not intended to be consequential, at least not among those who could manipulate public opinion: White male enslavers, overseers, and patrollers who communicated their dominance over the whole enslaved community through random and routine acts of sexualized violence and exploitation. For Petigru, Moultrie had already paid too high a price with no end to his suffering in sight.[18]

Petigru was astounded by Alexander's audacity. He found it preposterous that an enslaved woman could generate so much trouble for Moultrie, himself, and their associates. He wrote frankly that Alexander's scheme "would not be tolerated even in the case of a white woman."[19]

With a successful law practice in the heart of downtown Charleston, Petigru knew the state statutes and city ordinances that regulated behavior of enslaved and free Black people. The statutes set limits on when and where Black people could be, what they could physically possess, and with whom they could form partnerships. The law required White people to surveil their free or enslaved Black neighbors, marking all Black Carolinians as subordinate to all White people. Monitoring enslaved people's activities, especially in Charleston, became an even greater obsession after Denmark Vesey's thwarted revolt in 1822. Petigru anticipated that Alexander, if reported, would "deserve the severity of the code," and asked Pagan to convey to Alexander that "the doctors friends would not be passive under such provocation as her threats imply; but would surely hand her over to the police."[20]

Undoubtedly, Julia Alexander knew how daring and dangerous her actions were. She broke the law every time she put pen to paper. To write out her demands of a White enslaver marked an even bolder move. A man who assisted Moultrie concluded that "it is certainly an extraordinary letter for one to write in her position in life." When Alexander demanded monetary payments and requested that Moultrie give the child his last name, she could have been charged with "insolence to a white person," a crime punishable with violence "not extending to life or limb." Beyond penalty of law, Moultrie could have silenced her by incentivizing her enslaver to sell her to an out-of-state buyer, "removing her annoyance" forever, as Petigru imagined. Moultrie could have suggested the sale of her child, placing her daughter beyond her reach indefinitely. Despite these risks, Alexander appeared fearless in the eyes of Moultrie and his associates.[21]

Alexander knew well the burdens of enslavement, and she determined to shield her daughter from the weight of subjection. This desire to protect children—and grieve over their futures in bondage—pervaded the writings of enslaved and self-emancipated women. Harriet Jacobs in her widely circulated memoir wrote at length about the despair enslaved mothers felt when they contemplated their children's future in bondage. Her owner, James Norcom, notoriously raped and impregnated enslaved women and then sold the mothers and children far away from their enslaved community to avoid conflict with his wife, Mary Norcom. Jacobs "shuddered to think of being the mother of children that should be owned by my old tyrant." Norcom constantly harassed Jacobs, trying to have sex with her at any opportunity. Desperate to evade rape and end Norcom's sexual harassment, Jacobs schemed to deter her enslaver and hopefully secure freedom for her future children. When Samuel Tredwell Sawyer, a young White bachelor in Jacobs's home of Edenton, North Carolina, expressed interest in having sex with Jacobs, she did not resist. Jacobs explained that due to "revenge, and a calculation of interest," and "seeing no other way of escaping the doom I so much dreaded, I made a headlong plunge." Sawyer promised to buy her and any children who resulted from their liaison. When Norcom refused to sell Jacobs and the two children to whom she subsequently gave birth, Jacobs ran away. She eventually hid in her grandmother's attic, only nine feet long, seven feet wide, and three feet high, where she lived for seven years. Norcom ultimately sold Jacobs's two children to Sawyer, who then sent the children to Jacobs's grandmother's house where they could live as virtually free, affording Jacobs the opportunity to hear her children's voices and catch glimpses of them playing outside through the holes and cracks in the attic's wooden frame. Despite being unable to stand upright or feel the sun's rays fall on her face for years, Jacobs declared, "You never exhausted your ingenuity in avoiding the snares, and eluding the power of a hated tyrant."[22]

Similarly, Julia Alexander's knowledge of southern White mores and her keen cultural and spatial awareness effectively prepared her for confrontations with James Moultrie and his allies. She understood the importance that southern White men like Moultrie placed on being perceived as honorable and used it to her advantage. It is unclear how well

Alexander knew Moultrie personally, how much time they spent together, or how the interpersonal dynamics of their relationship worked. Enslaved people testified that some White men who engaged in sexual liaisons with enslaved women gave gifts, extended privileges such as improved working conditions or better clothes, and even promised to free them and/or their children. Perhaps Alexander became familiar with Moultrie's ways and personality through the intimacy of their liaison or her assessment of Moultrie as an enslaver. Whether drawing from her experiences or intuition, Alexander determined the kinds of pressures to which Moultrie would be vulnerable, and she proceeded boldly.[23]

According to Petigru, Alexander conveyed in one of her letters that Moultrie as well as his friends would be "passive" in response to her threats and too "weak" to turn her over to authorities. Her audacity vexed Petigru, but Alexander's projections proved accurate. Moultrie did not respond with violence, although he could have done so with minimal consequences. Rather, he did everything in his power to create distance from her, soliciting Robert Pagan and Petigru to pass along what he hoped would be enough money to silence her for good. It was Petigru, not Moultrie, who considered reporting her to local magistrates if she persisted in her demands, which they viewed as harassment and extortion.[24]

Alexander's cultural awareness was astute, aided by an alliance with sympathetic White southerners. By virtue of their status, they could hurl accusations or spread rumors that would harm Moultrie's reputation. According to Petigru, they too considered Moultrie weak, encouraging Alexander to pressure him further. Their support and advice bolstered Alexander's confidence—which Petigru abhorred.

Still, Alexander had the most to lose. When Moultrie and his associates wrote letters back and forth regarding his dilemma, it was not fellow White Carolinians whom they demonized. They referenced Alexander by name, recalled private meetings with her, articulated her demands as threats, and spoke of the criminal charges she could face.

Enslaved women's tenacity in the face of such dangers was spurred by their understanding of the fragile and paradoxical nature of White southern honor. Like Julia Alexander, Harriet Jacobs understood the importance of honor to White men. Jacobs explicitly stated her intensions to appeal to Sawyer's honor for the sake of her children. Although Sawyer had purchased the children from Norcom, he had yet to emancipate them as he had promised. When Jacobs learned that Sawyer's wife intended to remove the children from their great-grandmother's care and place them under her own watchful eye, Jacobs became distraught. Just as Alexander risked jail and prosecution, Jacobs risked exposing her secret hiding place to remind Sawyer "of the promise he had made me, and to throw myself upon his honor for the performance of it."[25]

Similarly, when another bondwoman, Virginia Boyd, found herself in a slave trader's yard alongside her child and with another one in her womb, both of whom were fathered by her owner, Samuel Boyd of Natchez, Mississippi, she penned a message for Boyd that contained a stern warning. She declared that she would not "return to harass or protest his peace of mind & shall never try [to] get back if I am dealt with fairly." She urged Boyd to "relent & see his error for I still beleave that he is possest of more honor than that." Jacobs and Boyd acted boldly, but not out of arrogance or hubris. These enslaved women feared for their children's lives—wanting to save them from hard labor, physical violence, psychological torture, rape, and even death. Saving their children from bondage motivated them to push past fear and draw from their knowledge and experiences to determine their fates.[26]

Julia Alexander aspired to more than security, however. What she demanded of Moultrie tested the elasticity of southern honor. She wanted her daughter to benefit from her familial connection to an honorable southern gentleman: to secure freedom, financial stability, a name. If Moultrie refused, and if Alexander and her associates tarnished his reputation, he risked losing the social capital that came with being an honorable southern gentleman. And yet, if he satisfied her demands and publicly acknowledged his enslaved child, he also risked damaging his reputation, which might have undermined any aspirations that Alexander had for her daughter. She appeared to care about the consequences for Moultrie's status only in the context of her daughter. What did it matter to her if he was reputationally ruined in the process of meeting her demands?

Focused on how Moultrie could benefit her daughter, Alexander appeared willing to exhaust his social capital in exchange for her child's freedom and economic support. Freedom and financial stability would have instantaneously shifted her daughter's positionality in South Carolina society. Although Alexander's child could never experience the privileges of Whiteness, she would gain certain legal rights and be able to maneuver spaces and institutions inaccessible to enslaved people. Alexander was under no illusion that Moultrie and her daughter would have a traditional father-daughter relationship, where her child would walk the streets of Charleston with her arm curled around his, receive invitations to coveted social events, or be accepted into the Moultrie family. However, Moultrie could ensure that her daughter—as his daughter—escaped a life in bondage.[27]

In his 17 November 1859, letter to Robert Pagan, James Petigru conveyed how James Moultrie would entertain any "reasonable proposal" to stop Julia Alexander. In fact, Moultrie would "do not only as much but more than will satisfy the requirements of honor in such a case." Although Petigru omitted details on the actions under consideration, he established honorability as the benchmark and assured Pagan that Moultrie would certainly meet the standard. Petigru did, however, explicitly state what Moultrie refused to do, eliminating courses of action that might compromise his status: "His convictions as to the poor things paternity is immovable, and he never will countenance the impertinence of giving her his name or of assuming that which he has strenuously denied." Moultrie's refusal to bestow his name placed him and Alexander at a crossroads. Moultrie saw no way to meet Alexander's demands without damaging his reputation and his family's social standing.[28]

Over the next few months, with tensions over slavery brewing between the northern and southern parts of the United States as the presidential election of 1860 approached, Petigru continued to lobby on his friend's behalf. The letters that he wrote and received illustrate how a group of White men generated solutions and executed a plan that they hoped would at least neutralize the threat that Alexander and her allies posed to Moultrie's good name. Their ideas varied, ranging from punitive to compassionate, and their sympathies, while always with Moultrie, occasionally fell on the enslaved child whose existence brought them together.

Petigru declined to report Alexander to legal authorities, deciding instead to reason with her and penning a memorandum with a list of questions he intended to pose. The tone of Petigru's questions softened his initial frustrations and scorn for what he saw as Alexander's insubordination as an enslaved woman. They hinted of his consideration, if not deference, for Alexander's desires for her daughter's future. For example, he asked, "Is she to be brought up a white child or a colored?" and "Is she to be brought up in the country or in town?" Petigru's questions were unfathomable to most enslaved parents, who, because their children did not legally belong to them, rarely were given the authority to contribute to such decisions. By offering Alexander the choice to determine her daughter's race, Petigru positioned her to designate the girl not only as a free person but as a free White person—that is, if her physical features allowed her to easily pass into White society. Per South Carolina law, a person's skin color could be "prima facie evidence" for enslavement, and "the party bearing the color of a negro, mulatto or mestizo, is a slave" until proven otherwise. Alexander had ample reasons to believe her daughter would have greater opportunities if raised as a White child. While free Black people could marry other free people, purchase and sell property, and work for wages, they were not citizens but denizens of the state with limited freedoms. They experienced segregation in public spaces such as churches, hotels, and restaurants. In Charleston, free Black residents had to pay a yearly capitation or "head" tax for their skin color. They also bore the burden of proving their free status whenever questioned. It is an understatement to say that Petigru offered Alexander extraordinary choices, but why did he do so?[29]

Dr. Alexander P. Wylie, who had treated Alexander numerous times, including for a lung hemorrhage, provided insight into why Petigru adopted a more diplomatic tone with Alexander. From everything that Wylie had learned from James Moultrie, James Petigru, Julia Alexander, and her enslaver Charles, he concluded "that your friend whilst he was not willing to publicly acknowledge the child—still was satisfied that it was his—that he was a man of considerable means without a child by his wife—that he wished to give the child some education & provide for it in a quiet way with the design that it might ultimately enter society in a free state as a white person." The crux of Wylie's assessment was that Moultrie felt a sense of duty to provide his only child with a decent life that reflected his social status. But because the child was enslaved, born to an enslaved mother, such a life would require unorthodox measures, giving context to Petigru's memorandum to Alexander. The memorandum, then, belied the traditional enslaver-enslaved power dynamic and set the stage for how these men talked about and engaged Alexander and her child moving forward. Petigru had stated to Robert Pagan that Moultrie wished to "satisfy the requirements of honor in such a case." From Wylie's assessment, Moultrie appeared willing to provide his child with a pathway to Whiteness and freedom, even though he remained steadfast about never publicly acknowledging his paternity.[30]

If Wylie's assumptions were true, Moultrie was prepared to stretch the limits of southern honor but not hurl himself beyond the borders in the process. Prior to Alexander's extortion, his life had followed a traditional and prescribed path. For southern men, being married and leading independent households was crucial to affirming their manhood. Moultrie met his first obligation by marrying a suitable woman and establishing a household. When James and Louisa Moultrie married in 1818, they were expected to quickly welcome a child, followed by another and another. Southern elite society looked favorably on having large numbers of children. Moultrie's glaring reputational shortcoming, then, was his and Louisa's failure to have children.

When Alexander confronted Moultrie in 1859, he and Louisa had reached their sixties without having any children together. Although respected for their tremendous contributions to the Charleston community, the Moultries' infertility was surely a topic of gossip as well as a source of pain and conflict for the couple. James and Louisa had not had children to nurture into southern gentlemen and proper ladies, or to inherit an estate that included twenty-six enslaved people, land, and federal and bank stock, all valued at $60,000. Having no other way to leave a legacy, Moultrie concluded that securing an economic future and possibly freedom for his only child was the honorable thing to do.[31]

Any drama or social embarrassment over failing to produce legitimate heirs would have paled in comparison to his sexual liaison with Alexander and the fathering of her enslaved child becoming the talk of Charleston's high society. The child not only symbolized Moultrie's failure to be discreet but exposed his wife as the source of their infertility. Motherhood was central to southern women's identities. Being barren in and of itself was a heavy burden for a woman of this era and class to carry. The wife was often blamed for a couple's inability to have children, although either spouse could have been the cause of infertility. Mary Boykin Chesnut, also of South Carolina, moved in the most elite social circles. Yet she experienced tremendous shame and isolation because of her childlessness, noting it repeatedly in her diaries. Her father, Stephen Decatur Miller, had been a governor of South Carolina, and her husband, James Chesnut Jr., was a US senator. Like most southern women, she understood her value and identity as entwined with motherhood. After listening to her father-in-law, Colonel James Chesnut Sr., praise his wife for having twenty-seven great-grandchildren, Chesnut turned to her diary, decrying, "Me a childless wretch ... no good have I done myself or anyone else." Additionally, if a wife became jealous or scornful that an enslaved woman provided her husband with a child that she could not, their marriage might suffer. Divorce was prohibited in South Carolina, and marital discord also drew unwanted public scrutiny.[32]

White men had no obligation—by law or social mores—to care for or free their enslaved children. Moultrie's plan in fact contradicted the expectations of an honorable southern gentleman and savvy businessman. Enslaved children, whether an enslaver's progeny or not, represented labor and capital. Yet Moultrie's decision to finance his daughter's education and emancipate her was not unprecedented. Some southern White men felt obliged to do so, all while understanding the consequences for their reputations. Nonetheless, they pursued legal action, when necessary, to emancipate their children, remove them to free states and territories, and bequeath money, land, and other property. In 1821, for example, when Rene Peter David petitioned the South Carolina senate to pass an act to emancipate his three enslaved children, he proclaimed that he was "possessed of the humble feelings of a parent," and he anxiously hoped the body would "confer on them the blessings of emancipation." Like Moultrie, Thomas Cox of Texas had no White children of his own but fathered four enslaved children: Lotty, Commodore, Perry, and Frederick. He petitioned the Texas legislature to manumit his children, declaring that he "sincerely regrets the situation in which he finds these his only children." While penitent for stumbling outside societal norms, Cox publicly acknowledged how "he entertains for them, to its full extent, the attachment of the parent for his offspring." Further, he questioned whether his children "should be held to mortification and disadvantages of a situation into which they have been thrown, not by any agency of their own, but by the improper action of the authors of their existence."[33]

From the beginning of Julia Alexander's demands, Moultrie stealthily decided to take a less conspicuous approach to securing his daughter's future. Even before Petigru wrote his memorandum to Alexander, Moultrie established a trust to pay for his daughter's "support and education in a way suitable to her condition till she is of age or married." Because the child was legally enslaved, he needed someone he could rely on as a fair-handed guardian to honor his wishes for her education and well-being. He turned to Alexander Quay Dunovant, a wealthy planter in Chester who enslaved over seventy people. Like Moultrie, he was known throughout the state and served in the South Carolina House of Representatives during the 1850–51 session. Moultrie fronted the money for Dunovant to purchase the girl, and Pagan oversaw the sale. Afterward, Dunovant wrote to Petigru, confirming, "The child of Julia Alexander so far as the legal title is concerned, is already in me. I am willing to act for the child as trustee."[34]

Once Dunovant became a trustee, Petigru continued the work of determining how much money Moultrie should annually invest in the trust. Initially, the child would receive fifty dollars per year, but when Petigru consulted Wylie, the latter replied, "The amt proper to be given to the child of this kind depends upon so many contingencies that I feel very diffident in giving an opinion. If its paternity is doubted & it is intended that it should occupy the position of a free person of colour (always) probably $500 of $600 properly vested might be ample." Although Wylie recognized that Moultrie wanted the child to quietly "enter society in a free state as a white person," he questioned the feasibility. "They are most unfortunate where they are too white to be satisfied with the condition of a negro & tainted with African blood so that they can't enter white society," he warned. "They are to be pitied truly." As a White man, Wylie's consideration for the child seems extraordinary given White southerners' preoccupation with maintaining clear distinctions between White people and people of color, especially those whose light skin color might allow them to cross racial lines undetected. Ultimately, Wylie's concern lay with Moultrie: "But however we may sympathise with this unfortunate child—still we should not forget that justice is due your friend who I highly esteem."[35]

On 24 January 1860, James Petigru wrote to Alexander Wylie what appears to be his last letter regarding Moultrie's paternity scandal. The letter began with Petigru acknowledging Wylie's kind words and well wishes for Moultrie. Petigru confirmed that, while they all held Moultrie in high esteem, Moultrie sensed that this good will would soon expire. According to Petigru, Moultrie felt "no doubt it will be generally considered as great weakness to yield so much to the species of extortion that has been practiced on him." Petigru just as easily could have penned these words for himself, Wylie, or Pagan. Alexander had met with each of them when they served as Moultrie's couriers, delivering messages or money. Even if they did so with contempt, they helped Alexander to extort money and negotiate for the education and potential freedom of her daughter. Although Moultrie feared being seen as weak, he feared scandal and the tarnishing of his honorable reputation more. "He is extremely sensitive to the sort of persecution that he has undergone, and is ready to comply with the demand for a settlement to the extent of $1000 dollars," related Petigru. Moultrie likely considered Wylie's suggestion of $500 or $600, but he was most concerned with reaching an amount that would quiet Alexander forever. According to Petigru, $1,000 was the amount "which the girl now says she will be content with, if a trustee can be found."[36]

Although an amount had been reached, Petigru sensed the fight was far from over, confiding in Wylie that, although Dunovant had consented to be trustee, he had not detailed his long-term plans for Alexander and Moultrie's daughter. Petigru knew only that Dunovant would "take charge of the child & see it brought up decently." Did he plan to emancipate the child in South Carolina or send her to a free state where she could live as free? Petigru understood that Alexander would be unsatisfied with anything less than her daughter's emancipation and, "if the child is to be really held in servitude, the mother will find in that an excuse for a renewal of the same annoyances." He explained that "she has again and again received money on her promise to ask for nothing more. The experience of the past shows that there is no use in paying money for peace with no better assurance than her word." As long as Moultrie's reputation remained at risk, he had "a direct interest in stipulating for her the interest of the child." Even should the daughter be freed in South Carolina, Petigru suspected that "the same sort of appeals will be sure to be made if the child should be in want."[37]

Trying to force the issue, Petigru insisted that Dunovant receive no more money until he confirmed receipt of Moultrie's initial payment and his intensions to apply it "towards her maintenance or support till she is married when the principal or so much as is left shall be paid to her and she allowed to go where she pleases." Although Petigru never explicitly directed Dunovant to emancipate the child, he implied as much by his mention of marriage and relocation. Since South Carolina prohibited enslaved people from marrying, entering legal contracts, or going where they pleased, Moultrie and Alexander's daughter would have to be free to enjoy the rights that Petigru listed. He appeared convinced that Moultrie's freedom from extortion and fear was inseparable from Moultrie's daughter's freedom from bondage. Alexander had made it so.[38]

IN JANUARY 1860, James Petigru wrote Alexander Wylie: "I wish that you would see the girls letters burnt—for I am ashamed to think that he has borne so much calumny." It is unknown whether Wylie destroyed all of Julia Alexander's letters, but their absence from any archive renders a deafening silence, which is what Moultrie and Petigru wanted. What happened to Julia Alexander and her daughter also remains unknown. No clues remain to trace the happenings of their lives beyond January 1860. Throughout the correspondence, no one named the child, making it virtually impossible to track her down in surviving records. There are no bills of sale involving Moultrie, Dunovant, or Pagan that mention a young girl with the Moultrie or Alexander last name.[39]

As the Civil War raged, Alexander and Moultrie's daughter grew, and if she remained enslaved, she found freedom once US troops carried emancipation into the crumbling Confederacy. If Dunovant had freed her early in the war, she was likely trapped for some time in South Carolina. With war's end and Reconstruction, she may have joined the thousands of Black southerners who fled northward and westward. Or she may have chosen to remain in South Carolina. There were many possibilities for her life, further contributing to the historian's difficult task of figuring out what became of her.

More verifiable is that James Moultrie's fears of losing his honorable reputation went unrealized. He went to his grave with the admiration of his peers. After his death in 1869, the Medical Society of South Carolina published a twenty-two-page memoir lauding Moultrie's life and contributions to the medical profession in South Carolina and beyond. They celebrated the soundness of his home life, proclaiming that "his domestic attachments were the polished chains that bound him to life." There was "no home more happy than his." To earn such esteem, particularly considering he and his wife's inability to have children, testifies to the exhaustive efforts that Moultrie, Petigru, and their associates made to conceal his sexual liaison with Julia Alexander and his paternity of her child. White men put much work into constructing their public selves. As an enslaved woman, Julia Alexander should have been an improbable threat to James Moultrie. His race and gender empowered him to dominate and cajole enslaved women. At the expense of his good name, however, it was not enough to *act* honorably. It was essential to be *perceived* as honorable, even if that meant acting surreptitiously in the process—working in the shadows of the South's culture of honor to battle the strong will of an enslaved mother.[40]

Questions to Consider

1. For elite southern men, why was honor so important, and how could engaging in interracial sex damage men's social standing in public and private spaces?
2. Beyond their enslavement, why were Black women especially vulnerable to sexual exploitation and violence?

Notes

1. For fear of consequence, many enslaved women did not discuss the paternity of their mixed-race children outside the enslaved community or trusted confidants. Historian Darlene Clark Hine argued that due to Black women's systemic rape and sexual abuse, they developed behaviors and attitudes that "created the appearance of openness and disclosure but actually shielded the truth of their inner lives and selves from their oppressors"; see Hine, *Hine Sight: Black Women and the Re-Construction of American History* (Bloomington: Indiana University Press, 1997), 37.
2. On the sexual exploitation of enslaved women, see Deborah Gray White, *Ar'n't I a Woman? Female Slaves in the Plantation South,* rev. ed. (1985; New York: Norton, 1999); Thelma Jennings, "Us Colored Women Had to Go Through a Plenty: Sexual Exploitation of African-American Slave Women," *Journal of Women's History* 1, no. 3 (Winter 1990): 45–74; Jennifer L. Morgan, *Laboring Women: Reproduction and Gender in New World Slavery* (Philadelphia: University of Pennsylvania Press, 2004); and Shannon C. Eaves, *Sexual Violence and American Slavery: The Making of a Rape Culture in the Antebellum South* (Chapel Hill: University of North Carolina Press, 2024). On enslaved men and boys and sexual exploitation, see Martha Hodes, *White Women, Black Men: Illicit Sex in the Nineteenth-Century South* (New Haven, CT: Yale University Press, 1997), and Thomas A. Foster, *Rethinking Rufus: Sexual Violations of Enslaved Men* (Athens: University of Georgia Press, 2019). On White fathers, enslaved children, and inheritance, see Bernie D. Jones, *Fathers of Conscience: Mixed-Race*

Inheritance in the Antebellum South (Athens: University of Georgia Press, 2009), and Amrita Chakrabarti Myers, *Forging Freedom: Black Women and the Pursuit of Liberty in Antebellum Charleston* (Chapel Hill: University of North Carolina Press, 2011).

3. James Henry Hammond, "Hammond's Letters on Slavery," in *The Pro-Slavery Arguments as Maintained by the Most Distinguished Writers of the Southern States* (Charleston, SC: Walker, Richards, 1852), 119. On sexual exploitation of enslaved women as a mode of reinforcing White patriarchal authority and gender roles, see Eaves, *Sexual Violence and American Slavery*, 5–10. On southern honor, see Bertram Wyatt-Brown, *Southern Honor: Ethics and Behavior in the Old South* (New York: Oxford University Press, 1982); Stephanie McCurry, *Masters of Small Worlds: Yeoman Households, Gender Relations, and the Political Culture of the Antebellum South Carolina Low Country* (New York: Oxford University Press, 1995); and Lorri Glover, *Southern Sons: Becoming Men in the New Nation* (Baltimore: Johns Hopkins University Press, 2007).

4. See Glover, *Southern Sons*, esp. 19–20, and Craig Thompson Friend, "Belles, Benefactors, and the Blacksmith's Son: Cyrus Stuart and the Enigma of Southern Gentlemanliness," in *Southern Manhood: Perspectives on Masculinity in the Old South*, ed. Craig Thompson Friend and Lorri Glover (Athens: University of Georgia Press, 2004), 92–112.

5. A. P. Wylie to James Petigru, 20 January 1860, James Louis Petigru Papers, 1816–63, South Carolina Historical Society, Charleston.

6. Enslaved men had more opportunities to travel between plantations and towns to labor as blacksmiths, stevedores, or coopers. Enslaved women had more opportunities to work in cities like Charleston; see Bernard E. Powers Jr., *Black Charlestonians: A Social History, 1822–1885* (Fayetteville: University of Arkansas Press, 1994); Alexandra J. Finley, *An Intimate Economy: Enslaved Women, Work, and America's Domestic Slave Trade* (Chapel Hill: University of North Carolina Press, 2020); and Tamika Y. Nunley, *At the Threshold of Liberty: Women, Slavery, and Shifting Identities in Washington, D.C.* (Chapel Hill: University of North Carolina Press, 2021).

7. The Moultries enslaved twenty-seven people in 1850, situating the family among the state's elite; 1850 US Census, Charleston District, SC, Slave Schedules.

8. Stephen Shrewsbury, Last Will and Testament, 4 February 1814, Will Book 3 (1807–18), 503–5, South Carolina Probate Court (Charleston County), microfilm, South Carolina Department of Archives and History, Columbia; "The Moultries," *South Carolina Historical and Genealogical Magazine* 5, no. 4 (October 1904): 229–60.

9. "The Moultries," 229–60.

10. Moultrie and his associates never identified Julia Alexander's allies by name, occupation, race, or gender in their surviving correspondence.
11. James Petigru to Robert Pagan, 17 November 1859, James Louis Petigru Papers.
12. James Petigru, memorandum to Julia Alexander, n.d., James Louis Petigru Papers.
13. James Moultrie to James Petigru, 15 November 1859; Petigru to Robert Pagan, 17 November 1859, James Louis Petigru Papers.
14. William H. Pease and Jane H. Pease, *James Louis Petigru: Southern Conservative, Southern Dissenter* (Athens: University of Georgia Press, 1995), 12–36.
15. Petigru to Pagan, 17 November 1859. In 1860, Pagan owned three enslaved people. In 1859, he was lead signatory on a petition requesting that free Black people be placed in bondage or moved to Liberia to "relieve the state of their contaminating influence"; see 1860 US Census, Chester District, SC, Slave Schedules; Petition of Citizens of Chester District to the South Carolina Legislature, ca. 1859, Records of the General Assembly, no. 1843, South Carolina Department of Archives and History.
16. Petigru to Pagan, 17 November 1859; envelope with Petigru's handwriting, n.d.; A. P. Wylie to Petigru, 20 January 1860, James Louis Petigru Papers.
17. Petigru to Pagan, 17 November 1859.
18. Petigru to Pagan, 17 November 1859. For context, see Victoria E. Bynum, *Unruly Women: The Politics of Social and Sexual Control in the Old South* (Chapel Hill: University of North Carolina Press, 1992); Hodes, *White Women, Black Men*; and Joshua D. Rothman, *Notorious in the Neighborhood: Sex and Families Across the Color Line in Virginia, 1787–1861* (Chapel Hill: University of North Carolina Press, 2003).
19. Petigru to Pagan, 17 November 1859.
20. Petigru to Pagan, 17 November 1859. For the Vesey revolt, see Douglas R. Egerton, *He Shall Go Out Free: The Lives of Denmark Vesey* (Indianapolis: Madison House, 1999), and David Robertson, *Denmark Vesey: The Buried History of America's Largest Slave Rebellion and the Man Who Led It* (New York: Knopf, 1999).
21. Wylie to Petigru, 20 January 1860; John Belton O'Neall, *The Negro Law of South Carolina* (Columbia, SC: J. G. Bowman, 1848), 32; Petigru to Pagan, 17 November 1859.
22. Harriet Jacobs, *Incidents in the Life of a Slave Girl*, ed. Jean Fagan Yellin (Cambridge, MA: Harvard University Press, 2009), 71.
23. In his narrative, William Craft, an enslaved person, argued that White male enslavers gave trinkets to elicit enslaved women's affections and trust and promised to free and educate their children; see Craft, *Running*

a Thousand Miles for Freedom, in *African American Slave Narratives: An Anthology,* ed. Sterling Lecater Bland Jr., 3 vols. (Westport, CT: Greenwood Press, 2001), 3:902–3.
24. Petigru to Pagan, 17 November 1859.
25. Jacobs, *Incidents in the Life of a Slave Girl,* 176.
26. Jacobs, *Incidents in the Life of a Slave Girl,* 176; Virginia Boyd to R. C. Ballard, 6 May 1853, Rice C. Ballard Papers, Southern Historical Collection, University of North Carolina at Chapel Hill.
27. White men attempting to integrate their mixed-race children, enslaved and free, into White society often faced public ridicule and rejection; see Amrita Chakrabarty Myers, *The Vice President's Black Wife: The Untold Life of Julia Chinn* (Chapel Hill: University of North Carolina Press, 2023), 117–27.
28. Petigru to Pagan, 17 November 1859.
29. Petigru, memorandum to Alexander, n.d.; O'Neall, *The Negro Law of South Carolina,* 5; Myers, *Forging Freedom,* 4.
30. Wylie to Petigru, 20 January 1860.
31. Glover, *Southern Sons,* 132; Anya Jabour, *Scarlett's Sisters: Young Women in the Old South* (Chapel Hill: University of North Carolina Press, 2007), 234; 1860 US Census, Charleston District, SC, Slave Schedules; Shrewsbury, Last Will and Testament.
32. Entry for 19 March 1861, in Mary Boykin Chesnut, *Mary Chesnut's Civil War,* ed. C. Vann Woodward (New Haven, CT: Yale University Press, 1981), 32.
33. Jones, *Fathers of Conscience,* xxi; Rene Peter David, petition, Charleston, South Carolina, 1821, Records of the General Assembly; Thomas Cox, petition, Texas, 1850, Records of the Legislature, Memorials and Petitions, Archives Division, Texas State Library, Austin.
34. James Petigru, note to himself, 19 December 1859; Petigru to A. P. Wylie, 24 January 1860; A. Q. Dunovant to Petigru, 5 January 1860, James Louis Petigru Papers; 1850 US Census, Chester District, SC, Slave Schedules.
35. Petigru, memorandum to Alexander, n.d.; Wylie to Petigru, 20 January 1860.
36. Petigru to Wylie, 24 January 1860.
37. Petigru to Wylie, 24 January 1860.
38. Petigru to Wylie, 24 January 1860.
39. Petigru to Wylie, 24 January 1860. Julia Alexander's name does not appear in any South Carolina newspaper advertisements or in Charleston's register of free Blacks; presumably she remained enslaved until the passage of the Thirteenth Amendment in 1865.
40. William T. Wragg, *Memoir of Dr. James Moultrie* (Charleston, SC: William G. Mazyck, 1869), 6–7.

The "Black Douglass" and the "White Douglas"

EMBODYING SECTIONAL POLITICS IN LATE ANTEBELLUM AMERICA

Joshua A. Lynn

In September 1858, *Stephen* Douglas attracted national attention while campaigning throughout Illinois for reelection to the US Senate against Abraham Lincoln. Understandably, a notable public figure with a similar name caused quite a stir when he stopped for the night in Smithboro, New York. As *Frederick* Douglass later told his newspaper audience, upon leaving his hotel room the next day, he saw that "the bar room was speedily filled up in the morning, under the impression that STEPHEN A. DOUGLAS had passed the night there!" He recounted how one "rather awkward looking chap, bolder than the rest, who evidently found me a *little* darker than he had painted STEPHEN, resolved to test my identity, and proceeded to address me as the veritable STEPHEN. I found it hard, however, to undeceive him, for he had, he said, never heard of any other DOUGLAS but the one of Illinois!"[1]

While his misidentification as Stephen Douglas "might have wounded my pride a little," Frederick Douglass drew a lesson from the mix-up. Residents of Smithboro did not read many newspapers, and the "character of the place" contrasted unfavorably with a strongly antislavery community in Pennsylvania he had visited. The home where he had stayed "was thronged" by those who knew which Douglass they clamored to see. As he so often did, Frederick Douglass employed humor to deliver a sharp political critique—only an ignorant community preferred a visit from Stephen over Frederick.[2]

Throughout the 1850s, Americans across the political spectrum juxtaposed Frederick and Stephen to make arguments about the constituencies and principles each represented. Frederick Douglass relished that he, America's most prominent Black man, shared a surname with Stephen A. Douglas, America's most famous White politician. Their name facilitated rhetorical linkages between a radical Black activist and a White supremacist Democrat. The "Black Douglass" and the "White Douglas," as contemporaries called them, came to embody the increasingly zero-sum antagonism over slavery that characterized 1850s politics.

To evaluate their political principles and cultural values, politicians appraised each man's gender and sexuality. Antebellum political parties and reform movements advanced distinct understandings of gender differences and race relations. Political figures personified their coalitions' worldviews so that discussing individual bodies meant debating larger issues. Stephen and fellow Democrats pointed to Frederick's mixed-race body to warn about a racially amalgamated body politic should antislavery forces upset racial hierarchies. For Frederick and antislavery Americans, Stephen evinced the ruffian manhood of southern enslavers. A northern man with a southern body, Stephen symbolized not only slavery's expansion but also the national consolidation of the slaveholding South's gender order. The two men embodied radically different futures for the body politic. Assessing Frederick's and Stephen's manhood, late antebellum Americans used gender to make sense of, and exacerbate, the sectional crisis that led to the Civil War.[3]

When Frederick laughed about New Yorkers confusing him with Stephen in 1858, he knew his readers got the joke because he and countless others had told it for years. The pairing of "Judge Douglas and Fred. Douglass—the white and the black" began in the early 1850s. Political developments in 1854 cemented the connection. That year, Stephen secured passage of the Kansas-Nebraska Act, which repealed the longstanding prohibition against slavery in those territories. Stephen and the Democratic Party sought to remove the acrimonious issue of slavery's expansion from Congress by empowering local majorities of White male settlers to decide whether to legalize slavery under the doctrine of "popular sovereignty." By opening free territory to slavery, however, the Kansas-Nebraska Act galvanized antislavery Americans and intensified sectionalism.[4]

Slavery's opponents, especially Frederick, focused their ire on Stephen. By the mid-1850s, Frederick had achieved international renown. Born in Maryland in 1818, he escaped to the free states in 1838. After liberating himself, Frederick became a famous orator, political activist, radical reformer, and newspaper editor. Stephen, meanwhile, cultivated his national reputation. Born in 1813, he grew up in Vermont and New York but traded the Northeast for the West and settled in Illinois. By the 1850s, he had established himself as a senator, presidential aspirant, and Democratic Party leader.[5]

Frederick wanted to challenge Stephen personally over Kansas-Nebraska. The senator stumped in Illinois for the fall 1854 elections amid fierce blowback over the legislation. Frederick left his home in Rochester, New York, and embarked on a midwestern speaking tour. As his newspaper explained, "Important truths connected with the cause of human freedom, are sometimes better taught by antitheses. Ebony and ivory are thought to look better standing together than when separated. A white Douglas, canvassing the State for slavery, has suggested the idea of having black Douglass there to canvass the State for freedom." Hoping to debate Stephen, Frederick arrived in Aurora, Illinois, where the senator planned to speak. Citing illness, Stephen refused to leave his hotel. Or, as one skeptical newspaper related, "It was currently rumored that Senator Douglas was attacked with the chills as soon as he heard that Frederick was to be on the ground."[6]

Stephen's critics savored Frederick's pursuit of the senator, particularly its racial implications. Frederick recalled that "there was some little suspicion expressed, that Stephen's sickness was less physical than moral, in its character—and arose more from a dislike of meeting a black opponent before the people than from any other cause," but he magnanimously concluded that Stephen had not avoided him for "fear either of our eloquence, or ability." Douglass nevertheless supposed that "a man who is wont to debate with Senators may hardly be expected to have a taste for debating with negroes," given Douglas's desire to placate "Southern gentlemen, and Northern negro-haters." Others noted the consequences of Stephen engaging with Frederick. A Massachusetts newspaper remarked, "During the late canvass in Illinois, his namesake, a person of color, has been continually at his heels, and what was worse, getting the best audiences, and absolutely making the best speeches." Stephen surely could not handle this affront to his racial identity. "It must have taken down the little giant's pride a peg or two, thus to be persecuted by 'a runaway n——,'" the paper concluded.[7]

Nicknamed "the Little Giant" for his five-feet-four-inch stature, Stephen Douglas would not have agreed with Frederick Douglass that ebony and ivory should appear together. Placed alongside Frederick, the senator's body would have undermined Democrats' claims of White racial superiority. At six feet one inch, Frederick stood slightly shorter than Lincoln, another rival who towered over the Little Giant. As one correspondent told Frederick, "You are yourself a living argument against the great wrong of slavery." Frederick's newspaper printed a fictional dialogue between two Illinoisans discussing the 1854 canvass. A supporter of Stephen fumed that "they've got n—— Douglass out here to answer our Steve on Nebraska! It is a deliberate insult!" His sparring partner countered, "If your little man isn't a match for one big one, you may withdraw him and put up another. We want the best you've got."[8] Even without an actual confrontation, observers found significance in physically comparing the two men.

Jokes about "The Little Dug." ridiculed his size to assail his politics. Political observers dubbed him "the petit prodigy," "a little Senator," and the "most diminutive of giants."[9] And because antebellum politicians enjoyed flaunting their classical knowledge, a Republican Party poem rendered Stephen as "some dwarf Polyphemus," while in private a Supreme Court justice snarkily Latinized Stephen's nickname as "Microgigas."[10]

Such jibes transcended simple jest. Politicians embodied their political values. An individual's praiseworthy manhood testified to his party's sound philosophy, while a degenerate body indicated corrupt principles. Mocking the Little Giant impugned his principles and his party. "Without the stature of a full-grown man," Stephen resembled, according to a poem in William Lloyd Garrison's *Liberator*, a "Tom Thumb Titan [who] is not seen, / Save when he climbs upon a negro's back, / Or struts and spouts upon an auction-block." Another poem portrayed Douglas as "a dapper little demagogue" who "climbed on the shoulders of a sturdy slave."[11] The Little Giant, these poems insinuated, depended on the institution of slavery to enhance his standing physically and politically.

Stephen was, in other words, a proslavery "doughface." Northern politicians earned the epithet by kowtowing to enslavers for political advancement. Frederick referred to such men as "that amphibious animal called a Northern man with Southern principles."[12] As "amphibious" suggested, doughfaces occupied liminal space. Neither northern nor southern, their indeterminate sectional identity made their race and gender ambiguous. Such men forfeited White manhood by politically enslaving themselves to the South.[13] Considering Stephen's unwillingness to debate Frederick, a Wisconsin newspaper remarked that "the doughface Douglas dared not meet him, but sneaked back to his hotel, leaving the field to his victor." For many northerners, Stephen personified doughfaces' unmanly submission to enslavers. Speaking at an 1855 convention demanding Black suffrage in his home state of New York, Frederick analogized White southerners' treatment of doughfaces such as Stephen to a boy teasing his dog: "That is what the South has done to the North. That is what they did to Douglas," adding as an aside, "I wish he had another name." Frederick continued, "They held up the cracker of the Presidency, and said to him, 'Stand up' and 'Speak,' and he did both." Frederick used Stephen to excoriate White northerners who appeased enslavers.[14]

Unmanly doughfaces provided a foil for asserting Black manhood. Frederick and many other Black activists emphasized Black manhood to combat racism's threatened emasculation. William J. Watkins, assistant editor of *Frederick Douglass' Paper,* petitioned to form a Black militia company in Massachusetts, demanding equal recognition of Black manhood even as "the Juggernaut of American Prejudice would feign crush the manhood out of us." Watkins used similar language attacking Stephen Douglas and the Kansas-Nebraska Act, explaining that doughfaces, "by their spaniel-like obsequiousness, and lick-the-dust servility, give unmistakable evidence of their pro-slavery affinities." To please the South, "they must suffer their manhood to be 'crushed out' of them, by the juggernaut of American despotism, and then upon their bellies must they crawl." Black men wanted to avoid the fate that Watkins assigned to White doughfaces.[15]

Yet by the 1850s, the unmanly doughface no longer captured the peril of the "Slave Power." Enslavers' heightened aggression inaugurated a new phase of the sectional crisis. Antislavery Americans responded with a compelling conspiratorial narrative by which the Slave Power plotted to nationalize slavery by spreading it to territories and even to free states. Enslavers' dominance of the federal government, their expansionist foreign policy, and their projection of a carceral apparatus into the North through the rendition of fugitives from slavery lent substance to northerners' anxieties. The Slave Power extended far beyond the South.[16]

To articulate the Slave Power's infiltration of the free states, antislavery forces needed sinister northern villains. "Stephen A. Douglas, the agent of this power," as Frederick designated him, fit the role. Stephen attained notoriety for orchestrating the Compromise of 1850, including the infamous

Fugitive Slave Act. Four years later, he opened free soil to slavery with the Kansas-Nebraska Act. Activist Martin R. Delany predicted "a reduction of the now nominally free into slave States" and counseled Black northerners to leave the country. The free states no longer promised safety because of slavery's northern accomplices such as Stephen, whom Delany reviled as "some hired spy of the slave power, residing in Illinois." Unsavory White men, including "miserable, half-starved, servile Northern slave-catchers," according to Delany, proved "ready and willing to do the bidding of their contemptible southern masters." Frederick regarded northern men who enforced the Fugitive Slave Act as "scoundrels." Black women and men adopted more confrontational forms of resistance in response to the homegrown threat of "Northern ruffians."[17]

Stephen served this antislavery agenda by giving the Slave Power a human face. His bodily presence in the free states heralded the ascendance of a proslavery and racist political culture shared by the South's enslavers and the North's doughfaces and ruffians. Antislavery Americans feared Stephen's pro-southern cultural values, including his offensive manhood.

The increasingly aggressive Slave Power took concrete form in the aggressively masculine Stephen. Although he fit the caricature of the unmanly doughface, Stephen's critics saw him as a ruffian whose masculinity aligned with that of enslavers. Portraying Stephen not as unmanly but as evincing unrestrained manhood made more sense. Stephen's nickname—"The Little Giant"—reflected not only his stature but also his charisma and political prowess.[18] Frederick regaled his newspaper audience with a firsthand account of the Little Giant speaking in Illinois in 1854: "He is a short man, firmly knit, has a large head, short neck, broad chest, a youthful face, and is exceedingly ready of speech. He is a man who would be at once recognized by an intelligent observer, as a dangerous man." Four years later, a correspondent in Illinois discerned a similarly noxious brew of outsized presence, magnetic oratory, and malice as Stephen campaigned against Lincoln. He told Frederick, "I was thinking of you all the while this bad man was speaking. I did most earnestly desire that you could have been here to have seen and heard him." After complaining about the bad man's racist remarks, the writer conceded, "a good, a noble, a lion-like voice, good oratorical powers, with rather a fine personal appearance." Little or not, Stephen had earned his giant status. "He is no trifling opponent," Frederick remarked in 1858, concluding, "He is one of the most restless, ambitious, boldest and most unscrupulous enemies with whom the cause of the colored man has to contend."[19]

Many northerners found Stephen and other Democrats' masculinity distasteful, especially as it evoked the perceived licentiousness of southern enslavers. The entire party seemed to consist of ruffians, whether northern or southern. Democrats made an asset of this perception. More than simply a pro-southern party, Stephen's Democrats defied sectionalism by championing the political equality of White men nationwide, including European immigrants, religious minorities, and enslavers. Southern Democrats praised their doughfaces for their supposedly disinterested defense of enslavers' rights. Georgia's Herschel V. Johnson, who served as Stephen's vice-presidential running mate after the Democratic Party split along sectional lines during the 1860 presidential election, explained his support for the Little Giant: "I knew his great ability, his firmness, his courage and tried friendship for the South. I knew that we could trust him, however we might differ from him." An Arkansas Democrat agreed that the Illinois senator "has been always and everywhere the bold, able, and eloquent defender of the rights of the southern people." Antislavery northerners saw men such as Stephen as lackeys to southern political interests; southern Democrats regarded these northerners as paternal figures who protected them as an insecure minority in national politics.[20]

The Little Giant seemed at home in a party of bad men lacking self-control and respectability. When Stephen proposed to the socially prominent Adele Cutts to become his second wife, a naval officer gossiped that "the ladies object to the match on the dissimilarity of personal cleanliness between the parties." Stephen struck many as profane, pugnacious, and unkempt. He had the reputation of being a hard drinker. Moral reformers associated intemperance with slaveholding, with imbibers and violent enslavers similarly eschewing self-control. A newspaper ridiculed Stephen's ignominious departure from Aurora, Illinois, after declining to debate Frederick: "Poor Douglas! The victim of the Slave power and brandy, once the honored son of Illinois."[21] Mocking Stephen's intemperance attacked Democrats as a party of unbridled masculinity, typified by anti-temperance and proslavery views.

Democrats' ruffian manhood also manifested through vulgar racism. Northern Democrats' White supremacist political culture aligned them with southern enslavers.[22] Having watched Stephen speak in 1858, one observer depicted him as "illiberal and ungenerous, and black-hearted and bitter to the last and lowest degree—pursuing the poor 'Negro, Indian, Chinaman,' and even 'Coolies,' . . . with fiendish and wolfish ferocity." In 1854, a newspaper correspondent recalled that "violence and vulgarity" and a "Bowery style" characterized one of Stephen's Senate speeches. Addressing antislavery senator William H. Seward, Stephen employed a racist epithet, leading the writer to specify that "He always used the word 'n——' and not 'negro' as it appears in his printed speeches." Black activists such as Frederick stressed the need to resist both southern slavery and northern racism. Frederick's newspaper foregrounded Stephen's racism upon the Little Giant's 1861 death: "In his exhibition of contempt for the negro, he was malignant, unscrupulous, coarse, vulgar and brutal, to a degree which made him the favorite exponent of this peculiar American malignity."[23]

Black activists cited dissipated White bodies to undermine Democrats' belief that Whiteness alone merited political rights. Frederick clarified that "the 'body politic' is not more immaculate than many other bodies." He recounted that on election day, he "saw the gambler, the horse jockey, the pugilist, the miserable drunkard just lifted from the gutter, covered with filth, enter and deposit his vote." He "saw Pat, fresh from the Emerald Isle, requiring two sober men to keep him on his legs, enter and deposit his vote for the Democratic candidate." A physically degraded body denoted immorality and unfitness for self-government. With such White men enjoying political rights, Frederick reckoned that America's body politic "could not suffer in its composition even should it admit a few sober, industrious and intelligent colored voters." In a racist political culture in which color-blind appeals to rights fell flat, some Black leaders focused on more tangible markers of Black respectability and fashioned their own stereotypes, especially regarding White immigrants, as one of many strategies for demanding inclusion. Class and culture thus joined race and gender as fault lines in late antebellum politics.[24]

White antislavery politicians ranked Black respectable manhood over Democratic ruffianism for their own purposes. Speaking in the House of Representatives in 1859, Illinois Republican John F. Farnsworth critiqued Illinois Democrats as "a man-worshiping party" who "blindly follow and worship Mr. DOUGLAS." Illinois Democrat Philip B. Fouke countered, "We worship STEPHEN A. DOUGLAS and you worship Fred Douglass." Democrats often referenced "Fred Douglass" to discredit members of the "Black Republican" Party as racial egalitarians. Farnsworth denied that

Republicans advocated "the social and political equality of the negro." Still, when choosing between Frederick and Stephen, he quipped, "I am inclined to think that Fred is the likelier man of the two." Farnsworth did not support racial equality, but he did argue that African Americans deserved the legal right to testify in court alongside any White man "who comes into court covered all over, from head to foot, with moral corruption and pollution." Without this right, African Americans could not defend themselves against crimes perpetrated "by some villainous, scoundrely Democratic white man—some Democratic doughface."[25]

After the Civil War, Republicans such as Farnsworth evolved to embrace Black male suffrage but still fended off accusations that they desired racial equality. Republicans manipulated Frederick's image to make both points. They justified extending suffrage by weighing Black respectability, newly enhanced by wartime loyalty, against the treason of Confederates and southern-sympathizing northern Democrats. In 1866, Farnsworth acknowledged that enfranchising Black men could alter the makeup of Congress. Even so, he told the House that "if it were true that they would send one of their own race here, I would still vote for it. For on the whole, however my reputation for good taste might be called in question by some, I would prefer to sit by the side of Fred. Douglass in this Hall rather than by the side of Fernando Wood." Farnsworth's partiality for Douglass over Wood, a notorious, pro-southern New York City Democrat, made his colleagues laugh. Illinois senator Richard Yates likewise contrasted Democrats to loyal African Americans to advance Black suffrage. But he also invoked Frederick to skirt Democrats' charge that Republicans would legislate equality, asking, "From what a lofty, shining light would Frederick Douglass have to fall, to reach the low level of Andrew Johnson?" White Republicans' flippant argument that men such as Wood and Johnson could never equal the exceptional Douglass allowed them to jab at White adversaries and countenance some rights for African Americans while deflecting questions of substantive equality.[26]

More than a decade before Farnsworth consented to sit beside Frederick in the House of Representatives, the nation's press indulged in a flurry of speculation that, as a Georgia newspaper put it, "'Fred' Douglass, the negro, is to be brought out for Congress." New York representative Gerrit Smith, a radical abolitionist, moral reformer, and close friend of Frederick, resigned his House seat in 1854. A nationwide brouhaha over whether Frederick should replace him provided opportunity to use Black manly respectability to besmirch White ruffianism. Smith, a devoutly religious teetotaler, groused about his congressional colleagues to Douglass: "How ludicrous a figure . . . is that member of Congress . . . who, in one breath, swears, that he would not so disgrace himself, as to sit by the side of 'Fred. Douglass;' and who, in the next breath, squirts his tobacco juice upon the carpet!" A northern newspaper maintained that "Mr. Douglass would make a very sorry figure among the 'pure Caucasians' in Congress, if in debate, the use of bowie knives, pistols, dirks, and other instruments of ruffianism, were to indicate a man's preiminary status." Frederick's "energy, eloquence, manliness, and good sense" contrasted with congressional ruffianism.[27]

Stephen, conversely, wallowed in a Congress full of "Southern bullies." By the 1850s, many northerners had lost patience with White southerners who, according to Frederick's newspaper, "have, been allowed to 'crack their whips' over the heads of Northern Representatives, too long already." Northerners cheered when their congressmen stood up to southerners' threats and violence. But the North had its bullies too, particularly Stephen, who allegedly tried to cow fellow White northerners into submission to the Slave Power.[28] Senator Charles Sumner admonished Stephen in May 1856 for his "gusts of vulgarity," reminding him "that the bowie-knife and bludgeon are not the proper emblems of senatorial debate." After South Carolina representative Preston Brooks caned Sumner two days later, accusations circulated about the Little Giant's complicity. An antislavery minister in Chicago claimed that "Douglas, of giant infamy, stood by with his hands in his pocket."[29]

Stephen even took on the persona of an enslaver when bullying others. An editorial in *Frederick Douglass' Paper* noted that one of Stephen's speeches attacking clergy who petitioned against the Kansas-Nebraska Act "sounds like an address made by a slave-driver, while untwisting a rope, with which means to tie up a victim, preparatory to laying on his back nine-and-thirty lashes." Stephen purportedly bullied his own constituents in Chicago during an infamous 1854 speech on Kansas-Nebraska. He grew noticeably frustrated when a rowdy audience refused to let him speak. A Democratic newspaper condemned "the mob spirit which prevailed in that hot-bed of abolitionism, Chicago, by which Judge Douglas was prevented from addressing his constituents," an insult worsened by the fact that Chicagoans had previously welcomed "Fred. Douglass, the negro orator of abolitionism." The Little Giant's critics faulted Stephen, not his audience. Another newspaper reported, "The spirit of a *dictator* flashed out from his eye, curled upon his lips, and mingled its cold irony in every tone of his voice and every gesture of his body." By interacting with his constituents "rather as *master* than a servant," Stephen had "lost sight of a very important and essential feature of our republican government." Even White northerners unsympathetic to African Americans resented the Slave Power, personified in Stephen, when it violated their republican equality and sectional autonomy. As a Massachusetts newspaper put it, "Douglas in leaving the stage at Chicago, declared that if he could not rule the rabble there, *he could command obedience on his plantation. He is better fitted for a slave driver* than for a leader of freemen."[30]

As a "Northern man with a 'Southern plantation,'" Stephen appeared more menacing than the typical doughface, defined merely as a northern man with southern principles. Upon his first marriage to a North Carolinian in 1847, Stephen rebuffed his father-in-law's offer of a Mississippi plantation for political reasons. But he did profit from the plantation, which he superintended for his wife after she inherited the land and its enslaved labor force, and later for their minor sons, who became heirs upon Martha Douglas's 1853 death. This "technical dodge," as one newspaper writer derided the legal niceties Stephen used "to escape the odium and censure of Northern public opinion," did not prevent his portrayal as an enslaver.[31] A Boston meeting protesting Kansas-Nebraska chastised "the slaveholding adventurer of Illinois." References to "the Mississippi slave plantation Senator from Illinois" and "the Illinois Senator, and Mississippi slaveholder," as editor William Watkins styled him, conveyed Stephen's sectional indeterminacy. After the Little Giant's hostile reception in Chicago, a correspondent told Frederick's newspaper that Stephen "will either go to his Southern plantation, and tyrannize over his wretched slaves, or go to Nebraska and aid in carrying out his idea of popular sovereignty, by assisting his Southern allies in establishing a slaveholding government."[32] Simultaneously an Illinois doughface, Mississippi enslaver, and Kansas border ruffian, Stephen embodied a national coalition of bad men dedicated to slavery and its expansion.

But his sectional fluidity made his manhood unstable. Antislavery northerners decried what they interpreted as Democrats' infidelity to the gender norms that made the free-labor North superior to the slaveholding South. To register the magnitude of Stephen's betrayal, many northerners not only praised Frederick as a better man than the Little Giant but extolled the formerly enslaved southerner as a better *northern* man than the native New Englander and Illinois senator. A poem appearing in multiple newspapers titled "The Douglasses—A Swop" captured this inversion: "Let Slavery now stop her mouth, / And quiet be henceforth: / We've got Fred Douglass from the South— / She's got Steve from the North!" Many northerners agreed that "we've made so much the better trade."[33]

Despite Stephen's record of sectional mediation, many southern Democrats and their proslavery northern allies disowned the Little Giant in the late 1850s for opposing efforts to turn Kansas into a slave state. In 1858, a South Carolina newspaper editor regretted that Stephen, who "has been, for years past, our beau ideal of a great and noble Senator," seemed to be "going, like a *black traitor*, into the ranks of the Black Republicans." Transforming Stephen into a northern antislavery radical tarnished his White manhood. A writer for the *Constitution*, the organ of the Democratic Party's anti-Douglas wing, sexualized the Little Giant's purported scheming with Black Republicans. The 1860 presidential election saw Stephen "getting ready to lie down with Lincoln," prompting the writer to muse, "We shall see how many in the South are ready to sanction his acceptance of a black-republican bed-fellow." The anti-abolitionist and anti-Douglas *New York Herald* contended that "red-hot radical abolitionists" including William Lloyd Garrison and "the black Douglass" had aligned with Democrats such as "the white Douglas" who opposed Kansas becoming a slave state. Seeking sectional harmony, Stephen had long hedged on the morality of slavery, putting him at odds with Americans who expected statesmen to espouse sectional values. That some Americans depicted the White Douglas as the Black Douglass's antislavery ally while others vilified him as an enslaver reveals how Stephen's attempt to surmount sectionalism led many to dismiss him as the racialized and gendered personification of either northern antislavery extremism or southern proslavery radicalism.[34]

Earlier, in the 1850s, one newspaper writer critiqued both Stephen and Frederick for such slippery sectional identities. Both men, in effect, practiced doughface politics: "In regard to the sectional character of their sentiments, they do not greatly differ—the one being a Southern man with Northern principles, and the other a Northern man, with Southern principles." Each man's adherence to another section's expectations did not highlight principled differences but rather a common lack of principle. The writer suggested another similarity: "Nor are they, in blood, so far removed as might at first appear." Having blurred the racial boundaries, they elaborated, "Fred being Anglo-Saxon upon the side of his father, while Stephen may be said to be eminently worthy of an eulogy similar to that pronounced by the negro over his master, that 'if he was a white man, he had a black heart.'"[35]

By minimizing sectional and racial distinctions within "the Douglass family," the writer hinted at amalgamation, one of nineteenth-century America's greatest taboos. Frederick and Stephen did share a political strategy: they both focused on interracial sex to make political arguments. Amalgamation constituted a crude metaphor but not a blunt one. Diverse politicians leveled carefully crafted charges of sexual impropriety to advance their agendas.[36] Frederick and Stephen embodied transgressive sexuality for their opponents, who referenced their degraded bodies to argue about sectional values, proper manhood, and the body politic.

Stephen used Frederick to indict Republicans for encouraging sexual and political amalgamation. During his 1858 debates with Lincoln, Douglas told the audience in Freeport, Illinois, "The last time I came here to make a speech ... I saw a carriage, and a magnificent one it was, drive up and take a position on the outside of the crowd; a beautiful young lady was sitting on the box-seat, whilst Fred Douglass and her mother reclined inside, and the owner of the carriage acted as driver." Stephen did not invent the story. Frederick had attended the Little Giant's speech in Freeport when they both toured Illinois in 1854.[37] Stephen dredged up the moment four years later to insinuate that Republicans condoned sexual amalgamation.

Stephen also employed the incident to arraign Republicans for promoting political amalgamation, snarling "that those of you who believe that the negro is your equal and ought to be on an equality with you socially, politically, and legally, have a right to entertain those opinions, and of course will vote for Mr. Lincoln." For Democrats, interracial politics accompanied sexual and social mixing—Stephen located Frederick's proximity to White women at a political event. Earlier in his campaign against Lincoln, Stephen had affirmed, "I am in favor of preserving not only the purity of the blood, but the purity of the government from any mixture or amalgamation with inferior races." Sexual amalgamation and political amalgamation went together for Democrats.[38]

Frederick's mixed-race body personified both sexual and political mixing. A Democratic newspaper in Kentucky linked interracial sex to interracial politics when speculating about Frederick serving in Congress, reminding readers that "this Fred is a mulatto" and positing that Frederick's election would have a salutary result. It would "open the eyes of men in the free States. It will be similar in effect to a negro's marrying a white woman—a war against nature." Frederick's amalgamated body forecast an amalgamated, and unnatural, body politic.[39]

Antislavery rivals undercut Democrats' handwringing over amalgamation by hurling the accusations right back. Frederick foregrounded his racial identity as often as his opponents, using his body to make White Americans confront the coercive sexuality at the heart of slavery. "My father was a white man," Frederick bluntly announced in his popular 1845 autobiography. Two years later, he joked about a harrowing altercation when "a little white man" objected to his presence in a train car, telling Frederick, "Why, you know you are a negro." Frederick recollected that he "denied" the claim, explaining, "I am but half a negro; betwixt and between, as they say." He found himself violently ejected nonetheless.[40] Frederick made sure that Americans understood his paternity.

With Frederick self-embodying amalgamation, the Little Giant likely cringed whenever Frederick Douglass invoked his "good friend and namesake, Stephen A. Douglas." Quips about Frederick's "lighter-skinned, but black-hearted namesake," as one correspondent labeled Stephen, proved irresistible.[41] As early as 1851, several newspaper editors, including at least one Democrat, laughed about a familial connection by reprinting a fabricated exchange between Stephen and Daniel Dickinson, a former Democratic senator and ardent anti-abolitionist. Dickinson "was anxious to know if Judge Douglas was any relation to another gentleman bearing his cognomen, somewhat prominent in public life. 'His name,' says the Senator, 'is Frederick; I believe he is not a cousin of yours?'"[42] We can picture Frederick's mischievous grin when calling Stephen his "distinguished namesake" in speeches or identifying himself as Stephen's "namesake" in his newspaper. Based on how politically useful he found their shared surname, Frederick was disingenuous when he told a Scottish audience that "he wished the scamp had another name."[43]

Frederick's waggish allusions to amalgamation made serious the point that Democrats upheld an institution that countenanced abusive sexuality. Antislavery Americans routinely dismissed hysteria over interracial sex as hypocritical. Enslavers' sexual coercion of Black women had long saturated antislavery print and visual culture. Democrats, by defending slavery, presumably condoned such violence. An article reprinted in Frederick's newspaper echoed the standard rebuttal: "Anti-Slavery men, when charged—as they frequently used to be—with being amalgamationists, have ever made the unanswerable retort, that the system of *Slavery* is the very hot-bed of amalgamation." When presenting Stephen as an enslaver, adversaries drew on established themes of sexual abuse including "slave breeding."[44]

These depredations supposedly gave Stephen a financial stake in slavery's expansion. Demand for enslaved labor in Kansas promised profit if the Little Giant sold a woman he enslaved, "especially if she be a good breeder." Such allegations challenged Stephen's boasted neutrality regarding slavery's expansion under his doctrine of popular sovereignty. His exploitation of Black women's reproductive labor led to a striking juxtaposition with Frederick. Anticipating a showdown between the two men, a newspaper writer reflected that "Fred is a man and a nobleman by the side of the 'n——' breeding Senator." Another writer implied that Stephen raped enslaved women by mentioning "his crops of picanninies of African, American and Senatorial paternity."[45] Villainizing Stephen as a sexually abusive enslaver reinforced antislavery Americans' claims that Democrats sanctioned sexual violence.

Stephen's party, critics warned, would spread slavery's sexual crimes through their territorial policy. When the Kansas-Nebraska Act allowed slavery's extension, proslavery "border ruffians" flocked to Kansas. Armed with "bowie knives, revolvers and bludgeons," southern ruffians bullied antislavery settlers and, screamed a White Republican in 1856, "passed over the virgin bride of Kansas liberty, bound hand and foot, to the tender mercies of the Southern Black Aristocracy!" Black activist Robert Purvis lambasted "the unscrupulous demagogueism of that traitor to humanity and to his country, Stephen Arnold Douglas . . . a man who would offer up to the bloody Moloch of Slavery, the unpolluted and virgin soil of a territory larger than the original thirteen States."[46] Metaphors of raping virgin territory complemented sensationalist accounts of border ruffians raping and murdering antislavery settlers.

Border ruffians symptomatized an unregulated masculinity that the Democratic Party spread alongside slavery. An 1856 political cartoon showcased their atrocities. The bad men in the cartoon do not consist of southern men but prominent northern Democrats—Secretary of State William L. Marcy of New York, presidential aspirant James Buchanan of

FIG. 1. John L. Magee, "Liberty, the Fair Maid of Kansas—in the Hands of the 'Border Ruffians'" (Philadelphia, 1856). (Courtesy, Political Cartoons Collection, The Library Company of Philadelphia)

Pennsylvania, President Franklin Pierce from New Hampshire, Michigan senator Lewis Cass, and of course Illinois senator Stephen A. Douglas—behaving as southern men and border ruffians. Pierce and Cass menace a White woman symbolizing "Liberty, the Fair Maid of Kansas." By foregrounding White female victims, anti–Slave Power appeals prioritized slavery's impact on White Americans. Stephen, meanwhile, scalps a fellow White man who opposed slavery in Kansas.[47] The cartoon conveyed fears that when northern White men acted like southern White men, Democrats' cultural and gender values threatened the free-labor North. Whether bullying colleagues in the Senate, swaggering on the stump in Illinois, courting besotted Irish Catholic voters, enslaving Black Mississippians, or encouraging ruffians along the Missouri-Kansas border, Stephen personified the masculine ethos of this national party of bad men.

Stephen's ruffian manhood and Frederick's respectable manhood reveal the complex interaction of gender, race, and sectionalism on the eve of the Civil War. Slavery produced a sectional crisis because it sundered northerners and southerners in their politics and culture, including their thoughts about manhood. Yet, competing conceptions of masculinity jostled within the North where antislavery men squared off against

Democrats and where politicians manipulated ideas of Black and White manhood. Debates about the masculinity and sexuality of the Black Douglass and the White Douglas illustrate how American political culture fractured over gender.

Dividing men within the free states, gender also connected White men across the sectional chasm. Northern and southern Democrats touted their shared dedication to White male mastery, warning that Frederick Douglass portended a racially amalgamated nation, hardly an accurate reflection of most antislavery northerners' politics. By playing that role for northern and southern Democrats, Frederick gave tangible form to many White men's anxieties over the loss of their racially exclusive polity.

A party uniting northerners and southerners, however, proved a liability in an age of sectional absolutism. By 1860, sectionalized understandings of gender contributed to undermining national coalitions and obscuring diversity with each section. In that climate, Stephen's collaboration with southern White men amounted to treason against the antislavery North and its idealized gender roles. Depicting Stephen Douglas as a proslavery ruffian did not accurately reflect his politics. But by playing that role for antislavery northerners, Stephen made the Slave Power's threat to their cultural values comprehensible.[48] Gender could unite or divide; it could forge intersectional partnerships or intensify sectionalism. By distilling the messiness of the 1850s political crisis over slavery into two fundamentally different raced, gendered, and sectionalized bodies, diverse Americans used gender to clarify complex issues and ease their way toward civil war.

Questions to Consider

1. Along with disagreements over slavery, how did disagreements over gender and manhood divide northerners and southerners before the Civil War?
2. How did gender relate to other aspects of late antebellum Americans' identities, such as their political or regional identities?

Notes

1. "A Letter from the Editor," *Frederick Douglass' Paper* (Rochester, NY), 24 September 1858.

2. "A Letter from the Editor."
3. On parties' gender ideologies, see Michael D. Pierson, *Free Hearts and Free Homes: Gender and American Antislavery Politics* (Chapel Hill: University of North Carolina Press, 2003), and Pierson, *The Wild Woman of Cincinnati: Gender and Politics on the Eve of the Civil War* (Baton Rouge: Louisiana State University Press, 2023), 77–95. For embodied politics, see Nancy Isenberg, "The 'Little Emperor': Aaron Burr, Dandyism, and the Sexual Politics of Treason," in *Beyond the Founders: New Approaches to the Political History of the Early American Republic,* ed. Jeffrey L. Pasley, Andrew W. Robertson, and David Waldstreicher (Chapel Hill: University of North Carolina Press, 2004), 129–51, and Joshua A. Lynn, "A Manly Doughface: James Buchanan and the Sectional Politics of Gender," *Journal of the Civil War Era* 8, no. 4 (December 2018): 591–620.
4. *New York Herald,* quoted in *Illinois State Register* (Springfield), 8 February 1854; Tekla Ali Johnson, "Frederick Douglass and the Kansas-Nebraska Act: From Reformer to Revolutionary," in *The Nebraska-Kansas Act of 1854,* ed. John R. Wunder and Joann M. Ross (Lincoln: University of Nebraska Press, 2008), 118–22.
5. David W. Blight, *Frederick Douglass: Prophet of Freedom* (New York: Simon and Schuster, 2018); Robert W. Johannsen, *Stephen A. Douglas* (New York: Oxford University Press, 1973); James L. Huston, *Stephen A. Douglas and the Dilemmas of Democratic Equality* (Lanham, MD: Rowman and Littlefield, 2006); Martin H. Quitt, *Stephen A. Douglas and Antebellum Democracy* (New York: Cambridge University Press, 2012); Michael E. Woods, *Arguing Until Doomsday: Stephen Douglas, Jefferson Davis, and the Struggle for American Democracy* (Chapel Hill: University of North Carolina Press, 2020).
6. "Going to Illinois," *Frederick Douglass' Paper,* 29 September 1854; "Anti-Nebraska at Aurora. Speech from Frederick Douglass! The White Douglas Taken Sick! Meeting in the Congregational Church—Speeches from B. Chapman of Ohio, and S. S. Beman of New York," *Chicago Tribune,* reprinted in *Frederick Douglass' Paper,* 27 October 1854; Johannsen, *Stephen A. Douglas,* 447–61.
7. "The Campaign in Illinois," *Frederick Douglass' Paper,* 1 December 1854; "Douglas Against Douglas," *Boston Daily Atlas,* 18 November 1854 (euphemism employed).
8. "Emigration and Colonization," *Frederick Douglass' Paper,* 17 September 1858; *Frederick Douglass' Paper,* 3 November 1854 (euphemism employed); Blight, *Frederick Douglass,* 75, 102–4, 111, 112–14, 176, 209, 761; Huston, *Stephen A. Douglas and the Dilemmas of Democratic Equality,* 10, 14, 23, 144.

9. "New Nursery Ballads, for Good Little Democrats," in *The Bobolink Minstrel; or, Republican Songster for 1860*, ed. George W. Bungay (New York: O. Hutchinson, 1860), 72 (first and third quotes); George W. Bungay, "The Presidential Chair for Sale," *The Liberator* (Boston), 17 February 1854 (second quote); "The Final Finality," *New Orleans Crescent*, reprinted in *Boston Daily Atlas*, 13 March 1854 (fourth quote).
10. Almon H. Benedict, *A "Wide Awake" Poem; in Which Are Recounted the Political Death and Burial of the Unlamented Buchanan; and the Wanderings of the Little Giant "In Search of His Mother": In It Are, Also, Briefly Set Forth the Merits of "Honest Old Abe," Our Next President* (Cortland Village, NY: Edward D. Van Slyck, 1860), 13; Robert C. Grier to Jeremiah Sullivan Black, 15 September 1859, Jeremiah S. Black Papers, microfilm, Manuscript Division, Library of Congress, Washington, DC.
11. George W. Bungay, "Nebraska and the Little Giant," *The Liberator*, 10 February 1854; Bungay, "The Presidential Chair for Sale."
12. Frederick Douglass, "The Proclamation and a Negro Army: An Address Delivered in New York, New York, on 6 February 1863," in *The Frederick Douglass Papers. Series One: Speeches, Debates, and Interviews*, ed. John W. Blassingame et al., 5 vols. (New Haven, CT: Yale University Press, 1979–92), 3:550.
13. Joanne B. Freeman, *The Field of Blood: Violence in Congress and the Road to Civil War* (New York: Farrar, Straus and Giroux, 2018), 62–68; Joshua A. Lynn, *Preserving the White Man's Republic: Jacksonian Democracy, Race, and the Transformation of American Conservatism* (Charlottesville: University of Virginia Press, 2019), 22–24.
14. "It Won't Do!" *Wisconsin Free Democrat* (Milwaukee), reprinted in *Frederick Douglass' Paper*, 17 November 1854; Frederick Douglass, "We Ask Only for Our Rights: An Address Delivered in Troy, New York, on 4 September 1855," in Blassingame et al., eds., *Frederick Douglass Papers. Series One*, 3:96.
15. William J. Watkins, *Our Rights as Men. An Address Delivered in Boston, Before the Legislative Committee on the Militia, February 24, 1853, by William J. Watkins, in Behalf of Sixty-Five Colored Petitioners, Praying for a Charter to Form an Independent Military Company* (Boston: Benjamin F. Roberts, 1853), 4, Samuel J. May Anti-Slavery Collection, Division of Rare and Manuscript Collections, Digital Collections, Cornell University Library, Ithaca, NY; [Watkins], "Douglas, the Nebraska Bill, and the Administration," *Frederick Douglass' Paper*, 17 February 1854; Christopher James Bonner, *Remaking the Republic: Black Politics and the Creation of American Citizenship* (Philadelphia: University of Pennsylvania Press, 2020),

151–54, 231n12; A. Kristen Foster, "'We Are Men!': Frederick Douglass and the Fault Lines of Gendered Citizenship," *Journal of the Civil War Era* 1, no. 2 (June 2011): 143–75.

16. Matthew Karp, *This Vast Southern Empire: Slaveholders at the Helm of American Foreign Policy* (Cambridge, MA: Harvard University Press, 2016); Leonard L. Richards, *The Slave Power: The Free North and Southern Domination, 1780–1860* (Baton Rouge: Louisiana State University Press, 2000); Jonathan Daniel Wells, *The Kidnapping Club: Wall Street, Slavery, and Resistance on the Eve of the Civil War* (New York: Bold Type Books, 2020).

17. Frederick Douglass, "We Are in the Midst of a Moral Revolution: An Address Delivered in New York, New York, on 10 May 1854," in Blassingame et al., eds., *Frederick Douglass Papers. Series One,* 2:482; Martin R. Delany, "Political Destiny of the Colored Race on the American Continent," in *Martin R. Delany: A Documentary Reader,* ed. Robert S. Levine (Chapel Hill: University of North Carolina Press, 2003), 272–79 (quotes on 277, 274, and 279); Frederick Douglass, "Northern Ballots and the Election of 1852: An Address Delivered in Ithaca, New York, on 14 October 1852," in Blassingame et al., eds., *Frederick Douglass Papers. Series One,* 2:403 ("Northern ruffians"), 418 ("scoundrels"); Ali Johnson, "Frederick Douglass and the Kansas-Nebraska Act," 113–28; Blight, *Frederick Douglass,* 236–47, 264, 269–73, 277–79; Kellie Carter Jackson, *Force and Freedom: Black Abolitionists and the Politics of Violence* (Philadelphia: University of Pennsylvania Press, 2019); Walter C. Rucker, "Unpopular Sovereignty: African American Resistance and Reactions to the Kansas-Nebraska Act," in Wunder and Ross, eds., *The Nebraska-Kansas Act of 1854,* 129–58.

18. Huston, *Stephen A. Douglas and the Dilemmas of Democratic Equality,* 5–6, 10, 14–15; Quitt, *Stephen A. Douglas and Antebellum Democracy,* 65–86; Woods, *Arguing Until Doomsday,* 40–41, 57–60.

19. "The Campaign in Illinois"; "From H. O. Wagoner," *Frederick Douglass' Paper,* 23 July 1858; Frederick Douglass, "Freedom in the West Indies: An Address Delivered in Poughkeepsie, New York, on 2 August 1858," in Blassingame et al., eds., *Frederick Douglass Papers. Series One,* 3:236–37.

20. "Letter from Ex-Gov. H. V. Johnson. He Endorses the Philadelphia Convention," *Augusta [GA] Chronicle and Sentinel,* reprinted in *Macon [GA] Daily Telegraph,* 9 September 1866; Albert Rust, *Address of Hon. Albert Rust, to the People of Arkansas* (Washington, DC: Lemuel Towers, [1860]), 13, J. L. M. Curry Pamphlet Collection, Alabama Department of Archives and History, Montgomery; Thomas J. Balcerski, *Bosom Friends: The Intimate World of James Buchanan and William Rufus King* (New York: Oxford University Press, 2019); Lynn, *Preserving the White Man's Republic;* Pierson, *Free Hearts and Free Homes,* 97–114; Pierson, *The Wild Woman*

of Cincinnati, 81–85; Mark Power Smith, "The Young America Movement and the Crisis of Household Politics," *Panorama*, 7 July 2021, https://thepanorama.shear.org/2021/07/07/the-young-america-movement-and-the-crisis-of-household-politics/; Amy S. Greenberg, *Manifest Manhood and the Antebellum American Empire* (New York: Cambridge University Press, 2005), esp. chaps. 4–5; Robert E. Cray, *A Notable Bully: Colonel Billy Wilson, Masculinity, and the Pursuit of Violence in the Civil War Era* (Kent, OH: Kent State University Press, 2021).

21. Henry Augustus Wise to Edward Everett, 27 September 1856, Edward Everett Papers, microfilm, Massachusetts Historical Society, Boston; "Black vs. White," *Aurora [IL] Guardian*, 19 October 1854; Huston, *Stephen A. Douglas and the Dilemmas of Democratic Equality*, 5–6, 14–15, 34, 35–36, 52–53, 98–99; Woods, *Arguing Until Doomsday*, 148.

22. Jean H. Baker, *Affairs of Party: The Political Culture of Northern Democrats in the Mid-Nineteenth Century* (1983; rpt. New York: Fordham University Press, 1998), 177–258; Paul D. Escott, *The Worst Passions of Human Nature: White Supremacy in the Civil War North* (Charlottesville: University of Virginia Press, 2020); Lynn, *Preserving the White Man's Republic*; Jonathan Daniel Wells, "Inventing *White Supremacy*: Race, Print Culture, and the Civil War Draft Riots," *Civil War History* 68, no. 1 (March 2022): 42–80; Joshua A. Lynn, "Stephen Douglas's Enlightenment: Democracy, Race, and Rights in Civil War–Era Political Thought," *Civil War History* 66, no. 3 (September 2020): 272–94; Woods, *Arguing Until Doomsday*, 150–55, 172–73.

23. "From H. O. Wagoner"; "The Last Night in the Senate," *New York Tribune*, reprinted in *Frederick Douglass' Paper*, 24 March 1854 (euphemism employed); "The Late Stephan A. Douglas," *Douglass' Monthly* (Rochester, NY), July 1861; David W. Blight, *Frederick Douglass' Civil War: Keeping Faith in Jubilee* (Baton Rouge: Louisiana State University Press, 1989), 13–16; Carter Jackson, *Force and Freedom*.

24. Frederick Douglass, "The Present and Future of the Colored Race in America: An Address Delivered in Brooklyn, New York, on 15 May 1863," in Blassingame et al., eds., *Frederick Douglass Papers. Series One*, 3:578–79; Blight, *Frederick Douglass*, 416–17, 455–56; Bonner, *Remaking the Republic*, 11–37, 87–91. For a different analysis of this speech, see Nicholas Buccola, *The Political Thought of Frederick Douglass: In Pursuit of American Liberty* (New York: New York University Press, 2012), 65–75.

25. *Congressional Globe* (Washington, DC), 36th Congress, 1st session, 236, 239, 240.

26. J. F. Farnsworth, *Equal Suffrage. Speech of the Hon. J. F. Farnsworth, of Illinois. Delivered in the House of Representatives, on Thursday, January 11th,*

1866, upon the Bill Extending the Right of Suffrage to Colored Men in the District of Columbia (N.p.: N.p., 1866), 3 (quote), Samuel J. May Anti-Slavery Collection; Richard Yates, *Representation in Congress. Speech of Hon. Richard Yates, of Illinois, Delivered in the Senate of the United States, June 11, 1868* (Washington, DC: F. and J. Rives and Geo. A. Bailey, 1868), 12–15 (quote on 13); Richard Yates, *Speech of Senator Yates at Springfield, Illinois, August 22, 1868* (N.p.: N.p., 1868?), 7–8, 14, in Richard Yates, "Speeches and Governor's Messages, 1851–72," bound volume of pamphlets, Manuscript Division, Library of Congress; Bonner, *Remaking the Republic*, 154–70; Erik Mathisen, *The Loyal Republic: Traitors, Slaves, and the Remaking of Citizenship in Civil War America* (Chapel Hill: University of North Carolina Press, 2018), 100–117, 145–66.

27. "'Fred' Douglass for Congress," *Savannah [GA] Republican*, reprinted in *Georgia Telegraph* (Macon), 20 June 1854 (first quote); letter from Gerrit Smith, 28 August 1854, *Frederick Douglass' Paper*, 1 September 1854 (second quote); "Frederick Douglass in Congress," *Massachusetts Spy* (Worcester), reprinted in *Frederick Douglass' Paper*, 4 August 1854 (third and fourth quotes); "Gerrit Smith to His Constituents," *Frederick Douglass' Paper*, 18 August 1854; Philip S. Foner, *Frederick Douglass* (New York: Citadel Press, 1964), 165–67.

28. "O What a Fall Was There, My Countrymen," *Frederick Douglass' Paper*, 12 February 1858; Freeman, *The Field of Blood*, 183–84, 196–97, 269; Cray, *A Notable Bully*.

29. *Congressional Globe*, 34th Congress, 1st session, appendix, 547; J. E. Roy, *Kansas—Her Struggle and Her Defense. A Discourse Preached in the Plymouth Congregational Church of Chicago, Sabbath Afternoon, June 1, 1856, by the Pastor, Rev. J. E. Roy* (Chicago: Wright, Medill, Day, Tribune Office, 1856), 20–21 (quote on 21), Samuel J. May Anti-Slavery Collection.

30. "The Clergy Moving," *Frederick Douglass' Paper*, 24 March 1854; "Judge Douglas in Chicago," *Daily Indiana State Sentinel* (Indianapolis), 7 September 1854; *Democratic Press* (Chicago), reprinted in "Douglas at Home," *Ohio State Journal* (Columbus), 13 September 1854; "Well Known at Home," *Boston Daily Atlas*, 8 September 1854; Johannsen, *Stephen A. Douglas*, 453–55.

31. "Senator Douglas's Reception in Chicago," letter from "Egypt," September 1854, *Frederick Douglass' Paper*, 15 September 1854 (first quote); "Douglas and His Negroes," *Cleveland Leader*, reprinted in *Ohio State Journal*, 11 October 1854 (second and third quotes); Huston, *Stephen A. Douglas and the Dilemmas of Democratic Equality*, 53–54; Quitt, *Stephen A. Douglas and Antebellum Democracy*, 186–94.

32. "Boston Hunkerism Against the Nebraska Bill," *The Liberator*, 3 March 1854; "Quevedo," "From Cleveland. Taxes—Temperance—Nebraska—Cleveland Female Seminary," *Ohio State Journal*, 4 April 1854; [William J. Watkins], "Effect of the Nebraska Bill," *Frederick Douglass' Paper*, 3 March 1854; "Senator Douglas's Reception in Chicago."
33. "The Douglasses—A Swop," *New York Tribune*, reprinted in "Humors of the Day," *Frederick Douglass' Paper*, 31 March 1854 (quote); "The Douglases—A Swop," in "Humors of the Day," *New York Express*, reprinted in *Ohio State Journal*, 4 April 1854.
34. "Hon. T. S. Green's Speech," *Greenville [SC] Patriot*, reprinted in "Hopeful," *Charleston [SC] Mercury*, 23 January 1858; "Black-Republican Bed-Fellows," *Constitution* (Washington, DC), 3 November 1860, morning edition; "Monsiuer Tonson Come Again," *New York Herald*, 6 March 1858.
35. "The Black and White Douglass," *Cincinnati Commercial*, reprinted in *Frederick Douglass' Paper*, 4 August 1854.
36. "The Black and White Douglass"; Thomas Brown, "The Miscegenation of Richard Mentor Johnson as an Issue in the National Election Campaign of 1835–1836," *Civil War History* 39, no. 1 (March 1993): 5–30.
37. Stephen A. Douglas, "Mr. Douglas's Reply," at "Second Joint Debate, Freeport, August 27, 1858," in *The Lincoln-Douglas Debates of 1858*, ed. Robert W. Johannsen (New York: Oxford University Press, 2008), 92–93 (quote on 92). For Frederick's contemporary account of attending Stephen's speech, see "The Campaign in Illinois."
38. Douglas, "Mr. Douglas's Reply," 92–93 (quote on 93); Stephen A. Douglas, "Speech of Stephen A. Douglas, Chicago, July 9, 1858," in Johannsen, ed., *The Lincoln-Douglas Debates of 1858*, 34; Brown, "The Miscegenation of Richard Mentor Johnson," 8–15, 16–17; Stephanie M. H. Camp, *Closer to Freedom: Enslaved Women and Everyday Resistance in the Plantation South* (Chapel Hill: University of North Carolina Press, 2004), 111–13; James Brewer Stewart, "The Emergence of Racial Modernity and the Rise of the White North, 1790–1840," *Journal of the Early Republic* 18, no. 2 (Summer 1998): 198–205.
39. *Louisville [KY] Daily Democrat*, reprinted in *Frederick Douglass' Paper*, 4 August 1854.
40. Frederick Douglass, *Narrative of the Life of Frederick Douglass, an American Slave, Written by Himself, with Related Documents*, ed. David W. Blight, 3rd ed. (1845; Boston: Bedford/St. Martin's, 2017), 41–43 (quote on 41); Frederick Douglass, "The Skin Aristocracy in America: An Address Delivered in Coventry, England, on 2 February 1847," in Blassingame et al., eds., *Frederick Douglass Papers. Series One*, 2:6–7.

41. Frederick Douglass, quoted in *Ohio State Journal*, 30 May 1854; "Anti-Nebraska at Aurora. Speech from Frederick Douglass!" Martin H. Quitt speculates, without conclusive evidence, that Stephen changed the original spelling of his name from Douglass in 1846 to avoid association with Frederick after his 1845 autobiography appeared and when Stephen was courting North Carolinian Martha Martin; Quitt, *Stephen A. Douglas and Antebellum Democracy*, 56. James L. Huston dates the name change to 1847 without explanation; Huston, *Stephen A. Douglas and the Dilemmas of Democratic Equality*, 2.
42. *Journal of Commerce* (New York), reprinted in "Judge Douglas," *Daily Picayune* (New Orleans), 31 May 1851, evening edition (quote); *Journal of Commerce*, reprinted in *Daily Ohio Statesman* (Columbus), 24 May 1851; *New York Mirror*, reprinted in "Senatorial Wit," *Savannah [GA] Daily Republican*, 24 May 1851.
43. Frederick Douglass, "Slavery, Freedom, and the Kansas-Nebraska Act: An Address Delivered in Chicago, Illinois, on 30 October 1854," in Blassingame et al., eds., *Frederick Douglass Papers. Series One*, 2:541 (first quote); *Frederick Douglass' Paper*, 31 March 1854 (second quote); Frederick Douglass, "John Brown and the Slaveholders' Insurrection: An Address Delivered in Edinburgh, Scotland, on 30 January 1860," in Blassingame et al., eds., *Frederick Douglass Papers. Series One*, 3:319 (third quote).
44. "Amalgamation at the South—Some of the Consequences," *Indiana Standard* (LeGrange), reprinted in *Frederick Douglass' Paper*, 8 December 1854; Brown, "The Miscegenation of Richard Mentor Johnson," 15–16, 28–30; Rachel Hope Cleves, *The Reign of Terror in America: Visions of Violence from Anti-Jacobinism to Antislavery* (New York: Cambridge University Press, 2009), 104–52, 172–78, 230–75; Carol Lasser, "Voyeuristic Abolitionism: Sex, Gender, and the Transformation of Antislavery Rhetoric," *Journal of the Early Republic* 28, no. 1 (Spring 2008): 83–114; Pierson, *Free Hearts and Free Homes*, 64, 135–38, 148–49, 155, 157–59, 173–87, and on antislavery references to "slave breeding," 213n60; Ronald G. Walters, "The Erotic South: Civilization and Sexuality in American Abolitionism," *American Quarterly* 25, no. 2 (May 1973): 177–201; Pierson, *The Wild Woman of Cincinnati*, 81–85, 86–95, 109–10.
45. Letter from "A. Southron," in "Kansas—Douglas—and Slaves," *St. Louis Intelligencer*, reprinted in *Ohio State Journal*, 18 October 1854; *Cayuga Chief* (Auburn, NY), reprinted in *Frederick Douglass' Paper*, 6 October 1854 (euphemism employed); "Douglas and His Negroes."
46. Henry B. Pearson, *Freedom Versus Slavery. Letters from Henry B. Pearson, Late of the Philadelphia Bar, to Hon. Rufus Choate, on His Letter to the Whig Committee of the State of Maine* (Portland, ME: Daley and Lufkin,

1856), 3, Samuel J. May Anti-Slavery Collection; Robert Purvis, "Mr. Purvis's Speech," in "Twentieth Anniversary of the American Anti-Slavery Society," *The Liberator,* 19 May 1854.
47. John L. Magee, "Liberty, the Fair Maid of Kansas—In the Hands of the 'Border Ruffians'" (Philadelphia: N.p., 1856), Political Cartoons, 1856–59, Print Department, Library Company of Philadelphia; Kristen Tegtmeier Oertel, "'Nigger-Worshipping Fanatics' and 'Villain[s] of the Blackest Dye': Racialized Manhoods and the Sectional Debates," in *Bleeding Kansas, Bleeding Missouri: The Long Civil War on the Border,* ed. Jonathan Earle and Diane Mutti Burke (Lawrence: University Press of Kansas, 2013), 75–78.
48. Michael E. Woods offered an important corrective to pro-southern portrayals of Stephen in *Arguing Until Doomsday,* 5, 167–68. Antislavery Americans' proslavery depiction of him nonetheless helps explain the escalating sectional crisis. For the argument that sectionalized gender norms outweighed sectional convergence, see Pierson, *The Wild Woman of Cincinnati,* 77–110, 134.

READING BODIES

BODIES CONVEY a lot about gender and how it is represented. Think about how your manner of dress differs from how people your age dressed in the 1990s (have you seen pictures of their big hair?) or in the 1970s (such as the flower children and hippies) or even in the 1950s (with women in poodle skirts and bobby socks, and men sporting pompadour haircuts). Each manifestation was a generation saying something about how they understood bodies and genders. "Reading" the body can reveal a lot about how historical people thought about gender and society and how cultures change over time. For example, the paintings and portraits of leading members of the founding generation usually depicted them in knee britches and stockings and wearing wigs—the style of eighteenth-century European and Anglo-American elites. But by the end of the eighteenth century, powerful men increasingly abandoned their wigs and wore longer pants and elite women chose simpler fabrics and clothing designs. Such choices reflected their ideas of a more American, republican style of dress.

Beyond dress, anatomy, racial and ethnic appearances, bodily adornments, the ways in which bodies move and pose, physical disabilities and dismemberments, and many other considerations allow us to read bodies and draw conclusions about gender. The fact that we can make such conclusions suggests that gender is fluid and prone to reassertions and reconstructions.

In this section, authors read historical bodies to better comprehend how people in the early republic thought about gender. Rachel Walker argues that Americans applied phrenology—the study of the shapes of faces and skulls—to understand gender. Phrenology has since been dismissed as a pseudoscience, but in the early republic it was among the most popular "sciences," allowing practitioners to graft ideas about gender (and race) onto human bodies and create flexible understandings of human sexuality. Examining clothing, foodways, and sexuality, Rachel Hope Cleves interrogates the Fifth Avenoodle, a stereotype of flamboyant masculinity that arose from cultures of consumerism and self-making. Stephanie J. Richmond studies abolitionist representations of

Black women and examines how illness was an analytical category that early Americans layered onto bodies. Abolitionists made their subjects more sympathetic to readers who would never understand them through race. These essays raise important questions: In what ways did the reading of bodies differ between female and male subjects? Black and White? Wealthy and poor? Why did the differences exist? Who benefited more from reading bodies: the subjects or those who read them?

Reading the Gendered Body in Early America

Rachel Walker

For decades, scholars have described the nineteenth century as an era of "separate spheres." During the early national period, they have shown, Americans defended gender hierarchies by arguing that "the sexes" were inherently different beings who should occupy distinct realms within society. Peddling a "cult of true womanhood," early American authors suggested that home and family constituted the woman's domain, while politics was the province of men. Recent histories have complicated this narrative in productive ways, pointing out that "separate spheres" and "true womanhood" were rhetorical constructs rather than accurate depictions of people's lived experiences. Even when gender ideologies were stark and rigid, people's identities and behaviors inevitably varied according to race, class, and region. Scholars have nonetheless agreed on two major points: Americans embraced increasingly inflexible ideas about gender by the early decades of the nineteenth century, and they rationalized these ideas, at least in part, with the help of science.[1]

Both Americans and Europeans did indeed begin to think about sex and gender in new ways by the end of the eighteenth century. In the sixteenth and seventeenth centuries, scientists conceptualized women as inferior, underdeveloped versions of men. This "one-sex model" of humanity, as the historian Thomas Laqueur so famously put it, envisioned male and female bodies as essentially the same—different in degree but not in kind. Over the course of the eighteenth century, though, a new conception of sexual difference emerged.[2]

With the rise of Enlightenment rationalism, Europeans and Americans could no longer rationalize gender hierarchies by merely invoking a divinely sanctioned hierarchy of humanity. Existing inequities seemed to necessitate more empirical explanations, and physicians and anatomists stepped in with answers. Placing new emphasis on skeletons and reproductive organs, they argued that men and women were unique and complementary beings with distinct brains, bodies, and behaviors. This "two-sex model" posited that male and female bodies were innately, unalterably, and unmistakably different. If male and female bodies were opposites, the thinking went, then perhaps biology—not theology—justified existing gender relations.

Early American historians have generally agreed that these new scientific understandings of the body provided a conceptual bedrock for the restrictive gender ideologies which came to predominate by the mid-nineteenth century. As Rosemarie Zagarri argued, Americans were temporarily willing to embrace a more expansive political role for women during the revolutionary era. Yet by the early nineteenth century, this spirit of egalitarian possibility largely dissipated. Zagarri suggested that the two-sex model constituted part of the logic for this "revolutionary backlash" against women's political activism. As Americans came to view women and men as incommensurable opposites, she asserted, "the body became the basis for exclusion from the polity." John Wood Sweet similarly contended that "new anatomical understandings of male and female bodies helped justify the exclusion of women across the country from the emerging public sphere." Clare A. Lyons too showed that Americans found ways to "reconceptualize gender" in the post-Enlightenment era "by positing radical differences between men and women and fixing them in the anatomical body."[3]

This narrative is tidy and compelling: as gender ideologies became more rigidly defined, so too did scientific ideas about the body. On its own, though, the prevailing interpretation fails to fully explain how early Americans understood sex and gender in a practical sense. For one, much existing scholarship in the history of science and medicine focuses on the works of elite European naturalists. When gender historians cite this work, they typically imply that novel scientific theories shaped American society and politics, rather than demonstrating precisely *how* this happened. We know a great deal about how transatlantic intellectuals viewed anatomy and physiology. But how did the general population make meaning from the human body? Did they care about science? If so, what discourses and disciplines did they find most compelling? Where did people access scientific knowledge? How did Americans interpret bodies, on the ground, in everyday life? In other words, how did people see gender?

To answer those questions, we need to look beyond the two-sex model—and away from a study of European naturalists—and turn our attention to disciplines like phrenology, a popular science rooted in a simple assumption: that people's faces and skulls revealed their character and personality. Nowadays, we dismiss phrenology as the quintessential example of pseudoscientific quackery. But in the decades between the American Revolution and the Civil War, people perceived it quite differently. At a time before modern neuroscience and psychology existed—and when the boundary between popular and professional science proved murky at best—phrenology became one of the most popular and accessible tools that Americans had for understanding human minds and bodies.[4]

By focusing on phrenology, we can rethink established historiographical interpretations of sex, gender, and science in early America. It is certainly true that physicians and naturalists began describing bodies in new ways by the late eighteenth century. But when ordinary people interpreted bodies, they rarely engaged in abstruse debates about skeletons, gametes, and gonads. Rather than looking below the belt, they stared above the shoulders. Through phrenology, they fashioned a practical method for mapping cultural ideas about race and gender onto the human body. In the process, they developed a much more flexible understanding of sexual difference than most scholarship has acknowledged.

While the two-sex model depicted male and female bodies as incommensurable opposites, phrenologists popularized what I call the "one-brain model." The two-sex model emphasized the distinct and complementary reproductive systems of men and women: men had testes, women had ovaries; men had penises, women had vaginas; men had sperm, women had eggs. The one-brain model, by contrast, highlighted the basic similarity of all human beings. Like the older one-sex model, the one-brain model posited that men and women were different in *degree* rather than in *kind*. Shifting their focus from the genitals to the cranium, phrenologists saw the brain as the entity that made individuals who they fundamentally were as people. This made the brain the most important determinant of one's gender identity.

Phrenologists did not ignore bodily differences. In fact, they consistently emphasized "natural" distinctions between male and female forms. Yet they also repeated a constant refrain: all human beings shared more similarities than differences. They maintained that all people's brains contained the same basic organs, faculties, and propensities, regardless of race, sex, or ethnicity. This allowed phrenologists to make a clever (if sometimes confounding) argument. Even as they portrayed men and women as opposite sexes, they made allowances for individuals who eluded these binary categories. Such a framing created space for gender fluidity and allowed individuals to see themselves as potential exceptions to established gender stereotypes. Phrenology, in other words, encouraged all Americans to imagine themselves as cognitively distinctive beings who were naturally endowed with both feminine and masculine characteristics. By validating an older, more flexible conception of the human body, phrenology created space for Americans to challenge newly restrictive ideologies of gender complementarity, even as it provided a scientific foundation for those same ideas.

PHRENOLOGICAL THEORY rested on a few basic assumptions. First, practitioners claimed that the brain functioned as both the "dome of thought" and the "palace of the soul." Second, phrenologists argued that the brain was not a monolithic entity but rather a collection of distinct "organs" that controlled different aspects of character or personality. Third, they suggested that the brain quite literally imprinted itself on the skull, molding the skeletal structure from the inside out. In the phrenological worldview, the best way to understand the human mind was by analyzing the size and shape of the cranium.

The simplicity and practical elegance of phrenological theories made the science appealing in both popular culture and exclusive intellectual circles. Phrenology started as an elite European science in the 1790s but became ubiquitous in American society between the 1830s and 1850s. By midcentury, phrenological imagery saturated the nation's novels, newspapers, and magazines. Traveling lecturers conveyed cranial doctrines to rural and urban areas alike. Children learned about phrenology in school. Adults talked about it in public places and at private parties. Particularly for literate Americans, the science became an inescapable part of the nation's cultural fabric. Not everyone agreed with phrenological theories. Countless Americans ridiculed the science as "humbuggery" or

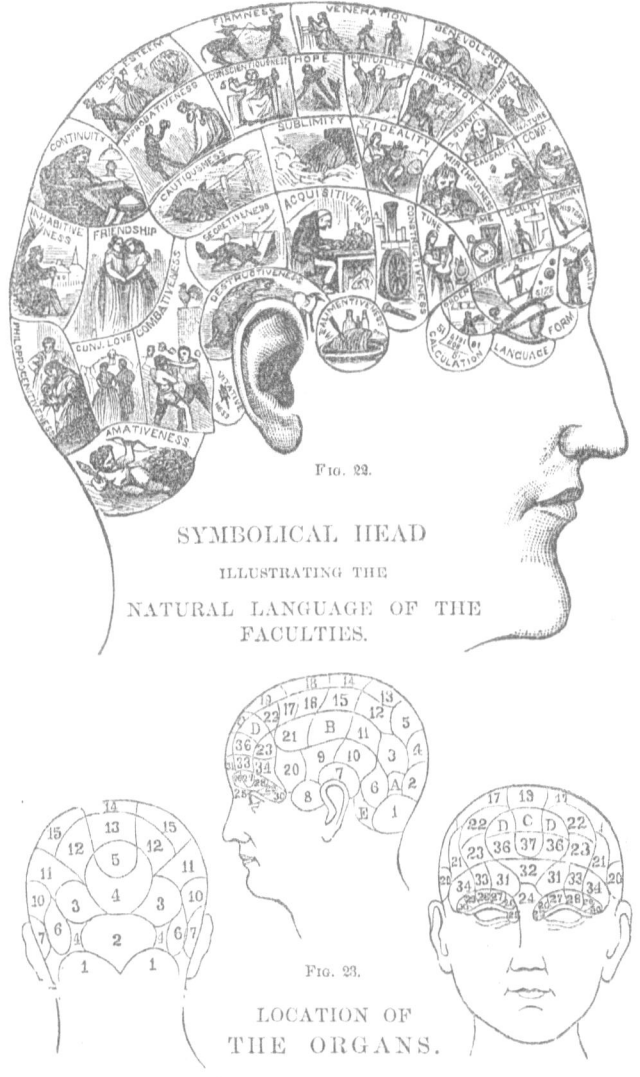

FIG. 1. "Symbolical Head Illustrating the Natural Language of the Faculties," in Samuel Wells, *How to Read Character: A New Illustrated Handbook of Phrenology and Physiognomy* (New York: Fowler and Wells, 1882), 36. (Courtesy, American Antiquarian Society)

"bumpology." Still, even the most skeptical dabblers attained at least a basic fluency in the language of skulls. The science became inescapable, if not irrefutable—compelling, if not universally convincing.[5]

What, then, made phrenology so popular? Part of its allure was its pledge to make the invisible visible. Phrenology suggested that bodies hid secrets in plain sight—and that people could uncover those secrets through empirical investigation. The practical benefits seemed limitless. Desperate for knowledge about themselves, Americans wondered, How smart am I? Am I generous? Thoughtful? Kind? Do I have a propensity for violence? Would I make a good parent? Could I become a famous writer? Am I a budding entrepreneur? Phrenology provided answers. It helped people believe, as one nineteenth-century woman put it, that "the whole map of the mind is drawn in legible marks on the skull." This was a beguiling promise. Science had taken a mysterious entity—the human mind—and made it finally seem "legible."[6]

Phrenology started as an elite science. Although always controversial, it initially garnered adherents from some of the most prominent intellectual circles in the transatlantic world. Yet phrenology soon developed into a more practical discipline that required neither a university education nor expensive medical training. It became quite simply a science of the people. At a time when "metaphysicians" and "mental philosophers" engaged in impenetrable debates about human cognition, phrenological apostles proclaimed that anyone could become an expert in cranial interpretation. They published cheap, user-friendly guidebooks with instructions on how to read heads and faces. Rather than excluding the working classes, White women, or people of color from scientific knowledge, they encouraged a diverse array of individuals to study the human mind. After all, everyone could stare at someone's skull or attend a free lecture. For a nominal fee, Americans could even get their heads examined or purchase a cranial bust. Mary Virginia Montgomery, for instance, was a young Black woman who not only subscribed to the *American Phrenological Journal* but also acquired a plaster bust to become a more proficient skull reader. Despite being born enslaved, she eventually became a free woman and an autonomous cranial interpreter. Phrenology was beyond useful. It was *accessible*.[7]

Mastering the phrenological method was relatively simple. The first step required learning about the tripartite division of the human brain. Phrenologists associated the frontal lobe with intellectual functions like

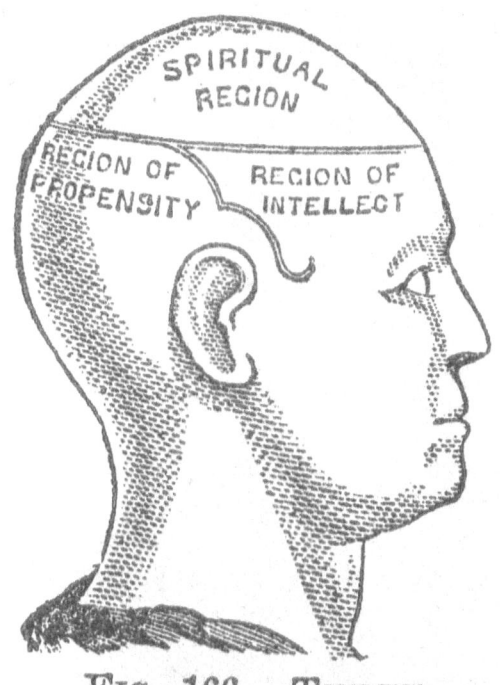

FIG. 166.—THREE REGIONS.

FIG. 2. "Three Regions," in Samuel Wells, *How to Read Character: A New Illustrated Hand-book of Phrenology and Physiognomy* (New York: Fowler and Wells, 1882), 124. (Courtesy, American Antiquarian Society)

reason, perception, and deliberation. In a smart person, they argued, the front part of the brain would grow strong and powerful, producing a robustly developed forehead or a "high brow." If a person lacked sophistication or refinement, though, they would exhibit a wide head that bulged out above the ears and at the base of the neck. This was because the lateral and posterior parts of the brain allegedly controlled the "animal propensities," which included characteristics like "combativeness," "destructiveness," and the visceral yearning for food and sex. By contrast, the brain's upper regions housed the "moral sentiments." In a person of particular benevolence, virtue, or religiosity, the crown of the head signaled a superior morality.[8]

Beyond these general rules, phrenological doctrines proved adaptable and malleable. Two individuals might look at the same head—and perhaps even agree about the size and shape of the organs—but come to radically different conclusions about a person's character. A large organ of "combativeness" could expose someone as unreasonably argumentative, but it might simply suggest their willingness to fight for their principles. A large organ of "acquisitiveness" might indicate a ravenous appetite for hoarding worldly possessions, but when tempered by strong intellectual faculties and moral sentiments, that organ might signal an admirable desire to establish personal independence through property ownership. Phrenology privileged the observations of the analyzer. Still, cranial subjects—who were themselves versed in the tenets of phrenology—could always contest the findings of their skull interpreters. In the end, every person held the power to decode the human brain.

The intellectual flexibility of phrenological doctrines allowed Americans to rationalize potentially contradictory propositions. On one hand, the science presumed the constitutional inequality of people's brains, bodies, and characters, suggesting that there were winners and losers in the hereditarian lottery. On the other hand, phrenology gave Americans hope that craniums did not invariably dictate one's destiny. Embedded within phrenological doctrines was the optimistic message that every human being could improve. As people refined their mental faculties and moral sentiments, their brains would develop, pressing on the skull in all the right areas until their internal reformation became palpably visible on their bodies.[9]

The *American Phrenological Journal* cited Laura Bridgman as a paradigmatic example of this phenomenon. After studying with Samuel Gridley Howe at the Perkins Institution for the Blind, she purportedly experienced a "perceptible change . . . in the size and shape of her head" and "a marked increase in the size of the forehead." The institution apparently misplaced the preliminary measurements of Bridgman's cranium, so they relied on anecdotal impressions of her mental and skeletal progress. For phrenological enthusiasts like Dr. Howe, the missing data was no problem. As he saw it, Bridgman's anatomical metamorphosis was dramatic enough to verify that the brain was not merely a gelatinous mass of mental activity but also a malleable and powerful organ that dictated the very shape of the skull.[10]

Phrenologists understood the brain as a formidable entity that both shaped people's character and determined their gender identities. In *The Phrenological Almanac for 1841*, one of the United States' most influential phrenologists, Lorenzo Fowler, articulated a theory about the gendered brain. Phrenology, he argued, was the best tool for understanding the "difference between the sexes" because even the briefest introduction to "phrenological principles" allowed someone to spot the distinctions between male and female craniums. For starters, men generally had bigger brains and broader heads with "a higher and deeper forehead." Since phrenologists associated the depth and breadth of the forehead with intelligence, they generally considered men to be smarter than women. At the very least, men's expansive foreheads meant their minds were more powerful. Female skulls, by contrast, appeared "higher and fuller in the coronal or upper region." Because the top of the skull revealed benevolence, virtue, and religiosity, women's soaring coronal regions allegedly illustrated their "stronger feelings and moral sentiments." In other words, men were thinkers while women were feelers, and men were more intelligent while women were more virtuous. How could one argue with a human skull?[11]

Following nineteenth-century gender conventions, phrenologists contended that men's skulls displayed a boldness and combativeness that female craniums lacked, whereas women's skulls revealed a natural propensity for rearing children. Yet even as phrenologists laid out such gendered expectations, they insisted those rules did not apply in every instance. Yes, women *generally* acted more virtuous, submissive, and caring than men. But some women were sneaky, assertive, violent, or aloof. Although most women could not match masculine genius, some possessed powerful brains and the cranial conformations to match. For instance, when the phrenologist Nelson Sizer analyzed Susan B. Anthony's skull in 1853, he complimented her exceptional brain: "Your intellect is active," he declared, "and your mind more naturally runs in the channel of intellect than of feeling." He then postulated that Anthony's "reasoning organs" were improving, becoming more powerful than her "perceptions." Through these remarks, he articulated a coded argument about gender.[12]

Nineteenth-century scientists regularly argued that women were excellent perceivers and imitators but not profound deliberators or inventive reasoners. Sizer reinforced the message with Anthony's diagnosis, though only in part: "At fifteen your mind was devoted to facts and phenomena; of late years you have been thinking of principles and ideas." Sizer ultimately concluded that Anthony's faculties had improved over time, setting her on the path toward masculine genius. At the very least, she was doing better than a Pennsylvania man named John Bancroft, who solicited an exam from Sizer just a year later. Although Bancroft had a good "knowledge of facts" and could "pick up practical information," he was not particularly impressive: "Your intellect is not naturally strong," Sizer penned. Anthony, by contrast, was a thinker. Through skull readings such as these, phrenologists simultaneously confirmed and counteracted scientific truisms about masculine and feminine brains.[13]

In cranial analysis, phrenologists allowed for exceptions to the gendered rules and made room for a person's individuality to shine through. Such a reality allowed phrenologists to simultaneously articulate antithetical arguments. For example, phrenologists maintained that the heads of the sexes were always distinguishable, boasting that when given a random skull, they could easily determine the gender. And yet, the one-brain model suggested that male and female brains were marked by "a difference in *degree,* although none in *kind.*"[14] Men and women exhibited all the same organs, just in different proportions. This held true even for the most dramatically gendered organs: "amativeness" (the desire for sex) and "philoprogenitiveness" (the love of children). Regardless of a person's sex or gender identity, these two organs existed in every human skull. It was not as if women had no libido and men felt zero love for their children. Phrenologists simply concluded that women typically had larger organs of philoprogenitiveness—making them more devoted parents—while men displayed larger organs of amativeness. Still, the rules were not universal. When a man named Thomas (his last name is illegible) got his head examined, he discovered that his organ of philoprogenitiveness was "VERY LARGE": a "7" on a "1" to "7" scale. The examiner concluded that Thomas would "be apt to spoil children."[15]

Phrenologists willingly admitted that their guidelines might not ring true for every individual. Any person's head could flout phrenological rules without undermining the science. This point became especially clear in the case of Phoebe George Bradford, a socialite from Wilmington, Delaware. Bradford solicited a cranial examination from Orson Fowler in 1838. During the reading, she learned that her organ of "Order" was "unusually developed," meaning that she liked to have "a place for everything" and that she always put "everything in its place." Bradford disagreed. "Quite a mistake," she declared in her journal. Still, she concurred with plenty of Fowler's other claims. The phrenologist told her that she was kind, honest, confident, energetic, and persevering. She accepted these conclusions without complaint. He also guessed that Bradford was a flighty individual who struggled to "think long on any subject," instead preferring to "fly from one thought to another." She conceded that "in this, he hit the truth exactly." Bradford did not hesitate to critique elements of Fowler's diagnosis. She nonetheless found herself "much amused" by her cranial adventures and carefully recorded the phrenologist's comments in her journal. Her case illustrates a phenomenon that many Americans experienced: they happily accepted the parts of phrenology that resonated with them, even when they rejected the conclusions that failed to match their personal beliefs.[16]

What makes Bradford's reading so compelling, though, is its depiction of how phrenologists used science to convey messages about gender, power, and proper womanhood. After reading Bradford's head, Fowler informed her that she was unique. She had the organ of "self esteem fully developed," when "not one woman in fifty has this organ even moderate." Such a skeletal conformation indicated that she was "entirely independent" in her viewpoints and firm to the point of "obstinacy." These might have been perceived as positive traits for a man, but as historian Barbara Welter so powerfully demonstrated, cheerful submission was an essential tenet of "true womanhood" during the mid-nineteenth century. Bradford thus flouted established gender roles through her firmness and unapologetic self-confidence.[17] Fowler reinforced this point when speculating about the gender dynamics in Bradford's home. After describing his client as an "ardent" lover and "a kind, but not indulgent parent," Fowler deduced that she must "love to command and not brook submission." He then suggested that her "husband was a meek, quiet man who was silent when [his wife] was finding fault." Bradford did not refute these suppositions, but she added a parenthetical disclaimer: "(not always the case certainly)."[18]

Based purely off Phoebe Bradford's cranium, Fowler felt comfortable dissecting the power dynamics of her marriage. The phrenologist never analyzed Mr. Bradford's head. He simply assumed that Phoebe's husband was "a meek, quiet man." After all, her skull suggested that she was obstinate, energetic, and eager to command. Such a cranium marked a woman who would "not brook submission." Fowler then formulated his hypothesis: if Bradford was failing to submit to her husband, then her husband must be submitting to her. Such role reversal violated nineteenth-century gender ideals, which required women to be docile, domestic, and solicitous of their husbands' needs. Intriguingly, though,

Fowler never criticized Bradford for her boldness. He merely noted it and moved on. Perhaps this was because of his own familiarity with spirited and independent women. His sister Charlotte Fowler Wells spearheaded the family's business empire throughout much of the nineteenth century, while his sister-in-law Lydia Folger Fowler became the second woman to earn a medical degree in the United States (behind only Elizabeth Blackwell). At a time when popular newspapers, magazines, and advice books lambasted "strong-minded women," American phrenologists instead nurtured the boldness of female activists and intellectuals.[19]

Phrenologists created space for women to buck existing gender conventions, despite reinforcing those conventions in their published works. Orson Fowler, for instance, published scores of books, articles, and almanacs declaring that men had greater firmness and self-esteem than women. This did not stop him from casually informing Phoebe Bradford that she was bolder, firmer, and more self-assured than her husband. While maintaining that established norms remained true in the aggregate, phrenologists suggested that any individual woman could defy expectations. Women in the abstract might be less profound, more sexually restrained, and less aggressive than men. Yet some women exhibited soaring brows (signaling impressive rational faculties), wide heads (revealing destructive tendencies), or large protuberances at the napes of their neck (exposing a propensity for amatory indulgence). Because each person's head was distinctive, there were unlimited potential permutations of faculties and propensities. As historian Carla Bittel argued, "Gender differences were made visible and tangible" through cranial analysis, but they were always "subject to negotiation." Phrenological doctrines were elastic enough to allow for versatile understandings of the gendered mind.[20]

CRANIAL THEORY encompassed similarly contradictory ideas about race and ethnicity. As a rule, phrenologists advocated for a one-brain model of human difference, which emphasized the common humanity of all individuals. Yet on numerous occasions they hinted that people of different ancestries were inherently dissimilar, suggesting that an experienced skull interpreter could identify the racial or ethnic background of a cranium without ever meeting the person. In an article on "The Superiority of the Caucasian Race," the *American Phrenological Journal* matter of factly asserted that Anglo-Saxon "brains are superior in size, and more perfect in figure, than the brains of any other variety." Orson

Fowler likewise contended that Black Americans had "small reasoning organs," which left "them but little depth and strength of intellect, and a feeble judgment." Phrenologists often proclaimed that Black Americans possessed receding foreheads and protruding jaws (traits that allegedly signaled weak intellects and high animal propensities). And while most phrenologists in the United States opposed slavery, some used the science to defend the institution.[21]

Phrenological doctrines were nonetheless malleable enough to allow for exceptions to these racist rules. When the influential Fowler family analyzed the head of Sarah Margru Kinson Green, a captive from the *Amistad* who went on to study at Oberlin College, they described her as exceptional—in both senses of the word. She had "unusual intellectual powers," which were visible in her "broad and high" forehead. Yet she was not merely an extraordinary human being in the general sense. She was, they claimed, "far superior to Africans generally." Through these few short sentences, the Fowlers deployed an insidious rhetorical strategy: they acknowledged Green's intelligence, only to suggest that she was different—better somehow—than other Black people. The sleight of hand allowed them to cling to racist ideas while elevating certain individuals as models of Black excellence. In the end, phrenology reinforced prevailing racial and gender stereotypes by suggesting that White men were smarter—and stronger—than all women, that White Americans were more intelligent and more capable than Black Americans, and that White women were more beautiful than women of color.[22]

Women of color, understandably, developed a fraught relationship with phrenology. Unlike White women and Black men, Black women did not seem to write publicly about the science. Yet that did not mean that they were unaware of or uninterested in it. In the years following her emancipation, Mary Virginia Montgomery "studied Bumpology," "enjoyed" reading her "Phren Journal," and "had a lively time" examining the heads of her fellow classmates at Oberlin College.[23] Journals of the poet, teacher, and abolitionist Charlotte Forten likewise show familiarity with phrenology.[24] Famous Black abolitionist and women's rights activist Sojourner Truth became a curious phrenological dabbler when she solicited a skull reading from Nelson Sizer (who analyzed Susan B. Anthony's skull in 1853). An abolitionist himself, Sizer declared that Truth was "ingenious" and lauded her "courage," "moral firmness," and "love of justice." Unlike white feminists, though, Truth never published her results.²⁵ The influential journalist and anti-lynching activist Ida B. Wells stayed similarly silent about phrenology in public, although she casually discussed the science with one of her romantic interests in 1886.²⁶ As all these examples show, Black women clearly knew about phrenology and sometimes used it to evaluate themselves and others. Yet doing so required trudging through a morass of discriminatory discourses that marked them as doubly inferior.

Phrenological texts were riddled with racial and gender biases. The science nonetheless achieved enormous popularity among abolitionists and women's rights activists. Why? Part of the reason lay in the fact that phrenologists self-identified as reformers, forging friendships with some of the era's most prominent activists and intellectuals. Perhaps more importantly, phrenologists presented the American public with a philosophy of mind that emphasized universal humanity—and improvability. In response, abolitionists and women's rights activists tended to embrace phrenology as a practical and potentially radical science that might support their crusades for social justice. Susan B. Anthony, Elizabeth Cady Stanton, Sojourner Truth, Theodore Dwight Weld, Abby Kelley Foster, Lucretia Mott, and William Lloyd Garrison comprise just a small sampling of the abolitionists who commissioned cranial examinations. This was of course a common thing to do in mid-nineteenth-century America. Soliciting a skull reading did not necessarily signal a sincere or lasting dedication to phrenology. Even so, many of these activists publicly discussed their fondness for the science. Garrison was so impressed with phrenology that he published his diagnosis in *The Liberator,* marveling that Lorenzo Fowler sketched his character with "striking accuracy" despite being "entirely ignorant of the person whose head he was examining." The article concluded that the precision of Garrison's skull reading could not "be accounted for in any other way, than by supposing the science of Phrenology to be founded in truth." Although Garrison's editorial team acknowledged that many people dismissed phrenology as "a humbug," they mused that even if it were a quack science, "Mr. Fowler beats all other yankees at *guessing!*"²⁷

Garrison's fondness for phrenology was hardly unique within his social and political circles. The woman's rights activist and dress reformer Amelia Bloomer published laudatory articles and advertisements about phrenology in her newspaper, *The Lily*. Harriet Beecher Stowe used phrenological imagery in her antislavery novels. Her brother, the famous minister Henry Ward Beecher, became a dedicated phrenological enthusiast who incorporated cranial doctrines into his sermons. In fact, it was Beecher who first got Orson Fowler interested in the science (they were college roommates). Black abolitionists such as Frederick Douglass, William J. Wilson, and William Wells Brown deployed phrenological language to advocate for racial justice, while Quaker abolitionists like Lucretia Mott, Abby Kelley Foster, and William Bassett invoked the science to physiologically rationalize their dedication to the antislavery crusade. Making the connection between science and politics explicit, Abby Kelley once lauded the "blunt radicalism" of phrenological thought.[28]

Elizabeth Cady Stanton became similarly enamored with phrenology, seeing it as a rational philosophy that might eventually demonstrate the intellectual equality of women and men. In a speech that she "delivered several times immediately after the first Woman's Rights Convention," Stanton discussed the one-brain model: "The Phrenologist says that woman's head has just as many organs as man's and that they are similarly situated," she explained, noting that phrenologists "do not divide heads according to sex." She also pointed to an exciting tenet of phrenology: people could improve their minds and bodies with cultivation. She saw this as a hopeful doctrine for women, who lacked the same educational opportunities as their male counterparts. Stanton nonetheless understood problems that phrenology posed for women. Phrenologists, she griped, had a habit of labeling "all the fine heads masculine and all the ill shaped feminine, for when a woman presents a remarkable large well developed intellectual region, they say she has a masculine head, as if there could be nothing remarkable of the feminine gender." Stanton grumbled that phrenologists gave "all the glory to masculinity," even when talking about female skulls. By contrast, whenever they encountered a man with "a small head very little reasoning power and the affections inordinately developed they say he has a woman's head." None of this dissuaded her from using the science. Despite its problems, phrenology provided Stanton with an expansive vision of the gendered mind.[29]

Abolitionists and women's rights activists must have been encouraged when the most famous phrenologists in the United States expressed sympathy for their political crusades. The influential Fowler and Wells family stayed cravenly silent on the question of slavery for the most part, but they also employed men such as John Brown Jr. (son of the famous abolitionist) and Nelson Sizer (who praised the Underground Railroad and reviled "pro-slavery sharks").[30] In a more direct way, the Fowler and Wells publishing house explicitly fashioned itself as an advocate of the "rights of woman" that aspired to use the power of science to expand "woman's sphere." Women, members of the family argued, should have access to scientific knowledge, be able to cultivate a profession, engage in political activism, attend college, and fully develop their mental faculties. The Fowlers even argued in favor of female suffrage and developed friendly professional relationships with feminist activists.[31]

By the 1850s, the Fowler and Wells firm had begun dutifully chronicling all the triumphs and tribulations of the women's rights movement in the pages of the *American Phrenological Journal*. Its editors printed flattering sketches of female suffragists and White abolitionists (though they conspicuously eschewed positive portrayals of most Black activists). They also published Elisha Hurlbut's treatise on human rights, which made a vociferous craniological argument for women's enfranchisement. The book presented readers with a rousing vindication of the one-brain model: "It is established by phrenological science," Hurlbut proclaimed, "that woman is endowed with precisely the same mental faculties as man—that, nevertheless, she enjoys some of these in a higher and some in a less degree than her sturdy brother." He never argued that male and female brains were exactly alike. In fact, he contended that women might indeed be intellectually inferior to men. Hurlbut nevertheless claimed that the minds of men and women were more similar than different, and he therefore saw no logical or scientific reason to prohibit women from voting. Through such publications, influential phrenologists provided Americans with innovative ways of thinking about gender difference, as well as a scientific rationale for women's political advancement. Not surprisingly, then, many female activists embraced cranial analysis.[32]

EVEN WHEN they were skeptical of phrenology, women used the science to make sense of their gender identities in very practical and quotidian ways. In May 1841, the Transcendentalist, author, and women's rights activist Caroline Healey visited her dentist "to have some teeth filled." As a Dr. Keep worked on her mouth, he broached the subject of phrenology. Healey expressed ambivalence, positing that it might well be a "charlatan faith." Still, she talked about phrenology with ease and had no trouble launching into a detailed discussion of her own organs. At one point, she mentioned that her closest friend and fellow New Englander

Martha Choate had urged her to get her head examined by one of the Fowler brothers. Healey balked. "I esteemed him one of many quacks," she recalled.³³

Her dentist expressed greater enthusiasm. He felt sure that Fowler would give Healey "a fine head," adding that he himself had been captivated by her cranium. Declaring that "he was phrenologist enough" to diagnose her character, Keep noted Healey's enormously large organs of "self-esteem" and "Firmness," interpreting them to mean that she was both self-confident and resolute. Despite these strengths, her musical talents apparently left much to be desired. Her organ of "Tune" was only a "3" on a scale that ran from "1" (very small) to "7" (very large). The dentist ranked Healey higher in other areas. Her organs of "Caution" and "Secretiveness" were quite large, and her "intellectual development was very wonderful." Keep nonetheless questioned the power of Healey's mind. She apparently lacked the dogged temperament of her father, which meant that she would struggle to achieve great things. Healey both internalized this message and scoffed at it: "Dr Keep—gave me—little mathematical genius—which was wrong—I have a great deal." Even so, her confidence coexisted with nagging doubts about her own capacities. If she indeed possessed all the "magnificent powers" that the dentist identified in her skull, then why did she always "sink" whenever she encountered "a difficulty"? Her current struggles seemed to belie his pronouncements.³⁴

At least the dentist graciously eschewed a discussion of her "passions," which would have been "somewhat embarrassing." Knowing herself, Healey assumed that her "amativeness" (sexual drive) and "philoprogenitiveness" (love of children) were "both at 7." Thankfully, the dentist stayed mum on the subject. In the privacy of her own journal, though, Healey felt comfortable tackling it. Her entry is a fascinating mix of frankness and coded language. When she speculated about her amativeness and philoprogenitiveness, Healey exhibited knowledge of phrenological principles. She knew that her skull marked her as a lover of children (and thus a model of proper womanhood). But she also bluntly admitted something that others might have found indecorous: she had a high sex drive and was fond of male company. For that reason, she breathed a sigh of relief when her dentist avoided a discussion of her passions. Other women were not so lucky.³⁵

In a cautionary tale about what could happen when women submitted their skulls for examination, Healey told the story of "H," a local woman who was outed as having a healthy appetite for male attention. Referring to this embarrassing episode, one of Healey's friends expressed anxiety about "what might be said" about her own character if she risked a cranial reading. Then, she turned the inquisition onto Healey. Why, this woman wondered, was Healey so hesitant to have her "head publicly examined"? Was she also "afraid" that the examiner would expose her bulging organ of amativeness to a live audience? "I told her no!" Healey exclaimed. If phrenology was a "just" science, then it would correctly identify "the strength of my passions—if only to add—that they are in the strong check of Reason."[36]

By carefully distinguishing between her animal propensities and the rational faculties that governed them, Healey repeated a common phrenological argument. Just because one possessed a powerful libido—or a tendency toward gluttony, destructiveness, or secrecy—it did not mean that one was ruled by those traits or unable to regulate them. In fact, phrenologists argued that there were no inherently bad characteristics. Everyone had the same organs after all. The goal was a "well-balanced head." So long as moral sentiments and intellectual faculties remained strong enough to govern baser passions, then it was perfectly fine to have robust amorous tendencies. Seizing on this argument, Healey willingly acknowledged the potency of her animal propensities, but in the same breath she insisted that her mental and moral developments were stronger. In any case, phrenology might turn out to be humbuggery. If that were true, she reasoned, "what should I care to be told as H. was the other day, that I could not exist out of the society of the other sex?"[37]

Healey's entry makes it clear that women used phrenology to assess and disclose their anxieties and self-doubts. Healey, for instance, was both confident and insecure. She believed she possessed "mathematical genius" and strong rational faculties. Yet she worried that her animal nature was too strong. Healey insisted that she was unashamed by the marks of libidinal appetite on her skull and maintained that she refused to allow Fowler to examine her head because she "did not care to encourage" a quack scientist. Even so, her hesitancy clearly sprung—at least in part—from fear of public exposure. She admitted that it would have been "somewhat embarrassing" to have her dentist expounding on her amorous tendencies. Surely it would have been more embarrassing to have those tendencies revealed before a live audience? Despite her protestation that she "need not fear the truth," Healey was evidently nervous about subjecting herself to a public examination.[38]

Healey's private musings reveal that early Americans thought about their identities in phrenological terms. She might have denounced phrenology as a "charlatan faith," but that did not stop her from using the science to analyze her own capacities. She also assumed that others would use phrenology to evaluate her. Healey might not have expected to have her character laid bare by her family dentist when she walked in for a filling. But she was neither surprised nor offended by the intrusion. After all, she had already been conversing about her phrenological organs with her friends.

Beyond giving people a way to make sense of their gendered identities, phrenology furnished Americans with a scientific language for discussing sex and desire. At a time when the nation's leading moralists insisted that women were fundamentally "passionless," phrenologists encouraged women to imagine themselves not just as wives and mothers but also as sexual beings.[39] As historian Carla Bittel brilliantly argued, phrenologists urged men and women to think about "cranial compatibility" when searching for a spouse. During the 1850s, the Fowler and Wells publishing house regularly printed courtship advice and provided readers with guidance on how to find someone with complementary phrenological endowments. It even allowed subscribers to write to the journal editors and ask for advice on what sorts of skeletal conformations they should seek in a potential partner.[40]

Some women took this advice seriously. In 1843, the influential abolitionist and women's rights activist Abby Kelley read Lorenzo Fowler's book on phrenology and matrimony while courting her fellow abolitionist Stephen Symonds Foster. She gave it a positive review and asked her partner to procure a copy as soon as he could.[41] Rachel Bowman similarly used phrenology to navigate her romantic pursuits. Bowman earned a degree from Otterbein University in Ohio during an era when higher education was inaccessible for most women. She met her future husband, Samuel Eckerman Cormany, while completing her studies. During their courtship, Rachel spent an evening poring over "a Phrenalogical Journal." She "found some good pieces, marked some," and thought about sending them to her beloved "S. E. C." She held back, though, worrying "that he would think me rather too fast." What did she mean? Why would phrenological articles mark her as "too fast"? The answer becomes clear in a later entry, where she mentioned that she had been "reading extensively" about phrenology and matrimony. If Rachel refrained from sending certain excerpts to Samuel, it was likely because they contained material about sex, the skull, and the phrenological foundations for marriage. Luckily, the match worked out. Rachel and Samuel were happily wedded in November 1860. Then, just a few months after the ceremony, they went to get their heads examined together.[42]

Phrenology ultimately gave women a language for talking about their bodies, brains, and gender identities. Regardless of whether they trusted in its scientific infallibility, they used it to evaluate others and make sense of their own identities and desires. In a very practical way, it furnished Americans with a method for reading the people they encountered each day.

AMERICAN WOMEN continued to rely on phrenology to understand their minds and bodies, long after most elite scientists turned their noses up at the science. Emily Hawlie Gillespie, for instance, was an Iowa feminist, wife, and mother who attended phrenological lectures and subscribed to the *American Phrenological Journal* well into the latter decades of the nineteenth century. In both 1882 and 1883, Gillespie took her children to get their heads examined. Each experience delighted her. Her son Henry received "a model Chart." Whether he chose a career as a mechanic, doctor, photographer, merchant, or dentist, his head predicted success. "All of it was good," Gillespie buoyantly recounted. She was also thrilled with her daughter Sarah's reading: "I *am so glad* she has got it, it is a splendid examination." When the phrenologist told Sarah that her daughter should go into medicine, Gillespie could barely contain her excitement: "Only think of it both my Children *Doctors*—well I am proud of it & will help them all I can."[43]

Despite being fiercely proud of her children, Gillespie could not help but wonder what she might have achieved had she not become a mother. When one phrenologist told her that she had "the most remarkable head he ever examined," she sunk into wistful melancholy. "I could be one of the finest poets, one of the best authors, & in the finest arts I could have reached the very highest," Gillespie lamented. Of course, she never reached such heights. She had given up the dream of literary fame to care for her family. Her cranium only revealed the disjuncture between her extraordinary capabilities and what she had in fact accomplished. Finding another way to mobilize her literary talents, Gillespie paraphrased the famous poet John Greenleaf Whittier: "The saddest words from tongue or pen, / Are these—it might have been." Phrenology brought both joy and sadness into Gillespie's life. On the one hand, it assured her of her family's exceptionality. On the other hand, it reminded her of all the dreams she had forsaken. What good was it to know that you could have been one of the world's most impressive poets if you abandoned your literary ambitions for motherhood? "All is well," she insisted. "My Children amply repay me for all I have been obliged to—well—give up." It was an unconvincing attempt at cheerful resignation.[44]

Gillespie penned these words in 1885, long after phrenology had receded in popularity. Although elite White men had once embraced phrenology, the United States' medical and scientific establishment no longer considered it a legitimate discipline by the late nineteenth century. In the 1850s and 1860s, these men had started aggressively distinguishing themselves from the phrenological "quacks" of the past and began forming societies that emphasized the value of professional credentials and university degrees. Turning away from phrenology, they embraced disciplines like craniology, evolutionary biology, physical anthropology, and eugenics. In the process, they ignored how foundational phrenology had been for their own intellectual development in the preceding decades. But even as professional men abandoned the more flexible phrenological model of the early national and antebellum decades, women like Emily Gillespie held onto it.[45]

Phrenology appealed to American women not only because they saw it as a tool of self-knowledge but also because it provided the intellectual flexibility to craft and negotiate their own gender identities. At a time when scientists and political thinkers insisted that men and women were innately distinct beings who should occupy "separate spheres," phrenologists encouraged women to see themselves as neurologically distinctive individuals who might be anyone, go anywhere, and do anything they desired. They laid out a series of gendered rules, to be sure, but they also made it clear that women could break those rules when necessary. Women who were happy with existing norms could take comfort in their "feminine" identities, but those who resented societal expectations could emphasize their distinctiveness or relish how their craniums contradicted dominant stereotypes.

Until recently, historians of gender in the early republic have mostly ignored the study of phrenology. When they grapple with it at all, they largely denounce it as harmful to women—an early form of biological essentialism or, at the very least, a science that strengthened society's commitment to theories like "separate spheres" and gender complementarity. Early American women, though, saw something in phrenology that scholars are just beginning to take seriously. Phrenology was clearly a problematic and discriminatory science, but it was also a flexible discipline that allowed women to think creatively about their gender identities and envision alternate possibilities for their lives. By examining women's uses of this science, scholars can reconstruct an early American world where gender ideologies were not as rigid or confining as we often assume.

Of course, twenty-first-century historians should not romanticize phrenology. At best, it was a misguided method for studying human character and cognition. At worst, it was a toxic discipline that weaponized the rhetoric of empirical discovery and deployed it to perpetuate gender and racial discrimination. Phrenology rested on a series of problematic assumptions: that external beauty revealed internal character, that some brains were inherently superior to others, and that social inequities could be legitimate—so long as they reified the "natural" differences that already divided human beings. Phrenology helped both elite thinkers and ordinary people make excuses for scientific racism and gender essentialism. It not only set the stage for later forms of biological determinism and eugenics; it also helped make these concepts popular.

Despite its many problems, phrenology appealed to scores of women in the early United States—particularly those who self-identified as intellectuals, abolitionists, and women's rights activists. These women saw phrenology as a flawed but flexible science that gave women a nuanced and practical method for thinking about human difference and gender identity and armed them with tools to carve out a place in the world. Through intimate and personalized cranial readings, phrenologists highlighted women's strengths and idiosyncrasies, assuring them that they were unique and special, confident and intelligent, firm and bold, and perhaps even masculine. For those who felt trapped by existing gender conventions, phrenology must have been liberating. By confirming that everyone's brain was unique, the science assured Americans that there was more than one way to be a "true woman."

Questions to Consider

1. How did Americans use phrenology to think about gender identity in the early republic?
2. What problems did phrenology pose for women? What possibilities did it open for those who wanted to challenge prevailing gender stereotypes?

Notes

1. For rigidity of nineteenth-century gender ideologies, see Barbara Welter, "The Cult of True Womanhood: 1820–1860," *American Quarterly* 18, no. 2 (Summer 1966): 151–74; Nancy F. Cott, *The Bonds of Womanhood: "Woman's Sphere" in New England, 1780–1835* (New Haven, CT: Yale University Press, 1977); and Jeanne Boydston, *Home and Work: Housework, Wages, and the Ideology of Labor in the Early Republic* (New York: Oxford University Press, 1990). For intersections between science and gender, see Carroll Smith-Rosenberg and Charles Rosenberg, "The Female Animal: Medical and Biological Views of Woman and Her Role in Nineteenth-Century America," *Journal of American History* 60, no. 2 (September 1973): 332–56; Elizabeth Fee, "Nineteenth-Century Craniology: The Study of the Female Skull," *Bulletin of the History of Medicine* 53, no. 3 (Fall 1979): 415–33; Cynthia Eagle Russett, *Sexual Science: The Victorian Construction of Womanhood* (Cambridge, MA: Harvard University Press, 1989); Carla Bittel, *Mary Putnam Jacobi and the Politics of Medicine in Nineteenth-Century America* (Chapel Hill: University of North Carolina Press, 2009); and Kimberly A. Hamlin, *From Eve to Evolution: Darwin, Science, and Women's Rights in Gilded Age America* (Chicago: University of Chicago Press, 2014). For "separate spheres" and the "cult of true womanhood" reflecting ideology rather than lived reality, see Linda K. Kerber, "Separate Spheres, Female Worlds, Woman's Place: The Rhetoric of Women's History," *Journal of American History* 75, no. 1 (June 1988): 9–39; Carol Lasser, "Beyond Separate Spheres: The Power of Public Opinion," *Journal of the Early Republic* 21, no. 1 (Spring 2001): 115–23; and Cathy N. Davidson and Jessamyn Hatcher, eds., *No More Separate Spheres! A Next Wave American Studies Reader* (Durham, NC: Duke University Press, 2002).
2. Thomas Laqueur, *Making Sex: Body and Gender from the Greeks to Freud* (Cambridge, MA: Harvard University Press, 1990), 4, 149. See also Londa Schiebinger, "Skeletons in the Closet: The First Illustrations of the Female Skeleton in Eighteenth-Century Anatomy," *Representations* 14 (Spring

1986): 42–82; Ludmilla Jordanova, *Sexual Visions: Images of Gender in Science and Medicine Between the Eighteenth and Twentieth Centuries* (Madison: University of Wisconsin Press, 1989); Schiebinger, *The Mind Has No Sex? Women in the Origins of Modern Science* (Cambridge, MA: Harvard University Press, 1989); and Schiebinger, *Nature's Body: Gender in the Making of Modern Science* (Boston: Beacon Press, 1993). For scholars who have challenged or provided more nuance for Laqueur's argument, see Michael Stolberg, "A Woman down to Her Bones: The Anatomy of Sexual Difference in the Sixteenth and Early Seventeenth Centuries," *Isis* 94, no. 2 (June 2003): 274–99; Karen Harvey, "The Substance of Sexual Difference: Change and Persistence in Representations of the Body in Eighteenth-Century England," *Gender and History* 14, no. 2 (December 2002): 202–23; and Helen King, *The One-Sex Body on Trial: The Classical and Early Modern Evidence* (New York: Routledge, 2013).

3. Rosemarie Zagarri, *Revolutionary Backlash: Women and Politics in the Early American Republic* (Philadelphia: University of Pennsylvania Press, 2007), 184; John Wood Sweet, *Bodies Politic: Negotiating Race in the American North, 1730–1830* (Baltimore: Johns Hopkins University Press, 2003), 296; Clare A. Lyons, *Sex Among the Rabble: An Intimate History of Gender and Power in the Age of Revolution, Philadelphia, 1730–1830* (Chapel Hill: University of North Carolina Press, 2006), 2. See also Bruce Burgett, *Sentimental Bodies: Sex, Gender, and Citizenship in the Early Republic* (Princeton, NJ: Princeton University Press, 1998), 95; Kirsten Fischer, *Suspect Relations: Sex, Race, and Resistance in Colonial North Carolina* (Ithaca, NY: Cornell University Press, 2001), 4; Catherine Kerrison, *Claiming the Pen: Women and Intellectual Life in the Early American South* (Ithaca, NY: Cornell University Press, 2006), 55–56; Sheila L. Skemp, *First Lady of Letters: Judith Sargent Murray and the Struggle for Female Independence* (Philadelphia: University of Pennsylvania Press, 2009), 307; Donald Ratcliffe, "The Right to Vote and the Rise of Democracy, 1787–1828," *Journal of the Early Republic* 33, no. 12 (Summer 2013): 246; and Susan Ware, *American Women's History: A Very Short Introduction* (New York: Oxford University Press, 2015), 23.

4. I use the word "science" deliberately. As numerous scholars have argued, "pseudoscience" is a problematic word. It suggests that disciplines like phrenology do not count as real sciences, simply because they were later discredited. Phrenology was always a contested form of knowledge, but elite thinkers and ordinary people took it seriously in the nineteenth century. On the overlap between "popular" and "proper" science in the nineteenth century, see Richard Yeo, *Defining Science: William Whewell, Natural Knowledge and Public Debate in Early Victorian Britain* (New

York: Cambridge University Press, 1993); Daniel Patrick Thurs, *Science Talk: Changing Notions of Science in American Culture* (New Brunswick, NJ: Rutgers University Press, 2007); Ralph O'Connor, "Reflections on Popular Science in Britain: Genres, Categories, and Historians," *Isis* 100, no. 2 (June 2009): 333–45; Katherine Pandora, "Popular Science in National and Transnational Perspective: Suggestions from the American Context," *Isis* 100, no. 2 (June 2009): 346–58; Sherrie Lynne Lyons, *Species, Serpents, Spirits, and Skulls: Science at the Margins in the Victorian Age* (Albany: SUNY Press, 2009); and Britt Rusert, *Fugitive Science: Empiricism and Freedom in Early African American Culture* (New York: New York University Press, 2017).

5. On European origins, see Roger Cooter, *The Cultural Meaning of Popular Science: Phrenology and the Organization of Consent in Nineteenth-Century Britain* (New York: Cambridge University Press, 1984). On rising popularity in the United States, see John D. Davies, *Phrenology, Fad and Science: A 19th-Century American Crusade* (New Haven, CT: Yale University Press, 1955); Madeleine Stern, *Heads and Headlines: The Phrenological Fowlers* (Norman: University of Oklahoma Press, 1971); Cynthia S. Hamilton, "'Am I Not a Man and a Brother?' Phrenology and Anti-Slavery," *Slavery and Abolition* 29, no. 2 (June 2008): 173–87; Carla Bittel, "Woman, Know Thyself: Producing and Using Phrenological Knowledge in 19th-Century America," *Centaurus* 55, no. 2 (May 2013): 104–30; Susan Branson, "Phrenology and the Science of Race in Antebellum America," *Early American Studies* 15, no. 1 (Winter 2017): 164–93; James Poskett, *Materials of the Mind: Phrenology, Race, and the Global History of Science, 1815–1920* (Chicago: University of Chicago Press, 2019); Bittel, "Testing the Truth of Phrenology: Knowledge Experiments in Antebellum American Cultures of Science and Health," *Medical History* 63, no. 3 (July 2019): 352–74; Courtney E. Thompson, *An Organ of Murder: Crime, Violence, and Phrenology in Nineteenth-Century America* (New Brunswick, NJ: Rutgers University Press, 2021); Rachel E. Walker, "Facing Race: Popular Science and Black Intellectual Thought in Antebellum America," *Early American Studies* 19, no. 3 (Summer 2021): 601–40; and Walker, *Beauty and the Brain: The Science of Human Nature in Early America* (Chicago: University of Chicago Press, 2022).

6. Rebecca Gratz to Maria Gist Gratz, 9 March 1834, in *Letters of Rebecca Gratz*, ed. David Philipson (Philadelphia: Jewish Publication Society, 1929), 195.

7. Mary Virginia Montgomery, diary, in *We Are Your Sisters: Black Women in the Nineteenth Century*, ed. Dorothy Sterling (New York: Norton, 1984), 462–72.

8. For an early articulation of such ideas in American phrenological thought (built on and replicating conclusions of European thinkers such as Franz Gall, Johann Gaspar Spurzheim, and George Combe), see Orson Squire Fowler, *Fowler's Practical Phrenology* (Philadelphia: O. S. Fowler and L. N. Fowler, 1840).
9. To improve patients' craniums and characters, phrenologists encouraged deliberate "mental exercise"; see "Mental Exercise as a Means of Health," *American Phrenological Journal* 2, no. 2 (November 1839): 85–93. Rebecca Gratz, a Jewish educator and philanthropist, articulated this idea in her private manuscripts; see Rebecca Gratz to Maria Gist Gratz, 9 March 1834.
10. "The Case of Laura Bridgman," *American Phrenological Journal* 3, no. 12 (September 1841): 563. On Howe's relationship to phrenology, see Harold Schwartz, "Samuel Gridley Howe as Phrenologist," *American Historical Review* 57, no. 3 (April 1952): 644–51. See also Ernest Freeberg, *The Education of Laura Bridgman: First Deaf and Blind Person to Learn Language* (Cambridge, MA: Harvard University Press, 2001).
11. Lorenzo N. Fowler, *The Phrenological Almanac for 1841* (New York: W. J. Spence, 1840), 8.
12. "Phrenological Reports, 1853," in *The Elizabeth Cady Stanton and Susan B. Anthony Reader: Correspondence, Writings, Speeches*, ed. Ellen Carol Dubois (1981; rpt. Boston: Northeastern University Press, 1992), 275–76. On cranial interpretations of women as having superior minds, see, for example, "Phrenological Developments of Gottfried, a Murderess," *American Phrenological Journal* 2, no. 12 (September 1840): 542–44.
13. "Phrenological Reports, 1853," 275–76; Nelson Sizer Phrenological Character of Mr. John B. Bancroft, 24 February 1854, Historical Medical Library, College of Physicians of Philadelphia.
14. Elisha Hurlbut, *Essays on Human Rights and Their Political Guaranties* (New York: Fowlers and Wells, 1845), 12.
15. Adeline Barnes, a woman who solicited a cranial reading around the same time, had only a "LARGE" development of this organ, coming in at a "6." Both readings appeared in marked-up copies of *Fowler's Practical Phrenology* (1840) held by the Library Company of Philadelphia.
16. Phoebe George Bradford, diary, 20 December 1838, in *Phoebe George Bradford Diaries*, ed. W. Emerson Wilson (Wilmington: Historical Society of Delaware, 1975), 87–88.
17. Welter, "The Cult of True Womanhood," 152.
18. For further discussion, see Bittel, "Testing the Truth of Phrenology."
19. Phoebe George Bradford, diary, 20 December 1838, 87–88. For critiques of strong-minded women and laudatory portrayals of female modesty, see J. C., "The Blue-Stocking," *New World: A Weekly Family Journal of Popular*

Literature, Science, Art and News 2, no. 11 (13 March 1841): 171; "My Cousin Nell," *Journal of Agriculture* 2, no. 11 (2 June 1852): 83–86; "Strong-Minded Women," *Gleason's Pictorial Drawing-Room Companion* 5, no. 2 (9 July 1853): 29; Horace Greeley, "A Fable for Strong-Minded Women: Respectfully Addressed to Lucy Stone," *Prisoner's Friend: A Monthly Magazine Devoted to Criminal Reform, Philosophy, Science, Literature, and Art* 7, no. 11 (1 July 1855): 372; and Genio C. Scott, "For the Home Journal: Interesting to Ladies," *Home Journal* 26, no. 542 (28 June 1856): 4. For phrenologists' defenses of intellectual women, see "Sketchings," *The Crayon* 2, no. 2 (11 July 1855): 24–25, and "High Foreheads, Beauty, and Intellect," *American Phrenological Journal* 23, no. 3 (March 1856): 61–62.

20. Carla Bittel, "Unpacking the Phrenological Toolkit: Knowledge and Identity in Antebellum America," in *Working with Paper: Gendered Practices in the History of Knowledge,* ed. Carla Bittel, Elaine Leong, and Christine von Oertzen (Pittsburgh: University of Pittsburgh Press, 2019), 107.

21. "The Superiority of the Caucasian Race," *American Phrenological Journal* 3, no. 3 (December 1840): 124–26; Fowler, *Fowler's Practical Phrenology,* 32. Also see "The Negro and Caucasian Brain Compared," *American Phrenological Journal* 3, no. 6 (March 1841): 282–83, and O. S. and L. N. Fowler, *New Illustrated Self-Instructor in Phrenology and Physiology* (New York: Fowlers and Wells, 1854), 41. Charles Caldwell, an enslaver and early phrenological expert, used phrenology to support slavery. For analysis, see Branson, "Phrenology and the Science of Race in Antebellum America," and Hamilton, "'Am I Not a Man and a Brother?'" For Black intellectuals embracing and repurposing phrenology, see Rusert, *Fugitive Science,* 121–26, and Walker, "Facing Race."

22. "Sarah Kinson, or Margru," *American Phrenological Journal* 12, no. 1 (1 July 1850): 231, reprinted in *The Illustrated Phrenological Almanac for 1851* (New York: Fowler and Wells, 1850), 30. See also Thompson, *An Organ of Murder,* 24, and Poskett, *Materials of the Mind,* 62.

23. Mary Virginia Montgomery, diary, entries for 29 March, 24, 30 November 1872, in Sterling, ed., *We Are Your Sisters,* 462–72.

24. Forten extolled Nathaniel Hawthorne's "splendid head" and said it bore "the unmistakeable impress of genius and superior intellect"; see entry for 10 July 1854, in *The Journals of Charlotte Forten Grimké,* ed. Brenda Stevenson (New York: Oxford University Press, 1988), 84.

25. For Sojourner Truth's relationship to phrenology, see Darcy Grimaldo Grigsby, *Enduring Truths: Sojourner's Shadows and Substance* (Chicago: University of Chicago Press, 2015), 13–14, and Margaret Washington, *Sojourner Truth's America* (Urbana: University of Illinois Press, 2009), 179.

26. Ida B. Wells, journal, entries for 21–28 January 1886, in Sterling, ed., *We Are Your Sisters*, 481–82.
27. For William Lloyd Garrison's relationship with phrenology, see Goldwin Smith, ed., *The Moral Crusader: William Lloyd Garrison—A Biographical Essay* (New York: Funk and Wagnalls, 1892), 115. For Garrison's phrenological reading, see "Miscellaneous," *The Liberator* (Boston, MA), 21 September 1838. Also see "Prospectus of the American Phrenological Journal and Miscellany," *The Liberator*, 16 November 1838, and "Phrenology," *The Liberator*, 29 November 1839.
28. Abby Kelley to Stephen S. Foster, 30 January 1843, Abigail Kelley Foster Papers, American Antiquarian Society, Worcester, MA. For examples of phrenology in *The Lily*, see "The Phrenological and Water Cure Journals," *The Lily* (Seneca Falls, NY), 1 May 1853; Senex, "Harper's Editor and the Women. No. VI," *The Lily* (Mount Vernon, Ohio), 15 August 1854; and "What Woman Needs," *The Lily* 6, no. 12 (Mount Vernon, Ohio), July 1854. For Henry Ward Beecher's relationship with phrenology, see T. J. Ellinwood, ed., *Autobiographical Reminiscences of Henry Ward Beecher* (New York: Frederick A. Stokes, 1898), 38. For physiognomy and phrenology in *Uncle Tom's Cabin*, see Harriet Beecher Stowe, *Uncle Tom's Cabin; or, Life Among the Lowly*, 2 vols. (Boston: John P. Jewett, 1852), 1:13–14, 16, 40–41, 98, 133, 184, 211–12, 229, 269; 2:12, 32, 70, 102, 112, 114, 164, 166, 181, 189. On Black intellectuals and popular sciences, see Walker, "Facing Race." On Quakers using phrenology to understand political radicalism, see Lucretia Mott to George Combe, 13 June 1839, in *Selected Letters of Lucretia Coffin Mott*, ed. Beverly Wilson Palmer (Urbana: University of Illinois Press, 2002), 53. See also William Bassett to Abby Kelley, 12 November 1838, and Kelley to Mr. and Mrs. Hudson, 12 April 1841, Abigail Kelley Foster Papers.
29. "Address by ECS on Woman's Rights," in *The Selected Papers of Elizabeth Cady Stanton and Susan B. Anthony: In the School of Anti-Slavery, 1840 to 1866*, ed. Ann D. Gordon (New Brunswick, NJ: Rutgers University Press, 1997), 103. For Stanton's phrenological analysis (and Susan B. Anthony's), see "Phrenological Reports, 1853," 269–76. For Stanton's response, see *Elizabeth Cady Stanton as Revealed in Her Letters, Diary and Reminiscences*, ed. Harriet Stanton Blatch and Theodore Stanton, 2 vols. (New York: Harper and Brothers, 1922), 2:46–47. For Stanton's relationship to phrenology, see also Bittel, "Woman, Know Thyself," 118–19, and Walker, *Beauty and the Brain*, 134–35.
30. See Samuel Wells to John Brown Jr., 2 March 1854; Nelson Sizer to Brown, 26 March 1860, Charles E. Frohman Collections, Rutherford B. Hayes Presidential Library, Fremont, OH.

31. For examples, see "The Worcester Female Convention," *American Phrenological Journal* 12, no. 9 (September 1850): 291–92; "Reform in the Condition of Woman," *American Phrenological Journal* 12, no. 10 (October 1850): 318–22; Peggoty, "Woman's Rights," *American Phrenological Journal* 14, no. 4 (October 1851): 89–90; "Woman's Rights Convention," *American Phrenological Journal* 14, no. 4 (October 1851): 90; Anna, "Woman! Her Rights and Duties," *American Phrenological Journal* 14, no. 6 (December 1851): 127–28; "Woman's Rights Convention," *American Phrenological Journal* 15, no. 4 (October 1852): 91–92; and "Woman's Rights Convention," *American Phrenological Journal* 17, no. 2 (February 1853): 43–44. For the journal's glowing profiles of female activists, see "Character and Biography of Amelia Bloomer: Biographical Sketch," *American Phrenological Journal* 17, no. 3 (March 1853): 50–53; "Biography: Paulina Wright Davis," *American Phrenological Journal* 17, no. 6 (June 1853): 11–13; "Biography: Elizabeth Oakes Smith," *American Phrenological Journal* 18, no. 5 (November 1853): 109–11; "Grace Greenwood: A Portrait, Biography, and Phrenological Character," *American Phrenological Journal* 19, no. 1 (January 1854): 5–8; and "The Champions of Social Reform," *American Phrenological Journal* 49, no. 3 (March 1869): 93–96.
32. Hurlbut, *Essays on Human Rights,* 113. The Fowler and Wells publishing house gave both material and intellectual support to the suffrage movement and forged friendships with leading activists. Stanton and her coeditors enlisted the aid of Charlotte Fowler Wells when publishing the first volume of *The History of Woman Suffrage;* see Elizabeth Cady Stanton, Susan B. Anthony, and Matilda Joslyn Gage, eds., *The History of Woman Suffrage, 1848–1861,* 6 vols. (New York: Fowler and Wells, 1881), 2:45.
33. Entry for 13 May 1841, in *Selected Journals of Caroline Healey Dall,* ed. Helen R. Deese (Charlottesville: University of Virginia Press, 2006), 1:79–80.
34. Entry for 13 May 1841, in Deese, ed., *Selected Journals of Caroline Healey Dall,* 1:79–80.
35. Entry for 13 May 1841, in Deese, ed., *Selected Journals of Caroline Healey Dall,* 1:79–80.
36. Entry for 13 May 1841, in Deese, ed., *Selected Journals of Caroline Healey Dall,* 1:79–80.
37. Entry for 13 May 1841, in Deese, ed., *Selected Journals of Caroline Healey Dall,* 1:79–80.
38. Entry for 13 May 1841, in Deese, ed., *Selected Journals of Caroline Healey Dall,* 1:79–80.
39. Nancy F. Cott, "Passionlessness: An Interpretation of Victorian Sexual Ideology, 1790–1850," *Signs* 4, no. 2 (Winter 1978): 219–36. See also Helen

Lefkowitz Horowitz, *Rereading Sex: Battles over Sexual Knowledge and Suppression in Nineteenth-Century America* (New York: Knopf, 2002), 115–18, 328–31, and April R. Haynes, *Riotous Flesh: Women, Physiology, and the Solitary Vice in Nineteenth-Century America* (Chicago: University of Chicago Press, 2015), 145–46.

40. Carla Bittel, "Cranial Compatibility: Phrenology, Measurement, and Marriage Assessment," *Isis* 112, no. 4 (December 2021): 795–803.
41. Abby Kelley to Stephen S. Foster, 30 January 1843, Abigail Kelley Foster Papers.
42. Rachel Bowman Cormany, diary, entries for 10 October 1859, 26 March 1860, March 1861, in *The Cormany Diaries: A Northern Family in the Civil War*, ed. James C. Mohr (Pittsburgh: University of Pittsburgh Press, 1982), 38–39, 68, 136.
43. Entries for 18 July 1882 and February 1883, in *A Secret to Be Buried: The Diary and Life of Emily Hawley Gillespie, 1858–1888*, ed. Judy Nolte Lensink (Iowa City: University of Iowa Press, 1989), 469, 481.
44. Entry for 8 June 1885, in Lensink, ed., *A Secret to Be Buried*, 540.
45. Russett, *Sexual Science*, 16–48.

Fifth Avenoodles
EFFEMINATE DANDIES IN ANTEBELLUM NEW YORK

RACHEL HOPE CLEVES

AT THE halfway point of the nineteenth century, a new personage took his first elegant steps through the streets of the booming metropolis of New York City and into public consciousness. He made his initial print appearance in an 1851 article by Nathaniel Parker Willis. This original character was a rich young man, a progeny of Fifth Avenue's brownstone mansions, who perambulated the city's boulevards dressed to dazzle: "His pantaloons are so diligently renewed that knee marks never protuberate. His gloves look like primroses, new-blown with thumb and fingers. His head, smooth from the curling-tongs, sits in his collar like a marigold in a paper holder. The tie of his cravat, so broad and so long, is a marvel of untumbled dexterity. With his hat at the angle agreed upon by his set, booted like the model foot in the show-case of the maker, laced, and with a violet in his button-hole, he walks Broadway." During the eighteenth century, flamboyantly attired young men of leisure had been denigrated as "macaronis." Now Willis caricaturized the new generation of New York dandies as "Fifth-ave-noodles."[1]

The Fifth-ave-noodle—alternatively spelled "avenoodle," "avenudle," or "avenuedle"—challenged normative American constructions of White, middle-class, northern masculinity. Northern men had a reputation as business-minded vulgarians who wore sober, dark clothes and wolfed down their meals at double-speed, not to lose a minute that could be devoted to making money. Initially, the market-oriented masculinity of such middle-class workers provoked anxiety over the nation's transition to capitalism, but by midcentury the "self-made man" epitomized American manliness.[2]

The avenoodle, however, consumed rather than produced wealth. He was the son of the self-made man, supported by his father's largesse. He lived for pleasure, attending the theater, lingering at restaurant tables, and speaking knowledgeably about gastronomy. His focus on aesthetics made the avenoodle suspiciously effeminate.

In the 1850s, male effeminacy had not yet become fixed as a signifier of homosexuality, as it would be by the end of the century. Critics accused dandies of using their effeminacy to seduce young women, forging intimacies through their shared love of clothes, a charge that dated back to ancient Rome.³ But like ancient Roman dandies and eighteenth-century macaronis, effeminate avenoodles could also be negatively linked to same-sex desire.⁴ Historian Valerie Traub described these recurring metalogics linking sex and gender variance over time as "cycles of salience." In the Victorian sensibility, the violet that Willis's avenoodle wore in his buttonhole linked him to the classical world and to the supposed classical predilection for love between men. (Such symbolism applied to women too: the Greek poetess Sappho was associated with violets.)⁵

The heyday of the avenoodle was brief, and he has been almost entirely neglected by historians.⁶ Taking a close look at this forgotten urban archetype affords fresh, important insights into men's experiences, gender roles, and sexual variance in antebellum America, before the emergence of modern sexual identity categories. The recovery of the avenoodle reveals how male effeminacy in the mid-nineteenth century was simultaneously linked to womanizing and to same-sex sexuality, and how the links between male effeminacy and epicureanism laid the groundwork for twentieth-century characterizations of gourmet tastes as gay.

IN THE mid-nineteenth century, New York City entered a period of rapid growth, increasing in population from around 300,000 in 1840 to over 1 million by 1860. During this intensive urbanization, a sophisticated pleasure culture emerged in the city. Nathaniel Parker Willis, who had traveled extensively in Europe, gushed about the "Parisification of New-York." The globe was "an amphitheater whose civilized radii have an irresistible declivity toward one centre—*the point where money is spent most freely for pleasure.*" Paris had long been that center point, but New York, with its growing wealth, was taking its place. The city attracted world-class performers including Jenny Lind and Franconi's Circus, as well as "the prettiest glove-fitters, the most inspired milliners, the best portrait painters, the neatest equipages," and "the best cooks."⁷

During the 1840s, wealthy young men who patronized these performers and tradespeople in Paris acquired the label *flâneurs*, best translated as strollers, or men who idly walked the grand boulevards, looking and being seen. The Parisification of New York City gave rise to a new American variation of the *flâneur,* with a new name. Antebellum New Yorkers shared what scholar Irving Lewis Allen described as "a distinctive lexical culture of new slang about city life" that, thanks to the concentration of the nation's publishing industry in Manhattan, came to dominate American vernacular. Words such as "smart-aleck" and "shyster" originated in New York during the 1840s.[8] Out of this crucible of linguistic creativity emerged the "avenoodle."

The new slang term had layers of meaning. In British English, a "noodle" was a fool. In the 1840s, the London satirical magazine *Punch* created a character named "Yankee Noodle," a long-limbed, heavy-booted clod with lank hair. The name played on the song "Yankee Doodle," which originated as a British satire on vulgar, foolish North American colonials who imagined that merely by sticking a feather in their cap they could transform into fashionable macaronis. During the American Revolution, rebelling colonists appropriated the song as a point of pride.[9]

Similarly, in the mid-1840s, American humorists reclaimed the character of Yankee Noodle from *Punch,* establishing a magazine in New York called *Yankee Doodle* with a column titled "Politico-Editorial Noodles." The editors made puns about "Yankee Doodle's noodles" and joked about Yankee Doodles "who starting as Doodles Doo, become in a short time most particularly Doodles did and Noodles done." Building on this foundation, the portmanteau *avenoodle* also mocked New Yorkers' habit of pronouncing the word *avenue* as "AVE-noo," rather than as "AV-en-new." In sum, avenoodles represented a specifically New York variant of dandy who strolled the city's most wealthy and stylish thoroughfares, such as Fifth Avenue.[10]

Nathaniel Parker Willis most likely coined the term "Fifth Avenoodle" in his 1851 *Home Journal* article. Willis was famous for his neologisms, or "Willicisms," which included the expression "Upper Ten Thousand" to refer to the city's elite.[11] However, an 1866 author credited George William Curtis, another midcentury New York humorist who satirized high society, saying it was Curtis "who, fashion getting further uptown, called its votaries 'Fifth Avenoodles.'" Curtis only moved to New York City in 1850, but it is possible that he invented the term before Willis.[12] South Carolina writer William M. Bobo used the variants "avenuedle" and "avenudle" in his 1852 book *Glimpses of New York City,* a critique of the northern metropolis that included an entire chapter devoted to the flashy young men. Walt Whitman used the expression "Fifth Avenoodledom" in 1856.[13] By mid-decade, the term had become widespread and was applied to dandies throughout the United States, demonstrating how New York's urban slang became the vernacular of the nation.

Early descriptions of the avenoodle highlighted his effeminacy. An 1854 article noted his "foppish dress, [and] effeminate air." Like women, the avenoodle devoted himself to appearances. He "looks upon labor as ignoble, and flatters himself that his porcelain person was ordained for ornament rather than for use."[14] The emergence of separate-spheres ideology in the nineteenth century fueled a growing bifurcation between masculine and feminine dress in the United States. Men began favoring dark solid textiles that signified sober respectability. Their dress dispensed with ornamentation, which signified their putative role as producers in the public sphere, rather than consumers in the domestic sphere. Conversely, women's dress in the 1850s became more ornamental, as the sewing machine made it easier to add on all sorts of trimmings.[15] The avenoodle transgressed this gender divide.

William Bobo mocked the Avenuedle's velvet coats. An 1855 novel, also possibly by Bobo, described avenoodles wearing "varioloid waistcoats" and "elongated skirts."[16] *Varioloid,* a term used to describe smallpox infections in people previously inoculated, made the presumably polka-dotted waistcoats of the avenoodle sound diseased, while the long "skirts" of the New York dandies' jackets undoubtedly resonated as feminine in an era when social norms confined women to dresses. Willis's passage about the avenoodle in the *Home Journal* also called attention to the archetype's feminine fussiness about his clothing: he took such diligent care of his "pantaloons" that "knee marks never protuberate." Just the use of the multisyllabic words "pantaloons" and "protuberate," in place of shorter, more common synonyms like "trousers" and "bulge," suggested the avenoodle's extravagance.[17]

Willis's physical description connected the avenoodle to a flower three times. Along with the avenoodle's primrose gloves, his head resembled a marigold, and he wore a violet in his buttonhole. The link between flowers and femininity was at its height in the mid-nineteenth century, when "sentimental flower books" for women readers proliferated, including anthologies of flower poetry, flower folklores, sentimental botanies, and lexicons of the so-called language of flowers. Flowers represented women because they shared the stereotyped feminine qualities of smallness, fragility, and beauty.[18]

Men of the period often wore flowers in their buttonholes for special occasions such as weddings, but the practice did not disrupt the strong association between flowers and femininity. Willis's reference to the avenoodle's violet associated the character with Sappho, reinforcing the femininity of the avenoodle's choice to wear it as a boutonniere. The analogy of the avenoodle's hair to the golden marigold signified his wealth. The primrose gloves were pale greenish-yellow, a color beloved by eighteenth-century macaronis and similar in hue to the carnation that became Oscar Wilde's hallmark later in the century and the suits worn by so-called pansies in 1920s New York.[19]

Willis's description also called attention to the avenoodle's use of "curling-tongs" to smooth his hair. Several descriptions of the avenoodle emphasized that he styled his hair in distinctively feminine ways. Sources diverged on the exact hairstyle favored by avenoodles, probably because fashions shifted rapidly in the mid-nineteenth century, but all linked curled hair to effeminate dandyism. Willis himself, as an example of "Fifth Avenoodledom," apparently had a fondness for "curling tongs." One source from 1860 ridiculed avenoodles who wore their hair "be-oiled" and their bodies "be-scented."[20] An 1875 satirical poem made fun of a young man whose "enemies called him a Fifth-Avenoodle / 'Cause he parted his hair in front, like a poodle." And an 1871 newspaper column described an avenoodle who wore "his hair powdered and parted in the middle," along with "embroidered collars and cuffs trimmed with fluted lace." These fashion choices, according to a Massachusetts newspaper, were "a premonition of a startling change to take place in our American society, which will be so revolutionized that the 'curled and perfumed darling' will no longer be the gentle, loving, confiding woman—she will change places with the 'coming man' who, conferring political power on the female aspirants so eager to possess it, will devote himself exclusively to the aesthetics of fashion and toilet."[21]

Accusations that male dandies happily exchanged political power for curling tongs demonstrated the semiotic significance of dress in the nineteenth century. As urbanization and industrialization destabilized traditional gender roles, dress served to reassert male dominance and female subordination. Transgressions of binary dress codes signified a threat to male power, and threats to male power were signified through dress.

Men wearing effeminate clothing threatened patriarchy by denaturalizing masculine superiority, and men who threatened patriarchy by supporting women's rights were lampooned in feminized dress. The rise of the suffrage movement sparked attacks on "mannish women" who dressed in masculine fashions and their feminine male supporters who donned aprons.[22] Conversely, critics ridiculed dandyish young men, like avenoodles, as supporters of women's rights.

Not all critiques of avenoodles flowed from the pens of defenders of the gender order. Willis was himself an infamous dandy who had been attacked for his effeminacy from his youth, long before the emergence of the avenoodle. Born in Maine in 1806, Willis attended Yale in the late 1820s and then moved to Boston, where he edited periodicals, published poetry, and cultivated a reputation as a womanizer and a fop. In 1830, the editor of the *Hartford Review* ridiculed Willis as "not quite a woman, by no means a man." Another newspaper editor, William Snelling, joked, "When W–ll–s saw the light, 'tis said his sex / Did for a month the neighborhood perplex." He was mocked as "Niminy-Piminy Willis."[23]

Willis moved to New York in 1831, joining the staff of the *New York Mirror*. After a visit to Europe, he returned to New York City and became one of the most famous magazine writers of the day. In the 1840s, Willis took full advantage of the city's thriving concert halls and theaters, and he carried on multiple affairs with women. In 1850, Shakespearean actor Edwin Forrest attacked Willis in Washington Square Park, beating the journalist with a whip for conducting an adulterous affair with his wife, Catherine Forrest. Accounts of the battle between the muscular, bull-like Forrest and the effeminate and elegant Willis, as well as accounts of Willis's role in the subsequent Forrest divorce trial, attracted a vast readership.[24] In short, when Willis printed the first account of the Fifth Avenoodle, he was himself one of the most famous dandies in the United States.

Attacks on Willis as a dandy appeared in newspapers and periodicals throughout the mid-nineteenth century. The *United States Democratic Review* disparaged Willis in 1854 for being "so largely indebted to female clothing for his similes, as to justify the suspicion that he must have surprised his Bethsheba in her bath, and stolen her petticoats." An 1844 etching of Willis published in *Graham's Magazine* portrayed him standing by a vase of flowers, a feminine signifier, and dressed in a long-skirted jacket with a tightly pinched waist, fine gloves, and dainty, pointed boots.

He wore his long hair in curls, brushed forward over his forehead. A character sketch of Willis that accompanied the etching acknowledged that "a man in pursuit of refinement may verge upon effeminacy," but argued that when it came to individuals of great merit, "a liberal mind will overlook and forget little defects and weaknesses." Not all could forgive Willis, however. His sister, writer Sarah Payson Willis, who used the pen name "Fanny Fern," satirized him in her autobiographical novel *Ruth Hall* (1854). She named a character modeled after her brother "Hyacinth," another purple flower with homoerotic associations rooted in antiquity. In Greek mythology, Hyacinthus was a beautiful boy beloved by Apollo.[25]

Attacks on Willis's character exemplified the ambiguous relationship between male effeminacy and same-sex sexuality in the mid-nineteenth-century United States, before the ascendance of sexology—the study of human sexual interests and behaviors—toward the end of the century and the solidification of the homo/hetero binary. Willis's effeminacy simultaneously made him vulnerable to attacks about his sexual behavior with women and with men. His womanliness was seen as attractive to women readers and authors. Writer Sarah Hale called him "the keeper of a Harem, who itches to be kissing all the pretty girls he sees, and who courts all that consent to flirt with him among his passionate admirers." In private letters, Willis wrote explicitly about his pursuit of sex with a wide variety of women. Yet his reputation as a Lothario did not stop his critics from accusing him of same-sex inclinations. Frederic Hill, a Scottish reformer and the editor of the *Galaxy*, attacked Willis for promoting pederasty. And Willis's private letters contained homoerotic allusions. He wrote to his friend George Pumpelly that he thought he could love him "like a woman."[26] As an antebellum dandy, Willis's sexuality was suspicious but unfixed.

The same confusion characterized accounts of the avenoodle. On the one hand, critics maligned avenoodles for associating with "fast" women. According to William Bobo, avenoodles picked up prostitutes from the third tier of New York City theaters and could be seen cavorting with girls at the Abbey, a resort on the banks of the Hudson River popular with "*fast* people." The Abbey had "pistol-galleries, billiard-tables, card-rooms, dancing-rooms, ten-pin alleys, eating and sleeping-rooms." The last in this list likely referred to the *cabinets particuliers,* or private rooms, attached to restaurants at the time, furnished with tables, chairs, and a couch. Men favored these private rooms as prime locations to take

FIG. 1. George W. Flagg, "Nathaniel Parker Willis," in "Our Contributors, No. XI." (Courtesy, Print Collection, New York Public Library)

mistresses and prostitutes for sex. Encounters with female sex workers were part of the avenoodle repertoire. An 1860 article in the *Brooklyn Daily Eagle* reported a police raid on a brothel in an uptown neighborhood, noting that the customers were in "the form of the Fifth-avenoodle stamp." Other articles described avenoodles as constantly flirting with women.[27]

On the other hand, some critics insinuated that avenoodles' effeminacy revealed their penchant for same-sex mischief. An 1854 article about avenoodles published in Mississippi's *Yazoo Democrat* commented on the young men's "half-amorous stare at the ladies" but also explained that these "dainty" dandies often traveled to Europe where they attended "the gay *salons* of Paris" and became familiar with "the whole gamut of cosmopolitan vices."[28] The description of his "half-amorous stare" suggested that the avenoodle's flirtations were ineffectual or only suggestive. In keeping with the standards of the time, the author declined to articulate the avenoodle's specific vices, knowing readers would understand, or at least imagine, that in Paris the "whole gamut" extended beyond sexual encounters with girls and women to sexual encounters with boys and men.

The sexual ambiguity of the avenoodle contrasts with the homoerotic fixity of the macaroni. Perhaps the macaroni's queerness has been overstated by historians.[29] It is also possible that the profound cultural flux of the rapidly urbanizing and industrializing late antebellum era destabilized gender and sexuality, leaving Americans uncertain about *how* to read this new dandy archetype. Men who curled their hair could be seeking sex with other men, or they could exemplify a new urban masculinity oriented toward sex with prostitutes, or they could be interested in sex both with other men and with female prostitutes. In short, although the avenoodle's name punned on the macaroni, the American archetype had distinctive qualities.

Along with a liking for colorful clothing, another quality that the two types of dandy did share in common was a love for fine food. The macaronis' name spoke to the idea that their aesthete tastes, picked up during the Grand Tour of Europe, included an appetite for pasta that spoke as much to their queerness as did their perfume, powder, and pantaloons. This perceived connection between alimentary and erotic subjectivities also informed the avenoodle. Historians have argued that sexuality was not carved off as a distinct domain of human desire and behavior until the late nineteenth century. David M. Halperin and others have posited that the idea of sexuality as a fixed, intrinsic, autonomous, core aspect of personhood is a modern, bourgeois production. Before the 1870s, eros constituted only one among many intersecting aspects of the self. In this pre-sexological modality, eating was closely linked to sex in what philosopher Giles Deleuze referred to as "the alimentary-sexual regime."[30] Like the macaroni, the avenoodle transgressed normative antebellum masculinity not only by his mode of dress but by his indulgence in the pleasures of the table.

Descriptions of the avenoodle often placed him in eating rooms. An 1853 article described the New York dandies' habit of frequenting Taylor's ice cream saloon, which a guidebook described as "the largest and most elegant restaurant in the world." Taylor's had eighteen-foot ceilings; inlaid marble floors; corner niches with marble, bronze, and gilt statuary; enormous gilt-framed mirrors; and chairs and sofas upholstered in crimson and gold. It was decadent and devoted entirely to pleasure. Its menu featured ice cream, patisseries, and other light dishes; people ate at Taylor's for enjoyment, not nutrition. Other sources depicted avenoodles as aficionados of decadent comestibles like turtle soup and sherry cobblers.[31]

Taylor's and other eating places exemplified a remarkable cultural transformation in the United States. As author Katharina Vester reveals, during the revolutionary and early national periods American political culture elevated a simplified "republican cuisine" as a signifier of national virtue. Cookbook authors, medical authorities, poets, and painters "promoted cooking that was deliberately bland," pushing citizens toward "constant control over and rejection of pleasures" as an expression of the self-discipline required from ideal citizens.[32] European visitors criticized Americans for grossly shoveling down their meals. From a domestic perspective, however, lack of discernment at the national table signaled Americans' freedom from corruption. Political rivals attacked Thomas Jefferson and Martin Van Buren for their effeminate tastes for fine French food. Restaurants, which first emerged in prerevolutionary Paris, were exclusively associated with French food by the early nineteenth century. Still, few restaurants existed in the United States until the 1840s and 1850s, when New York City's restaurant scene exploded. By 1869, one writer counted over five thousand restaurants in the city ranging from fine establishments such as Taylor's and Delmonico's to subterranean oyster cellars and lunch counters. "To a stranger, New-York must seem to be perpetually engaged in eating," he marveled.[33]

Fifth Avenoodles led the charge in this epicurean revolution, at least according to their critics. Ridiculing avenoodles for their taste for fine food was yet another way to highlight their effeminacy. When a group of wealthy New Yorkers organized themselves into a "Vigilance Committee" in 1859, their political enemies ridiculed them as "Fifth Avenoodles" who wore silk gloves, silk stockings, and pumps, and would "choke you with canvass-back and smother you in old Heidsieck." Canvasback ducks were a beloved game bird eaten by eastern elites at restaurants, and Heidsieck was a luxurious brand of champagne. Another article ridiculed these "Fifth Avenoodle Committees" as "Champagne-Verzenay-Silk-Stocking combinations."³⁴ Several news stories poked fun at the avenoodles' enthusiasm for buying up the fine silver and china of impoverished noblemen and deposed monarchs. Even their own debts failed to stop avenoodles from gastronomic self-indulgence. An anecdote circulated about an avenoodle who hosted a dinner party costing a thousand dollars but who could not pay his butcher bill.³⁵

Critics lambasted avenoodles for their excessive drinking of alcohol. Drunkenness defied the norms of masculine self-control requisite for a virtuous republic. An 1854 news item titled "Fashionable Drunkenness," reprinted many times over, reported on the new "habit among our Fifth Avenoodles, of getting 'a little tight' at parties." The author recommended ostracizing young men who got "disgustingly drunk."³⁶ The suggestion fell flat. Drunkenness soon became a defining characteristic of avenoodledom.³⁷ According to a humorous anecdote printed repeatedly in 1863, after a dinner party, "a jolly Fifth-avenudle said to his guests, as the ladies left the room, 'let us understand each other; are we to drink like men, or like beasts?' The guests, somewhat indignant, exclaimed, 'Like men!' 'Then,' he replied, 'we are going to get jolly drunk, for brutes never drink more than they want.'" Avenoodles were also ridiculed for being too particular about their alcohol. They drank fashionable cocktails, like sherry cobblers, and spent their time debating the merits of dry wines and pale brandies.³⁸

The personal celebrity of Nathaniel Parker Willis helped to cement the association between Fifth Avenoodledom and epicureanism. Willis was a noted gourmand. His popular travel book *Pencillings by the Way* detailed his alimentary adventures at Paris's premier restaurants, seeking out the best dishes at Grignon's, Rochers de Cancale, and Les Trois Frères Provençaux. Willis continued his search for the finest foods when he returned to New York, often writing about food in the *Home Journal*.³⁹ He was frequently spotted at Delmonico's. Social critic George G. Foster wrote about seeing him at the restaurant:

> A tall, shapely man, daintily dressed, and in a style that lets peep out here and there an all-pervading and inextinguishable love for the beautiful, which even, as in woman, seeks to expend itself upon the dress. The upper part of his face, with the long, clustering, glossy ringlets, 'brown in shadow, golden in the sun,' has something cherubic in its expression—but the eye is small and sensual; and the irrepressible pout of the under-lip,

and the white, full-swelling throat, add at once mortality to the composition. He is, as perhaps he himself might not disdain to express it, a sort of human julep, composed of spirits and sugar, with a pungent flavor of the mint, which makes the very air spicy around him.[40]

Foster's portrait of Willis as an effeminate dandy highlighted womanly clothing, hairstyle, and features ("the white, full-swelling throat"), and culminated by likening him to a mint julep. In the Western artistic and literary tradition, women were often metaphorized as food, in the trope of the "edible woman."[41] Notably, Foster instead described Willis as an alcoholic drink, a *cock*tail to be precise.

Another popular midcentury writer, Charles Astor Bristed, rivaled Willis in combining a reputation for avenoodledom and epicureanism. A grandson of John Jacob Astor, the wealthiest man in New York City, Bristed was described as "half a dandy, half a scholar" by those who knew him. He wrote frequently about his native city, including a series of sketches about "the upper ten thousand" that he initially published under the pseudonym "A New Yorker" but later acknowledged in a letter to Willis published in the *Home Journal*.[42] A collection of these sketches had a frontispiece depicting Bristed, labeled with another of his pseudonyms, "Carl Benson," mixing a sherry cobbler for a friend. The image portrayed Bristed wearing a pinch-waisted, long-skirted jacket, along with tight trousers with a flashy striped design. The introduction promised a portrait of the "fast boy of Young America . . . whose great idea of life is dancing, eating supper after dancing, and gambling after eating supper." Bristed's own ideas differed little from the fast boys he characterized. Under the Benson name, he published perhaps the first American work of gastronomy: an 1848 essay titled "Table Aesthetics," which appeared in New York's *Knickerbocker* magazine. Bristed filled the essay with racy comments linking an interest in food with sexual hedonism. After describing the "genesiac powers" of truffles, for example, Bristed concluded, "Give whatever weight you may to the fact of its being an exotic and an erotic, it must be confessed to impart an exquisite flavor."[43] Like Willis, Bristed's food writing and dandy aesthetic linked epicureanism to male effeminacy and suspect sexuality.

Originally coined to describe a specific archetype of New York City dandy, the term *avenoodle* eventually expanded to encompass a wide range of meanings. In the 1860s and 1870s, writers increasingly used the

Fig. 2. Charles Astor Bristed, labeled as his authorial alter-ego, Carl Benson, dressed in the tight-fitting coat of an avenoodle, mixing a sherry cobbler, a popular nineteenth-century cocktail, for a male friend. C. Astor Bristed, *The Upper Ten Thousand* (New York: Stringer and Townsend, 1852), frontispiece. (Courtesy, Library of Congress)

term as a general descriptor for the city's wealthy class or those of "high social position." After an 1858 winter snowstorm, an article in the *New York Herald* extolled sleighing, which brought out "mechanics" and "Fifth avenoodles" alike—in other words, men from across the social spectrum.[44] Even as the term's use broadened, its pejorative valence persisted. Avenoodles were often equated with parvenus, or new money, who spent ostentatiously on the latest trends.[45] In the 1860s and 1870s, writers made fun of avenoodles' indulgence in trendy pets, entertainers, vacations, and real estate. Avenoodles were mocked for allegedly dyeing their lap-dogs green or pink in imitation of Parisian dandies. Another frequent complaint was over-the-top avenoodle weddings, such as brides and grooms getting married in hot-air balloons or importing their attire and invitations from Paris.[46]

The nouveau riche tendency to clamor after aristocracy also sparked charges of avenoodledom. Newspapers attacked the Fifth Avenoodles who bent over backward to entertain the Prince of Wales when he visited New York in the fall of 1860. A widely reprinted 1868 item, which appeared in newspapers in Baltimore, Louisville, Richmond, and Detroit, noted that "some of the Fifth avenoodles of New York are now dressing their male servants in scarlet breeches and cream-colored coats, in imitation of English snobbery." An 1874 news report from Naples, New York, accused Fifth Avenoodles of employing "carriages with liveried coachman and footman." An 1884 article in a Louisville, Kentucky, newspaper joked about American avenoodle families who married off their daughters to titles and felt "in the shade if they cannot announce an expected visit from 'our daughter, the Marchioness of Dryrot,' or 'our dear Countess Carbuncle.'" By the 1880s, the avenoodle had shifted from a type of dandy to a synonym for a "vulgar" rich person.[47]

Avenoodles likewise expanded beyond New York to encompass wealthy people who enjoyed the high life in towns and cities throughout the nation. As early as 1855, an advertisement for a satiric novel about Philadelphia high society, *Our First Families,* described it as a book in which "Fifth Avenoodles catch a first rate showing up." A Cleveland newspaper in 1865 complained about "Euclid Avenoodles," referring to the industrializing city's major thoroughfare, also known as "Millionaire's Row."[48] The *Chicago Evening Press* in 1867 complained about the pretensions of the city snob who "lives in an alley, and calls it an avenue," saying by that standard "fully half our people will have become Avenoodles." In Milwaukee, the wealthy denizens of Grand Avenue even copied the fashionable pronunciation "Avenoo," reinforcing their status as "Grand Avenoodles." Southerners picked up the term too. The *Richmond Daily Whig* complained about "Brooke Avenoodles."[49]

Some writers applied the term beyond the limits of the male sex. Initially, the avenoodle was a specifically male archetype. Nathaniel Parker Willis reputedly said that "gentlemen may be Avenoodles, but the ladies are Avenudities." This witticism alluded to "the decolette style of dress," or low necklines, in fashion among wealthy New York women by the late 1850s. Willis also referred to this feminine class as the "fifth avenudity." The amusing term circulated widely in articles about women's fashions. William Bobo referred to women who accompanied Fifth Avenoodles to the Abbey or Taylor's as "Avenudle daisies."[50] A book of minstrel songs published during the Civil War included a comic tune titled "The Fifth Avenoodle Belle," about a tradesman whose flashy clothes tricked a rich young woman into marrying him. On occasion, writers used "avenoodle" as a term for rich and fashionable women, without affixing a modifier like "daisy" or "belle." "A feminine Fifth Avenoodle in New York triumphs in three hundred dresses," reported another widely reprinted item.[51]

The "avenoodle" lost its categorical integrity as conceptualizations of sexuality underwent significant transformation. At the beginning of the 1850s, the relationship between male effeminacy and same-sex sexuality was ambiguous. By the early 1870s, sexologists began to describe male effeminacy as a fixed characteristic of men who were oriented toward sex with men. New queer archetypes that equated gender variance with homosexuality, such as the "fairy" and the "pansy," replaced the dandy.[52] The fairy's or the pansy's sexuality was explained by his gender variance. His womanly nature dictated his desire for male penetration. This new framework diverged from the idea of the avenoodle, a man whose effeminacy spoke both to his womanizing and to his potential for same-sex encounters. The Fifth Avenoodle thus proved a transitional figure between the macaroni and the homosexual.

Many characteristics of the avenoodle carried over to the homosexual. A proclivity to effeminate dress and a tendency toward gourmet tastes both became associated with homosexuality.[53] However, the gender anxieties provoked by men's consumerism in the industrializing economy of the late antebellum era gave way with the ascendance of the market. Spending money on ornamental commodities like watches, suits, and cars became popular strategies for signaling masculinity in the twentieth century, not suspicious evidence of effeminacy. In the twentieth century, excessive consumerism might mark a man as gauche or classless but it would not undermine his gender.[54] The Fifth Avenoodle was forgotten, a relic of a time when urbanization, industrialization, and shifting economic roles for middle-class men created anxieties around masculinity that ultimately resolved into a new gender order, which legitimized male consumerism while coding other "feminine" tastes, like gourmet cooking and tight-fitting clothing, as decisively homosexual.

Questions to Consider

1. What does the archetype of the Fifth Avenoodle reveal about the relationship between male effeminacy and sexuality in the mid-nineteenth century?
2. Should the avenoodle be understood as a queer identity category?

Notes

1. The article is collected in N. Parker Willis, *The Rag-Bag, a Collection of Ephemera* (New York: Charles Scribner's Sons, 1855), 28–31. Willis's article offers commentary on and a translation of an article that first appeared in New York City's Francophone newspaper *Le Courrier des États-Unis*. Willis's essay was republished in national newspapers, including "The New York Dandy Daguerreotyped," *Buffalo [NY] Daily Republic*, 1 May 1851.
2. Bryan C. Rindfleisch, "'What It Means to Be a Man': Contested Masculinity in the Early Republic and Antebellum America," *History Compass* 10, no. 11 (November 2012): 853.
3. Kelly Olson, "Masculinity, Appearance, and Sexuality: Dandies in Roman Antiquity," *Journal of the History of Sexuality* 23, no. 2 (May 2014): 182–205. This complaint was made about Willis; see Thomas N. Baker, *Sentiment and Celebrity: Nathaniel Parker Willis and the Trials of Literary Fame* (New York: Oxford University Press, 1999), 48. Young male retail clerks in the mid-nineteenth century also were accused of both "rapacious male sexuality and foppish unmanliness"; see Brian P. Luskey, "Jumping Counters in White Collars: Manliness, Respectability, and Work in the Antebellum City," *Journal of the Early Republic* 26, no. 2 (Summer 2006): 179.
4. On British macaronis, see Peter McNeil, "'That Doubtful Gender': Macaroni Dress and Male Sexualities," *Fashion Theory: The Journal of Dress, Body and Culture* 3, no. 4 (1999): 411–47, and Freya Gowrley, "Representing Camp: Constructing Macaroni Masculinity in Eighteenth-Century Visual Satire," *ABO: Interactive Journal for Women in the Arts, 1640–1830* 9, no. 1 (2019): art. 4. For American macaronis, see Kate Haulman, *The Politics of Fashion in Eighteenth-Century America* (Chapel Hill: University of North Carolina Press, 2011), 135–38.
5. Valerie Traub, "The Present Future of Lesbian Historiography," in *A Companion to Lesbian, Gay, Bisexual, Transgender, and Queer Studies*, ed. George E. Haggerty and Molly McGarry (Oxford: Blackwell, 2007), 124–45; Christy Stevens, "Symbols," in *Lesbian Histories and Cultures: An Encyclopedia*, ed. Bonnie Zimmerman (New York: Garland, 2000), 747.
6. The avenoodle has never been the subject of historical focus, but the term is briefly analyzed in Irving Lewis Allen, *The City in Slang: New York Life and Popular Speech* (New York: Oxford University Press, 1993), 22, 221.
7. Willis, *The Rag-Bag, a Collection of Ephemera*, 45–48.
8. Allen, *The City in Slang*, 20.
9. Winifred Morgan, *An American Icon: Brother Jonathan and American Identity* (Newark: University of Delaware Press, 1988), 86; Henry Abelove, "Yankee Doodle Dandy," *Massachusetts Review* 49, nos. 1–2 (Spring 2008):

13–21. Abelove argued that the term also connoted a masturbator (one who *yanks* his doodle).
10. "Politico-Editorial Noodles," *Yankee Doodle* 1, no. 11 (19 December 1846): 185; "Various Attempts 'To See the Elephant,'" *Yankee Doodle* 2 (1847): 148; Allen, *The City in Slang*, 221.
11. "A New Willicism," *Burlington [VT] Free Press*, 9 February 1857. A long list of Willicisms can be found in S. S. Haldeman, *American Dictionaries* (Baltimore: A. T. Bledsoe, 1869), 59–60.
12. "Town Talk," *New Orleans Times*, 13 June 1866.
13. William M. Bobo, *Glimpses of New York City by a South Carolinian (Who Had Nothing Else to Do)* (Charleston, SC: J. J. McCarter, 1852), 26, 50–51, 156, 168–77; Walt Whitman, "New York Dissected: Wicked Architecture," *Life Illustrated*, 19 July 1856, 93, The Walt Whitman Archive, https://whitmanarchive.org/published/periodical/journalism/tei/per.00270.html#n2. Footnote 2 indicates that the term "Fifth Avenoodledom" was not Whitman's coining but appeared earlier, in "Nathaniel Parker Willis," *United States Democratic Review* 33 (June 1854): 340–44.
14. "Snobs . . . Squirts . . . Noodles," *Yazoo [MS] Democrat*, 31 May 1854.
15. Gayle V. Fischer, *Pantaloons and Power: A Nineteenth-Century Dress Reform in the United States* (Kent, OH: Kent State University Press, 2001), 3–4, 19–23. Macaronis also wore pastel colors and eccentric patterns that stood out from the sober clothing then becoming normative for British men; see McNeill, "'That Doubtful Gender,'" 412.
16. Bobo, *Glimpses of New York City*, 26; "A Child of the Sun," *The Summer-Land: A Southern Story* (New York: Appleton, 1855), 161. Scholars have not identified the pseudonymous author of this novel, but the use of the term "avenoodle" raises the possibility that William M. Bobo wrote it.
17. Willis, *The Rag-Bag, a Collection of Ephemera*, 28–31.
18. Beverly Seaton, *The Language of Flowers: A History* (Charlottesville: University Press of Virginia, 1995), 2, 9, 17–35, 101.
19. McNeill, "'That Doubtful Gender,'" 440.
20. "Nathaniel Parker Willis," 341; Daniel R. Hundley, *Social Relations in Our Southern States* (New York: Henry B. Price, 1860), 177. The description comes from Hundley's section anatomizing the "cotton snob," whose hair style and perfume he likened to the Fifth Avenoodle.
21. J. Brander Matthews, "Nine Tales of a Cat: A Legend of Murray Hill," in *Lotos Leaves: Stories, Essays, and Poems by Members of the Lotos Club*, ed. John Brougham and John Elderkin (Boston: William F. Gill, 1875), 351; "Spice Box," *Lawrence [MA] American and Andover Advertiser*, 12 January 1871.
22. Wendy L. Rouse, *Public Faces, Secret Lives: A Queer History of the Women's Suffrage Movement* (New York: New York University Press, 2022), 15–36.

23. Baker, *Sentiment and Celebrity*, 48, 49; Elizabeth Robins Pennell, *Charles Godfrey Leland, a Biography* (Boston: Houghton Mifflin, 1906), 232.
24. *The Forrest Divorce Case: Catharine Norton Forrest vs. Edwin Forrest, Before the Superior Court of New York* (Boston: N.p., 1852).
25. "Nathaniel Parker Willis," 341; "Our Contributors—No. XI: Nathaniel Parker Willis," *Graham's Lady's and Gentleman's Magazine* 25, no. 4 (April 1844): 146; Baker, *Sentiment and Celebrity*, 170; Ed Madden, "Flowers and Birds," in *Gay Histories and Cultures*, ed. George E. Haggerty (New York: Garland, 2000), 331. Nathaniel Parker Willis had angered his sister by withholding support for her literary career and calling her talentless.
26. Baker, *Sentiment and Celebrity*, 45–48; Nathaniel Parker Willis to George James Pumpelly, September 1827, quoted in Baker, *Sentiment and Celebrity*, 33.
27. Bobo, *Glimpses of New York City*, 29, 51; "Disorderly House in an Up-Town Neighborhood," *Brooklyn [NY] Daily Eagle*, 7 August 1860; "The New York Dandy Daguerreotyped"; "A Child of the Sun," *The Summer-Land*, 161.
28. "Snobs . . . Squirts . . . Noodles."
29. McNeill, "'That Doubtful Gender,'" 418.
30. David M. Halperin, "Is There a History of Sexuality?" *History and Theory* 28, no. 3 (October 1989): 257–74. See also Kim M. Phillips and Barry Reay, *Sex Before Sexuality: A Premodern History* (Malden, MA: Polity, 2011). Deleuze quoted in Elspeth Probyn, "Beyond Food/Sex: Eating and an Ethics of Existence," *Theory, Culture and Society* 16, no. 2 (1999): 215.
31. "New-York Daguerreotyped," *Putnam's Monthly Magazine of American Literature, Science, and Art* 1, no. 4 (April 1853): 131–34; Bobo, *Glimpses of New York City*, 175.
32. Katharina Vester, *A Taste of Power: Food and American Identities* (Berkeley: University of California Press, 2015), 46. See also Keith Stavely and Kathleen Fitzgerald, "Plainness and Virtue in New England Cooking," in *Food and Morality: Proceedings of the Oxford Symposium on Food and Cookery 2007*, ed. Susan R. Friedland (Blackawton, UK: Prospect Books, 2008), 269–78, and Meg Muckenhoupt, *The Truth About Baked Beans: An Edible History of New England* (New York: New York University Press, 2020).
33. Mark McWilliams, *Food and the Novel in Nineteenth-Century Literature* (Lanham, MD: Rowman and Littlefield, 2012), xiv; Cindy R. Lobell, "'Out to Eat': The Emergence and Evolution of the Restaurant in Nineteenth-Century New York City," *Winterthur Portfolio* 44, nos. 2–3 (Summer–Autumn 2010): 193–211; Junius Henri Browne, *The Great Metropolis; A Mirror of New York* (Hartford, CT: American Publishing, 1869), 260–66.

34. "Both Branches of the Democratic Party," *Burlington Free Press*, 1 November 1859; "Fifth Avenoodle Committees," *Sunday Dispatch* (New York), 29 December 1861. The label "Fifth Avenoodles" continued to occasionally be used for wealthy factions of New York City Democrats over the next two decades. See "Letter from New York," *Daily Evening Bulletin* (San Francisco), 22 September 1860; "Isaac C. Delaplaine," *Chicago Tribune*, December 14, 1860; and "An Organ Out of Tune," *St. Louis Globe-Democrat*, 6 September 1879.
35. "Aristocracy 'Run Down at the Hells,'" *Baton Rouge [LA] Tri-Weekly Gazette and Comet*, 2 October 1859; "A Fifth Avenoodle," *Bangor [ME] Daily Whig and Courier*, 2 March 1872; "Our New York Letter," *St. Johnsbury [VT] Caledonian*, 26 January 1877.
36. "Fashionable Drunkenness," *Rock Island [IL] Weekly Argus*, 29 March 1854.
37. See, for example, "Tragical Fate of Ali Ghalib Pacha, Son-in-Law of the Sultan," *Frank Leslie's Illustrated Newspaper* (New York), 11 December 1858.
38. Bobo, *Glimpses of New York City*, 27; "Primitive Animalism," *National Reformer* (Sheffield, UK), 22 February 1863. This anecdote is also attributed to the Irish playwright Richard Sheridan, who died in 1816; see Lionel Strachey, ed., *The World's Wit and Humor: An Encyclopedia of the Classic Wit and Humor of All Ages and Nations*, 15 vols. (New York: Review of Reviews, 1910), 7:219. The anecdote appears to have circulated prior to the emergence of "avenoodle."
39. N. Parker Willis, *Pencillings by the Way: Written During Some Years of Residence and Travel in Europe* (1835; New York: Charles Scribner's Sons, 1856), 112; Maura D'Amore, "Suburban Men at the Table: Culinary Aesthetics in the Mid-Century Country Book," in *Culinary Aesthetics and Practices in Nineteenth-Century American Literature*, ed. Monika Elbert and Marie Drews (New York: Palgrave Macmillan, 2009), 21–33.
40. George G. Foster, *New York in Slices: By an Experienced Carver* (New York: William H. Graham, 1849), 74.
41. Joan Smith, *Hungry for You: From Cannibalism to Seduction* (London: Random House UK, 1996), 83–142; Margaret Atwood, *The Edible Woman* (Toronto: McClelland and Stewart, 1969).
42. "Art. II—Five Years in an English University," *North American Review* 75, no. 156 (July 1852): 47.
43. Charles Astor Bristed, *The Upper Ten Thousand: Sketches of American Society* (New York: Stringer and Townsend, 1852), 10; Carl Benson [Charles Astor Bristed], "Table Aesthetics," *Knickerbocker; or, New-York Monthly Magazine of Literature, Art, Politics and Society* 31, no. 4 (April 1848): 302.

William Bobo described the sherry cobbler as a favorite drink of avenoodles, in Bobo, *Glimpses of New York City*, 27.

44. George Washington Bungay, *Pen and Ink Portraits of the Senators, Assemblymen, and State Officers of the State of New York* (Albany: J. Munsell, 1857), 11; "The Sleighing Yesterday," *New York Herald*, 22 February 22, 1858.
45. This attack on avenoodles as new money dated back to Bobo, *Glimpses of New York City*, 173. See also "New York Correspondence," *Cleveland Daily Herald*, 26 December 1856.
46. "Ristori," *Daily Ohio Statesman* (Columbus), 28 November 1866; "The Summer Season," *Times Union* (Brooklyn, NY), 11 July 1867; "Rural Felicity," *Weekly Caucasian* (Lexington, MO), 26 July 1873; "A Princess in India," *Burlington Free Press*, 9 October 1882; "The Piccolomi Excitement," *New York Daily Star*, 27 October 1885; "Mrs. Banks's Reception," *Times-Picayune* (New Orleans), 28 April 1865; "A High Old Time," *Gold Hill [NV] Daily News*, 14 December 1865; "The Fifth Avenoodles," *Buffalo [NY] Commercial*, 10 December 1866.
47. "Letter from New York"; "Why We Honor the Prince," *Cincinnati Daily Press*, 26 September 1860; "Some of the Fifth," *Baltimore Sun*, 15 May 1868; *Louisville Daily Journal*, 18 May 1868; *Daily Dispatch* (Richmond, VA), 18 May 1868; *Detroit Free Press*, 6 June 1868; *Naples Record* (New York), 3 January 1874; "Marrying Titles," *Evening World* (New York), 14 November 1888. See also "Bric-a-Brac," *Ohio County News* (Hartford, KY), 6 January 1875, and "Multiple New Items," *Galveston Daily News*, 7 May 1885.
48. "Our First Families," *Spirit of the Age* (Raleigh, NC), 1 August 1855; "An English Tit-for-Tat," *Cleveland Daily Leader*, 13 November 1865. See also Danielle Rose, "Millionaire's Row: Cleveland's Famous Euclid Avenue," Cleveland Historical, https://clevelandhistorical.org/items/show/10.
49. "Avenoodledom," *Chicago Evening Post*, 15 May 1867; "A Genius for Affairs," *Daily Dispatch* (Richmond, VA), 6 January 1868; "Brevities," *Milwaukee Daily Sentinel*, 5 December 1876; "City Items: Brooke Avenue," *Richmond [VA] Daily Whig*, 26 January 1861.
50. "A New York Paper," *Evening Star* (Washington, DC), 21 May 1857; "A New Willicism." The term "avenudities" also appeared in "High Life in Gotham from the Top of a Coachman's Box," *Sunday Delta* (New Orleans), 5 April 1857; "Letter from Boston," *Times-Picayune*, 8 November 1857; "A New Rage," *Baton Rouge Tri-Weekly Gazette and Comet*, 4 April 1858; "Various Items," *Summit County Beacon* (Akron, OH), 7 December 1859; and Bobo, *Glimpses of New York City*, 156.
51. "The Fifth Avenoodle Belle," in *Frank Converse's "Old Cremona" Songster* (New York: Sick and Fitzgerald, 1863), 61–62; "A Feminine Fifth Avenoodle," *Wheeling [WV] Daily Intelligencer*, 24 January 1868; *Muscatine [IA]*

Weekly Journal, 13 March 1868. The earliest reference to a female avenoodle is "The Lady's Page," *Ballou's Dollar Monthly Magazine* 4, no. 1 (July 1856): 92.
52. George Chauncey, *Gay New York: Gender, Urban Culture, and the Making of the Gay Male World, 1890–1940* (New York: Basic Books, 1994).
53. Rachel Hope Cleves, *Lustful Appetites: An Intimate History of Good Food and Wicked Sex* (Cambridge, UK: Polity Books, 2024).
54. Lizabeth Cohen, *A Consumer's Republic: The Politics of Mass Consumption in Postwar America* (New York: Knopf, 2003).

Black Women, Illness, and Refinement in Antislavery Literature

STEPHANIE J. RICHMOND

A TEN-YEAR-OLD girl stood beside her siblings with a bundle of clothing over her shoulder. Her mother had died, and her father could no longer keep all his children at home. Her younger brother cried and begged her to stay, but she had to walk away from her family to work for a White family in town. She was Elleanor Eldridge, daughter of a Black Revolutionary War veteran and his Indigenous wife.[1] Elleanor's story was one of many captured by antislavery activists before the American Civil War.

Antislavery writers crafted biographies of Black women to illustrate the horrors of slavery, but such books also demonstrated the difficulties that Black women faced as free people. Two overarching, interconnected themes emerge from the stories: the power of faith to transform lives and the isolation that free Black women faced once they "rose above" their original status. Stories emphasized how their subjects, because of their race, could not join the ranks of godly White women even as they no longer fit within the Black community. In many tales, illness featured as prominently as race, particularly among those of women who died from consumption or, in post-nineteenth-century terminology, tuberculosis. Typified as an illness that, ironically, enhanced women's beauty, frailty, and pallor, consumption appeared in literature as transformative. Black women, particularly mixed-race women—"mulattas"—became figures for whom race was secondary to illness and spirituality.

Development of the consumptive tragic mulatta character may be traced through memorials and biographies of Black women, including the memoirs of Chloe Spears and Elleanor Eldridge (published as Sunday school literature), and memorials to abolitionist Susan Paul. Semi-autobiographical novels written by Black women, including Harriet Jacobs's *Incidents in the Life of a Slave Girl* and Harriet Wilson's *Our Nig*, also developed the motif to appeal to antebellum readers, specifically White women.[2] The tragic, consumptive mulatta character merged two literary tropes that arose from disparate genres written and read by White women: antislavery literature, and serialized romance and pulp novels (which originally ran in newspapers). By intertwining the tropes in writings and stories about Black women, White authors redeemed their subjects through motifs easily recognized by audiences, thereby obscuring the real motivations and experiences of the Black women about whom they wrote.

Although historians and literary critics use memorials, biographies, and memoirs as sources of information about Black women's lives and the racialized perspectives of White antebellum women, such primary sources, particularly memorials, have received little critical attention from historians. In the 1970s, John Blassingame cautioned his peers about using White-authored sources to understand Black American lives because some "contained so many of the editor's views that there was little room for the testimony of the fugitive." Still, scholars have not been particularly critical in employing narratives of Black women. Religion scholar Laurie F. Maffly-Kipp examined community memoirs and memorials in her *Setting Down the Sacred Past* (2010), but her community-centered focus does not adequately include Black women's memorials or voices. Historians Catherine Adams and Elizabeth H. Pleck's *Love of Freedom* (2010) used memorials as sources on the lives of Black women in colonial and early republican New England, but they did not grapple with the narratives' problems as sources written by White women.[3]

Literary scholars have paid more attention to the challenges posed by such sources and to the figure of the tragic mulatta, examining her in antislavery and popular fiction throughout the Atlantic world. Lois Brown surveyed memorials of several Black women who lived and died in New England, including Chloe Spears, arguing that such narrative writers attempted to rewrite the history of New England slavery by erasing its horrible past, focusing on individuals' transcendence of enslavement without recognizing enslavement's continued role in their personal developments. In *The "Tragic Mulatta" Revisited* (2004), Eve Allegra Raimon concluded that, as a literary trope, "the 'tragic mulatto' allows for considerations of such important questions as whether mixed-race slaves can achieve freedom and independence, whether they can become integrated into the larger culture. . . . It functions as a device to investigate what place mixed-race persons can occupy in the new republic and indeed whether the Union itself can survive such profound divisions over race." Kimberly S. Manganelli expanded this idea in *Transatlantic Spectacles of Race* (2012), claiming that the tragic mulatta's body was problematic: as mixed-race rather than White, she was depicted as sexually available by default. She and her story became spectacles to be consumed. Karen Sánchez-Eppler's groundbreaking *Touching Liberty* (1993) elaborated on intersections of abolitionism and feminism in nineteenth-century abolitionist depictions of Black women's bodies. She argued that although abolitionist literature appeared mutually supportive, it was ultimately discriminatory and exploitative. Scholars of Black women abolitionists and writers emphasized ways in which Black authors subverted and used prevailing literary tropes to illuminate realities of Black life. Literary scholar P. Gabrielle Foreman, for example, noted that mixed-race characters written by Black authors often signaled the vulnerability of their mothers, not the inheritance of Whiteness.[4]

Literature on illness was also very popular in the nineteenth century, with "consumption" a catch all term for any wasting illness, including tuberculosis. The figure of the consumptive woman also appeared in a variety of literary genres in the late 1830s and early 1840s, coinciding with the rise in antislavery literary production. In *Tuberculosis and Victorian Literary Imagination* (2011), Katherine Byrne explored tuberculosis as a trope in Victorian British literature, concluding that society viewed the disease as transformative, not only physically but morally and spiritually. She found that in novels such as Elizabeth Gaskell's stories of working-class invalids, the disease elevated protagonists' social status and "brings traces of nobility to even its poorest sufferers."[5] Many Black American women, stricken by consumption, received praise for their continued efforts to end slavery and, after their deaths, received memorials for their sacrifices for noble causes. They became celebrated as examples of Black womanhood. Only in their illnesses and deaths did they earn the recognition of wider antislavery audiences.

As subjects of illness and death, Black women—or more precisely, literary representations of Black women—became objects of "voyeuristic consumerism." Historian Carol Lasser coined this term to describe the attitude many abolitionists in the 1830s took toward the sexual exploitation of enslaved women and the ways in which they centered nudity and sexual assault when describing enslaved women's lives. Lasser argued that such eroticized voyeurism receded in the 1840s as abolitionists grappled with internal struggles and played respectability politics.[6]

Building on the historiographical foundation laid by Lasser, Foreman, and other scholars, I trace the ways in which abolitionist writers transformed their early sexual voyeurism into stories of moral and racial uplift, and how they shifted the voyeuristic gaze from sexual predation to the impact of illness on the Black female body, justifying and shaping how their reading audiences understood the horrors and long-term impacts of enslavement. Abolitionist voyeurism did not go away: authors buried it beneath a veneer of evangelical Christianity and interest in the body, health, and illness. Black authors such as Harriet Wilson and Harriet Jacobs specifically understood the tensions between the voyeuristic gaze and White middle-class evangelical interests. They used that knowledge to subvert the standard narrative and sell books.

The figure of the tragic, consumptive mulatta continued a process of stripping women of kinship and the status conveyed by motherhood that had begun with the transatlantic slave trade. As Jennifer L. Morgan outlined in *Reckoning with Slavery* (2021), colonizers, enslavers, and traffickers justified commodification of people of African descent by framing Black women as capable of reproduction without the status that motherhood and kinship conveyed in the early modern Atlantic world.[7] This calculated cultural excision has had deep implications in American culture, implications that we still struggle as a society to untangle and repair. As on plantations and the auction block, nineteenth-century authors replicated the separation of Black women from their families and their status as mothers. Even in the work of authors who advocated for the end of slavery, Black women became kinless, motherless, and childless when, in fact, they were at the center of close-knit and large families.

Such literary portraits contrasted with contemporary ideals of motherhood—the cult of true womanhood and its earlier version, republican motherhood—which situated American women's identity solely in relationship to their families. Black women were not depicted as tied to family as were their White counterparts. The stories that White abolitionists told about Black women whom they had worked alongside, known, or simply read about twined literary themes with reality, categorizing women who were significantly more complex with stylized, simplified monoliths.

The voyeuristic abolitionist gaze became layered atop the literary trope of the victimized mixed-race woman, and it requires historians to interrogate the assumptions, literary license, and innuendo to find Black women's voices and experiences. Through the lens of both the tragic mulatta narrative and the tragic consumptive, we can tease out how these literary tropes extended out of the texts and unpack the ways in which reality and literary license intersect in such sources.

IN 1832, James Loring, the largest antislavery publisher in Boston, printed "The Memoir of Mrs. Chloe Spear," written by a "Lady of Boston."[8] The memoir relates the life story of a woman brought from Africa to Boston and enslaved. Her religious devotion and hard work impressed her enslaver, eventually leading to baptism and freedom. Despite marrying a man who did not share her values, Chloe Spear developed a successful business as a laundress and supported her family. In her old age, after her husband's death, she opened her home to religious meetings, created a religious community in Boston, and, despite or even because of illness and infirmity from years of work, became a pillar of the Second Baptist Church. The memorial depicts Spear as a woman whose suffering elevated her to a higher spiritual plane.

One of Spear's White neighbors and a fellow member of Second Baptist Church, Mary Webb, possibly authored the memorial. Webb was an advocate of antislavery and religious education in Boston's African American community, including helping to open a Sunday school for Black children in 1816. She knew Spear from church and probably had read a short account of Spear's life in the *Massachusetts Baptist Missionary Magazine*, written by Reverend Thomas Baldwin of the Second Baptist Church.[9]

Webb also had personal reasons to sympathize with Spear, having been confined to a wheelchair since contracting a "usually fatal" illness as a child. She depended on her parents and then a married sister for her entire life, and she was able to devote time to religious and reform activities because of her family's financial stability.[10] As an aging and disabled woman who could barely walk a few steps, Webb sympathized with pain and illness in others, but she also wrote through the lens of her own racial and financial privilege and, despite her disability, her own general good health.

Spear's religious adherence was the first trait that separated her from other Black figures in the memoir, most notably her husband, who Webb depicted as a spendthrift interested only in parties and fine clothing. Webb framed Spear's religious devotion as making her more feminine, even as an older woman. Webb reported that a "Christian" visitor who heard Spear speak said, "She is black, but comely." Spear's lack of education also was evident, as when Webb transcribed a speech that Spear made as given in broken English and full of dropped consonants. Despite Spear's educational shortcomings, however, she was a powerful and widely appreciated orator, as many "found it pleasant and profitable to . . . converse with her."[11]

By this point in her life, Spear had lost her husband, her children, and all her grandchildren except one. Spear emerges as a tragic figure in the story—an aging, lonely woman—effectively forced by Webb into the role of the tragic mulatta whose religion trumped her race, age, and life experience. Webb recounted how Spear's religious faith brought White women to her home and inspired them to call her a friend, even as she continued to treat them with a deference that belied those friendships.[12] We cannot know what Spear thought of the middle-class White women who took tea with her, but Webb used the example to frame Spear's racial metamorphosis.

Spear's illness grounded her work. She dried laundry in her bedroom at night, seemingly leaving her vulnerable to rheumatism as she aged. Webb recounted that Spear suffered from attacks of rheumatism every winter, and "some of her fingers were drawn double with the violence of the disorder." She endured the pain with Christian fortitude: "On recovering so as to be able to participate again in the public worship and ordinances of God's house, she seemed filled with gratitude and holy joy." Webb, although likely sympathetic to Spear's pain, cast the pain as a morally uplifting experience, one that left her subject full of gratitude and joy, a theme of uplift that continued through the last chapter of the book. As Webb described Spear's later life, she quoted from the original biography: "As she advanced in life, she seemed to ripen for glory. Few Christians with whom we have been acquainted, have appeared to maintain so near a walk with God, or to enjoy so much of heaven. During her last sickness, which was of several months continuance, she was favoured with an almost uninterrupted peace of Mind." In Spear's final months of illness, Webb dropped the colloquial speech patterns when quoting Spear and depicted her words as fluent and echoing patterns of speech in the Bible.

By employing new speech patterns and changing descriptions of Spear's mannerisms from subservient to those of a woman who was still humble but "comely" and eloquent, Webb emphasized Spear's "ripening."[13]

Webb's conclusions, borrowed from Reverend Baldwin's earlier, shorter account, established precedent for how future biographers conceptualized Spear's illness as imbuing her with a peace of mind and a closeness to God that was visible to observers. Illness provided a vehicle to fulfill Spear's spiritual quest, elevating her above others still striving to find spiritual certainty.

Spear faced a lifetime of struggle to educate herself, support her family once freed, and in her old age live with a degenerative illness. That her biographers spun her final months of pain and suffering to signify the reward for a lifetime of hard work and struggle mirrors a notable literary arc of the era. Elizabeth Gaskell, Charles Dickens, and other popular nineteenth-century authors created characters who suffered from lifelong illnesses and poverty. Victorian-era literature touted the idea that illness—particularly conditions that kept sickly and incapacitated women confined to the home—morally and spiritually elevated the sufferer. Few novelists experienced such illness, suffering, and poverty themselves. (Mary Webb did live with a disability, but her family's wealth insulated her from poverty.) Webb's biography of Spear offered an early nonfictional engagement with themes previously addressed in novels. Her familiarity with the trope pervades the memoir and shaped its messages, making the life of a woman of color familiar and accessible to White middle-class readers.[14]

While emphasizing Spear's infirmity and spirituality, Webb obscured her subject's connections to family and community. Webb hardly mentioned Spear's children, and she made Spear's husband a minor and antagonistic character. Spear's entrepreneurship, family ties, and community are stripped from her in the narrative. Spear, as a Black woman entrepreneur, would have served as an example for her community. As an elder and a religious woman, she also likely served as a mentor and surrogate mother and grandmother to her neighbors and extended family network. Even after most of her own kin had passed, Spear would likely have retained deep connections to the community in which she lived and worked. Ignoring all those ties, Webb centered Spear in her connection to the White Christian community: the main relationships Webb develops in the memorial are between Spear and White women. Spear's position as a Black woman in Boston's Black community is absent, her roles as mother, wife, and business owner overwritten by the trope of the tragic consumptive.

In 1838, Elleanor Eldridge, a free woman of African and Native American ancestry who lived in Rhode Island, became the subject of *The Memoir of Elleanor Eldridge,* coauthored by antislavery activist and author Frances Harriet Whipple.[15] Eldridge worked in a variety of women's trades, saving enough money to eventually purchase a dwelling in Providence, where she lived and rented out apartments. According to the *Memoir,* Eldridge fell sick with typhus while traveling for work, becoming so ill that her mortgage-holder believed she had died. When informed of his mistake, he allowed her to continue the original mortgage terms, but when she left town again, this time to care for a family stricken by cholera, he sold the house out from under her. Eldridge wanted to raise funds to repurchase the property, so when Whipple approached her with the idea of a biography, she accepted. Unlike Spear and the other women discussed in this essay, Eldridge did not suffer from a deadly illness. She was alive and healthy at the time her biography hit the market.

Still, disease helped to define her reputation. In the waning years of the cholera epidemic of the 1830s, her ability to continue working as a nurse despite her bout of typhus elevated her as a hard worker and selfless individual. Death runs through the work: Eldridge lost her mother when she was only ten years old, her siblings fell ill with an unnamed disease, and her nieces and nephews died from poisoning. Unlike other illness-driven narratives, the *Memoir* emphasizes Eldridge's strength and abled-ness. She worked as a nurse, contracted and overcame typhus multiple times, and traveled from home to treat patients suffering from cholera. Whipple remarked on Eldridge's "vigorous constitution" as she recovered from her first bout of typhus, and the narrative depicts her repeated employments as a nurse and aid to ill family members as "skillful and fearless." Whipple often compared Eldridge's physical strength to her moral strength, determination, and upright character.[16]

Yet, to replicate the narrative arc that seemed most successful with audiences, Whipple was willing to bend the truth. For example, she rearranged the order of events that led to the loss of Eldridge's property, and she compressed the chronology. According to court records, Eldridge was in Providence when the mortgagee sued for nonpayment.

Furthermore, three months passed between the seizure of Eldridge's property for unpaid debt and when it was sold at public auction. Eldridge's case against her mortgagee for the return of her furniture and personal effects dragged on much longer than Whipple reported. Using the memoir as a vehicle for discussions about the importance of hard work and morality, Whipple clearly hoped to downplay financial failure in the narrative arc, and she focused instead on Eldridge's illness and devotion to nursing cholera patients. Whipple's own experiences as a teenager, when she lost family members to illness, likely prompted her to express gratitude for skilled nurses.[17]

Although titled a memoir, the narrative of Eldridge's life was not written in the first person. Instead, Whipple acted as narrator, depriving Eldridge of agency and voice. Whipple apparently based her research on copies of letters and other written materials, raising questions about the extent of Eldridge's cooperation with the project. Much like Webb's memorial of Chloe Spear, Whipple's memoir of Eldridge contained an ulterior motive: to raise money for Eldridge and to launch Whipple's writing career. The book succeeded on both accounts. Eldridge's property holdings doubled after the publication of the *Memoir,* and Whipple became a well-known author.[18]

The relationship between Whipple as narrator and Eldridge as both subject and gatekeeper of knowledge about her life was quite tense however. When Whipple could not get the information she wanted, she hinted at what she thought Eldridge hid from her. For example, Eldridge tried to conceal her courtship by her cousin Christopher, who later died in a shipwreck. When Whipple asked why Eldridge had never married despite being a "belle" as a young woman, Eldridge cryptically replied, "She had a cousin." Eventually, Eldridge gave Whipple access to some personal papers mixed in with household records and receipts, and Whipple printed several of Christopher's letters, offering fleeting insights into the relationship Eldridge wanted to keep private. When recounting Eldridge's reunion with Christopher, Whipple wrote, "And here, dear reader the curtain drops;—since it is not meet that the sacred scene should be witnessed by the cold eye of a stranger."[19]

Readers were to imagine the reunion, a voyeurism popular in nineteenth-century literature and akin to the conceit that abolitionist writers used to direct readers' attentions to the sexual abuse of enslaved women.[20] Whipple masked her lack of knowledge about this part of Eldridge's life by appealing to her readers' sense of propriety. Despite Eldridge's reticence about the kind of story that Whipple was telling, the author shaped the memoir to follow the standard narrative of the tragic mulatta, with a romantic tragedy at the center of the story. Eldridge works hard to create financial stability despite her difficult childhood and the loss of her one true love, but a case of typhus endangers her success and safety, and nearly takes her life. The heroine's illness brings about her downfall while also signaling her moral superiority: she selflessly cares for White former employers despite their contagious illnesses and the threats to her financial stability.

Four years later, Whipple, writing under her married name of Green, published *Elleanor's Second Book,* containing an abridged version of the full memoir and a long introduction explaining the origins of the first memoir, when mutual acquaintances who knew of Eldridge's situation sought to raise funds to help her as well as reveal the poor treatment that she had received. Illness features in the second memoir as well. Whipple recounted that the last time she saw Eldridge, "she was almost sick with a bad cold on the lungs, and so exhausted by her severe day's labor as to be hardly able to speak." Whipple then emphasized Eldridge's willingness to work hard with an account of how Eldridge was up before dawn and on her way to work. The depiction contrasts to longer descriptions of Whipple's White friends that she included in the introduction, friends endowed with "natural fitness" and "energy of character."[21] In Whipple's portrayal, Eldridge's illness derived from her need to work hard and her losses of both family and property.

In both biographies, Whipple forced Eldridge's life story into the arc of the traditional literary theme of the tragic consumptive mulatta, reorganizing events, hinting at salaciousness, and connecting themes of interracial identity, illness, and morality. Eldridge, who led a fascinating and singular life, emerged on the page as nearly interchangeable with any other interracial female character. In altering Eldridge's story, Whipple distorted her subject's true life, depriving her of the agency and self-determination she developed as a property-owning, single, mixed-race woman. As in Webb's treatment of Spear, Whipple centered Eldridge's relationships with White women and families, obscuring her position within the Black and Indigenous communities and her own family. We cannot fully understand Eldridge's life and her legal struggles without the context of the community she lived within, which would have been predominately Black and Indigenous. While we cannot know if Whipple made the choice to leave Eldridge's neighbors and wider network out of her life story, or, as with her relationship with Christopher, Eldridge chose not to open that part of her life to her White biographer, the lack of community presented in the two books is striking.

NARRATIVES WRITTEN by and about Susan Paul, an active member of the Boston Female Anti-Slavery Society and a teacher at a school for Black children, also engaged tropes of the tragic mulatta and the consumptive woman. Paul was the daughter of one of Boston's prominent Baptist ministers, but his early death left her to support her mother and nieces. As a fixture in Boston's antislavery scene, Paul's hard work and success as a teacher, particularly her direction of the Juvenile Choir and their performances at meetings and bazaars around Boston, received positive mentions in *The Liberator* and other antislavery newspapers. But she did not speak publicly, write often, or attract attention to herself (perhaps fearing treatment such as that of her fellow parishioner Maria W. Stewart, who was ostracized for her public comments).[22] In 1835, Paul published a memoir of one of her students, James Jackson, who died at age six, the first Black-authored memoir published in the United States and similar in style and message to Webb's memorial of Chloe Spear.

In her memorial to James Jackson, Paul used many of the tropes we see in other memorials to Black women, but unlike Webb and Whipple, Paul saw young Jackson as part of a large and caring family and community. His frailty and spiritual power are evident to his mother, siblings, and neighbors, whose testimony fills the pages of her memorial. Historian Lois Brown argues that Paul both used and subverted Victorian literary conventions to make her points about the impact of racism and slavery on Black children. Although the text is a memoir of a child, Mrs. Jackson plays a prominent role in the story. Mrs. Jackson was a widow with several children and is portrayed as a loving and understanding mother who tempers her children's piety with practicality and good sense.[23] The Jackson family is embedded in a vibrant Black community, with friends, neighboring families, doctors, and classmates filling the pages of James Jackson's memoir. Unlike the memorials written by White women, Susan Paul's memorial emphasizes the community that surrounded the vibrant young boy she remembered.

Paul's memorial to Jackson constructs a world of godly Black families in a thriving neighborhood that included Paul as the teacher, daughter of a minister, and friend to the families described in its pages. Paul's own struggles as the sole breadwinner supporting her mother, niece and nephew, and teenaged brother contrasted with her role as a teacher and community leader. The Paul family had a complicated relationship to the Black community they lived in and served. Thomas Paul resigned from the church he helped found over disputes regarding racial integration and politics, and his family remained partly estranged from much of Boston's Black community thereafter. Susan Paul, although employed by the Abiel Smith School, was not particularly active in the Black community outside of her work as a teacher and manager of the Juvenile Choir. Her association with the Boston Female Anti-Slavery Society apparently further damaged relationships with Black organizations as there are hints that others perceived her as aloof or acting too White. In fact, abolitionist and writer Anne Warren Weston noted that Paul was not seen as part of the Black community because of her close association with White abolitionists.[24]

Paul suffered from tuberculosis, which took her life in 1841, leaving her young brother to support their elderly and ill mother and their sister's young children. Her obituary, published in *The Liberator* and reprinted in other antislavery papers, described her as both the tragic mulatta, out of place because of her race, and as the consumptive woman whose disease lent her moral authority as she struggled to continue to work while ill. Paul's final act before retiring to her death bed, according to the obituary, was to preside over a table at the National Anti-Slavery Bazaar in December. Of her illness, one sentence summed it up: "Her disease was consumption."[25]

By 1841, "her disease was consumption" evoked in the minds of the readers an image of a woman wasting away physically while growing spiritually. In Paul's case, her final act of working at a charity bazaar reinforced the imagery of a selfless but wasting woman. Her obituary recounted a litany of troubles she faced as an adult, including poverty and growing responsibility for supporting her family, and praised her character in the face of such hardships: "Her lot, since she arrived at womanhood, has been a very severe one—marked all along by sorrow, disappointment, adversity; yet it was met with an indomitable spirit and extraordinary fortitude."[26] The obituary characterized Paul as a survivor, persisting through her trials despite toiling alone, and her story was made more poignant by a reminder that she had been engaged to a man who died only a year before she passed.

Focus on the losses that Paul sustained rather than the career successes she achieved as a teacher, choir leader, fundraiser, and activist cast her as a victim when she was, in fact, a trailblazing leader. This fit a common theme of literature: a Black woman could not be seen as a strong role model and breadwinner, only as a persistent victim of her circumstances. Lost in this version of Paul's life is her resilience, her agency in making choices about how she levied her allegiances and friendships to further the cause of antislavery, the support of her students, and her success in supporting her extended family.

Susan Paul is particularly illustrative of the power of the tragic consumptive mulatta ideal because she generated some of the antislavery and religious literature that shaped the tropes of consumptive Blackness. In her one published work, the *Memoir of James Jackson,* Paul described Jackson as a child with deep faith, generosity, and an old soul who contracted a terrible disease. Through his painful illness, he continued to believe in God and spread kindness and cheer. Paul relied heavily on the model of the tragic consumptive in memorializing her young student. Similarly, the power of that motif overshadowed her own life and work, including her leadership in helping to grow and integrate the Boston Female Anti-Slavery Society and the organization's annual Boston Anti-Slavery Bazaar.[27] The story of the tragic consumptive mulatta encapsulated her life. After her obituary appeared, she was often referenced in newspaper articles commemorating lost antislavery advocates, always depicted as a tragic figure. Paul's tenuous relationship with Boston's Black community makes it evident that the tropes of the tragic mulatta and tragic consumptive were meant for White audiences.

BLACK AMERICAN authors understood the power of literary conventions to sell books, direct readers' attentions, and signal intended audiences for a novel. But as historians and literary critics have rediscovered more early African American literature, Black female authors have received greater recognition for challenging literary conventions and stereotypes to push back against prevailing narratives about race, gender, and morality in the early United States. Harriet Jacobs, for example, was particularly astute in her use of silences to justify her right to tell her story and strengthen her position. Harriet Wilson in *Our Nig* grappled with questions of religion and morality, framing religion as a tool of both oppression and liberation in order to signal African Americans as "equal descendants of Adam, mirroring his power."[28] Both Jacobs and Wilson flipped prevailing paradigms by positioning mothers of mixed-race children as "fallen" figures in their novels, opening up the question of whether it was better to be a victim or to willingly engage in an extramarital relationship to preserve one's bodily autonomy. Their conclusions were vastly different and spoke directly to the role of race in women's agency. Despite their different conclusions regarding the role of the fallen woman in their novels, both Jacobs and Wilson wrote about unmarried mothers to complicate the figures of the tragic mulatta and the tragic consumptive as they had been constructed in White-authored works.

In 1859, Wilson published *Our Nig*, a novelized autobiography that many scholars interpret as a response to *Uncle Tom's Cabin*. The main character, Frado, is the daughter of a poor White woman and her Black husband. After her father's death from consumption, her mother abandons Frado with a neighboring White family with a reputation for cruelty, the Bellmonts. Illness pairs with goodness and faith throughout the novel. Frado's father is a kind and good person, lost to consumption. Jane and James, the two Bellmont children who are kind to Frado, are both sickly. Frado falls ill when she selflessly tends to James in his final months.

Wilson employed tropes of the tragic mulatta and the redemptive power of religion to explore the racialized world in which Frado lives. After bouts of sickness, Frado begins to accept Christianity, despite being forbidden to attend church or read the Bible. She muses aloud about how she does not want to be saved or go to heaven if Mrs. Bellmont, the cruel neighbor who takes her in, would be there. She searches for faith during difficult times, at one point asking, "*Is* there a heaven for the Black? She knew there was one for James, and Aunt Abby, and all good White people; but was there any for blacks?"[29] From the point of her questioning the existence of heaven, which happens midway through the story, Wilson paralleled Frado's physical weakness and suffering with her spiritual questioning, both of which become more intense as James approaches death. Through faith and illness, Frado escapes the clutches of Mrs. Bellmont. Frado's faith leads her to discuss her situation with Mr. Bellmont and to seek out pious women beyond the Bellmont family, women who take her in when she becomes too ill to work. Through her faith, Frado is both saved from her illness and from her suffering in the Bellmont household.

In *Our Nig*, Wilson played with what, by 1859, were strongly established literary conventions, making the broad outlines of her novel fit the tropes but turning those models on their heads. Wilson subverted the usual behaviors and patterns of the tragic mulatta and the tragic consumptive to highlight the problems of these tropes. Frado's faith comes to her with difficulty, and in her struggle to convert she openly questions the Christianity of White people, including the cruel Mrs. Bellmont and her daughter Mary, and even those who acted kindly, such as Aunt Abby and a minister. Frado remarks that "it was all for white people."[30] Wilson subverted the tragic mulatta narrative, casting Frado not as the child of rape but as the daughter of a legally married White woman and Black man. Frado's mother resents her and places her in the service of the cruel Mrs. Bellmont. But this protagonist does not bear her burdens quietly. Instead, Frado fights back, enlisting the aid of the Bellmont men in defending herself. Although a victim of poor parenting and a cruel mistress, Frado seizes her own agency and makes her own decisions once she is old enough to do so. Although Frado never marries, she is a caregiver and businesswoman, and her story has a positive trajectory rather than the arc of redemption and death that typified so many other memoirs.

Harriet Jacobs similarly used the novel form to tell her life story on her own terms. *Incidents in the Life of a Slave Girl* was published in 1861 under a pseudonym. Jacobs told the story of her abuse and harassment at the hands of the physician who owned her as a young woman, the difficult choices she made to evade his sexual predations, and her harrowing escape by spending seven years in her grandmother's attic. Admitting to willingly becoming a White man's mistress and bearing him two children, Jacobs opened herself to the social stigma of unwed motherhood. When she first escaped to Philadelphia, she confided in a minister who warned her not to let her unwed status become public knowledge, and Jacobs styled herself as a widow while she created her new life.[31] Jacobs's depiction of her life as a young woman otherwise neatly fits in the mold of the tragic mulatta who resists the moral and sexual depredations of enslavement through her own moral fortitude.

Yet Jacobs's discussion of her concubinage to a White man highlights the formulaic and unrealistic strictures of the tragic mulatta model. Her challenge of the literary model stems from her interactions with Harriet Beecher Stowe, whom Jacobs asked to write her biography. Stowe was initially sympathetic to Jacobs's situation as a supposedly widowed mother struggling to support her children. As Jacobs and Stowe became more well acquainted, Stowe began to ask questions about the origins of Jacobs's children as she prepared to hire Jacobs's daughter Louisa as a companion for her children. Once Stowe suspected that Louisa was born out of wedlock, she did not wish to hire her as a governess, and their relationship deteriorated as Stowe's skepticism and racist attitudes infuriated Jacobs. Ironically, the schism initiated Jacobs's career as an author. She began writing letters documenting some of her experiences and what she had witnessed while in Edenton, North Carolina. Newspapers published Jacobs's accounts, although she hesitated to reveal too much of her own situation. It was not until her grandmother passed away that Jacobs felt she should and could tell her full story on her own terms.[32]

Had Harriet Beecher Stowe been convinced to write Harriet Jacobs's life story, *Incidents in the Life of a Slave Girl* would likely fit fully into the literary tropes that Stowe employed so heavily in *Uncle Tom's Cabin*. Instead, Jacobs's autobiographical novel broke the narrative arc of the tragic mulatta. The beautiful, light-skinned protagonist who she called Linda Brent exercised agency. Faced with the sexual abuse of her enslaver, Brent adheres to her own morals and defends herself the only way she can: by accepting a less distasteful sexual relationship. Unlike other tragic mulatta characters, Brent negotiates the circumstances of her own fall from grace. After her fiancée is sent away by her enslaver, Brent attracts the attention of a young gentleman who courts her. Jacobs explained, "There is something akin to freedom in having a lover who has no control over you, except that which he gains by kindness and attachment." It was a metaphor for her own life. Jacobs's biographer Janet Yellin noted that we cannot know if Jacobs pursued Samuel Sawyer, the White man who fathered her children, or if he pursued her, but either way, the decision seems to have been hers to begin the relationship.[33] The choice to engage in a physical relationship outside of marriage and across racial lines shocked nineteenth-century audiences.

Illness became less central to Jacobs's writing than race or tragedy. However, the discussion of Brent's seven-year confinement in an attic has many parallels with mid-nineteenth-century consumption narratives. Tormented by insects, forced to spend most of her days lying quietly as her muscles atrophied, and breathing in the alternately stiflingly hot or freezing cold air, Brent suffers through the years in hiding. Jacobs's description of Brent's physical reactions to her confinement read much like descriptions of rheumatism and other illnesses. One winter her "limbs were benumbed by inaction, and the cold filled them with cramp."[34] Her physical suffering mirrors her emotional state, as she is separated from her children and only interacts with the adult members of her family late at night and in whispers. The impact of Brent's confinement on her body and her emotional state are central to building sympathy for Jacobs's fictional personification, demonstrating the lengths to which she would go to avoid being forced into concubinage. Despite her physical isolation, family is central to Brent's survival. Her grandmother and uncles hide her and make sure she can see her children regularly. They bring her news and food, provide her with the only link to the outside world, and ultimately help her connect with the Underground Railroad and freedom in the North. Family and the Black community are central to the story Jacobs crafted about her life.

In telling her story, Jacobs resisted the narrative that would likely have been placed on her life by a White author. She justified her choices to bear children out of wedlock and build a life as a single mother in the North. Instead of ending her story with an appeal for funds, Jacobs showed strength and resourcefulness as a Black mother, casting blame for her position as an unwed mother on White enslavers. Brent's role as a mother becomes all important in the conclusion of the novel: she has ensured that her daughter will not be a tragic mulatta. She is also never separated from the support of her family, even when in hiding. Her grandmother, uncles, aunts, brother, and other family members support her and her children through their trials and prevent White enslavers from ripping the family apart. Family, not faith, saves Linda Brent and her children.

Both Harriet Wilson's *Our Nig* and Harriet Jacobs's *Incidents in the Life of a Slave Girl* challenged the narrative arc found in many other stories of mixed-race women. Both authors confronted the voyeuristic gaze of antebellum readers and their fascination with the bodies and morals of Black women. By focusing on the agency of their main characters and the ways in which both Frado and Linda Brent navigate moral and physical perils to which they were subjected, Wilson and Jacobs called attention to the voyeurism and victimization underlying the construction of tragic mulatta and tragic consumptive characters. Unlike the memoirs of Chloe

Spears, Elleanor Eldridge, and Susan Paul, these two novelists assumed audiences would be well versed in nineteenth-century evangelical Christianity. Although the characters find religion over the course of the stories, the role that faith plays aligns secondary themes to larger narrative arcs of the evils of slavery and racism. Because the novels appealed to a slightly different audience than the Sunday school memoirs, the specifics of conversion became less central to convincing the audience of the message.

IMAGES OF consumptive Black women detail the intrusion of literary tropes into the ways in which the lives of real people were discussed when used for antislavery propaganda and religious uplift. When memoirs featured mixed-race women whose trials highlighted moral strength and their inability to fit into either Black or White society, they collided with the imagery of the consumptive woman. Her sins and moral failings were corrected by illness that led to a greater faith in God, building moral strength as physical strength failed. In the case of Chloe Spear, the trope situated her rheumatism as a vehicle for greater spirituality after a life of enslavement, hard labor, and a troubled marriage. As a narrative written early in the literary development of the tragic mulatta and consumptive woman tropes, her story does not fully engage the idea of illness leading to spiritual power, but the incipient idea is present enough. In 1838, Elleanor Eldridge's memoir depicted a living and not quite consumptive tragic mulatta whose White biographer employed the emerging narrative arc but rejected the accompanying model of the Protestant religious memoir. By the 1840s, the image of the consumptive woman was so deeply ingrained in American minds that only one sentence was needed to inform readers of the scene cast by Susan Paul's death. Each of these memoirs elided many of the realities of life, family, and community that supported and surrounded their subjects, replacing their subjects' stories with the framework of the White-run church and tropes of the tragic consumptive and tragic mulatta.

Susan Paul, Harriet Wilson, Harriet Jacobs, and other Black authors were well aware of the stereotypical Black characters in abolitionist and sentimental literature. They created characters who both fit the molds of the tragic mulatta and tragic consumptive and challenged the boundaries of those tropes. Paul's memoir of her student very closely followed conventions of the tragic consumptive, and it was heavily influenced by other

Sunday school texts for young children. Twenty years later, Frado and Linda Brent both broke the rules for Black, female protagonists, illustrating the damage that restrictive tropes could do to fiction and nonfiction accounts of women's lives. However, Black women authors did not isolate their characters from their extended families and Black communities. Instead, the main characters in Paul's memorial and Wilson's and Jacob's novels are depicted as embedded in extended families and communities who care for them through sickness and deprivation.

The literary tropes so popular in American and English literature in the early to mid-nineteenth century obscured the lives of Black women. By erasing or minimizing their roles as mothers, wives, daughters, and neighbors, White authors framed Black women as victims of circumstances in need of saving by White women. In novels written by Black authors, however, the main characters assert their own moral and personal autonomy and save themselves. As historians, we need to use our literary imaginations and rewrite the stories told about nineteenth-century Black women to recenter them in their own families, communities, and lives.

Questions to Consider

1. How did nineteenth-century writers craft narratives about Black women's bodies to affirm or challenge stereotypes about race, gender, and morality?
2. How did authors frame biographies, memoirs, and novelized autobiographies as texts meant for women readers?

Notes

1. Elleanor Eldridge and Frances Harriet Green, *Memoirs of Elleanor Eldridge* (Providence, RI: St. Albro-Printer, 1838), 24–25.
2. Literary scholars debate the amount of personal information in Wilson's *Our Nig*. Certainly, the overarching details of Wilson's life story match the contents of her novel, including being hired out as a young girl and her interactions with White employers. But how much of Fredo's personal journey is autobiographical remains under debate; see John Ernest, "Economies of Identity: Harriet E. Wilson's *Our Nig*," *PMLA* 190, no. 3 (May 1994): 424–25, and Barbara A. White, "'Our Nig' and the She-Devil:

New Information about Harriet Wilson and the 'Bellmont' Family" *American Literature* 65, no. 1 (March 1993): 43–45.
3. John W. Blassingame, "Using the Testimony of Ex-Slaves: Approaches and Problems," *Journal of Southern History* 41, no. 4 (1975): 478; Laurie F. Maffly-Kipp, *Setting Down the Sacred Past: African-American Race Histories* (Cambridge, MA: Harvard University Press, 2010); Catherine Adams and Elizabeth H. Pleck, *Love of Freedom: Black Women in Colonial and Revolutionary New England* (New York: Oxford University Press, 2010).
4. Lois Brown, "Memorial Narratives of African Women in Antebellum New England," *Legacy* 20, no. 1 (2003): 38–61; Eve Allegra Raimon, *The "Tragic Mulatta" Revisited: Race and Nationalism in Nineteenth-Century Antislavery Fiction* (New Brunswick, NJ: Rutgers University Press, 2004), 68–71; Kimberly S. Manganelli, *Transatlantic Spectacles of Race: The Tragic Mulatta and the Tragic Muse* (New Brunswick, NJ: Rutgers University Press, 2012), 152; Karen Sánchez-Eppler, *Touching Liberty: Abolition, Feminism, and the Politics of the Body* (Berkeley: University of California Press, 1993); Pier Gabrielle Foreman, *Activist Sentiments: Reading Black Women in the Nineteenth Century* (Urbana: University of Illinois Press, 2009), 5–6.
5. Katherine Byrne, *Tuberculosis and Victorian Literary Imagination* (New York: Cambridge University Press, 2011), 6, 12, 64.
6. Carol Lasser, "Voyeuristic Abolitionism: Sex, Gender, and the Transformation of Antislavery Rhetoric," *Journal of the Early Republic* 28, no. 1 (Spring 2008): 92–95.
7. Jennifer L. Morgan, *Reckoning with Slavery: Gender, Kinship, and Capitalism in the Early Black Atlantic* (Durham, NC: Duke University Press, 2021), 19–20.
8. The first edition of the Chloe Spears memorial was unsigned, and Loring attributed later editions to Rebecca Warren Brown. Historians recently uncovered a copy with Mary Webb's name attached, although other editions naming Maria Weston Chapman as the author also exist; see Margot Minardi, *Making Slavery History: Abolitionism and the Politics of Memory in Massachusetts* (New York: Oxford University Press, 2010), 201n32.
9. Brown, "Memorial Narratives of African Women in Antebellum New England," 51; Thomas Baldwin, "Biography of Mrs. Chloe Spear," *Massachusetts Baptist Missionary Magazine* 4, no. 5 (March 1815): 157–58. Author Mary Webb should not be confused with her contemporary Mary E. Webb, the Black abolitionists and activist; see Adams and Pleck, *Love of Freedom*, 73–75; Minardi, *Making Slavery History*, 113; and Albert L. Vail, *Mary Webb and the Mother Society* (Philadelphia: American Baptist Publication Society, 1914), 96.

10. Vail, *Mary Webb and the Mother Society*, 2–3.
11. *Memoir of Mrs. Chloe Spear, a Native of Africa, Who Was Enslaved in Childhood, and Died in Boston, January 3, 1815 . . . Aged 65 Years* (Boston: James Loring, 1832), 71–72, 83.
12. *Memoir of Mrs. Chloe Spear*, 72.
13. *Memoir of Mrs. Chloe Spear*, 83, 86.
14. Byrne, *Tuberculosis and Victorian Literary Imagination*, 6–12. Webb's memoir follows many of the stylistic and narrative trends detailed by Joanna Bowen Gillespie in "'The Clear Leadings of Providence': Pious Memoirs and the Problems of Self-Realization for Women in the Early Nineteenth Century," *Journal of the Early Republic* 5, no. 2 (Summer 1985): 197.
15. Frances Harriet Whipple was unmarried when she wrote *The Memoir of Elleanor Eldridge*. She married Charles Green in 1842, divorced him in 1847, and married William McDougall in 1862. I use her maiden name; see Sarah C. O'Dowd, *A Rhode Island Original: Frances Harriet Whipple Green McDougall* (Hanover, NH: University Press of New England, 2004).
16. Whipple was prone to exaggerations. Her biographer dismissed these as common artistic liberties; see O'Dowd, *A Rhode Island Original*, 28.
17. O'Dowd, *A Rhode Island Original*, 13–14, 27–28.
18. O'Dowd, *A Rhode Island Original*, 29. Joycelyn K. Moody and Sarah R. Robbins argued for a complex and contentious relationship between the two authors of the text, and pointed out that Whipple's name disappeared from the title page after the first edition; see Moody and Robbins, "Seeking Trust and Commitment in Women's Interracial Collaboration in the Nineteenth Century and Today," *MELUS: Multi-Ethnic Literature of the United States* 38, no. 1 (March 2013): 55–57.
19. Eldridge and Green, *Memoirs of Elleanor Eldridge*, 32–33, 57. Joanna Bowen Gillespie argued that the growing body of pious memoirs in the early nineteenth century provided a public presence for the emerging recognition of the "ego"; see Gillespie, "'The Clear Leadings of Providence,'" 218.
20. Lasser, "Voyeuristic Abolitionism," 107.
21. Frances Harriet Green, *Elleanor's Second Book* (Providence, RI: B. T. Albro, 1842), 9–10.
22. Maria W. Stewart was the first American woman to speak publicly against the slave trade, but the content of her speeches, given in 1833–34, fueled animosity from Boston's Black community, and she was ostracized for her criticism of Black men; see Lois Brown, "Out of the Mouths of Babes: The Abolitionist Campaign of Susan Paul and the Juvenile Choir of Boston," *New England Quarterly* 75, no. 1 (March 2002): 59–61.

23. Susan Paul, *Memoir of James Jackson: The Attentive and Obedient Scholar Who Died in Boston, October 31, 1833, Aged Six Years and Eleven Months*, ed. Lois Brown (1835; Cambridge, MA: Harvard University Press, 2000), 62, 94–95.
24. Anne Warren Weston to Deborah Weston, 18 April 1837, Ms. A.9.2.v.9, 28, Antislavery Collection, Boston Public Library; Stephanie J. Richmond, "Race, Class, and Antislavery: African American Women in the Transatlantic Antislavery Movement," *Journal of Women's History* 31, no. 3 (Fall 2019): 62.
25. "Died," *The Liberator*, 23 April 1841. Lois Brown argued that Paul embodied the new ideal of antebellum evangelical womanhood in which women linked reform work with religion to access the public sphere in ways available under the model of female virtue in the early republic; see Brown, "Out of the Mouths of Babes," 61.
26. "Died," *The Liberator*, 23 April 1841.
27. Debra Gold Hansen, *Strained Sisterhood: Gender and Class in the Boston Female Anti-Slavery Society* (Amherst: University of Massachusetts Press, 1993), 19–20. Surprisingly, Paul has received very little historical attention; see Brown, "Out of the Mouths of Babes," 52n1.
28. Foreman, *Activist Sentiments*, 25–27, 51.
29. Harriet E. Wilson, *Our Nig* (Boston: Rand and Avery, 1859), 84.
30. Wilson, *Our Nig*, 84.
31. Jean Fagan Yellin, *Harriet Jacobs: A Life* (New York: Basic Books, 2003), 66. P. Gabrielle Foreman interpreted *Incidents* as an assertion of Jacobs's reproductive agency and personal power; see Foreman, *Activist Sentiments*, 21.
32. Yellin, *Harriet Jacobs*, 120–24.
33. Yellin, *Harriet Jacobs*, 27. Karen Sánchez-Eppler noted that Stowe was particularly problematic in her treatment of Black characters, focusing on the bodies and sexuality of her Black characters to the exclusion of their facial features and personalities, and consequently dehumanizing them; see Sánchez-Eppler, *Touching Liberty*.
34. Harriet Jacobs, *Incidents in the Life of a Slave Girl*, ed. Francis Smith Foster and Richard Yarborough, 2nd Norton Critical Edition (1861; New York: Norton, 2019), 103.

HISTORIOGRAPHIES

UNLIKE THE other essays in this collection, these two do not derive from original research into eighteenth- and early nineteenth-century sources. Instead, Lorri Glover and Ami Pflugrad-Jackisch and Craig Thompson Friend and Timothy J. Williams reflect on the larger scholarly contexts in which historians have written about gender. Individual authors of the twelve preceding essays provide some historiographical contexts, often at the outsets and conclusions of their essays and sometimes in footnotes. Their historiographical frameworks are necessarily specific to the topics at hand. These two historiographical essays, in contrast, take wider and longer views of how, since the emergence of the field of women's history in the 1970s, historians of the early republic have interpreted women, gender, men, and sexuality. Still, they offer interpretations of which books and articles the authors consider central to shaping (and reshaping) the fields, which methodological and conceptual innovations were most influential, and the cultural and political contexts that shaped historiographical interpretations.

Reflecting on these two historiographical essays, consider for yourself: What do you conclude were the most significant innovations in scholarship on women, men, gender, and sexuality? How did social, political, and cultural changes influence historians' topics and the questions they asked? Why does it matter how scholars interpret trends in gender history? With the advantage of this broader perspective on so many books and articles, what questions would you like to answer for yourself, through further reading or original research into gender in the early American republic? Thinking as well about how these historiographical essays frame the original research essays, have you gained fresh insights into the studies you read? Do you see larger historical patterns that the authors did not emphasize? What historiographical connections can you trace across the essays in this collection?

Histories of Women in the Early American Republic

Lorri Glover and Ami Pflugrad-Jackisch

As the essays in this collection reveal, scholarship on women in the early American republic is rich, multifaceted, and transformational. It is also very long. Mercy Otis Warren published one of the earliest histories of the new nation in 1805, Elizabeth F. Ellet compiled her three-volume history of women in the American Revolution a few decades later, and Julia Cherry Spruill's *Women's Life and Work in the Southern Colonies* appeared in 1938.[1] Across the nineteenth and early twentieth centuries, historians authored many other works about early American women, but the topic first became a distinctive and sustained focus of study in the 1970s.

The field expanded across ensuing decades, with some women's historians pursuing studies that intersected with traditional historical frameworks centered on politics and the nation-state. Their works reshaped scholars' understanding of the new nation's origins, politics, social structures, and values. Other women's historians took a different tack, emphasizing woman-centered narratives that challenged and even abandoned the political demarcations of colonial, revolutionary, and early national periodizations. In moving away from the nation-state and its White male–centered framework, women's historians expanded the geography and chronology of early American history. Scholars also illuminated the experiences of diverse groups of women and embraced intersectional analyses. And they stood at the forefront of sexuality studies and medical humanities.

In short, the past fifty years of studying early American history through the lens of women's experiences and gender analysis has made significant contributions to the field. Historians of women and gender reinterpreted the meanings and functions of power, family, culture, race, class, religion, and work. It is difficult to imagine the field of early American history without the contributions of women's historians. At the same time, such sophisticated and wide-ranging enquiries produced overlapping and sometimes contradictory histories that defy easy categorization or even inventory. It is a happy commentary on the state of the field that our essay cannot be comprehensive. The scholarship is too vibrant and varied. Instead, we offer insights into the most influential turns in women's (and gender) history over the past five decades and outline the context in which the contributors to this collection are writing the next chapters in this historiography.[2]

AMONG THE influences shaping the origins of early American women's history, two stand out: feminism and the Bicentennial. In the 1960s and 1970s, feminist scholars including Gerda Lerner claimed a place for women's history in the male-dominated academy. Lerner's publications reflected the *zeitgeist* of late twentieth-century feminist movements, emphasizing women's shared culture, experiences, and oppression in a patriarchal world.[3] She and other Marxist-feminist scholars contributed to the framework of "separate spheres," which became central to interpreting early American women's history. They asserted that market forces and industrialization artificially separated work and home, especially in the northeastern United States. This partitioning of men's and women's worlds codified a sexual division of labor, with men's work assigned monetary value while women contributed to the household economy as unpaid laborers.[4] Historians adopting this framework described early American women's lives as circumscribed by the private, female world of the "domestic sphere," which stood apart from men's rough-and-tumble public sphere of politics and wage and professional labor.[5]

The most important study of early American women that emerged from this framework was Nancy F. Cott's *The Bonds of Womanhood* (1977).[6] Her pivotal book inaugurated still-unfolding debates about the place and power of women in the new nation—particularly in New England—and the roots of feminism. Cott argued that a unique women's culture emerged among reform-minded middle-class women in New England, which laid the foundation for the antebellum women's rights movement. Other key studies explored White women's networks and contributions to middle-class culture, including Mary P. Ryan's *Cradle of the Middle Class* (1981), Karen Halttunen's *Confidence Men and Painted Women* (1982), Nancy A. Hewitt's *Women's Activism and Social Change*

(1984), and Mary Kelley's *Private Woman, Public Stage* (1984). These innovative investigations of women's culture, moral reform activism, and relationships became instant classics, and they remain required reading in many graduate programs and for scholars of class and gender.[7]

Public planning for and nationwide commemorations of the 1976 Bicentennial of the Declaration of Independence sparked a profusion of academic conferences, public history projects, and publications focused on the founding era. Many of these initiatives moved beyond the "founding fathers" and pursued inclusivity.[8] Feminist historians asked innovative questions about the meanings of the American Revolution for women. In 1980, Linda K. Kerber's *Women of the Republic* and Mary Beth Norton's *Liberty's Daughters* explored the consequences of the American Revolution for White women. Kerber and Norton concluded that postrevolutionary Americans defined White women's proper role in society as mothers, infusing that role with new political meaning and responsibility for raising virtuous republican citizens from the confines of the domestic sphere. This "republican motherhood" was in many ways an extension of the separate spheres framework. Republican motherhood, Kerber remarked, brought "the older version of separate spheres into rough conformity with the new politics that valued autonomy and individualism" and defined "a place for women in post-revolutionary republicanism."[9] Jan Lewis also extended scholars' understanding of women's experiences with her influential 1987 essay "The Republican Wife."[10]

In the 1980s, many historians studying early American women either focused on or responded to White northeastern-centered narratives. As second-wave feminism reshaped twentieth-century American society, scholars sought to understand its antecedents, which they traced to northeastern female networks, reform movements, and the 1848 Seneca Falls Convention.

Historians of southern women, meanwhile, asserted that slavery stifled the development of White women's reform movements in the South. Catherine Clinton's *The Plantation Mistress* (1982) was an explicit counterpoint to Cott's *Bonds of Womanhood*. Clinton argued that, unlike in New England, slave societies aggressively censored and prohibited southern women from establishing reform movements or advocating for women's rights.[11] In *The Free Women of Petersburg* (1984), Suzanne Lebsock likewise found that slavery inhibited organized feminism in Virginia, although, she contended, the existence of a women's "sphere" and culture created positive change in women's lives.[12] These two studies propelled the growth of women's early American history beyond the northeastern United States and prompted scholars to interrogate how slavery altered Black and White women's experiences.

Early American women's history diversified throughout the 1980s, as scholars published a remarkable range of still-influential books. Historians studying working-class urban women and rural women addressed the complexities of class and regionalism, and their findings further dispelled assumptions of any homogenous women's culture. Christine Stansell's pioneering investigation of wage-earning women in New York City, *City of Women* (1986), alongside books by Mary H. Blewett, Jeanne Boydston, and Thomas Dublin, examined changing ideas about White women's labor, class status, and efforts to navigate their "proper" place in society as wage earners.[13] Joan M. Jensen's study of women in rural Pennsylvania, *Loosening the Bonds* (1986), disrupted scholarly assumptions about the rural South and industrializing North. Writing at the end of that pivotal decade in women's historiography, Joan E. Cashin blended women's and family history in *A Family Venture* (1991) to reveal White women's experiences as they migrated into the Old Southwest.[14]

Other historians writing in the 1980s moved women's historiography into dialogue with scholarship on slavery and Black people's experiences. No book published in that decade exerted a greater influence on women's historiography than Deborah Gray White's *Ar'n't I a Woman?* (1985). A major innovation in scholarship, the book became widely adopted within college courses, reshaping generations of students' perceptions of gender, race, and power in early American history.[15] White, along with Paula Giddings and Jacqueline Jones, led the way in decentering White New Englanders and emphasizing the necessity of studying gendered elements in racial slavery. Of particular importance was White's argument that although patriarchy constrained the autonomy of both enslaved and elite White women, living under a common patriarchal authority did not translate into a shared women's culture or set of experiences. By examining race and gender together, scholars highlighted the limits of the separate spheres framework and launched important scholarly conversations about intersectionality.[16]

This generation of women's historians, by employing multiple perspectives rather than defaulting to a White, male-centered periodization, reshaped scholars' chronological framing of early America too.

Years previously perceived to be of sweeping importance—1776, 1787, 1803—were recast or rendered irrelevant when historians prioritized women's points of view.[17]

The proliferation of women's histories did not, of course, occur in a vacuum. Historians were in dialogue with other scholars studying women's history across a variety of locations and eras. Indeed, the field of women's history grew at such a pace in the 1970s and 1980s that when Johns Hopkins University Press launched the *Journal of Women's History* in 1989, the opening statement of purpose proclaimed, "The field of women's history has expanded so rapidly that it is difficult to keep track of the latest interpretations and publications."[18] Theda Perdue, a leading expert in Cherokee history, authored the first essay in the journal's inaugural issue. Perdue, like many scholars at the time, was turning her attention toward women's history. "Cherokee Women and the Trail of Tears" reflected the capaciousness of early American women's history in the 1980s and the transformations wrought by the still-innovative inclusion of women's perspectives. Perdue's essay also underscored how historians needed to broaden their vision to include all women in their understanding of the past.[19]

Scholars writing in the 1970s and 1980s were unsure, as some historians today remain, what result they sought for women's history writ large: Should it become a separate discipline or strive for integration into and revision of existing narratives? Should women-centered histories adopt different chronological frameworks? To what degree should the nation-state influence topics? Such foundational questions—and consequent debates about chronology, geography, and frameworks—shaped early American women's histories over the ensuing decades. Some historians traced the origins of the modern feminist movement, while others sought to recover the histories of women who struggled, sometimes in obscurity and in vain, against patriarchal oppression. Women's historians also debated how best to integrate activism and advocacy with scholarship.

BETWEEN THE 1990s and the 2020s, women's history became a distinct field, with proliferating subfields and divergent schools of thought. The vibrancy of women's history led to a multiplication of academic conferences, organizations, journals, programs, centers, and departments. Women's historians were early practitioners of interdisciplinarity and transnational perspectives, and they inclined toward intersectionality decades before the term and approach became widely adopted. Scholars debated how class, region, and race influenced (even outweighed) gender in shaping women's lives and perceptions. The rise of sexuality and masculinity studies expanded those debates. The results made women's historiography exciting, diverse, vast, and increasingly specialized. To use an analogy deriving from a traditional form of women's labor, the field came to resemble a patchwork quilt.

One of the most significant changes to the emerging discipline came in the wake of Joan W. Scott's transformational 1986 article "Gender: A Useful Category of Historical Analysis," as growing numbers of scholars pivoted from women's history to gender history.[20] Scott asserted that historians' efforts at recovering women's experiences, while laudable, failed to explain structural inequalities. She posited that histories of women's culture tended to isolate women from systems of economic and political power. Historians, Scott argued, needed a theoretical construct to better analyze how relationships between women and men signified and legitimized power. Poststructuralist ideas such as Scott's propelled early American women's history into the realms of political, cultural, and diplomatic history and beyond. Scholars undertook fresh topics, approaches to sources, and theoretical frameworks, and pursued investigations into masculinities and sexualities. However, this emphasis on social constructions of gender and gendered power dynamics sometimes had the unintended effect of decentering women's experiences.

As twenty-first-century scholars debated the merits of women's history and gender history, women's studies programs and departments reimagined their missions. Many academic units consequently changed their names from women's studies to women's and gender studies or women's, gender, and sexuality studies.[21] Transformations in institutional identity dovetailed with the topics women's historians pursued in the 1990s–2010s, which explored intersectional, geographically expansive, and diverse gendered histories. That scholarship advanced understandings of race, ethnicity, sexuality, consumption, science, law, medicine, and political culture. Moreover, new questions about gendered power led scholars to reconsider traditional topics such as women's education, labor, marriage, and religion.

As HISTORIANS of early American women incorporated gender analysis into their scholarship and pushed beyond the separate spheres paradigm, they uncovered the significance of women in traditionally "male" spaces. Their research recast histories of the nation's founding and women's civic responsibilities and identities.

The Revolutionary War became a rich topic for exploration. Holly A. Mayer and Carol Berkin, among other historians, concentrated on women's wartime experiences.[22] The 2019 collection *Women in the American Revolution,* edited by Barbara B. Oberg, captured the breadth of scholarship. Contributors wrote about enslaved midwives; Philadelphia loyalists; Haudenosaunee targets of patriot troops; and writers, planters, and entrepreneurs during the long revolutionary era. Another volume, edited by Mayer, focused on the Revolutionary War while employing the same commitment to the diversity of women's experiences. A third volume, edited by Charlene M. Boyer Lewis and George W. Boudreau, considered the many women who influenced George Washington. These three collections—all appearing with the University of Virginia Press—recentered the history of North American opposition to British authority and the Revolutionary War around women's perspectives and experiences.[23]

The challenges of nation-building offered further opportunities to reassess traditional understandings of public and private and investigate the degrees to which women entered and transformed sites of power in the early republic.[24] In *Revolutionary Backlash* (2007), Rosemarie Zagarri explored how revolutionary impulses challenged Americans' perceptions of women's capacity for political thought, women's involvement in the political sphere, and the conservative backlash against those changes.[25] In her investigation of the power wielded by presidential wives, *Parlor Politics* (2000), Catherine Allgor redirected conversations about women's roles in the nation's founding and the nature of political culture. Susan Branson's study of 1790s Philadelphia uncovered women's centrality in the print culture, theaters, and salons propelling political culture in the nation's temporary capital. Carolyn Eastman's *A Nation of Speechifiers* (2009) moved beyond elites to reveal how women and men created a new conception of the public and national identity. Susan E. Klepp's *Revolutionary Conceptions* (2009) charted how women in the early republic asserted greater agency over the timing and number of children they bore, changing long-entrenched ideals about family and gendered social roles. With *In Dependence* (2023), Jacqueline Beatty crossed regions and traditional chronologies to illuminate how experiences with dependence under the patriarchal state fueled women's self-perceptions as rights-bearing citizens.[26]

Biographers also enabled readers to reimagine this long revolutionary era from women's perspectives: prominent subjects included Phyllis Wheatley and Mercy Otis Warren; famous wives such as Martha Washington, Abigail Adams, and Dolley Madison; and surprisingly independent women like Ona Judge, Elizabeth Murray, and Eliza Lucas Pinckney.[27] Taken together, these works demonstrated how much women and ideas about gender influenced every aspect of the origins of the nation, further challenging separate spheres paradigms and illuminating the diversity of meanings to independence and citizenship.

OVER THE past forty years, one major trend has linked the ever-expanding studies of early American women's histories: attention to racial diversity and intersectionality.[28] Although much work remains to be done, historians devoted deep consideration to the interplay of gender and race, with major implications for understanding every region within the young nation. Southern historians, inspired by Deborah Gray White's debunking of the existence of a transracial sisterhood, debated elite White women's complicity in or exploitation under the antebellum South's increasingly "peculiar" institution. In *Within the Plantation Household* (1988), Elizabeth Fox-Genovese explored the lives of elite and enslaved women, emphasizing White women's role as part of the enslaving class. Thavolia Glymph's *Out of the House of Bondage* (2008) and Stephanie E. Jones-Rogers's *They Were Her Property* (2019) reinterpreted how race and gender operated in the slaveholding South. Both scholars foregrounded the point of view of enslaved women in their explorations of the violence endemic in slaveholding: Glymph focused on plantation households and Jones-Rogers centered slave markets. Their findings demolished the notion of cross-racial gender solidarity and documented how White women sought power, exercised racial violence, and perpetrated patriarchalism.[29]

Other historians of southern women extended their research beyond plantations. Michele Gillespie and Elizabeth R. Varon examined the roles of middling and wage-earning White women, further demonstrating the heterogeneity of southern women's lives.[30] Cynthia A. Kierner focused much of her extensive scholarship on interrogating White southern women's experiences and roles in the early republic.[31] Anya Jabour and Christie Anne Farnham produced enlightening interpretations of girls' coming-of-age and educational experiences.[32] Kirsten E. Wood's *Masterful Women* (2004) explored the roles played by independent White slave-owning widows.[33] Together, these works showcased the importance of life-course analysis for understanding women's experiences.

Explorations of the lives of enslaved women likewise grew richer and more varied in the 2000s. Stephanie M. H. Camp's *Closer to Freedom* (2004) and Daina Ramey Berry's *"Swing the Sickle for the Harvest Is Ripe"* (2007) emphasized Black women's resistance, agency, and family relations, alongside their exploitation, exemplifying the greater depth and dimension to scholars' understanding of enslaved women's experiences.[34] In the 2010s and 2020s, Amrita Chakrabarti Myers, Jessica Millward, and Tamika Y. Nunley published innovative works reimagining freedom from the perspectives of Black women. Kabria Baumgartner focused on Black women advocating for educational rights. Tera W. Hunter centered marriages among enslaved and free couples spanning the nineteenth century. Alexandra J. Finley, adopting a biographical framework, revealed the centrality of enslaved women to antebellum slave markets.[35]

Such studies enhanced and transcended the field of Black women's history, with implications for how scholars interpret chronological and geographic boundaries. Led by Jennifer L. Morgan and Daina Ramey Berry, a new generation of Black women historians reshaped American historiography. Morgan foregrounded gender and race into broader narratives of colonization, and Berry emphasized nation-making and sectional divisions. With Kali Nicole Gross, Berry recast the narrative of US history—and, indeed, the notion of comprehensive narratives—in *A Black Women's History of the United States* (2020).[36] Erica Armstrong Dunbar's acclaimed *Never Caught* (2017), which recovered the life and successful quest for freedom of Ona Judge, reoriented the focus of revolutionary historiography from the most famous of the founding fathers to the Black woman he enslaved and who declared her independence in 1792. Vanessa M. Holden's *Surviving Southampton* (2021) reinterpreted the 1831 slave revolt in Southampton County, Virginia, to foreground women's voices and experiences. Biographies including Nell Irvin Painter's *Sojourner Truth: A Life, a Symbol* (1996), Nikki M. Taylor's *Driven Toward Madness* (2016), and Amrita Chakrabarti Myers's *The Vice President's Black Wife* (2023) deepened understanding of the lives, struggles, and triumphs of Black women in the nineteenth century.[37]

Historians of Native American women expanded conceptualizations of race and gender too, as well as geography and chronology. Theda Perdue forcefully reminded historians of the limitations of a biracial framework in her transformational *Cherokee Women* (1998). Perdue's interrogation of Cherokee women's cultural influences resulted in a longer chronological timetable than most Anglo-centered historians adopted. Juliana Barr redefined not only the chronology but also the geography of early American women's history with *Peace Came in the Form of a Woman* (2007). Her gender-centered history crossed academic categories and won book prizes in women's, southern, southwestern, and Latin American history. Susan Sleeper-Smith's extensive work on the Great Lakes region similarly centered gender and reframed power, chronology, and geography.[38]

For historians studying Native American cultures, gender often afforded a more relevant framework than women's history. As Perdue pointed out, Cherokee women and men balanced each other: understanding women requires consideration of men. At the same time, surviving sources, many created by Anglo traders and early ethnographers, often ignored or distorted Indigenous women's lives. Moreover, as both Perdue and Barr exemplified, ethnohistorians understand and thus write toward tribal and national distinctiveness with a keen appreciation of the perils of generalization. Perdue warned against using Cherokee women's experiences to understand other nations. Barr reflected that same understanding, paying careful attention to the differences among the gender values of Caddo, Wichita, and Comanche peoples. Tiya Miles's *Ties That Bind* (2005) emphasized similar perspectives on sources, chronology, and cultural nuances while recovering an Indigenous-Black family history that was at once singular and transcendent. Honor Sachs's research into descendants of a seventeenth-century Apalachee woman opens fresh insights into racial categories and fights for freedom.[39]

Studies of women in the eighteenth- and early nineteenth-century West—members of Indigenous nations, Anglo migrants, enslaved and free African Americans—marked another vibrant field of inquiry. These historians tended to write toward ethnohistorical or western historiographies, as was the case with Anne F. Hyde's *Empires, Nations, and Families* (2011) and Lisbeth Haas's works on early California, including *Saints and Citizens* (2013).[40] Their insights enriched the ever-expanding field of early

American women's and gender history and checked scholars' tendency to default to eastern-centered frameworks.

Decades of research into the lives of women—living in and migrating into the West; members of varied Native nations; Black women, enslaved, free, and in liminal legal status; White women of varied classes and locales—affirmed the limited explanatory power of the model of White, northern, middle-class women who organized for self-empowerment and gender solidarity. Indeed, these varied works suggest that it was perhaps the New England reformers who were outliers.

IN THE last two decades, researchers launched innovative studies of sex, sexualities, and bodies. They advanced understanding of the early American republic's economy and the history of capitalism. And they provided fresh takes on well-established topics such as the legal status and rights of women, reform, labor, marriage, and religion.

Women's and gender historians shaped sexuality studies with works investigating women's sexual desires and constraints, same-sex relationships, sexual violence, the commodification of sex, and sex across the color line. Clare A. Lyons's *Sex Among the Rabble* (2006) was a signal achievement in sexuality studies. Engaging gender, class, race, print culture, ideology, and politics, she untangled how constructions of sexual propriety shaped gender expectations, and she demonstrated how gender underlay power dynamics in the early republic.[41] Scholars also began to uncover the histories of transgender identities and same-sex partnerships in early America. Through exemplary historical detective work, Rachel Hope Cleves brought to life the forty-year relationship of a New England couple in *Charity and Sylvia* (2014).[42]

Scholarship on the history of medicine and the body similarly benefited from—and were often led by—women's and gender historians. Deirdre Cooper Owens's *Medical Bondage* (2017) epitomized the potential to be gained from research in medical humanities, and her prodigious research advanced the histories of gender, race, health, medicine, ethnicity, and slavery.[43] Ernest Freeberg's 2001 biography of Laura Bridgman marked an early contribution to the emerging field of disability studies, which intersected with gender history in books published in the 2020s by Kim E. Nielsen and Jennifer L. Barclay.[44]

Important scholarship on the history of rape and sexual violence also intersected with women's history. In *Celia, a Slave* (1991), Melton A.

McLaurin interrogated legal and cultural ideas about rape and race in antebellum Missouri, based on the sometimes-opaque story of a young enslaved woman named Celia and her predatory enslaver. Sharon Block's *Rape and Sexual Power in Early America* (2006) offered a geographically and chronologically expansive interrogation of sexual violence. Alexandra J. Finley's *An Intimate Economy* (2020) contributed a nuanced analysis of traders' and enslavers' sexual abuse of enslaved women, showing how the commodification of Black women and their imagined sexual availability proved central to the domestic slave trade.[45]

Other scholars investigated sexual relationships that defied norms and laws. Victoria E. Bynum and Joshua D. Rothman added new perspectives to histories of sex across racial lines in the antebellum South. Both scholars demonstrated the importance of social, economic, and political forces in setting racial and sexual boundaries.[46] Annette Gordon-Reed's momentous research into Sally Hemings and Thomas Jefferson's relationship challenged longstanding biased interpretations, foregrounded enslaved people at Monticello, and inspired scholars toward more judicious textual analysis and more expansive sources.[47] Scholars studying transgressions of sexual boundaries often found it necessary to adopt extensive chronological frameworks. To explain the evolution of laws prohibiting marriages between White women and Black men, for example, Martha Hodes started her study in the seventeenth century and continued through the nineteenth.[48]

Scholars versed in women's and gender history produced nuanced investigations of sex workers. Building on Christine Stansell's classic *City of Women,* historians debated the empowerment and exploitation of sex workers, and weighed how region, class, and race intersected with commercialized sex. Patricia Cline Cohen's *The Murder of Helen Jewett* (1998) used a sensationalized crime to recast interpretations of prostitution and elucidate challenges women faced earning a living wage. Cohen and others explored how gendered conceptions of proper sexual behavior became pivotal to defining middle- and working-class identity in nineteenth-century America. Investigations into the commercialization of sex and brothel culture, including Judith Kelleher Schafer's *Brothels, Depravity, and Abandoned Women* (2009) and Katie M. Hemphill's *Bawdy City* (2020), advanced understanding of the new culture of leisure and entertainment that went hand in hand with the expansion of capitalism and urbanization.[49]

WOMEN'S HISTORIANS added immeasurably to historical understandings of labor, economy, and capitalism. As with other topics, scholars interrogating the intersections of gender and labor, industrialization, and market-centered economies found themselves needing to adopt divergent chronologies. And frameworks varied too as scholars centered diverse types of labor and women of different classes and locales.

Since 2000, scholars have investigated gendered patterns embedded in capitalist development and women's labor both inside and outside the household, transcending the sticky dichotomy of home and work. In *The Ties That Buy* (2009), Ellen Hartigan-O'Connor concentrated on urban centers to reveal the centrality of Black and White women to marketplaces and commercial culture. Marla R. Miller used a biographical approach in *The Needle's Eye* (2006) to recover the experiences of female tailors and dressmakers in a rural Massachusetts community. Kathleen M. Brown's *Foul Bodies* (2009) studied early Americans' gendered and racialized ideas about sickness, cleanliness, and housework, which bolstered the cultural construction of domesticity and idealized notions of female beauty and character.[50]

Scholars also examined how capitalist developments affected Black women. Daina Ramey Berry's pathbreaking *The Price for Their Pound of Flesh* (2017) took an unflinching look at how capitalists and enslavers gauged the value of enslaved people for the market and how their perceptions of gender and race shaped enslaved women's market value. Berry contrasted this dehumanizing process with an examination of how enslaved people reacted to the commodification of their bodies, explicating a private sense of self-worth and "soul value." In *Scraping By* (2008), Seth Rockman explored how the emerging labor market in early Baltimore affected the lives and work of free Black and enslaved women. In *Slaves for Hire* (2012), John J. Zaborney elucidated the experiences of hired-out enslaved women in Virginia and explained how the sexual division of labor among enslaved people sometimes afforded women greater opportunities for resistance.[51]

AT THE turn of the twenty-first century, historians' longstanding interest in the origins of women's rights and women's involvement in reform movements benefited from innovative frameworks, diverse perspectives, and field-crossing research. No longer solely the story of White middle-class women in the northeastern United States, scholarship on nineteenth-century reform efforts explored women of color, women who lived in western states and territories, and connections to European feminists. Shirley J. Yee's *Black Women Abolitionists* (1992) and Martha S. Jones's *All Bound Up Together* (2007) led the way in uncovering African American women's reform work. Stephanie J. Richmond contributed fresh insights into Black women's transatlantic antislavery efforts.[52] Tiya Miles investigated Native American women's antiremoval efforts.[53] Stacey M. Robertson, Julie Roy Jeffrey, and Elizabeth Jameson examined women's activism in the Midwest and West.[54] Bonnie S. Anderson's *Joyous Greetings* (2000) established a transnational connection between women reformers in the United States and Europe, contextualizing women's reform and rights within European radicalism. And Bruce Dorsey's *Reforming Men and Women* (2002) offered a gendered reinterpretation of men's and women's collective reform activities.[55] Scholars, particularly those investigating abolitionism, continued to debate the degree to which Black and White reformers worked as partners, drawn together in opposition to patriarchal power structures, or whether White women reinforced, intentionally or inadvertently, racial hierarchies.

The women's rights movement drew sustained attention from feminist scholars. Seneca Falls loomed large, as did biographies of leading nineteenth-century feminists and activists, including Susan B. Anthony, Angelina and Sarah Grimké, Harriet Jacobs, Elizabeth Cady Stanton, Lucy Stone, and Sojourner Truth. With *Sex and Citizenship in Antebellum America* (1998), Nancy Isenberg challenged the centrality of Seneca Falls and advanced a wider interpretation of the origins and implications of feminism than scholars had previously pursued.[56] Lori D. Ginzberg, Anne M. Boylan, Judith Wellman, and Alison M. Parker authored important studies exploring women's political identities, citizenship rights, and methods for creating political change. In *The Myth of Seneca Falls* (2014), Lisa Tetrault interrogated the origin myth of Seneca Falls, demonstrating that a more disparate set of actors participated in the early suffrage movement and suggesting a revised chronology.[57] Authors illuminated the effects of women's participation in antislavery, temperance, and other reforms; the power of local actors and contexts; religious diversity among activists; and debates over moral suasion and petitioning versus electoral action and suffrage. Collectively, the literature reveals a far richer story of the roots of women's rights movements and feminism—pillars of the field of women's history.

Other scholars revisited the legal status of women as property owners, wives, mothers, and citizens, and advanced scholarly knowledge of systems of law and power in the young nation. The legal rights women exercised—or were denied—have long been central to women's history. Because property rights and divorce laws were state matters, scholars studying women's legal history in the early republic tended toward regional and local frameworks. In her classic and still essential *Women and the Law of Property in Early America* (1986), Marylynn Salmon examined how inheritance laws and coverture shaped women's ability to acquire property.[58] While some historians continued to probe the changing intricacies of laws, others shifted their focus to how property rights were practiced and policed. Laura F. Edwards's *The People and Their Peace* (2009) demonstrated that some married women in the early South exercised control over property they did not legally own and that communities often valued social order over adherence to laws.[59]

Divorce proceedings, child custody disputes, and other family crises garnered scholarly attention: both the legal structures created by states and the lived experiences within families. Scholars including Norma Basch, Thomas E. Buckley, Merril D. Smith, and Jacqueline Beatty studied how state divorce laws and adjudications of child custody cases affected women's rights and family values.[60] Since states needed to draft constitutions and create legal structures after breaking from Great Britain, chronology in this subfield has been more consistent than in many others. Scholars mined a variety of sources, including legal treatises, legislative records, court proceedings, probate records, and estate inventories to piece together how laws defined women's rights and how women asserted authority over property and in families and courts. The two—policy and practice—did not always meet so smoothly as male legislators and lawyers envisioned. Many scholars writing about women and the law focused on how women pushed back against patriarchal legal systems. In *Scandal at Bizarre* (2004), Cynthia A. Kierner used an allegation of infanticide to reveal how law, gender conventions, racial hierarchies, and social values worked in early national Virginia.[61]

In the 2010s and early 2020s, some of the most significant innovations in the history of gender and the law centered on the actions of African Americans. Kelly M. Kennington's study of freedom suits in St. Louis and Kimberly M. Welch's research into the Natchez district illuminated how Black women and men asserted their rights before the law and compelled a broadening of legal systems and citizenship.[62] Martha S. Jones's *Birthright Citizens* (2018) traced the many ways in which free Blacks in Baltimore used the law to secure rights and recast the definition of citizenship in the United States.[63]

GREATER ATTENTION to diversity and intersectionality enriched studies of more traditional topics in women's history, including familial roles, educational experiences, and religious practices. From Mary P. Ryan's study of Oneida County, New York, to Theda Perdue's investigation of Cherokee women, to Tera W. Hunter's exploration of African American marriages, family—in all its varied forms—remained central to many women's histories.[64] The lines between women's history and family history sometimes blurred to the point of indecipherability. Scholars studied marital ages, laws, traditions, and purposes, including the much-discussed rise of affectionate, companionable marriage. Scholars undertook imaginative research into motherhood, framed by divergent chronologies and attracting wide-ranging debate.[65]

In the early 2000s, scholars also reconsidered women's education and intellectual pursuits, with key works including Margaret A. Nash's *Women's Education in the United States, 1780–1840* (2005), Mary Kelley's *Learning to Stand and Speak* (2006), and Catherine Kerrison's *Claiming the Pen* (2006). In the next decade Lucia McMahon fruitfully adopted a life-course analysis in *Mere Equals* (2012), while Kabria Baumgartner recovered the leadership of Black educators and educational activists in *In Pursuit of Knowledge* (2019), and Ann Taylor Allen revealed United States and German educational networking in *The Transatlantic Kindergarten* (2017). Reflective of these scholars' field-crossing research, their works also made important contributions by interrogating racial hierarchies, appreciating regional variations, employing life-course analysis, and tackling underutilized sources.[66]

Women's religious history likewise grew more nuanced and capacious. Beginning in the 1970s and led by Barbara Welter and Ann Douglas, scholars inaugurated sustained consideration of women's roles within New England's middle-class congregations, centering much of their analyses on the Second Great Awakening and the "feminization" of American religion.[67] But the subfield, like so many others, soon diversified and scholarship moved geographically, chronologically, and interpretively. In *Southern Cross* (1997), Christine Leigh Heyrman wove gender analysis into her explanation of how evangelicals compromised their values to gain inroads in the South, and Susan Juster tracked the transformation of gender roles among New England evangelicals in the revolutionary era in *Disorderly Women* (1994).[68] Scholars working at the intersection of women's and religious history undertook research as varied as the radicalizing impacts of spiritualism, Cherokee seminarians, and Ursuline nuns in New Orleans.[69] The innovations and intersections continue, more than we can do justice to in a single essay.

SOME THEMES and commitments connect the rich, sometimes dizzying patchwork of late eighteenth- and early nineteenth-century women's histories. Scholars working across subfields share a determination to recover women's lives on their own terms and to write histories that respect the diversity of women's experiences. Some works, by virtue of deep scholarly consideration, celebrate women's achievements and their fortitude in the face of patriarchal power structures that diminished, disfranchised, enslaved, and erased women. Other historians reveal how women exercised power, including consideration of racialized and gendered violence. Linking these scholars is a commitment to refraining from universalizing womanhood and to depicting subjects as actors, not passive victims or spectators, in history. Women's and gender historians also share a clear understanding of the contours of patriarchy embedded in the politics, laws, and cultures of the early American republic. Indeed, patriarchy may be the single greatest interpretive link connecting all these histories. Scholars study women brutalized and marginalized by patriarchal power, women fighting patriarchy in its varied forms, and women upholding patriarchy.

Over the past five decades, women's and gender historians determined to recover stories obscured by White, male-centered archival preservation consistently sought out new and untapped sources, undertook new evidentiary approaches, and read traditional sources in innovative ways. Their rethinking of the historical archive benefited the larger profession.[70] Women's historians, alongside scholars studying African American and Native American histories (and often working at the intersections of those topics), motivated historians in all fields to ask more inclusive questions. Historians studying women and gender in the early republic also broke down ill-fitting disciplinary boundaries by redefining what politics and citizenship meant, how identities formed, and who drove cultural changes. In requiring the expansion of history to include their scholarship, women's historians transformed the profession and understandings of the nation's past.

The essays in this collection reflect and extend the achievements wrought by this half-century of scholarship on women in the (broadly defined) early republic era. Individually and collectively, the authors traverse fields, frameworks, and methodologies. Perhaps the best anthology, then, is not a quilt but a kaleidoscope.

Notes

1. Mercy Otis Warren, *History of the Rise, Progress and Termination of the American Revolution*, 3 vols. (Boston: Manning and Loring, 1805); Elizabeth F. Ellet, *The Women of the American Revolution*, 3 vols. (New York: Baker and Scribner, 1848–50); Julia Cherry Spruill, *Women's Life and Work in the Southern Colonies* (Chapel Hill: University of North Carolina Press, 1938). See also Kathryn Kish Sklar, "American Female Historians in Context, 1770–1930," *Feminist Studies* 3, nos. 1–2 (Autumn 1975): 171–84.
2. We are not systematically exploring works that foreground colonialism, Atlantic historiography, or the Civil War. We focus on scholarship centering the 1760s to 1850s.
3. Gerda Lerner, "The Lady and the Mill Girl: Changes in the Status of Women in the Age of Jackson," *Midcontinent American Studies Journal* 10, no. 1 (Spring 1969): 5–15; Lerner, *The Grimké Sisters from South Carolina: Pioneers for Women's Rights and Abolition* (New York: Schocken Books, 1967); Lerner, *The Creation of Patriarchy* (New York: Oxford University Press, 1986).
4. See, for example, Jeanne Boydston, *Home and Work: Housework, Wages, and the Ideology of Labor in the Early Republic* (New York: Oxford University Press, 1990).
5. See, for example, Barbara Welter, "The Cult of True Womanhood: 1820–1860," *American Quarterly* 18, no. 2 (Summer 1966): 151–74, and Carroll Smith-Rosenberg, "The Female World of Love and Ritual: Relations Between Women in Nineteenth-Century America," *Signs* 1, no.1 (Autumn 1975): 1–29. See also Leila J. Rupp, "Women's History in the New Millennium: A Retrospective of Barbara Welter's 'The Cult of True Womanhood, 1820–1860,'" *Journal of Women's History* 14, no. 1 (Spring 2002): 149–73.
6. Nancy F. Cott, *The Bonds of Womanhood: "Woman's Sphere" in New England, 1780–1835* (New Haven, CT: Yale University Press, 1977).

7. Mary P. Ryan, *Cradle of the Middle Class: The Family in Oneida County, New York, 1790–1865* (New York: Cambridge University Press, 1981); Karen Halttunen, *Confidence Men and Painted Women: A Study of Middle-Class Culture in America, 1830–1870* (New Haven, CT: Yale University Press, 1982); Nancy A. Hewitt, *Women's Activism and Social Change: Rochester, New York, 1822–1872* (Ithaca, NY: Cornell University Press, 1984); Mary Kelley, *Private Woman, Public Stage: Literary Domesticity in Nineteenth-Century America* (New York: Oxford University Press, 1984).
8. For the Bicentennial Commission, see https://www.archives.gov/research/guide-fed-records/groups/452.html.
9. Linda K. Kerber, *Women of the Republic: Intellect and Ideology in Revolutionary America* (Chapel Hill: University of North Carolina Press, 1980); Mary Beth Norton, *Liberty's Daughters: The Revolutionary Experience of American Women, 1750–1800* (Boston: Little, Brown, 1980). For Kerber's reflections on the field, see "Separate Spheres, Female Worlds, Woman's Place: The Rhetoric of Women's History," *Journal of American History* 75, no. 1 (June 1988): 9–39; "Beyond Roles, Beyond Spheres: Thinking About Gender in the Early Republic" *William and Mary Quarterly*, 3rd series, 46, no. 3 (July 1989): 565–85; and "Separate Spheres, Female Worlds, Woman's Place: The Rhetoric of Women's History," in *Toward an Intellectual History of Women: Essays by Linda K. Kerber* (Chapel Hill: University of North Carolina Press, 1997), 159–99 (quote on 174). See also Carroll Smith-Rosenberg, "Dis-Covering the Subject of the 'Great Constitutional Discussion,' 1786–1789," *Journal of American History* 79, no. 3 (December 1992): 841–73; Ronald J. Zboray and Mary Saracino Zboray, "Whig Women, Politics, and Culture in the Campaign of 1840: Three Perspectives from Massachusetts," *Journal of the Early Republic* 17, no. 2 (Summer 1997): 277–315; and Zboray and Zboray, *Voices Without Votes: Women and Politics in Antebellum New England* (Durham: University of New Hampshire Press, 2010).
10. Jan Lewis, "The Republican Wife: Virtue and Seduction in the Early Republic," *William and Mary Quarterly*, 3rd series, 44, no. 4 (October 1987): 689–721. See also Joan Hoff Wilson, "Illusions of Change: Women and the Revolution," in *The American Revolution: Explorations in the History of American Radicalism*, ed. Alfred F. Young (DeKalb: Northern Illinois University Press, 1976), 383–95, and Ronald Hoffman and Peter J. Albert, eds., *Women in the Age of the American Revolution* (Charlottesville: University of Virginia Press, 1989).
11. Catherine Clinton, *The Plantation Mistress: Woman's World in the Old South* (New York: Pantheon, 1982). For an important precursor, see Anne

Firor Scott, *The Southern Lady: From Pedestal to Politics, 1830–1930* (Chicago: University of Chicago Press, 1970).
12. Suzanne Lebsock, *The Free Women of Petersburg: Status and Culture in a Southern Town, 1784–1860* (New York: Norton, 1984). For female enslavers, see Thavolia Glymph, *Out of the House of Bondage: The Transformation of the Plantation Household* (New York: Cambridge University Press, 2008), 20–24.
13. Christine Stansell, *City of Women: Sex and Class in New York, 1789–1860* (New York: Knopf, 1986); Mary H. Blewett, *Men, Women, and Work: Class, Gender, and Protest in the New England Shoe Industry, 1780–1910* (Champaign: University of Illinois Press, 1988); Boydston, *Home and Work*; Thomas Dublin, *Women at Work: The Transformation of Work and Community in Lowell, Massachusetts, 1826–1860* (New York: Columbia University Press, 1979). Lerner, "The Lady and the Mill Girl," was a foundational study of women's labor and ideals of femininity.
14. Joan M. Jensen, *Loosening the Bonds: Mid-Atlantic Farm Women, 1750–1850* (New Haven, CT: Yale University Press, 1986); Joan E. Cashin, *A Family Venture: Men and Women on the Southern Frontier* (New York: Oxford University Press, 1991). See also Jane Turner Censer, *North Carolina Planters and Their Children, 1800–1860* (Baton Rouge: Louisiana State University Press, 1984).
15. Deborah Gray White, *Ar'n't I a Woman? Female Slaves in the Plantation South* (New York: Norton, 1985). For White's wide-ranging influences, see "Women, Slavery, and Historical Research," *Journal of African American History* 92, no. 1 (Winter 2007), and the roundtable on White's *Ar'n't I a Woman?* in *Journal of Women's History* 19, no. 2 (Summer 2007): 139–69. For the challenges she faced, see White, "'Matter Out of Place': *Ar'n't I a Woman?* Black Female Scholars and the Academy," *Journal of African American History* 92, no. 1 (Winter 2007): 5–12.
16. Paula Giddings, *When and Where I Enter: The Impact of Black Women on Race and Sex in America* (New York: William Morrow, 1984); Jacqueline Jones, *Labor of Love, Labor of Sorrow: Black Women, Work, and the Family from Slavery to the Present* (New York: Basic Books, 1985). See also Deborah Gray White, "Mining the Forgotten: Manuscript Sources for Black Women's History," *Journal of American History* 74, no. 1 (June 1987): 237–42.
17. For a wide-ranging reflection on periodization, see Manisha Sinha, "What Made Early America," *William and Mary Quarterly*, 3rd series, 81, no. 1 (January 2024): 65–72.
18. "Statement of Purpose of the Journal of Women's History," *Journal of Women's History* 1, no. 1 (Spring 1989): 6.

19. Theda Perdue, "Cherokee Women and the Trail of Tears," *Journal of Women's History* 1, no. 1 (Spring 1989): 14–30.
20. Joan W. Scott, "Gender: A Useful Category of Historical Analysis," *American Historical Review* 91, no. 5 (December 1986): 1053–75. For Scott's influence, see Jeanne Boydston, "Gender as a Question of Historical Analysis," *Gender and History* 20, no. 3 (November 2008): 558–83, and Joanne Meyerowitz, "A History of 'Gender,'" *American Historical Review* 113, no. 5 (December 2008): 1346–56.
21. The first women's studies program in the United States began at San Diego State College in 1970; see Roberta Salper, "San Diego State 1970: The Initial Year of the Nation's First Women's Studies Program," *Feminist Histories and Institutional Practices* 37, no. 3 (Fall 2011): 656–82.
22. Holly A. Mayer, *Belonging to the Army: Camp Followers and Community During the American Revolution* (Columbia: University of South Carolina Press, 1996); Carol Berkin, *Revolutionary Mothers: Women in the Struggle for America's Independence* (New York: Knopf, 2005). See also Nancy K. Loane, *Following the Drum: Women at the Valley Forge Encampment* (Lincoln: University of Nebraska Press, 2009), and Alfred F. Young, *Masquerade: The Life and Times of Deborah Sampson, Continental Soldier* (New York: Knopf, 2004).
23. Barbara B. Oberg, ed., *Women in the American Revolution: Gender, Politics, and the Domestic World* (Charlottesville: University of Virginia Press, 2019); Holly A. Mayer, ed., *Women Waging War in the American Revolution* (Charlottesville: University of Virginia Press, 2022); Charlene M. Boyer Lewis and George W. Boudreau, eds., *Women in George Washington's World* (Charlottesville: University of Virginia Press, 2022). See also Karen Cook Bell, *Running from Bondage: Enslaved Women and Their Remarkable Fight for Freedom in Revolutionary America* (New York: Cambridge University Press, 2021); Lauren Duval, "Mastering Charleston: Property and Patriarchy in British-Occupied Charleston, 1780–82," *William and Mary Quarterly*, 3rd series, 75, no. 4 (October 2018): 589–622; Kate Haulman, *The Politics of Fashion in Eighteenth-Century America* (Chapel Hill: University of North Carolina Press, 2011); and Serena Zabin, *The Boston Massacre: A Family History* (New York: Houghton Mifflin Harcourt, 2020).
24. The feminist political theorist Carole Pateman influenced historical scholarship exploring women's roles and status, including with *The Sexual Contract* (Redwood City, CA: Stanford University Press, 1988). Also influential in broadening understandings of politics was Elsa Barkley Brown, "Negotiating and Transforming the Public Sphere: African American Political

Life in the Transition from Slavery to Freedom," *Public Culture* 7, no.1 (Fall 1994): 107–46.

25. Rosemarie Zagarri, *Revolutionary Backlash: Women and Politics in the Early American Republic* (Philadelphia: University of Pennsylvania Press, 2007). See also Ruth H. Bloch, "The Gendered Meaning of Virtue in Revolutionary America," *Signs* 13, no. 1 (Autumn 1987): 37–58; Joan R. Gunderson, *To Be Useful to the World: Women in Revolutionary America, 1740–1790* (New York: Twayne, 1996); Hoffman and Albert, eds., *Women in the Age of the American Revolution*; Cynthia A. Kierner, *Beyond the Household: Women's Place in the Early South, 1700–1835* (Ithaca, NY: Cornell University Press, 1998); and Marylynn Salmon, *The Limits of Independence: American Women 1760–1800* (New York: Oxford University Press, 1994).

26. Catherine Allgor, *Parlor Politics: In Which the Ladies of Washington Help Build a City and a Government* (Charlottesville: University Press of Virginia, 2000); Susan Branson, *These Fiery Frenchified Dames: Women and Political Culture in Early National Philadelphia* (Philadelphia: University of Pennsylvania Press, 2001); Carolyn Eastman, *A Nation of Speechifiers: Making an American Public After the Revolution* (Chicago: University of Chicago Press, 2009); Susan E. Klepp, *Revolutionary Conceptions: Women, Fertility, and Family Limitation in America, 1760–1820* (Chapel Hill: University of North Carolina Press, 2009); Jacqueline Beatty, *In Dependence: Women and the Patriarchal State in Revolutionary America* (New York: New York University Press, 2023). For Black women in Washington, DC, see Tamika Y. Nunley, *At the Threshold of Liberty: Women, Slavery, and Shifting Identities in Washington, D.C.* (Chapel Hill: University of North Carolina Press, 2021).

27. Vincent Carretta, *Phillis Wheatley: Biography of a Genius in Bondage* (Athens: University of Georgia Press, 2011); David Waldstreicher, *The Odyssey of Phillis Wheatley: A Poet's Journey Through American Slavery and Independence* (New York: Farrar, Straus and Giroux, 2023); Rosemarie Zagarri, *A Woman's Dilemma: Mercy Otis Warren and the American Revolution,* 2nd ed. (1995; Malden, MA: Wiley Blackwell, 2015); Patricia Brady, *Martha Washington: An American Life* (New York: Viking, 2005); Woody Holton, *Abigail Adams* (New York: Free Press, 2009); Catherine Allgor, *A Perfect Union: Dolley Madison and the Creation of the American Nation* (New York: Henry Holt, 2006); Erica Armstrong Dunbar, *Never Caught: The Washingtons' Relentless Pursuit of Their Runaway Slave, Ona Judge* (New York: Atria, 2017); Patricia Cleary, *Elizabeth Murray: A Woman's Pursuit of Independence in Eighteenth-Century America*

(Amherst: University of Massachusetts Press, 2000); Lorri Glover, *Eliza Lucas Pinckney: An Independent Woman in the Age of Revolution* (New Haven, CT: Yale University Press, 2020). Other excellent biographies include Mary Sarah Bilder, *Female Genius: Eliza Harriot and George Washington at the Dawn of the Constitution* (Charlottesville: University of Virginia Press, 2022); Catherine Kerrison, *Jefferson's Daughters: Three Sisters, White and Black, in a Young America* (New York: Ballantine Books, 2018); Cynthia A. Kierner, *Martha Jefferson Randolph, Daughter of Monticello: Her Life and Times* (Chapel Hill: University of North Carolina Press, 2012); Kierner, *The Tory's Wife: A Woman and Her Family in Revolutionary America* (Charlottesville: University of Virginia Press, 2023); Charlene M. Boyer Lewis, *Elizabeth Patterson Bonaparte: An American Aristocrat in the Early Republic* (Philadelphia: University of Pennsylvania Press, 2012); Jill Lepore, *Book of Ages: The Life and Opinions of Jane Franklin* (New York: Knopf, 2013); Lucia McMahon, *The Celebrated Elizabeth Smith: Crafting Genius and Transatlantic Fame in the Romantic Era* (Charlottesville: University of Virginia Press, 2022); and Shelia L. Skemp, *First Lady of Letters: Judith Sargent Murray and the Struggle for Female Independence* (Philadelphia: University of Pennsylvania Press, 2009).

28. See Leslie M. Alexander, "The Challenge of Race: Rethinking the Position of Black Women in the Field of Women's History," *Journal of Women's History* 16, no. 4 (Winter 2004): 50–60; Kimberle Crenshaw, "Mapping the Margins: Intersectionality, Identity Politics, and Violence Against Women of Color," *Stanford Law Review* 43, no. 6 (July 1991): 1241–99; Elsa Barkley Brown, "'What Has Happened Here': The Politics of Difference in Women's History and Feminist Politics," *Feminist Studies* 18, no. 2 (Summer 1992): 295–312; and Evelyn Brooks Higginbotham, "African-American Women's History and the Metalanguage of Race," *Signs* 17, no. 2 (Winter 1992): 251–74.

29. Elizabeth Fox-Genovese, *Within the Plantation Household: Black and White Women of the Old South* (Chapel Hill: University of North Carolina Press, 1988); Glymph, *Out of the House of Bondage*; Stephanie E. Jones-Rogers, *They Were Her Property: White Women as Slave Owners in the American South* (New Haven, CT: Yale University Press, 2019). See also Jones, *Labor of Love, Labor of Sorrow*; Marli F. Wiener, *Mistresses and Slaves: Plantation Women in South Carolina, 1830–80* (Champaign: University of Illinois Press, 1998); Brenda E. Stevenson, *Life in Black and White: Family and Community in the Slave South* (New York: Oxford University Press, 1996); Stephanie McCurry, *Masters of Small Worlds: Yeoman Households, Gender Relations, and the Political Culture of the Antebellum South Carolina Low*

Country (New York: Oxford University Press, 1995); and Stephanie M. H. Camp, *Closer to Freedom: Enslaved Women and Everyday Resistance in the Plantation South* (Chapel Hill: University of North Carolina Press, 2004).

30. Michele Gillespie, *Free Labor in an Unfree World: White Artisans in Slaveholding Georgia, 1789–1860* (Athens: University of Georgia Press, 2000); Susanna Delfino and Michele Gillespie, eds., *Neither Lady nor Slave: Working Women of the Old South* (Chapel Hill: University of North Carolina Press, 2002); Elizabeth R. Varon, *We Mean to Be Counted: White Women and Politics in Antebellum Virginia* (Chapel Hill: University of North Carolina Press, 1998).

31. Cynthia A. Kierner: *Southern Women in Revolution, 1776–1800* (Columbia: University of South Carolina Press, 1998); Kierner, *Scandal at Bizarre: Rumor and Reputation in Jefferson's America* (New York: Palgrave Macmillan, 2004); Kierner, *Martha Jefferson Randolph, Daughter of Monticello*; Kierner, *Beyond the Household*; Kierner, *The Tory's Wife*.

32. Anya Jabour, *Scarlett's Sisters: Young Women in the Old South* (Chapel Hill: University of North Carolina Press, 2007); Christie Anne Farnham, *The Education of the Southern Belle: Higher Education and Student Socialization in the Antebellum South* (New York: New York University Press, 1994). For Black children, see Marie Jenkins Schwartz, *Born in Bondage: Growing Up Enslaved in the Antebellum South* (Cambridge, MA: Harvard University Press, 2000), and Crystal Lynn Webster, *Beyond the Boundaries of Childhood: African American Children in the Antebellum North* (Chapel Hill: University of North Carolina Press, 2021).

33. Kirsten E. Wood, *Masterful Women: Slaveholding Widows from the American Revolution Through the Civil War* (Chapel Hill: University of North Carolina Press, 2004). For the colonial era, see Vivian Bruce Conger, *The Widows' Might: Widowhood and Gender in Early British America* (New York: New York University Press, 2009). For the Civil War era, see Angela Esco Elder, *Love and Duty: Confederate Widows and the Emotional Politics of Loss* (Chapel Hill: University of North Carolina Press, 2022).

34. Camp, *Closer to Freedom*; Daina Ramey Berry, *"Swing the Sickle for the Harvest Is Ripe": Gender and Slavery in Antebellum Georgia* (Champaign: University of Illinois Press, 2007).

35. Amrita Chakrabarti Myers, *Forging Freedom: Black Women and the Pursuit of Liberty in Antebellum Charleston* (Chapel Hill: University of North Carolina Press 2011); Jessica Millward, *Finding Charity's Folk: Enslaved and Free Black Women in Maryland* (Athens: University of Georgia Press, 2015); Nunley, *At the Threshold of Liberty*; Kabria Baumgartner, *In Pursuit of Knowledge: Black Women and Educational Activism in Antebellum America* (New York: New York University Press, 2019); Tera W. Hunter,

Bound in Wedlock: Slave and Free Black Marriage in the Nineteenth Century (Cambridge, MA: Harvard University Press, 2017); Alexandra J. Finley, *An Intimate Economy: Enslaved Women, Work, and America's Domestic Slave Trade* (Chapel Hill: University of North Carolina Press, 2020).

36. Jennifer L. Morgan, *Laboring Women: Reproduction and Gender in New World Slavery* (Philadelphia: University of Pennsylvania Press, 2004); Morgan, *Reckoning with Slavery: Gender, Kinship, and Capitalism in the Early Black Atlantic* (Durham, NC: Duke University Press, 2021); Berry, *"Swing the Sickle for the Harvest Is Ripe"*; Daina Ramey Berry, *The Price for Their Pound of Flesh: The Value of the Enslaved, from Womb to Grave, in the Building of a Nation* (Boston: Beacon Press, 2017); Berry and Kali Nicole Gross, *A Black Women's History of the United States* (Boston: Beacon Press, 2020). Other important works include Sharla M. Fett, *Working Cures: Healing, Health, and Power on Southern Slave Plantations* (Chapel Hill: University of North Carolina Press, 2002); Cynthia M. Kennedy, *Braided Relations, Entwined Lives: The Women of Charleston's Urban Slave Society* (Bloomington: University of Indiana Press, 2005); Wilma King, *The Essence of Liberty: Free Black Women During the Slave Era* (Columbia: University of Missouri Press, 2006); and Marie Jenkins Schwartz, *Birthing a Slave: Motherhood and Medicine in the Antebellum South* (Cambridge, MA: Harvard University Press, 2006).

37. Dunbar, *Never Caught*; Vanessa M. Holden, *Surviving Southampton: African American Women and Resistance in Nat Turner's Community* (Champaign: University of Illinois Press, 2021); Nell Irvin Painter, *Sojourner Truth: A Life, a Symbol* (New York: Norton, 1996); Nikki M. Taylor, *Driven Toward Madness: The Fugitive Slave Margaret Garner and Tragedy on the Ohio* (Athens: Ohio University Press, 2016); Amrita Chakrabarti Myers, *The Vice President's Black Wife: The Untold Life of Julia Chinn* (Chapel Hill: University of North Carolina Press, 2023). See also Erica Armstrong Dunbar, *A Fragile Freedom: African American Women and Emancipation in the Antebellum City* (New Haven, CT: Yale University Press, 2008); Margaret Washington, *Sojourner Truth's America* (Champaign: University of Illinois Press, 2009); and Tiya Miles, *All That She Carried: The Journey of Ashley's Sack, a Black Family Keepsake* (New York: Random House, 2021).

38. Theda Perdue, *Cherokee Women: Gender and Culture Change, 1700–1835* (Lincoln: University of Nebraska Press, 1998); Juliana Barr, *Peace Came in the Form of a Woman: Indians and Spaniards in the Texas Borderlands* (Chapel Hill: University of North Carolina Press, 2007); Susan Sleeper-Smith, *Indigenous Prosperity and American Conquest: Indian Women in the Ohio River Valley, 1690–1792* (Chapel Hill: University of North Carolina Press, 2018); Sleeper-Smith, *Indian Women and French Men:*

Rethinking Cultural Encounter in the Western Great Lakes (Amherst: University of Massachusetts Press, 2001). See also Brooke M. Bauer, *Becoming Catawba: Catawba Indian Women and Nation-Building, 1540–1840* (Tuscaloosa: University of Alabama Press, 2022).

39. Tiya Miles, *Ties That Bind: The Story of an Afro-Creek Family in Slavery and Freedom* (Berkeley: University of California Press, 2005); Honor Sachs, "It's All Relative: Finding Connection and Continuity Through Family History," *William and Mary Quarterly*, 3rd series, 81, no. 1 (January 2024): 83–92.

40. Anne F. Hyde, *Empires, Nations, and Families: A History of the North American West, 1800–1860* (Lincoln: University of Nebraska Press, 2011); Lisbeth Haas, *Saints and Citizens: Indigenous Histories of Colonial Missions and Mexican California* (Berkeley: University of California Press, 2013).

41. Clare A. Lyons, *Sex Among the Rabble: An Intimate History of Gender and Power in the Age of Revolution, Philadelphia, 1730–1830* (Chapel Hill: University of North Carolina Press, 2006).

42. Rachel Hope Cleves, *Charity and Sylvia: A Same-Sex Marriage in Early America* (New York: Oxford University Press, 2014). See also Clare A. Lyons, "Mapping an Atlantic Sexual Culture: Homoeroticism in Eighteenth-Century Philadelphia," *William and Mary Quarterly*, 3rd series, 60, no. 1 (January 2003): 119–54; "Special Issue: Beyond the Binaries: Critical Approaches to Sex and Gender in Early America," *Early American Studies* 12, no. 3 (Fall 2014): 459–678; and Jen Manion, *Female Husbands: A Trans History* (New York: Cambridge University Press, 2020).

43. Deirdre Cooper Owens, *Medical Bondage: Race, Gender, and the Origins of American Gynecology* (Athens: University of Georgia Press, 2017). Other important works include Fett, *Working Cures*; Gretchen Long, *Doctoring Freedom: The Politics of African American Medical Care in Slavery and Emancipation* (Chapel Hill: University of North Carolina Press, 2012); Schwartz, *Birthing a Slave*.

44. Ernest Freeberg, *The Education of Laura Bridgman: First Deaf and Blind Person to Learn Language* (Cambridge, MA: Harvard University Press, 2001); Kim E. Nielsen, *Money, Marriage, and Madness: The Life of Anna Ott* (Champaign: University of Illinois Press, 2020); Jennifer L. Barclay, *The Mark of Slavery: Disability, Race, and Gender in Antebellum America* (Champaign: University of Illinois Press, 2021).

45. Melton A. McLaurin, *Celia, a Slave* (Athens: University of Georgia Press, 1991); Sharon Block, *Rape and Sexual Power in Early America* (Chapel Hill: University of North Carolina Press, 2006); Finley, *An Intimate Economy*. See also Diane Miller Sommerville, *Rape and Race*

in the Nineteenth-Century South (Chapel Hill: University of North Carolina Press, 2004); Walter Johnson, *Soul by Soul: Life Inside the Antebellum Slave Market* (Cambridge, MA: Harvard University Press, 1999); Edward E. Baptist, "'Cuffy,' 'Fancy Maids,' and 'One-Eyed Men': Rape, Commodification, and the Domestic Slave Trade in the United States," *American Historical Review* 106, no. 5 (December 2001): 1619–50; Baptist, *The Half Has Never Been Told: Slavery and the Making of American Capitalism* (New York: Basic Books, 2014); Emily A. Owens, *Consent in the Presence of Force: Sexual Violence and Black Women's Survival in Antebellum New Orleans* (Chapel Hill: University of North Carolina Press, 2023); and John Wood Sweet, *The Sewing Girl's Tale: A Story of Crime and Consequences in Revolutionary America* (New York: Holt, 2023).

46. Victoria E. Bynum, *Unruly Women: The Politics of Social and Sexual Control in the Old South* (Chapel Hill: University of North Carolina Press, 1992); Joshua D. Rothman, *Notorious in the Neighborhood: Sex and Families Across the Color Line in Virginia, 1787–1861* (Chapel Hill: University of North Carolina Press, 2003).

47. Annette Gordon-Reed, *Thomas Jefferson and Sally Hemings: An American Controversy* (Charlottesville: University Press of Virginia, 1997); Gordon-Reed, *The Hemingses of Monticello: An American Family* (New York: Norton, 2008). See also Jan Ellen Lewis and Peter S. Onuf, eds., *Sally Hemings and Thomas Jefferson: History, Memory, and Civic Culture* (Charlottesville: University Press of Virginia, 1999); Mia Bay, "In Search of Sally Hemings in the Post-DNA Era," *Reviews in American History* 34, no. 4 (December 2006): 407–26; and Catherine Kerrison, "Harriet Hemings," in *Virginia Women: Their Lives and Times*, ed. Cynthia A. Kierner and Sandra Gioia Treadway, 2 vols. (Athens: University of Georgia Press, 2015–16), 1:222–43.

48. Martha Hodes, *White Women, Black Men: Illicit Sex in the Nineteenth-Century South* (New Haven, CT: Yale University Press, 1997).

49. Stansell, *City of Women*; Patricia Cline Cohen, *The Murder of Helen Jewett: The Life and Death of a Prostitute in Nineteenth-Century New York* (New York: Knopf, 1998); Judith Kelleher Schafer, *Brothels, Depravity, and Abandoned Women: Illegal Sex in Antebellum New Orleans* (Baton Rouge: Louisiana State University Press, 2009); Katie M. Hemphill, *Bawdy City: Commercial Sex and Regulation in Baltimore, 1790–1915* (New York: Cambridge University Press, 2020). See also Timothy J. Gilfoyle, *City of Eros: New York City, Prostitution, and the Commercialization of Sex, 1790–1920* (New York: Norton, 1992); Rodney Hessinger, *Seduced, Abandoned, and Reborn: Visions of Youth in Middle-Class America, 1780–1850* (Philadelphia: University of Pennsylvania Press, 2005); Helen Lefkowitz Horowitz, *Rereading Sex: Battles over Sexual Knowledge and Suppression*

in Nineteenth-Century America (New York: Knopf, 2002); and Amy Gilman Srebnick, *The Mysterious Death of Mary Rogers: Sex and Culture in Nineteenth-Century New York* (New York: Oxford University Press, 1995).

50. Ellen Hartigan-O'Connor, *The Ties That Buy: Women and Commerce in Revolutionary America* (Philadelphia: University of Pennsylvania Press, 2009); Marla R. Miller, *The Needle's Eye: Women and Work in the Age of Revolution* (Amherst: University of Massachusetts Press, 2006); Kathleen M. Brown, *Foul Bodies: Cleanliness in Early America* (New Haven, CT: Yale University Press, 2009). See also Sara T. Damiano, *To Her Credit: Women, Finance, and the Law in Eighteenth-Century New England Cities* (Baltimore: Johns Hopkins University Press, 2021).

51. Berry, *The Price for Their Pound of Flesh*; Seth Rockman, *Scraping By: Wage Labor, Slavery, and Survival in Early Baltimore* (Baltimore: Johns Hopkins University Press, 2008); John J. Zaborney, *Slaves for Hire: Renting Enslaved Laborers in Antebellum Virginia* (Baton Rouge: Louisiana State University Press, 2012). For the colonial era, see Felicia Y. Thomas, "'Fit for Town or Country': Black Women and Work in Colonial Massachusetts," *Journal of African American History* 105, no. 2 (Spring 2020): 191–212.

52. Shirley J. Yee, *Black Women Abolitionists: A Study in Activism, 1828–1860* (Knoxville: University of Tennessee Press, 1992); Martha S. Jones, *All Bound Up Together: The Woman Question in African American Public Culture, 1830–1900* (Chapel Hill: University of North Carolina Press, 2007); Stephanie J. Richmond, "Race, Class, and Antislavery: African American Women in the Transatlantic Antislavery Movement," *Journal of Women's History* 31, no. 3 (Fall 2019): 55–77. See also Dunbar, *A Fragile Freedom*; Manisha Sinha, *The Slave's Cause: A History of Abolition* (New Haven, CT: Yale University Press, 2016); Julie Winch, "Sarah Forten's Antislavery Networks," in *Women's Rights and Transatlantic Antislavery in the Era of Emancipation*, ed. Kathryn Kish Sklar and James Brewer Stewart (New Haven, CT: Yale University Press, 2007), 143–57.

53. Tiya Miles, "'Circular Reasoning': Recentering Cherokee Women in the Antiremoval Campaigns," *American Quarterly* 61, no. 1 (June 2009): 221–43. See also Claudio Saunt et al., "Rethinking Race and Culture in the Early South," *Ethnohistory* 53, no. 2 (Spring 2006): 399–406, and Mary Hershberger, "Mobilizing Women, Anticipating Abolition: The Struggle Against Indian Removal in the 1830s," *Journal of American History* 86, no. 1 (June 1999): 15–40.

54. Stacey M. Robertson, *Hearts Beating for Liberty: Women Abolitionists in the Old Northwest* (Chapel Hill: University of North Carolina Press, 2010); Julie Roy Jeffrey, *Frontier Women: The Trans-Mississippi West, 1840–1880* (New York: Hill and Wang, 1979); Jeffrey, *The Great Silent Army of*

Abolitionism: Ordinary Women in the Antislavery Movement (Chapel Hill: University of North Carolina Press, 1998); Elizabeth Jameson, "Women as Workers, Women as Civilizers: True Womanhood in the American West," in *The Women's West,* ed. Susan Armitage and Elizabeth Jameson (Norman: University of Oklahoma Press, 1987), 145–64; Jameson, "Toward a Multicultural History of Women in the Western United States," *Signs* 13, no. 4 (Summer 1988): 761–91. See also Tiya Miles, *The Dawn of Detroit: A Chronicle of Slavery and Freedom in the City of the Straits* (New York: New Press, 2017), and Peggy Pascoe, *Relations of Rescue: The Search for Female Moral Authority in the American West, 1874–1939* (New York: Oxford University Press, 1990).

55. Bonnie S. Anderson, *Joyous Greetings: The First International Women's Movement, 1830–1860* (New York: Oxford University Press, 2000); Bruce Dorsey, *Reforming Men and Women: Gender in the Antebellum City* (Ithaca, NY: Cornell University Press, 2002).

56. Nancy Isenberg, *Sex and Citizenship in Antebellum America* (Chapel Hill: University of North Carolina Press, 1998).

57. Lori D. Ginzberg, *Women and the Work of Benevolence: Morality, Politics, and Class in the Nineteenth-Century United States* (New Haven, CT: Yale University Press, 1990); Ginzberg, *Untidy Origins: A Story of Women's Rights in Antebellum New York* (Chapel Hill: University of North Carolina Press, 2005); Anne M. Boylan, *The Origins of Women's Activism: New York and Boston, 1797–1840* (Chapel Hill: University of North Carolina Press, 2002); Judith Wellman, *The Road to Seneca Falls: Elizabeth Cady Stanton and the First Woman's Rights Convention* (Champaign: University of Illinois Press, 2004); Alison M. Parker, *Articulating Rights: Nineteenth Century American Women on Race, Reform, and the State* (DeKalb: Northern Illinois University Press, 2010); Lisa Tetrault, *The Myth of Seneca Falls: Memory and the Women's Suffrage Movement, 1848–1898* (Chapel Hill: University of North Carolina Press, 2014). See also Susan Zaeske, *Signatures of Citizenship: Petitioning, Antislavery, and Women's Political Identity* (Chapel Hill: University of North Carolina Press, 2003).

58. Marylynn Salmon, *Women and the Law of Property in Early America* (Chapel Hill: University of North Carolina Press, 1986).

59. Laura F. Edwards, *The People and Their Peace: Legal Culture and the Transformation of Inequality in the Post-Revolutionary South* (Chapel Hill: University of North Carolina Press, 2009).

60. Norma Basch, *Framing American Divorce: From the Revolutionary Generation to the Victorians* (Berkeley: University of California Press, 1999); Thomas E. Buckley, *The Great Catastrophe of My Life: Divorce in the Old Dominion* (Chapel Hill: University of North Carolina Press, 2002);

Merril D. Smith, *Breaking the Bonds: Marital Discord in Pennsylvania, 1730–1830* (New York: New York University Press, 1991); Beatty, *In Dependence*, chap. 2. For legal context, see Peter W. Bardaglio, *Reconstructing the Household: Families, Sex, and the Law in the Nineteenth-Century South* (Chapel Hill: University of North Carolina Press, 1995). For marriage, see Nancy F. Cott, *Public Vows: A History of Marriage and the Nation* (Cambridge, MA: Harvard University Press, 2000); Hendrik Hartog, *Man and Wife in America: A History* (Cambridge, MA: Harvard University Press, 2000); and Nicholas L. Syrett, *American Child Bride: A History of Minors and Marriage in the United States* (Chapel Hill: University of North Carolina Press, 2016).

61. Kierner, *Scandal at Bizarre*.
62. Kelly M. Kennington, *In the Shadow of Dred Scott: St. Louis Freedom Suits and the Legal Culture of Slavery in Antebellum America* (Athens: University of Georgia Press, 2017); Kimberly M. Welch, *Black Litigants in the Antebellum American South* (Chapel Hill: University of North Carolina Press, 2018). See also Anne Twitty, *Before* Dred Scott: *Slavery and Legal Culture in the American Confluence, 1787–1857* (New York: Cambridge University Press, 2016).
63. Martha S. Jones, *Birthright Citizens: A History of Race and Rights in Antebellum America* (New York: Cambridge University Press, 2018). See also Corinne T. Field, *The Struggle for Equal Adulthood: Gender, Race, Age and the Fight for Citizenship in Antebellum America* (Chapel Hill: University of North Carolina Press, 2014).
64. Ryan, *Cradle of the Middle Class*; Perdue, *Cherokee Women*; Hunter, *Bound in Wedlock*. See also Martha Saxton, *Being Good: Women's Moral Values in Early America* (New York: Hill and Wang, 2002).
65. For companionate marriage, see Anya Jabour, *Marriage in the Early Republic: Elizabeth and William Wirt and the Companionate Ideal* (Baltimore: Johns Hopkins University Press, 1998). For motherhood, see Nora Doyle, *Maternal Bodies: Redefining Motherhood in Early America* (Chapel Hill: University of North Carolina Press, 2018); V. Lynn Kennedy, *Born Southern: Childbirth, Motherhood, and Social Networks in the Old South* (Baltimore: Johns Hopkins University Press, 2010); Klepp, *Revolutionary Conceptions*; Catherine M. Scholten, *Childbearing in American Society, 1650–1850* (New York: New York University Press, 1985); Katy Simpson Smith, *We Have Raised All of You: Motherhood in the South, 1750–1835* (Baton Rouge: Louisiana State University Press, 2013); and Laurel Thatcher Ulrich, *A Midwife's Tale: The Life of Martha Ballard, Based on Her Diary, 1785–1812* (New York: Knopf, 1990).

66. Margaret A. Nash, *Women's Education in the United States, 1780–1840* (New York: Palgrave Macmillan, 2005); Mary Kelley, *Learning to Stand and Speak: Women, Education, and Public Life in America's Republic* (Chapel Hill: University of North Carolina Press, 2006); Catherine Kerrison, *Claiming the Pen: Women and Intellectual Life in the Early American South* (Ithaca, NY: Cornell University Press, 2006); Lucia McMahon, *Mere Equals: The Paradox of Educated Women in the Early American Republic* (Ithaca, NY: Cornell University Press, 2012); Baumgartner, *In Pursuit of Knowledge*; Ann Taylor Allen, *The Transatlantic Kindergarten: Education and Women's Movements in Germany and the United States* (New York: Oxford University Press, 2017).
67. Barbara Welter, "The Feminization of American Religion, 1800–1860," in *Clio's Consciousness Raised: New Perspectives in the History of Women*, ed. Lois Banner and Mary S. Hartman (New York: Harper and Row, 1974), 137–57; Ann Douglas, *The Feminization of American Culture* (New York: Knopf, 1977).
68. Christine Leigh Heyrman, *Southern Cross: The Beginnings of the Bible Belt* (New York: Knopf, 1997); Susan Juster, *Disorderly Women: Sexual Politics and Evangelicalism in Revolutionary New England* (Ithaca, NY: Cornell University Press, 1994). See also Catherine A. Brekus, *Strangers and Pilgrims: Female Preaching in America, 1740–1845* (Chapel Hill: University of North Carolina Press, 1998).
69. Ann Braude, *Radical Spirits: Spiritualism and Women's Rights in Nineteenth-Century America* (Boston: Beacon Press, 1989); Devon A. Mihesuah, *Cultivating the Rosebuds: The Education of Women at the Cherokee Female Seminary, 1851–1909* (Champaign: University of Illinois Press, 1993); Emily Clark, *Masterless Mistresses: The New Orleans Ursulines and the Development of a New World Society, 1727–1834* (Chapel Hill: University of North Carolina Press, 2007). See also Rebecca Larson, *Daughters of Light: Quaker Women Preaching and Prophesying in the Colonies and Abroad, 1700–1775* (New York: Knopf, 1999); Emily Bingham, *Mordecai: An Early American Family* (New York: Hill and Wang, 2003); Ann M. Little, *The Many Captivities of Esther Wheelwright* (New Haven, CT: Yale University Press, 2016); and Ashley E. Moreshead, "'Beyond All Ambitious Motives': Missionary Memoirs and the Cultivation of Early American Evangelical Heroines," *Journal of the Early Republic* 38, no. 1 (Spring 2018): 37–60.
70. Marisa Fuentes, *Dispossessed Lives: Enslaved Women, Violence, and the Archive* (Philadelphia: University of Pennsylvania Press, 2016).

Men and Manhood in the Historiography of the Early American Republic

CRAIG THOMPSON FRIEND AND TIMOTHY J. WILLIAMS

IN 1800, Mason L. Weems told a story of when General Edward Braddock met a young Colonel George Washington, who, having been stripped of military command in the British Army, had retreated to Mount Vernon, taking up the plow "Cincinnatus-like." Upon hearing the Virginian's reason for retiring, Braddock declared him "a young man of sense and spirit, who knew and asserted his rights as became a soldier and British subject." Manhood, passion, rights, citizenship—from its earliest manifestations, the creation of the United States, hagiographic and otherwise, has been a story about men, or more specifically how men made national history and how national history made men.[1]

That is, until women's history. In the 1970s and 1980s, women's historians decentered men, confirming that women too made history, and as historian Laurel Thatcher Ulrich noted, those who did so were seldom "well-behaved." Yet men remained, if not as explicit nemeses, implicitly through patriarchal systems that they had constructed and fortified. After all, if some history-making women were not well-behaved, one must ask, "according to whose rules?" Men's lives continued to frame understandings of the emerging nation-state: "The Age of Washington," named for the war hero who embodied eighteenth-century republicanism and refinement. "The Age of Jefferson," christened for a man who penned that "all men are created equal" while enslaving hundreds and wrestling with the wolf by the ear throughout his life, epitomizing the nation's complex and conflicted racial history. "The Age of Jackson," styled after a man who symbolized unregulated violence, enslavement, and imperialism and yet became synonymous with greater democratic citizenship and market opportunities. As historian Joy Parr concluded in a 1995 essay, in portraying women as reactive to and dialogical with patriarchal structures, scholars "inadvertently enhanced the conceptual capacity of man to stand for all that was enduringly human."[2]

FEW HISTORIANS, even the earliest women's historians, challenged the early American republic's dominion of men. Instead, scholars scrutinized the influence and authority of patriarchy. In her pathbreaking *The Southern Lady* (1970), Anne Firor Scott concluded that the Southern Lady was an image created and perpetuated by patriarchy, arguing that it was not until the patriarchy "functionally" died as the Civil War ended that the "New Woman" appeared, coming "out of the domestic circle to work, live, and act in a broader society." In other words, women exerted their womanhood and individualisms "only so much as would not unfit them for their appropriate role in the patriarchy."[3]

As women's historians reassessed the early republic, the gay liberation movement began to influence other scholars' perspectives. In 1976, Jonathan Ned Katz published *Gay American History,* a collection of primary sources that added new ways of imagining manhood by documenting historical patterns of same-sex love, friendships, sexualities, communities, expressions, surveillances, and punishments. Still, Katz perplexed some readers by implying more than the evidence allowed. Some readers were happy to join Katz in his imaginative claims; others reacted against any suggestion that the works could be read as anything more than homosociality. All seemed willing, however, to accept that the American past entailed more complex relationships among men, and between men and women.[4]

Some intellectuals found empowerment in evidence of a gay American past; others were less convinced. Drew Gilpin Faust published *James Henry Hammond and the Old South* in 1982, personifying him so much as the anticipated Confederacy that Faust might easily have titled it "The Age of Hammond." And yet, Faust wrestled with a perplexing accusation against Hammond for "poking and punching a writhing Bedfellow with your long fleshen pole." A few years later, Carol Bleser insisted any reading of the episode as homosexual was "a rather tortured reading of passages."[5] Still, the emergence of gay history expanded how historians thought of manhood in the early American republic, more as a cultural construction rather than simply a default focus of eighteenth- and early nineteenth-century historians. And they investigated extra-heteronormative male-to-male stories as something formed primarily, if not solely, in relationship with and in contrast to womanhood.[6]

Like Scott, Faust, and Bleser, Bertram Wyatt-Brown looked southward to frame what might be deemed a proto-history of men in the early American republic: *Southern Honor* (1982). Wyatt-Brown viewed "honor" as a gendered construct, that is, "male honor." Yet, *Southern Honor* contained no index entries for "manliness," "manhood," or "masculinity." Only upon the book's twenty-fifth anniversary reprint in 2007, as masculinity studies evolved, did the index list "masculinity."[7] Still, the book had an outsized influence on manhood studies.

Drawing from anthropologists' fascination with honor-bound societies and kinship, Wyatt-Brown turned away from the men-as-personification model, understanding southern White men through their inherited honor-bound society—the "patriarchal dream" through which they constructed their lives and for which many would die in the Civil War. Wyatt-Brown's approach mirrored Scott's interpretation of women's experiences as framed by patriarchy: White men's lives could *only* be understood through the lens of patriarchy as evidenced through the culture of honor.[8]

PATRIARCHY, HOWEVER, generated anxiety among American men. Historians have portrayed every decade of the early republic with anxious men acting badly to retain their authority—and therefore their manhood—over women, children, and enslaved dependents.[9] The theme emerged among earlier women's historians, as when Scott concluded that "fear lay beneath the surface of the flowery praise of woman."[10] In 1975, Allan Stanley Horlick described how New Yorkers sought to harness young men's transitions from adolescence to adulthood lest they destabilize society. In 1983, David G. Pugh defined manhood primarily in terms of anxiety about women. In 1995, David Leverenz found that when ideologies of manhood historically intensified, they fostered "a compensatory response to fears of humiliation." By the turn of the twenty-first century, scholars' propensity to frame masculinity around anxieties became foundational to most studies of manhood. As Bryce Traister concluded, the "new historiography of American masculinity . . . locates instability at the base of all masculine identities constructed within American cultural matrices."[11]

Wyatt-Brown also established some methodological precedents through which many future scholars studied manhood. For example, he advanced the Self/Other paradigm that had emerged in gender studies, drawing from the anxiety theme to posit that men's performances resulted from "the misogyny that arose from male fear of female power." From anthropology, he framed rituals such as courtship and duels as measures of patriarchal performance. As anthropologist Pierre Bourdieu had concluded about the culture of honor, "the being and truth about a person are identical with the being and truth that others acknowledge in him."[12] From psychology, Wyatt-Brown explored the power of alternative honor traditions in the context of enslaved communities. In 1988, he concluded that enslaved men were bound not only by their enslavers but by a code of honor adapted from West African traditions. Maintaining honor in the face of "shame and humiliation" led enslaved men "to repress and maintain confident behavior under pressure" from enslavers. As among White southerners, honor defined manliness among enslaved men: "Male honor was richly prized in the slave quarters," Wyatt-Brown wrote, "and a defense of it established rank among fellow slaves."[13]

Only months after the publication of *Southern Honor*, David Pugh published *Sons of Liberty* (1983), similarly employing psychology to uncover a "masculinity cult." Pugh's study expanded beyond the South and beyond the early American republic, but the crux of his argument was that "the Jacksonian mystique" created the prototype of the "American man" which shaped masculinity into the late twentieth century. Pugh recognized that the history of the United States had always been one of "WASP males," which made "any effort to assess them historically as men" a "superfluous analysis." Although Pugh seemingly did not employ Carroll Smith-Rosenberg's 1971 "Beauty, the Beast and the Militant Woman," he similarly understood the promise of feminist history in unraveling manhood, framing his own study as "an effort to comprehend nineteenth-century manliness by examining how women were perceived from the male point of view and how they reacted because of it." *Sons of Liberty* did what Wyatt-Brown had not by asking, "Where are the women in men's history?"[14]

IN JOINING feminist perspectives to interpretations of masculine honor, performance, and selfhood, historians were slightly late to the party. In literary studies, sociology, cultural studies, and women's and gender studies, scholars already understood that critical engagement with masculinity was a necessary corollary to understanding women. In 1981, sociologist

R. W. Connell and colleagues introduced the concept of "hegemonic masculinity": men characterized by stoicism, physicality, aggression, competitiveness, achievement, and violence dominated women *as well as* nonhegemonic, subordinated men. Hegemonic manhood quickly became the most influential theory of manhood in early American republic scholarship.[15]

Growing interest in masculinity led to what Traister called "a critical renaissance": a "restoration of the representations of men—produced by men and analyzed for the most part by men—to the center of academic cultural criticism." The 1980s and 1990s flourished with social histories of men, overwhelmingly written by men. As one reviewer noted in 1988, "It seems as if every man and his dog is writing a book on masculinities." For some at least, the scholarship was personal, performing "a self-authorizing function" that intersected historians' own experiences with those of their historical subjects. David Leverenz acknowledged in *Manhood and the American Renaissance* (1995), "My rereadings emerge from several experiences in my own life, especially my involvement in childcare." Similarly, E. Anthony Rotundo confessed in *American Manhood* (1993), "I have been more aware of my inner discord on issues of manhood than of my inner coherence."[16]

As much as the new men's historians benefited from women's history, they also inherited an analytical construct that eventually stagnated the field. Marxist-feminist historians' emphasis on "separate spheres" led emergent masculinity studies to imagine a "men's sphere," resulting in a reductive understanding of men as "public" and women as "private." In *Women and Men on the Overland Trail* (1979), John Mack Faragher acknowledged that when historical men wrote, they "mainly left indications of their relationship to the productive aspects of their lives, while women contributed sources for an understanding of their relationship to domestic life." Despite his awareness of the sources' biases, Faragher uncritically replicated those separate spheres. Other studies—Mark C. Carnes's *Secret Ritual and Manhood in Victorian America* (1989), W. Jeffrey Bolster's *Black Jacks* (1997), and even George Chauncey's *Gay New York* (1994)— took for granted the distinctions between men's and women's spheres. A construct originally employed by women's historians to carve a place for the study of historical women became an indisputable point of departure for men's studies.[17]

In contrast to the honor paradigm that drew attention southward, analysis of men's social spheres grew in tandem with work explaining the social and cultural origins of the northern middle class. Some works came out of an American studies tradition emphasizing gender and culture, including Karen Halttunen's *Confidence Men and Painted Women* (1982) and John F. Kasson's *Rudeness and Civility* (1990). Instead of separating men and women, such works focused on how prescriptive literature prepared both for separate spheres and conjoined those spheres in marriage and family.[18]

Bridging the gendered divide required historians to find an intersection. In *Searching the Heart* (1989), Karen Lystra found one in romantic love. She critiqued how separate spheres "obscured the actual relativity of Victorian conceptions of male-female differences." Women's historians, she argued, had focused too narrowly on this trope, thus physically restraining women and emotionally confining men. Faragher had fallen into this trap too, concluding that men "hid their feelings from themselves" and found "comfort in the company of their similarly repressed brothers." Lystra disagreed, concluding, "There is hardly a trace of evidence that Victorians thought that men as a gender lacked the emotional capacity for true love." Separate spheres might explain where men's and women's bodies were, but the concept failed to account for their hearts.[19]

IN 1990, Judith Butler critiqued scholars' heteronormative presumptions about a gender binary that set up exclusionary gender ideals. For Butler, masculinity and femininity were contingent constructions. She promised to decenter "phallogocentrism and compulsory heterosexuality," which she saw as most influential in shaping gender studies. Butler's poststructural perspective was certainly familiar to Bruce Dorsey, who in 1995 conceptualized a syllabus for a new course on the "History of Manhood in America, 1750–1920." His premises were that "masculinity and manhood are social constructions." While these theorems required no articulation a decade later, they had to be expressly stated in the 1990s because it remained unclear whether men's history existed as a valid field of study separate from the rules that dictated women's history. Only months after Dorsey's proclamations and frustrated by the feminist cage in which men's history had become trapped, sociologist Michael Kimmel declared, "American men have no history." Social historians of the 1980s and early

1990s, he complained, had been concerned with issues more aligned with women than with the history of men "*as men*."[20]

Some historians, however, had explored men *as men*. In *Constructing Brotherhood* (1989), Mary Ann Clawson interpreted Freemasonry as "the vehicle by which fraternalism entered American society." Masculine sociability existed outside of the home at the nexus of friendship and politics. In Clawson's view, Masonry was a "masculine organization" and a separate male sphere that "rejected Enlightenment-era attitudes toward women, which emphasized their spiritual role in family and civic life."[21]

One element of this fraternal model was romantic friendship, as articulated by E. Anthony Rotundo. His survey from the revolutionary era to the twentieth century, *American Manhood* (1993), described an early nineteenth-century middle class that viewed children more romantically, resulting in gendered subcultures in which girls and boys learned to become women and men. "Boy culture" brought less parental supervision and more independence, less attachment to family and more participation in schooling, less work and more play. Boys formed emotional attachments to other boys—romantic friendships—that fostered competition, stoicism, aggression, self-control, and dominion over nature, and Rotundo assigned these characteristics to an emergent "self-made manhood."[22]

As the first historical survey of American manhood, Rotundo's work deserved the recognition it inspired, although it broke little historiographical ground beyond introducing various masculine typologies: "communal manhood" (colonial, rooted in small places, and contrasted with womanhood); "self-made manhood" (mostly nineteenth century, grounded in a largely northern market economy and an ascendant middle class that celebrated fatherhood); and "passionate manhood" (late nineteenth century, concerned with the self and the body, and a muted contrast with womanhood "from 'opposite' to merely 'different'"). Consider the impact of Rotundo's chronology: In *National Manhood* (1998), Dana D. Nelson traced the "homosocial construction of American manhood *qua* civic identity" to the emergence of self-made manhood's "boy culture," consequently situating American men as a brotherhood protecting "America-the-mother" through authority over Others. Mark E. Kann, in *A Republic of Men* (1998), seemed to agree with Rotundo's notion that the founding generation's recognition of the male Self—manifesting as "the traditional patriarch," "aristocratic manhood," "the genteel patriarch," "republican manhood," and of course "the self-made man"—precipitated "the breakup of corporate families and traditional communities, on the one hand, and legitimize[d] individual rights, entrepreneurship, contractual relations, and interest-based politics, on the other."[23]

DESPITE LYSTRA'S and Rotundo's interventions, scholars continued to focus on separate spheres and the middle class's revision of gender roles, albeit with regional differences. Interactions between genders that Rotundo, Halttunen, Kasson, Lystra, and others found among the northern middle class seemed foreign to those studying the South, where rather than acting as helpmates, men and women existed in tension. In *Intimacy and Power in the Old South* (1987), Steven M. Stowe argued that ideas about gender, marriage, sexuality, and intimacy were "sharply divided, even alienated, female from male." By 2001, when Wyatt-Brown returned to his honor-bound, kinship-framed masculinity with *The Shaping of Southern Culture*, he recognized the problem, quipping that scholars so greatly emphasized "allegedly effete tendencies in the urban and bourgeois world of Northern business and intellect" that they warped scholarly understanding of American gender roles. If historians avoided such "embourgeoisement" of honor, they would find an untarnished, unapologetic, unrelenting manhood—independent, of course, of womanhood. His southward gaze reinforced many historians' assumptions that the gendered rules and roles of the South were more unyielding and authoritative than those of the North, and that only hegemonic "men's honor" truly counted as manhood.[24]

Other scholars saw a more consistent *American* manhood grounded in honor. In *Affairs of Honor* (2001), for example, Joanne B. Freeman recognized that "southerners were quicker to duel than northerners, who withstood harsher insults but had their own breaking point." Levels and frequency of violence, not honor itself, distinguished southerners from other Americans. Wyatt-Brown conceded violence as the distinction between northern and southern White men, but he insisted the embourgeoisement of manhood—the middle class's materialistic dilution of things—led to the North's divergence. He found particularly troubling the failure of scholars, including Leverenz, Rotundo, and Gail Bederman (*Manliness and Civilization,* 1995) to interrogate embourgeoisement's effect on manhood. If embourgeoisement meant that the North evolved from traditional gender ways, the persistence of honor suggested that the South was insistently premodern.[25]

Not all historians were convinced. Anya Jabour challenged both Wyatt-Brown's concerns over embourgeoisement and Rotundo's framing of romantic male friendships as a northeastern middle-class phenomenon. Studying the worlds of Robert and William Wirt, Jabour uncovered how southern romantic friendships persisted into adulthood, evidence of middle-class values permeating supposed premodern traditions. Such values contributed to Americans' turn toward companionate marriage, in which husband and wife "value the love of the other above all else." Jabour's fresh portrait of southern manhood minimized the familiar context of honor-based patriarchal power and contextualized the South in the industrial and market economies where pressures to make money resulted in a "dual nature of nineteenth-century manhood," as Robert L. Griswold put it.[26]

WHEN SCHOLARS approached historical men through the contemporary lens of feminism, they prioritized male domination over women. The patriarchy needed to be smashed, or at least accounted for and thoroughly analyzed. But feminism was not the only political influence on masculinity studies. By the late 1980s, the gay rights movement and the AIDS epidemic had drawn attention to the privileging of heteromasculinity and the resulting Othering of nonhegemonic men. Leverenz's subjects—Nathaniel Hawthorne, Herman Melville, Henry David Thoreau, Frederick Douglass, Ralph Waldo Emerson, and Walt Whitman—were men of open feelings and thoughts, self-consciously deviant from the normative stoic patriarchy, and creating a self-making that envisioned mastery differently.[27]

Rotundo and Bederman were less willing to acknowledge Othering during the early to mid-1800s, situating it instead in the late nineteenth century. Rotundo agreed that emotions mattered but not in the manner that Leverenz claimed. For Rotundo, men became self-made only when they channeled emotions into ambitions, rivalry, and aggression. His chronology of manhood—communal, self-made, passionate—reinforced R. W. Connell's hegemonic model. Bederman also drew from the hegemonic model, intersecting it with race. Until Bederman, most gender historians had written about manhood as if it were assumed to be White manhood. Even Leverenz's discussion of Frederick Douglass emphasized self-making at the expense of race. Although Bederman focused on the turn of the twentieth century, her explicit attention to the Whiteness of hegemonic manhood in an imperial nation colonizing Black and Brown peoples provided a critical intercession in a historiographical conversation.[28]

Race could not be ignored. In fact, when scholars introduced race into analysis of manhood, regional distinctions diminished. Dana Nelson argued that White men's "investment in equality and inequality" destabilized their privilege. Wyatt-Brown considered that threat to racial privilege in his later writings on honor and kinship, concluding that White southern men ultimately went to war against their nation because they felt threatened "on the fundamental principle of honor, family, and race supremacy, one and indivisible." Nelson, Wyatt-Brown, and most early scholars of men's history concluded that men—White men—occupied "a lofty perch where they are depicted as complex beings who are equally capable of being brutish and noble," as sociologist Aldon D. Morris expressed in critiquing their scholarship.[29]

Not so loftily perched were Black men, whom, as Morris continued, gender scholars either ignored or portrayed "as the lesser side of humanity." Some scholars touched on masculinity in studying Black men as revolutionary soldiers, for example, but few analyzed Black manhood itself. James Oliver Horton and Lois E. Horton were notable exceptions. They demonstrated that when Black northern men attempted to act on manhood as White men did, their efforts resulted in increased White anxieties, anti-Black laws, and violence.[30]

In the late 1990s, scholars began to unravel Black manhood in the early United States. Martha Hodes tackled a prominent stereotype: Black men's oversexualization. White southerners considered Black men's sexual liaisons with White women scandalous and immoral, yet Hodes found little evidence of punitive violence and concluded that "toleration was mediated by limits of both patriarchy and class." Only with Black freedom did interracial sex become intolerable, partially because it represented Black men achieving manhood, "connoting the rights of citizenship and equality as well as autonomy."[31]

Darlene Clark Hine and Earnestine Jenkins's edited collection *A Question of Manhood* (1999), was already off to press when Hodes published her study, and so they did not consider it when they argued that scholars stereotyped Black manhood "as a negative and dismal experience." They contended that scholars had been corrupted by a historical negation of Black manhood that permeated the sources and persisted in the historiography. Although Hine and Jenkins did not cite *Roll, Jordan, Roll* (1976) as an example, their thinking certainly would have included Eugene D. Genovese's assessment of Black men: "The struggle to become and to remain men, not the 'boys' their masters called them, included some unattractive manifestations of male aggression." Violence was a common stereotype about Black men that Hine and Jenkins denounced, alongside their being "oversexed, ignorant, and immoral beings." Collectively, the essays in *A Question of Manhood* insisted that Black men historically grappled "with the same issues and questions of manhood and masculinity facing every other group of men in the nation." The authors elevated resistance as the dominant theme in studying Black men, many of whom not only faced enslavement but also a denial of their manhood that enslavers employed to diminish them.[32]

Unlike the regional distinctions attached to White manhood, scholars found Black manhood more uniform across geographies. Hodes hinted at how free Black men in the North faced similar legal and judicial toleration as enslaved Black men, until emancipation when all began to feel the same pressures against interracial sex. Essayists in *A Question of Manhood* found Black male resistance across the nation.

Despite growing attention to Black masculinity in the late 1990s, all men were not historiographically equal. White men seemed complex. Black men were one-dimensional at best. Indigenous men, Latino men, and Asian American men were nearly invisible, having appeared only when Hodes published *Sex, Love, Race* (1999), a collection which concluded that racial, ethnic, sexual, geographical, and class diversity "preclude the crafting of one master narrative." As Hodes anticipated, the first decade of the twenty-first century became a time of expanding subjects, overturning assumptions, and even rejecting paradigms that initially framed earlier works in men's history.[33]

WITH A new century, cultural histories of early American manhood outpaced the first generations of both women's and men's social histories. The advent of gender theory, with its poststructuralist, postmodernist deconstructions, challenged many tenets of gender history that had formed by the 2000s. Postmodern historians embraced the centrality of language and texts that Joan Scott had heralded. Yet, because gender is not only academic but also personal, many historians—particularly feminist scholars for whom women's history had been political activism—could not easily abandon the questions that had initiated their field and constrained their own lives. Cultural historians, enjoining anthropological interest in the objects and experiences of everyday life such as clothing, cuisine, and life rituals with analyses of values, assumptions, and prejudices, complicated—if not destabilized—older interpretations in gender history.[34]

Among the first tropes historians reexamined was anxiety over young men and their disruptive cultures. Unlike earlier studies that emphasized behavior without consideration of gender *qua* gender, cultural histories focused on how cultures of control, especially in popular discourse and print culture, emerged to construct "appropriate" manhood. Some scholars focused on reform and sex. From Bruce Dorsey's reform movements to Helen Lefkowitz Horowitz's "erotic canon" to Thomas Augst's character-producing conduct books to Jason Opal's "public-spirited" subjects, historians uncovered a variety of methods (usually not external enforcements but rather efforts to change hearts and minds) by which Americans directed young men into appropriate manhood.[35]

Many such works focused on northern urban milieus, but not all of them. In *All That Makes a Man* (2004), Stephen W. Berry II argued that young men might have desired distinction, which, like honor, brought social recognition, but unlike men of honor, those in search of éclat often struggled internally to develop a manliness worthy of the greatest novels, epic life journeys, and, importantly, the love of a woman. Three years later, Berry published *Princes of Cotton* (2007), an edited volume of the diaries that informed his monograph. Within their self-disclosures, Berry's subjects expressed an inner Self, shaped by "individualism, romanticism, and the secularization of evangelicalism." It was this "interiority of the self," formed in reaction to cultures of control, rather than the performance of manhood that provided new insight into southern manhood.[36]

As with Berry's schoolboys, interest in gender construction led to new scholarship about education and homosocialization. Robert F. Pace found the code of honor weighing heavily on college students, conflicting with their adolescent development. Lorri Glover concluded that "although honor accurately denotes a primal, perhaps the quintessential southern value," it did not explain the generation that saw themselves as Americans first, destined to bring the nation into being.[37]

Scholars such as Berry and Glover, writing in the wake of the 2001 terrorist attacks on the United States and the George W. Bush administration's engagement in Iraq, lived in a world where questions of a more national, if not altogether imperial, sense of masculine selfhood ran deep. In 2005, Amy S. Greenberg published *Manifest Manhood and the Antebellum American Empire* in which manhood in the era of the Mexican-American War existed along a continuum between "martial manhood" and "restrained manhood." These framing themes applied Rotundo's "self-made manhood" to imperial contexts: the former passionately embracing self-interest—personal and national—through aggression; the latter dedicated to self-making and domesticity, particularly fatherhood.[38]

Greenberg's attention to the trans-Mississippi West foregrounded a region that men's historians largely had ignored. The few scholars who wrote western men's history typically traced how American manliness, specifically White manhood, evolved as it traveled westward. Joan E. Cashin argued that in the Old Southwest, more intense notions of manly independence, violence, and patriarchalism emerged. Robert L. Griswold found continuity in chapters titled "Ideal Manhood in California" and "Manhood and the Companionate Ideal" in his survey of family and divorce.[39]

BEGINNING IN 1999, a flurry of scholarship emerged that demonstrated how very White previous masculinity histories had been. Albert L. Hurtado explored how the libertine culture of 1850s California constructed manhood among Indigenous, Hispanic, Chinese, mixed-race, and White Americans. Two years later, Susan Lee Johnson explored how gendered and sexual identities reshaped amid the diversity of California's Gold Rush—men and women of Mexican, White American, Black American, Indigenous, and Chinese backgrounds.[40]

These books heralded an expansion of men's history beyond White men. Although not particularly focused on manhood, scholars of Indigenous America could not avoid gender in explaining how American military conquest, extractive colonialism, settler colonialism, and capitalism transformed indigenous lives. Whether Cherokees, Choctaws, or Creeks, southern Indians' gender roles evolved in the eighteenth and nineteenth centuries. Where matrilineality had long dominated, patriarchy gained strength. Where traditional patterns of masculine behavior faded with declining opportunities for hunting and warfare, new patterns based on market relations and conspicuous consumption arose.[41]

Black manhood also received more attention in the early 2000s. Edward E. Baptist led the way with a series of essays that posited gender and sexuality as instruments of enslavement. His provocative *The Half Has Never Been Told* (2014) dealt little with gender but nevertheless characterized enslavement as an instrument of capitalism that denigrated male and female bodies.[42]

Much of the scholarship that focused on Black and Indigenous manhood developed from new attentions to market relations. In his study of working-class New Yorkers, Joshua R. Greenberg determined that working men shaped a sense of manliness out of their reactions to the challenges of a new industrial economy. L. Diane Barnes found capitalistic influences shaping manhood identities among *Artisan Workers in the Upper South* (2008).[43] The market loomed large in John Mayfield's poignant cultural history of humor in the Old Southwest, *Counterfeit Gentlemen* (2009). Mayfield concluded that "tentative manhoods" abounded in this liminal region which was unencumbered by traditional southern mores. Literary humor about the region, therefore, relied on a "fluid state of masculinity" and "many alternative models of manly behavior."[44]

While alternative, tentative, and even muted manhoods began to appear prominently in historians' studies of places like the Old Southwest, older traditions continued. Harry S. Laver showed how values of camaraderie and homosociability in militia service remained constant on trans-Appalachian landscapes. Mark R. Cheathem did the same for honor and kinship. Brian Steele focused on gender as an analytical category in "Thomas Jefferson's Gender Frontier," arguing that the president envisioned an American identity based on a seemingly natural domestic order with female domesticity at its center, an ideal that marginalized Native Americans, enslaved Blacks, and the French. Other scholars demonstrated the challenges in transferring gender ideals to western territories. In *Home Rule* (2015), Honor Sachs concluded that Jefferson's idyllic American domestic order was largely untenable. Would-be patriarchs found little more than poverty and disappointment in Kentucky's frontier, and little power to rule their homes, protect against raiding Native Americans, and engage in insurrections. Only common Whiteness among the new state's elites and poor Whites facilitated a political culture and government based on race and masculinity.[45]

The role of the state and politics in defining manhood became a prominent theme in gender scholarship in the early 2000s. Albrecht Koschnik found all-male literary societies and militia companies creating environments where young Federalists coalesced around political values and "initiated each other into organized Federalism." Gendered spaces provided havens for intellectuals too. In *Men of Letters in the Early Republic* (2008), Catherine O'Donnell Kaplan argued that public institutions such as the Boston Athenæum fostered intellectualism and republican manliness. Public debating societies for young men created forums for what Carolyn Eastman termed "gendered public participation." John Gilbert McCurdy's *Citizen Bachelors* (2009) showed how unmarried men occupied a liminal space within the body politic, suspicious for not heading households but admired for their independence and autonomy (especially when it came to sex). Between 1800 and the political ascendancy of one of the nation's best-known bachelors, James Buchannan, Americans "reconsider[ed] the single man" as a "legal identity, a cultural ideal, and a lived experience." Writing nine years after McCurdy, Joshua A. Lynn found that despite Buchanan's bachelorhood raising eyebrows and generating sensationalized stories, bachelorhood ultimately served him politically, signifying "a conservative temperament" that stood in contrast to northern antislavery "fanatics." In *Bosom Friends* (2019), Thomas J. Balcerski combined much of the analytical literature that bound politics to bachelorhood and manhood. His exploration of Buchanan's romantic friendship with William Rufus King did not resolve questions of homosexuality but underscored how homosociality so often fostered political advancement.[46]

Greater interest in men's gendered citizenship has led scholars to attend to how manhood shaped national and sectional politics. Christopher J. Olsen's *Political Culture and Secession in Mississippi* (2000) argued that local party politics created a sense of White "communal manhood" which united them behind the social values of a slave society. Masculinity and honor produced an antiparty political system sensitive to insults from party machines, Republicans, and Unionists. A protégée of Bertram-Wyatt Brown, Olsen interpreted honor as "the lingua franca of southern sectionalism," intrinsic to communal masculinity and Mississippi's gendered political culture. Carolyn Eastman similarly described masculinity coalescing men around political ideas in antebellum movements such as peace reformers and Garrisonian abolitionists. Men articulated different visions of the male reformer: peace advocates eschewed coercion and violence while some abolitionists saw those as important strategies for immediate antislavery action.[47]

In the 2000s and 2010s, scholars continued to investigate the role of capitalism in reshaping manhood and reimagined interpretive paradigms of honor and romantic friendship. In 2008, Jennifer R. Green showed how military academies "represented educational reform and the concerns of an emerging middle class that employed them to promote social stability and mobility." In 2009, Nicholas L. Syrett demonstrated how early fraternities emerged as challenges to faculty authority, constructing manhood around intellectual pursuits and personal autonomy. In 2010, Ami Pflugrad-Jackisch revealed how "market-oriented men" of fraternal organizations embraced "an alternative definition of southern White manhood and respectability that was rooted in self-discipline, moral character, and success at work rather than simply property ownership." And in 2015, Timothy J. Williams found young men in antebellum southern universities using education, self-making, and intellectual maturity to harmonize middle-class values and the honor-bound worldview.[48]

THE SECOND Great Awakening also garnered attention as historians mined archives for a sense of men's inner emotional lives. Such studies expanded on the trope of romantic friendships. Bruce Dorsey related how in New England, evangelical piety embodied desire and eroticism, only to be countered by the rise of evangelical reformers and their gospel of self-denial, sexual restraint, and policing of male pleasure.[49] In the South, evangelicalism influenced how men negotiated honor and manhood. James Hill Welborn III's *Dueling Cultures, Damnable Legacies* (2023) uncovered how men in Edgefield County, South Carolina, examined their own behavior and morality in lifelong pursuits of self-mastery, which proved crucial for perpetuating slavery. He found that as evangelical morality collided with manifestations of honor, men had to navigate intersecting (and sometimes conflicting) roles as fathers, clergy, politicians, and enslavers.[50]

Still, the methods employed to explore early nineteenth-century White men's emotions and inner lives became problematic when applied to Black manhood. Few enslaved or free Black men left behind the necessary evidence, so actions often had to speak louder than words. In 2016,

Sergio A. Lussana published *My Brother Slaves,* arguing that men's "homosocial recreational pursuits" created an "all-male world" where "they constructed markers of status, identity, and masculinity and forged lasting friendships." This community experience catalyzed and supported resistance to slavery. Published two years later, David Stefan Doddington's *Contesting Slave Masculinity in the American South* underscored what he characterized as "the fluidity of gender within slave communities" and that resistance, work, sex, power, violence, leisure, and family influenced enslaved men's public and private performances of masculinity. Doddington thus corrected past assumptions that enslaved men shared a singular identity derived from resistance and instead scrutinized one another and "passed judgment on the different forms of manhood they witnessed in their communities."[51]

Works on sex, especially sexual abuse, have also added nuance to historical understanding of enslaved men. Thomas A. Foster argued that, like enslaved women, enslaved men experienced "sexual vulnerability" within the power structures of chattel slavery, including but not limited to rape. This vulnerability, he concluded, "figured in developing concepts of masculinity."[52]

As Foster demonstrated, the intersection of sexuality and gender offered new historiographical possibilities, and his contributions to men's history in this regard have been invaluable. In many ways, Foster forged paths through the historiographical wilderness. In his introduction to *Long Before Stonewall* (2007), he articulated how Americans of the preindustrial United States viewed same-sex behavior as illegal and immoral but also as "distinct and unusual," presaging the rise of mid- to late nineteenth-century hegemonic ideals of gendered and sexualized personhoods. The early American republic's shift from "punishing the body to reforming the self" spoke to a dualism attached to same-sex sexuality, evidenced by Mark E. Kann's excellent chapter. In *New Men* (2011), Foster echoed Michael Kimmel's earlier critique that many historians viewed men "as un-gendered subjects," despite a quarter century of scholarship. Foster insisted that constructions of manliness during the colonial and revolutionary eras laid the foundation for "the notions of manhood [that] affected the development of what would become the United States." In *Sex and the Eighteenth-Century Man* (2006), Foster delineated how sexuality informed a man's communal standing, homosocial relationships, and business successes, making sexuality intrinsic to men's identities. In *Sex and the Founding Fathers* (2014), Foster unpacked how narratives associated with six founders naturalized heterosexuality as defining American manhood and, in turn, reified national identity as a straight White male inheritance.[53]

SINCE THE advent of men's history, scholars have been asking "who was a man?" and offering multivariant definitions. Still, they concurred on one thing: whether hegemonic or alternative, restrained or martial, self-regulated, enslaved, or intellectual, the masculine categories offered by scholars applied to biological males. Foster's scholarship began to demand greater elasticity to the concept of manhood. As some scholars of the 2010s pushed the historical analysis of manhood in that direction, the West again led the way. Although much of the scholarship on transness and cross-dressing stretches chronologically beyond the early republic, several scholars have grounded their studies in the antebellum era. In 2011, Peter Boag argued that the West offered a stage for gender and sexual transness. Women who cross-dressed as men enjoyed the benefits of manhood: adventure, economic opportunity, greater mobility, and anonymity. Drawing conclusions about men who cross-dressed as women proved more problematic to Boag, but he found among both groups individuals motivated by personal desires and emotions. Three years later, Clare Sears countered Boag's representation of a more libertine West with the story of how stabilizing gender and sexuality became central to state-making. The Gold Rush's male homosocial world might have resulted in a surprising array of gender and sexual practices, including cross-dressing, but as populations of cis-women grew, transness became a threat to the emerging heteronormative order. Women dressed as men challenged cis-male dominance, and cross-dressing and transness became increasingly associated with moral degeneracy. And Sears concluded that many cross-dressers were racialized Others threatening White heterogeneity. Boag too noted a racialized component to transness, and C. Riley Snorton showed how enslaved peoples performed "passing" as both a racial and gendered masquerade, the most famous example being Ellen Craft, who posed as a White man with her husband, William, as her enslaved "body servant."[54]

In 2020, Jen Manion studied women who "assumed the 'character of a man'" and sustained long-term relationships with women. As stories of "female husbands" circulated in popular literature, they came to represent "the idea that gender was malleable and not entirely linked to sex." Recovering such lives is not easy: Boag made the case for sexologists, historians, and archivists' complicity in covering up such stories, and Manion showed how the sources that do shed light are compromised by the sensationalism and moral judgment of their times.[55]

IN SOME ways, exploration of cross-dressing and transness brought gender history full circle. Manion's *Female Husbands* mirrored early scholars of men of the early republic and even earlier women's historians: history is personal, and the personal is political. The development of men's history showed a field necessarily bound by the social realities of the authors and their times. Movements for women's rights, gay liberation, Black freedom, and LGBTQ rights generated new questions and shaped the literature accordingly. The appearance of scholarship about cross-dressing and transness have appeared at a moment when the question of "what is a man?" proffers new possibilities for the history of manhood, the early American republic, and the twenty-first-century United States.

Notes

1. M. L. Weems, *The Life of George Washington* (Philadelphia: Joseph Allen, 1800), 40–41.
2. Laurel Thatcher Ulrich, "Vertuous Women Found: New England Ministerial Literature, 1668–1735," *American Quarterly* 28, no. 1 (Spring 1976): 20; Joy Parr, "Gender History and Historical Practice," *Canadian Historical Review* 76, no. 3 (September 1995): 354–76 (quote on 367). For a gendered critique of such representations, see Lorri Glover, *Founders as Fathers: The Private Lives and Politics of the American Revolutionaries* (New Haven, CT: Yale University Press, 2014), 64–70, 173–90.
3. Anne Firor Scott, *The Southern Lady: From Pedestal to Politics, 1830–1930* (Chicago: University of Chicago Press, 1970), xii, 52, 102.
4. Jonathan Ned Katz, *Gay American History: Lesbians and Gay Men in the U.S.A.: A Documentary History* (New York: Crowell, 1976).
5. Drew Gilpin Faust, *James Henry Hammond and the Old South: A Design for Mastery* (Baton Rouge: Louisiana State University, 1982), 19n18; Carol Bleser, ed., *Secret and Sacred: The Diaries of James Henry Hammond, a Southern Slaveholder* (New York: Oxford University Press, 1988), 5. Also see Martin Bauml Duberman, "'Writhing Bedfellows' in Antebellum South Carolina: Historical Interpretation and the Politics of Evidence," in

Hidden from History: Reclaiming the Gay and Lesbian Past, ed. Martin Bauml Duberman, Martha Vicinus, and George Chauncey Jr. (New York: New American Library, 1989), 153–68.

6. For a historiographical overview situating men's history in response to feminist studies, see Toby L. Ditz, "The New Men's History and the Peculiar Absence of Gendered Power: Some Remedies from Early American Gender History," *Gender and History* 16, no. 1 (April 2004): 1–35. Other useful historiographical essays include Bryce Traister, "Academic Viagra: The Rise of American Masculinity Studies," *American Quarterly* 52, no. 2 (June 2000): 274–304; Craig Thompson Friend and Lorri Glover, "Rethinking Southern Masculinity: An Introduction," in *Southern Manhood: Perspectives on Masculinity in the Old South*, ed. Craig Thompson Friend and Lorri Glover (Athens: University of Georgia Press, 2004), vii–xvii; Jeff Osborne, "Constituting American Masculinity," *American Studies* 49, nos. 3–4 (Fall–Winter 2008): 111–32; and Bryan C. Rindfleisch, "'What It Means to Be a Man': Contested Masculinity in the Early Republic and Antebellum America," *History Compass* 10, no. 11 (November 2012): 852–65.

7. Bertram Wyatt-Brown, *Southern Honor: Ethics and Behavior in the Old South* (New York: Oxford University Press, 1982), vii; Wyatt-Brown, *Southern Honor: Ethics and Behavior in the Old South: 25th Anniversary Edition* (1982; New York: Oxford University Press, 2007), 592. Also see Elliot J. Gorn, "'Gouge and Bite, Pull Hair and Scratch': The Social Significance of Fighting in the Southern Backcountry," *American Historical Review* 90, no. 1 (February 1985): 18–43, and Kenneth S. Greenberg, *Honor and Slavery: Lies, Duels, Noses, Masks, Dressing as a Woman, Gifts, Strangers, Humanitarianism, Death, Slave Rebellions, the Proslavery Argument, Baseball, Hunting, and Gambling in the Old South* (Princeton, NJ: Princeton University Press, 1997).

8. Wyatt-Brown, *Southern Honor* (1982), vii.

9. Kathleen M. Brown, *Good Wives, Nasty Wenches, and Anxious Patriarchs: Gender, Race, and Power in Colonial Virginia* (Chapel Hill: University of North Carolina Press, 1996); Judith A. Allen, "Men Interminably in Crisis? Historians on Masculinity, Sexual Boundaries, and Manhood," *Radical History Review* 82 (Winter 2002): 204n10.

10. Scott, *The Southern Lady*, 18; Stephanie McCurry, *Masters of Small Worlds: Yeoman Households, Gender Relations, and the Political Culture of the Antebellum South Carolina Low Country* (New York: Oxford University Press, 1995).

11. Allan Stanley Horlick, *Country Boys and Merchant Princes: The Social Control of Young Men in New York* (Lewisburg, NY: Bucknell University Press, 1975); Jay Fliegelman, *Prodigals and Pilgrims: The American Revolution*

Against Patriarchal Authority, 1750–1800 (New York: Cambridge University Press, 1982); David G. Pugh, *Sons of Liberty: The Masculine Mind in Nineteenth-Century America* (Westport, CT: Greenwood Press, 1983); David Leverenz, *Manhood and the American Renaissance* (Ithaca, NY: Cornell University Press, 1989), 3–4; Traister, "Academic Viagra," 276.

12. Pierre Bourdieu, "The Sentiment of Honor in Kabyte Society," in *Honour and Shame: The Values of Mediterranean Society*, ed. J. G. Peristiany (London: Weidenfeld and Nicholson, 1966), 212; Wyatt-Brown, *Southern Honor* (2007), 226–27. Performance—the need to *prove* manhood—as a dominant theme in American history is the central argument of Michael Kimmel's influential *Manhood in America: A Cultural History* (New York: Free Press, 1996).

13. Bertram Wyatt-Brown, "The Mask of Obedience: Male Slave Psychology in the Old South," *American Historical Review* 93, no. 5 (December 1988): 1246, 1249.

14. Pugh, *Sons of Liberty*, xv–xvii, xx; Carroll Smith-Rosenberg, "Beauty, the Beast and the Militant Woman: A Case Study in Sex Roles and Social Stress in Jacksonian America," *American Quarterly* 23, no. 4 (October 1971): 562–84.

15. Traister, "Academic Viagra," 274–304; Elaine Showalter, "Introduction: The Rise of Gender," in *Speaking of Gender*, ed. Elaine Showalter (New York: Routledge, 1988), 1–16; R. W. Connell et al., *Ockers and Disco-Maniacs: A Discussion of Sex, Gender and Secondary Schooling* (Stanmore, New South Wales, Australia: Inner City Education Centre, 1981); Connell, *Which Way Is Up? Essays on Sex, Class, and Culture* (Boston: Allen and Unwin, 1983); Connell, *Gender and Power: Society, the Person and Sexual Politics* (Stanford, CA: Stanford University Press, 1987); Connell, *Masculinities* (Berkeley: University of California Press, 1995); Connell and James W. Messerschmidt, "Hegemonic Masculinity: Rethinking the Concept," *Gender and Society* 19, no. 6 (December 2005): 829–59. On the importance of Connell's intervention, see Ditz, "The New Men's History and the Peculiar Absence of Gendered Power," 1–35.

16. Traister, "Academic Viagra," 276; Cameron Duff, review of John MacInnes, *The End of Masculinity: The Confusion of Sexual Genesis and Sexual Difference in Modern Society* (Buckingham, UK: Open University Press, 1998), *Journal of Sociology* 35, no. 3 (December 1999): 388; Leverenz, *Manhood and the American Renaissance*, 6; E. Anthony Rotundo, *American Manhood: Transformations in Masculinity from the Revolution to the Modern Era* (New York: Basic Books, 1993), x.

17. John Mack Faragher, *Women and Men on the Overland Trail* (New Haven, CT: Yale University Press, 1979), 1, 61, 171, 176; Mark C. Carnes, *Secret*

Ritual and Manhood in Victorian America (New Haven, CT: Yale University Press, 1989); W. Jeffrey Bolster, *Black Jacks: African American Seamen in the Age of Sail* (Cambridge, MA: Harvard University Press, 1997); George Chauncey, *Gay New York: Gender, Urban Culture, and the Making of the Gay Male World, 1890-1940* (New York: Basic Books, 1994).

18. Karen Halttunen, *Confidence Men and Painted Women: A Study of Middle-Class Culture in America, 1830-1870* (New Haven, CT: Yale University Press, 1982); John F. Kasson, *Rudeness and Civility: Manners in Nineteenth-Century Urban America* (New York: Hill and Wang, 1990). For a critique of scholars' avoidance of establishing broader intersections between women's history and men's history, see Nancy F. Cott, "On Men's History and Women's History," in *Meanings for Manhood: Constructions of Masculinity in Victorian America*, ed. Mark C. Carnes and Clyde Griffen (Chicago: University of Chicago Press, 1991), 205-12.

19. Karen Lystra, *Searching the Heart: Women, Men, and Romantic Love in Nineteenth-Century America* (New York: Oxford University Press, 1989), 123, 125; Faragher, *Women and Men on the Overland Trail*, 133.

20. Judith Butler, *Gender Trouble: Feminism and the Subversion of Identity* (1990; rpt. New York: Routledge, 1999), xxix; Bruce Dorsey, "History of Manhood in America, 1750-1920," *Radical History Review* 64 (Winter 1996): 19-30 (quotes on 20); Kimmel, *Manhood in America*, 1-2.

21. Mary Ann Clawson, *Constructing Brotherhood: Class, Gender, and Fraternalism* (Princeton, NJ: Princeton University Press, 1989), 28. Also see Steven C. Bullock, *Revolutionary Brotherhood: Freemasonry and the Transformation of the American Social Order, 1730-1840* (Chapel Hill: University of North Carolina Press, 1996), 260, and Michael Kaplan, "New York City Tavern Violence and the Creation of a Working-Class Male Identity," *Journal of the Early Republic* 15, no. 4 (Winter 1995): 591-617.

22. Rotundo, *American Manhood*, 31-46. See also Rotundo, "Body and Soul: Changing Ideals of American Middle-Class Manhood, 1770-1920," *Journal of Social History* 16, no. 4 (Summer 1983): 23-38; Rotundo, "American Fatherhood: A Historical Perspective," *American Behavioral Scientist* 29, no. 1 (Summer 1985): 7-23; Rotundo, "Learning About Manhood: Gender Ideals and Middle-Class Family in Nineteenth-Century America," in *Manliness and Morality: Middle Class Masculinity in Britain and America*, ed. J. A. Mangan and James Walvin (New York: St. Martin's Press, 1987), 35-51; Rotundo, "Romantic Friendship: Male Intimacy and Middle-Class Youth in the Northern United States, 1800-1900," *Journal of Social History* 23, no. 1 (Autumn 1989): 1-25; and Rotundo, "Boy Culture: Middle-Class Boyhood in Nineteenth-Century America," in Carnes and Griffen, eds., *Meanings for Manhood*, 15-36.

23. Rotundo, *American Manhood*, 2–7 (quote on 6); Dana D. Nelson, *National Manhood: Capitalist Citizenship and the Imagined Fraternity of White Men* (Durham, NC: Duke University Press, 1998), 50–51; Mark E. Kann, *A Republic of Men: The American Founders, Gendered Language, and Patriarchal Politics* (New York: New York University Press, 1998), 12–15, 159.
24. Steven M. Stowe, *Intimacy and Power in the Old South: Ritual in the Lives of the Planters* (Baltimore: Johns Hopkins University Press, 1987), xvii–xviii; Wyatt-Brown, *The Shaping of Southern Culture: Honor, Grace, and War, 1760s–1890s* (Chapel Hill: University of North Carolina Press, 2001), xi–xii, 305n5.
25. Joanne B. Freeman, *Affairs of Honor: National Politics in the New Republic* (New Haven, CT: Yale University Press, 2001), xvi–xvii. See also Freeman, *The Field of Blood: Violence in Congress and the Road to Civil War* (New York: Farrar, Straus and Giroux, 2018), and Craig Thompson Friend, "Sex, Self, and the Performance of Patriarchal Manhood in the Old South," in *The Old South's Modern Worlds: Slavery, Region, and Nation in the Age of Progress*, ed. L. Diane Barnes, Brian Schoen, and Frank Towers (New York: Oxford University Press, 2011), 246–65.
26. Anya Jabour, "Masculinity and Adolescence in Antebellum America: Robert Wirt at West Point, 1820–1821," *Journal of Family History* 23, no. 4 (October 1998): 393–416; Jabour, *Marriage in the Early Republic: Elizabeth and William Wirt and the Companionate Ideal* (Baltimore: John Hopkins University Press, 1998), 4, 46; Jabour, "Male Friendship and Masculinity in the Early National South: William Wirt and His Friends," *Journal of the Early Republic* 20, no. 1 (Spring 2000): 83–111; Robert L. Griswold, *Family and Divorce in California, 1850–1890: Victorian Illusions and Everyday Realities* (Albany: State University of New York Press, 1982), 92. On romantic friendships, also see Caleb Crain, *American Sympathy: Men, Friendship, and Literature in the New Nation* (New Haven, CT: Yale University Press, 2001), and Richard Godbeer, *The Overflowing of Friendship: Love Between Men and the Creation of the American Republic* (Baltimore: Johns Hopkins University Press, 2009).
27. Leverenz, *Manhood and the American Renaissance*, 1–8.
28. Rotundo, *American Manhood*, 3, 278; Gail Bederman, *Manliness and Civilization: A Cultural History of Gender and Race in the United States, 1880–1917* (Chicago: University of Chicago Press, 1995); Leverenz, *Manhood and the American Renaissance*, 108–34.
29. Nelson, *National Manhood*, 16, 176–203; Wyatt-Brown, *The Shaping of Southern Culture*, 202; Aldon D. Morris, "Foreword," in *A Question of Manhood: A Reader in U.S. Black Men's History and Masculinity*, vol. 1, "*Manhood Rights*": *The Construction of Black Male History and*

Manhood, 1750–1870, ed. Darlene Clark Hine and Earnestine Jenkins (Bloomington: Indiana University Press, 1999), xii.
30. Sidney Kaplan and Emma Nogrady Kaplan, *The Black Presence in the Era of the American Revolution* (Amherst: University of Massachusetts Press, 1989); James Oliver Horton, "Freedom's Yoke: Gender Conventions Among Antebellum Free Blacks," *Feminist Studies* 12, no. 1 (Spring 1986): 51–76; W. Jeffrey Bolster, "'To Feel Like a Man': Black Seamen in the Northern States, 1800–1860," *Journal of American History* 76, no. 4 (March 1990): 1173–99; James Oliver Horton and Lois E. Horton, "The Affirmation of Manhood: Black Garrisonians in Antebellum Boston," in *Courage and Conscience: Black and White Abolitionists in Boston,* ed. Donald M. Jacobs (Bloomington: Indiana University Press, 1993), 127–53; Daniel P. Black, *Dismantling Black Manhood: An Historical and Literary Analysis of the Legacy of Slavery* (New York: Garland, 1997); Diane Miller Sommerville, "Rape, Race, and Castration in Slave Law in the Colonial and Early South," in *The Devil's Lane: Sex and Race in the Early South,* ed. Catherine Clinton and Michele Gillespie (New York: Oxford University Press, 1997), 74–89.
31. Morris, "Foreword," xii; Martha Hodes, *White Women, Black Men: Illicit Sex in the Nineteenth-Century South* (New Haven, CT: Yale University Press, 1997), 1, 4, 143.
32. Darlene Clark Hine and Earnestine Jenkins, "Preface," in Hine and Jenkins, eds., *A Question of Manhood,* xvi, xvii, 2, 57; Eugene D. Genovese, *Roll, Jordan, Roll: The World the Slaves Made* (1972; rpt. New York: Vintage, 1976), 490. Centering resistance as a, if not *the,* primary analytic theme for Black manhood, *A Question of Manhood* proved transformative; see Sarah N. Roth, "'How a Slave Was Made a Man': Negotiating Black Violence and Masculinity in Antebellum Slave Narratives," *Slavery and Abolition* 28, no. 2 (2007): 355–75; Rebecca Fraser, "Negotiating Their Manhood: Masculinity Amongst the Enslaved in the Upper South, 1830–1861," in *Black and White Masculinity in the American South, 1800–2000,* ed. Lydia Plath and Sergio Lussana (Newcastle upon Tyne, UK: Cambridge Scholars, 2009), 76–94; Plath, "North Carolina and Nat Turner: Honour and Violence in a Slave Insurrection Scare," in Plath and Lussana, eds., *Black and White Masculinity in the American South,* 16–36; Lussana, "To See Who Was Best on the Plantation: Enslaved Fighting Contests and Masculinity in the Antebellum Plantation South," *Journal of Southern History* 76, no. 4 (November 2010): 901–22; Kenneth E. Marshall, *Manhood Enslaved: Bondmen in Eighteenth- and Early Nineteenth-Century New Jersey* (Rochester, NY: University of Rochester Press, 2011); A. Kristen Foster, "'We Are Men!': Frederick Douglass and the Fault Lines of Gendered Citizenship,"

Journal of the Civil War Era 1, no. 2 (June 2011): 143; and Lussana, *My Brother Slaves: Friendship, Masculinity, and Resistance in the Antebellum South* (Lexington: University Press of Kentucky, 2016).

33. Hodes, *Black Men, White Women*, 240n71; Martha Hodes, ed., *Sex, Love, Race: Crossing Boundaries in North American History* (New York: New York University Press, 1999), 1.

34. For an overview of men's history as it relates to gender and women's histories, see Sonya O. Rose, "Men and Masculinity," in *What Is Gender History?* (Malden, MA: Polity Press, 2010), 56–79.

35. Patricia Cline Cohen, "Unregulated Youths: Masculinity and Murder in the 1830s City," *Radical History Review* 52 (Winter 1992): 33–52; Bruce Dorsey, *Reforming Men and Women: Gender in the Antebellum City* (Ithaca, NY: Cornell University Press, 2002); Helen Lefkowitz Horowitz, *Rereading Sex: Battles over Sexual Knowledge and Suppression in Nineteenth-Century America* (New York: Knopf, 2002), 10; Thomas Augst, *The Clerk's Tale: Young Men and Moral Life in Nineteenth-Century America* (Chicago: University of Chicago Press, 2003), 4; J. M. Opal, *Beyond the Farm: National Ambitions in Rural New England* (Philadelphia: University of Pennsylvania Press, 2008), xi. Similar works include Timothy J. Gilfoyle, *City of Eros: New York City, Prostitution, and the Commercialization of Sex, 1790–1920* (New York: Norton, 1992); David Greven, "Troubling Our Heads About Ichabod: 'The Legend of Sleepy Hollow,' Classic American Literature, and the Sexual Politics of Homosocial Brotherhood," *American Quarterly* 56 (1 March 2004): 83–110; and C. Dallett Hemphill, "Isaac and 'Isabella': Courtship and Conflict in an Antebellum Circle of Youth," *Early American Studies* 2, no. 2 (Fall 2004): 398–434.

36. Stephen W. Berry II, *All That Makes a Man: Love and Ambition in the Civil War South* (New York: Oxford University Press, 2003); Berry, *Princes of Cotton: Four Diaries of Young Men in the South, 1848–1860* (Athens: University of Georgia Press, 2007), 5–6.

37. Robert F. Pace, *Halls of Honor: College Men in the Old South* (Baton Rouge: Louisiana State University Press, 2004); Lorri Glover, *Southern Sons: Becoming Men in the New Nation* (Baltimore: Johns Hopkins University Press, 2007), 2. Also see Glover, "An Education in Southern Masculinity: The Ball Family of South Carolina in the New Republic," *Journal of Southern History* 69, no. 1 (February 2003): 39–70, and Jeffrey A. Mullins, "Honorable Violence: Youth Culture, Masculinity, and Contested Authority in Liberal Education in the Early Republic," *American Transcendental Quarterly* 17, no. 3 (September 2003): 161–79.

38. Amy S. Greenberg, *Manifest Manhood and the Antebellum American Empire* (New York: Cambridge University Press, 2005), 11–12. For an

overview of how histories of manhood in the early republic influenced Civil War–era historiography, see James J. Broomall, "Wartime Masculinities," in *The Cambridge History of the American Civil War*, vol. 3, *Affairs of the People*, ed. Aaron Sheehan-Dean (New York: Cambridge University Press, 2019), 3–24, esp. 3–5.

39. Joan E. Cashin, *A Family Venture: Men and Women on the Southern Frontier* (New York: Oxford University Press, 1991); Griswold, *Family and Divorce in California*, 92–140. Also see Nicole Etcheson, "Manliness and the Political Culture of the Old Northwest, 1790–1860," *Journal of the Early Republic* 15, no. 1 (Spring 1995): 59–77.

40. Albert L. Hurtado, *Intimate Frontiers: Sex, Gender, and Culture in Old California* (Albuquerque: University of New Mexico Press, 1999); Susan Lee Johnson, *Roaring Camp: The Social World of the California Gold Rush* (New York: Norton, 2000). Also see Johnson's contribution, among those of others, in Matthew Basso, Laura McCall, and Dee Garceau, eds., *Across the Great Divide: Cultures of Manhood in the American West* (New York: Routledge, 2001), and Christopher Herbert, *Gold Rush Manliness: Race and Gender on the Pacific Slope* (Seattle: University of Washington Press, 2018).

41. Philip Gould, "Remembering Metacom: Historical Writing and the Cultures of Masculinity in Early Republican America," in *Sentimental Men: Masculinity and the Politics of Affect in American Culture*, ed. Mary Chapman and Glenn Hendler (Berkeley: University of California Press, 1999), 112–24; James Taylor Carson, *Searching for the Bright Path: The Mississippi Choctaws from Prehistory to Removal* (Lincoln: University of Nebraska Press, 1999); Claudio Saunt, *A New Order of Things: Property, Power, and the Transformation of the Creek Indians, 1733–1816* (New York: Cambridge University Press, 1999); Greg O'Brien, *Choctaws in a Revolutionary Age, 1750–1830* (Lincoln: University of Nebraska Press, 2002).

42. Edward E. Baptist, "The Absent Subject: African American Masculinity and Forced Migration to the Antebellum Plantation Frontier," in Friend and Glover, eds., *Southern Manhood*, 136–73; Baptist, "'Cuffy,' 'Fancy Maids,' and 'One-Eyed Men': Rape, Commodification, and the Domestic Slave Trade in the United States," *American Historical Review* 106, no. 5 (December 2001): 1619–50; Baptist, *The Half Has Never Been Told: Slavery and the Making of American Capitalism* (New York: Basic Books, 2014). Other notable studies of Black masculinity from the early 2000s include Fraser, "Negotiating Their Manhood," and Foster, "'We are Men!'"

43. Joshua R. Greenberg, *Advocating the Man: Masculinity, Organized Labor, and the Market Revolution in New York, 1800–1840* (New York: Columbia University Press, 2008); L. Diane Barnes, *Artisan Workers in the Upper*

South: Petersburg, Virginia, 1820–1865 (Baton Rouge: Louisiana State University Press, 2008). See also Greg O'Brien, "Trying to Look Like Men; Changing Notions of Masculinity Among Choctaw Elites in the Early Republic," in Friend and Glover, eds., *Southern Manhood*, 49–70; L. Diane Barnes, "Fraternity and Masculine Identity: The Search for Respectability Among White and Black Artisans in Petersburg, Virginia," in Friend and Glover, eds., *Southern Manhood*, 71–91; John Mayfield, "Being Shifty in a New Country: Southern Humor and the Masculine Ideal," in Friend and Glover, eds., *Southern Manhood*, 113–35; Brian P. Luskey, "Jumping Counters in White Collars: Manliness, Respectability, and Work in the Antebellum City," *Journal of the Early Republic* 26, no. 2 (Summer 2006): 173–219; and Luskey, *On the Make: Clerks and the Quest for Capital in Nineteenth-Century America* (New York: New York University Press, 2010).

44. John Mayfield, *Counterfeit Gentlemen: Manhood and Humor in the Old South* (Gainesville: University Press of Florida, 2009), xvi, xvii, 46. Timothy Stewart-Winter and Simon Stern offered a nuanced, queer reading of southwestern humor in "Picturing Same-Sex Marriage in the Antebellum United States: The Union of 'Two Most Excellent Men' in Longstreet's 'A Sage Conversation,'" *Journal of the History of Sexuality* 19, no. 2 (May 2010): 198.

45. Harry S. Laver, "Refuge of Manhood: Masculinity and the Militia Experience in Kentucky," in Friend and Glover, eds., *Southern Manhood*, 1–21; Laver, *Citizens More Than Soldiers: The Kentucky Militia and Society in the Early Republic* (Lincoln: University of Nebraska Press, 2007); Mark R. Cheathem, "'The High Minded Honourable Man': Honor, Kinship, and Conflict in the Life of Andrew Jackson Donelson," *Journal of the Early Republic* 27, no. 2 (Summer 2007): 265–92; Brian Steele, "Thomas Jefferson's Gender Frontier," *Journal of American History* 95, no. 1 (June 2008): 18; Honor Sachs, *Home Rule: Households, Manhood, and National Expansion on the Eighteenth-Century Kentucky Frontier* (New Haven, CT: Yale University Press, 2015); Sachs, "The Myth of the Abandoned Wife: Married Women's Agency and the Legal Narrative of Gender in Eighteenth-Century Kentucky," *Ohio Valley History* 3, no. 4 (Winter 2003): 3–20. Also see Thomas C. Buchanan, *Black Life on the Mississippi: Slaves, Free Blacks, and the Western Steamboat World* (Chapel Hill: University of North Carolina Press, 2004), and Ryan Dearinger, "Violence, Masculinity, Image, and Reality on the Antebellum Frontier," *Indiana Magazine of History* 100, no. 1 (March 2004): 26–55.

46. Albrecht Koschnik, *"Let a Common Interest Bind Us Together": Associations, Partisanship, and Culture in Philadelphia, 1775–1840* (Charlottesville:

University of Virginia Press, 2007); Catherine O'Donnell Kaplan, *Men of Letters in the Early Republic: Cultivating Forums of Citizenship* (Chapel Hill: University of North Carolina Press, 2008), 1, 41; Carolyn Eastman, "The Female Cicero: Young Women's Oratory and Gendered Public Participation in the Early American Republic," *Gender and History* 19, no. 2 (August 2007): 260–83; Eastman, *A Nation of Speechifiers: Making an American Public After the Revolution* (Chicago: University of Chicago Press, 2009), esp. 115–78; John Gilbert McCurdy, *Citizen Bachelors: Manhood and the Creation of the United States* (Ithaca, NY: Cornell University Press, 2009), 3–10; Joshua A. Lynn, "A Manly Doughface: James Buchanan and the Sectional Politics of Gender," *Journal of the Civil War Era* 8 (December 2018): 591–620; Thomas J. Balcerski, *Bosom Friends: The Intimate World of James Buchanan and William Rufus King* (New York: Oxford University Press, 2019).

47. Christopher J. Olsen, *Political Culture and Secession in Mississippi: Masculinity, Honor, and the Antiparty Tradition, 1830–1860* (New York: Oxford University Press, 2000), 9; Carolyn Eastman, "Fight Like a Man: Gender and Rhetoric in the Early Nineteenth-Century American Peace Movement," *American Nineteenth Century History* 10, no. 3 (September 2009): 247–71.

48. Jennifer R. Green, *Military Education and the Emerging Middle Class in the Old South* (New York: Cambridge University Press, 2008); Nicholas L. Syrett, *The Company He Keeps: A History of White College Fraternities* (Chapel Hill: University of North Carolina Press, 2009); Ami Pflugrad-Jackisch, *Brothers of a Vow: Secret Fraternal Orders and the Transformation of White Male Culture in Antebellum Virginia* (Athens: University of Georgia Press, 2010); Timothy J. Williams, *Intellectual Manhood: University, Self, and Society in the Antebellum South* (Chapel Hill: University of North Carolina Press, 2015).

49. Bruce Dorsey, "'Making Men What They Should Be': Male Same-Sex Intimacy and Evangelical Religion in Early Nineteenth-Century New England," *Journal of History of Sexuality* 24, no. 3 (September 2015): 345–77. Also see William Benemann, *Male-Male Intimacy in Early America: Beyond Romantic Friendships* (New York: Routledge, 2006), and Peter C. Baldwin, *Angel on a Freight Train: A Story of Faith and Queer Desire in Nineteenth-Century America* (Albany: State University of New York Press, 2020).

50. Christine Heyrman, *Southern Cross: The Beginnings of the Bible Belt* (New York: Knopf, 1997); James Hill Welborn III, *Dueling Cultures, Damnable Legacies: Southern Violence and White Supremacy in the Civil War Era* (Charlottesville: University of Virginia Press, 2023). Also see Janet Moore

Lindman, "Acting the Manly Christian: White Evangelical Masculinity in Revolutionary Virginia," *William and Mary Quarterly,* 3rd series, 57, no. 2 (April 2000): 393–416; Charity R. Carney, *Ministers and Masters: Methodism, Manhood, and Honor in the Old South* (Baton Rouge: Louisiana State University Press, 2011); Robert Elder, *The Sacred Mirror: Evangelicalism, Honor, and Identity in the Deep South, 1790–1860* (Chapel Hill: University of North Carolina Press, 2016); and Anna Koivusalo, *The Man Who Started the Civil War: James Chesnut, Honor, and Emotion in the American South* (Columbia: University of South Carolina Press, 2022).

51. Lussana, *My Brother Slaves,* 6–9; David Stefan Doddington, *Contesting Slave Masculinity in the American South* (New York: Cambridge University Press, 2018), 2–3, 19.

52. Thomas A. Foster, "The Sexual Abuse of Black Men Under Slavery," *Journal of the History of Sexuality* 20, no. 3 (September 2011): 445–64; Foster, "The Sexual Abuse of Black Men Under American Slavery," in *Sexuality and Slavery: Reclaiming Intimate Histories of the Americas,* ed. Daina Ramey Berry and Leslie M. Harris (Athens: University of Georgia Press, 2018), 124–44; Foster, *Rethinking Rufus: Sexual Violations of Enslaved Men* (Athens: University of Georgia Press, 2019), 4–5. Foster showed the possibilities of same-sex affection among enslaved men, a theme Jim Downs explored in "With Only a Trace: Same-Sex Sexual Desire and Violence on Slave Plantations, 1607–1865," in *Connexions: Histories of Race and Sex in North America,* ed. Jennifer Brier, Jim Downs, and Jennifer L. Morgan (Urbana: University of Illinois Press, 2016), 15–37.

53. Thomas A. Foster, "Introduction," in *Long Before Stonewall: Histories of Same-Sex Sexuality in Early America,* ed. Thomas A. Foster (New York: New York University Press, 2007), 8–10; Mark E. Kann, "Sexual Desire, Crime, and Punishment in the Early Republic," in Foster, ed., *Long Before Stonewall,* 279–302; Foster, ed., *New Men: Manliness in Early America* (New York: New York University Press, 2011), 3, 5; Foster, ed., *Documenting Intimate Matters: Primary Sources for a History of Sexuality in America* (Chicago: University of Chicago Press, 2012); Foster, *Sex and the Eighteenth-Century Man: Massachusetts and the History of Sexuality in America* (New York: Beacon Press, 2006); Foster, *Sex and the Founding Fathers: The American Quest for a Relatable Past* (Philadelphia: Temple University Press, 2014). Acts versus identities emerged as an early debate in the history of sexuality; see Michel Foucault, *The History of Sexuality: An Introduction,* trans. Robert Hurley (New York: Pantheon Books, 1978), and John D'Emilio and Estelle B. Freedman, *Intimate Matters: A History of Sexuality in America* (New York: Harper & Row, 1988).

54. Peter Boag, *Re-Dressing America's Frontier Past* (Berkeley: University of California Press, 2011); Clare Sears, *Arresting Dress: Cross-Dressing, Law, and Fascination in Nineteenth-Century San Francisco* (Durham, NC: Duke University Press, 2014); C. Riley Snorton, *Black on Both Sides: A Racial History of Trans Identity* (Minneapolis: University of Minnesota Press, 2017), esp. chap. 2. For the Crafts' story, see Illyon Woo, *Master Slave Husband Wife: An Epic Journey from Slavery to Freedom* (New York: Simon and Schuster, 2023).
55. Jen Manion, *Female Husbands: A Trans History* (New York: Cambridge University Press, 2020), 2, 13.

CONTRIBUTORS

JACQUELINE BEATTY is associate professor of history at York College of Pennsylvania and the author of *In Dependence: Women and the Patriarchal State in Revolutionary America* (2023). Her specializations are in early American history and women's and gender history with a particular focus on the American revolutionary era. She has published in the *South Carolina Historical Magazine, American Historian, Washington Post,* and *Time.*

RACHEL HOPE CLEVES is professor of history at the University of Victoria. She has authored multiple prize-winning books and articles, including *The Reign of Terror in America: Visions of Violence from Anti-Jacobinism to Antislavery* (2009), *Charity and Sylvia: A Same-Sex Marriage in Early America* (2014), *Unspeakable: A Life Beyond Sexual Morality* (2020), and *Lustful Appetites: An Intimate History of Good Food and Wicked Sex* (2024).

SHANNON C. EAVES is associate professor of African American history at the College of Charleston. She specializes in slavery and gender in the antebellum American South. Eaves is the author of *Sexual Violence and American Slavery: The Making of a Rape Culture in the Antebellum South* (2024) and has held research fellowships from Rutgers University and the American Association of University Women.

CRAIG THOMPSON FRIEND is professor of history and public history at North Carolina State University and a former president of the Society for Historians of the Early American Republic. He has authored five books including *Becoming Lunsford Lane: The Lives of an American Aeneas* (2025) and *Kentucke's Frontiers* (2012). He has edited or coedited eight collections, four with Lorri Glover, including *Southern Manhood: Perspectives on Masculinity in the Old South* (2004) and *Reinterpreting Southern Histories: Essays in Historiography* (2020).

LORRI GLOVER is the Bannon Endowed Chair in history at Saint Louis University. Her works include *Eliza Lucas Pinckney: An Independent Woman in the Age of Revolution* (2020), *Southern Sons: Becoming Men in the New Nation* (2007), and *Reinterpreting Southern Histories: Essays in Historiography* (2020), coedited with Craig Thompson Friend. She has served as president of the Southern Association for Women Historians and the Southern Historical Association.

ANTWAIN K. HUNTER is assistant professor of history at the University of North Carolina at Chapel Hill where he specializes in slavery and freedom in North America. His scholarship, including the forthcoming *A Precarious Balance: Firearms, Race, and Community in North Carolina, 1729–1865*, explores the legal and social dynamics of free and enslaved Black North Carolinians' access to, possession of, and use of firearms in the eighteenth and nineteenth centuries. He has published in the *Journal of Military History*, *Journal of Family History*, and *North Carolina Historical Review*.

LYNN KENNEDY is associate professor and chair in the Department of History and Religion at the University of Lethbridge (Canada), where she teaches American history. Her research focuses on issues of domesticity and household formation in the nineteenth-century South, including childbirth, motherhood, babies, gossip, sewing, and fashion. She is the author of *Born Southern: Childbirth, Motherhood, and Social Networks in the Old South* (2010) and coeditor of *Fat and the Body in the Long Nineteenth Century: Meanings, Measures, and Representations* (2025).

JOSHUA A. LYNN is associate professor of history at Eastern Kentucky University. He studies race, gender, and sexuality in nineteenth-century political culture and political thought. His first book was *Preserving the White Man's Republic: Jacksonian Democracy, Race, and the Transformation of American Conservatism* (2019). His work has appeared in the *Journal of the Civil War Era*, *Civil War History*, *Journal of the Early Republic*, and *Tennessee Historical Quarterly*.

KENNETH E. MARSHALL is professor of history at SUNY Oswego. He is the author of *Manhood Enslaved: Bondmen in Eighteenth- and Early Nineteenth-Century New Jersey* (2011), the first historical monograph specifically focused on the gendered lives of enslaved American men. His work on gender and northern slavery has appeared in scholarly journals including *Slavery and Abolition*, *Journal of African American History*, and *Journal of American Ethnic History*. He is currently writing a monograph on Silvia Dubois.

ASHLEY E. MORESHEAD is a lecturer of history at the University of Central Florida where she specializes in gender and religion in the nineteenth-century

United States. She has published essays in the *Journal of the Early Republic* and *Early American Studies*.

JAMIE MYERS is associate professor of history and American Indian Studies at the University of North Carolina at Pembroke. Her forthcoming *Cherokee Men: Masculinity and Gendered Power* explores Cherokee masculinity and how gender expectations informed men's political decisions in response to the pressures of colonialism. She is also coeditor of an upcoming anthology entitled *Gender in the Native South: A Reinterpretation of Women, Men, and Two-Spirit Peoples Before 1850* and serves on the *Native South* journal editorial board.

STEVEN PEACH is associate professor of history at Tarleton State University, a member of the Texas A&M University System. His research centers on politics, kinship, and leadership among Indigenous peoples of the eighteenth- and nineteenth-century South. He authored *Rivers of Power: Creek Political Culture in the Native South, 1750–1815* (2024) and is working on a book that explores race and gender in Indian Territory.

AMI PFLUGRAD-JACKISCH is professor and the chair of the history department at the University of Toledo. Her interests lie in questions about gender and citizenship in the early United States. She is the author of *Brothers of a Vow: Secret Fraternal Orders and the Transformation of White Male Culture in Antebellum Virginia* (2010) and the forthcoming *The World of Westover: Mary Willing Byrd, Gender, Slavery, and Citizenship in Revolutionary Virginia,* supported by a National Endowment for the Humanities Fellowship.

STEPHANIE J. RICHMOND is professor of history and director of the Roberts Center for the Study of the African Diaspora at Norfolk State University. A historian of gender and race in the Atlantic world, she has published work in the *Journal of Women's History, Women's History Review,* and *Programming Historian*. She is also the primary investigator of Sold Down River, a digital history project that traces more than twenty thousand enslaved people sold from Virginia to New Orleans.

RACHEL WALKER is associate professor of history at the University of Hartford, where she teaches courses on race, gender, and sexuality in American history. Walker's *Beauty and the Brain: The Science of Human Nature in Early America* (2022) won the Mary Kelley Book Prize from the Society for Historians of the

Early American Republic and was a finalist for both the Cheiron Book Prize and the Organization of American Historians' Frederick Jackson Turner Prize. Her next project focuses on sex, science, and Spiritualism in nineteenth-century radicalism.

TIMOTHY J. WILLIAMS is associate professor of history at the University of Oregon. He specializes in the history of education in the United States and intersections of gender and intellectual life in the Civil War era. He is the author of *Intellectual Manhood: University, Self, and Society in the Antebellum South* (2015) and coeditor of *Prison Pens: Gender, Memory, and Imprisonment in the Writings of Mollie Scollay and Wash Nelson, 1863–1866* (2018).

INDEX

Italicized page numbers refer to illustrations.

Abiel Smith School, 275
Abram, Susan, 9
Adams, Abigail, 296
Adams, Catherine, 265
adultery, 78–79, 148–53, 156, 158n1, 248
Affairs of Honor (Freeman), 327
AIDS epidemic, 328
Alexander, Elizabeth. *See* Dubois, Elizabeth
Alexander, Julia, 163–81
All Bound Up Together (Jones), 302
Allen, Ann Taylor, 304
Allen, Irving Lewis, 345
Allen, Myra, 36
Allgor, Catherine, 295
All That Makes a Man (Berry), 331
Alston, James, 59–60
Amazons, 84, 86, 94n43
a mensa et thoro. See divorce
American Bible Society, 23
American Board of Commissioners for Foreign Missions, 23, 121
American Education Society, 23
American Indian Center, 134n2
American Manhood (Rotundo), 324, 326–27, 328
American Medical Association, 164
American Museum (Carey), 71
American Phrenological Journal, 218, 220, 224, 228, 232
Ames, Lucy, 35
Amherst College, 23
Anderson, Bonnie S., 302
Anderson, Rufus, 31, 35
Andover Theological Seminary, 29
Anna Karenina (Tolstoy), 157

Anthony, Susan B., 221, 226
Armstead, Shaun, 96
Ar'n't I a Woman? (White), 292
Artisan Workers in the Upper South (Barnes), 333
Astor, John Jacob, 254
Astor Place theater riots, 152
Augst, Thomas, 331
avenoodle, 211, 243–57, 258n6, 259n13, 259n16, 259n20, 261n34, 262n45, 263n51

Badger, The (Chickamauga), 15, 20n23
Baird, William, 98
Balcerski, Thomas J., 334
Baldwin, Thomas, 268, 270
Balentine, Hamilton, 119, 126
Bancroft, John, 221–22
Baptist, Edward E., 333
Baptist Board of Foreign Missions, 34
Baptist Missionary Magazine, 36, 37
Baptists, 32, 34, 37, 121
Barclay, Jennifer L., 299
Barker, Theodosia, 33, 38
Barnes, Adeline, 238n15
Barnes, L. Diane, 333
Barr, Juliana, 298
Basch, Norma, 155, 303
Bassett, William, 227
Baumgartner, Kabria, 297, 304
Bawdy City (Hemphill), 300
Beatty, Jacqueline, 295, 303
Beauchamp, Pierre-Joseph de, 78, 80
"Beauty, the Beast and the Militant Woman" (Smith-Rosenberg), 323
Bederman, Gail, 327, 328–29

356 INDEX

Beecher, Henry Ward, 227
Benge, Bob (Chickamauga), 20n21
Benson, Carl. *See* Bristed, Charles Astor
Berkin, Carol, 295
Berlin, Ira, 105
Berry, Daina Ramey, 297, 301
Berry, Stephen W., II, 331, 332
Berthold, Michael, 96, 108, 111
Bicentennial, 290, 291
Billie (enslaved), 54–55
Birthright Citizens (Jones), 304
Bittel, Carla, 224, 231
Black American men: among Creek and Seminole nations, 122, 124; criticism of, 284n22; exclusion from citizenship, 107, 193; and fatherhood, 50; and firearms, 46–62; heroic manhood and, 55; historiography of, 46, 65n19, 99, 300, 323, 329–30, 335–36; honor among, 189, 323; mobility of, 102, 182n6; politicization of, 185–201; violence by, 68n40
Black American women: among Creek and Seminole nations, 120, 122–24, 125, 133–34; exclusion from citizenship, 107; and firearms, 48, 60–61; historiography of, 99, 265–66, 296–98, 300–301, 302, 303–4; and interracial progeny, 163, 181n1; literary victimhood of, 264–65, 274, 281, 282; mobility of, 102, 166, 182n6; and motherhood, 267; and phrenology, 225–26; resistance by, 96, 190; sexual abuse of, 108, 164, 169–72, 181n1, 183n23, 198–99, 266, 272; as tavernkeepers, 107; and voyeuristic gaze, 266–68, 280
Black Fox (Chickamauga), 15, 20n23
Black Jacks (Bolster), 324
Blackness, 141, 276
Black Women Abolitionists (Yee), 302
Black Women's History of the United States, A (Berry and Gross), 297

Blake, Doc, 60
Blake, Henry, 60
Blassingame, John, 265
Blewett, Mary H., 292
Bloch, Ruth H., 145–46
Block, Sharon, 300
Bloomer, Amelia, 226
Boag, Peter, 337, 338
Boardman, George Dana, 24, 32
Boardman, Sarah. *See* Judson, Sarah Hall Boardman
Bobo, William M., 245–46, 249, 256, 259n16, 262n43
bodies: and dandyism, 247–48; and disease, 267; enslaved, 108–9, 266, 280; gendering of, 108–9, 214, 220, 227, 232; historiography of, 299, 301, 333, 336; one-sex model of, 213; politicization of, 186, 188, 197–98, 214; racial distinctions among, 80, 84, 101, 186, 188, 192, 266, 280, 285n33; reading, 211–12; two-sex model of, 214, 215, 216; women's, 110
Bolster, W. Jeffrey, 324
Bonds of Womanhood, The (Cott), 290, 291
Boone, Arthur, 58, 62
Boone, Eliza, 58
Boone, J. F., 58
Bosom Friends (Balcerski), 334
Boston Athenæum, 334
Boston Female Anti-Slavery Society, 274, 275, 276
Boudreau, George, 295
Bourdieu, Pierre, 323
Bowdoin College, 23
Bowman, Rachel, 231
boy culture, 326
Boyd, Samuel, 176
Boyd, Virginia, 176
Boydston, Jeanne, 292
Boylan, Anne M., 302
Braddock, Edward, 320
Bradford, Phoebe George, 222–24

INDEX 357

Branson, Susan, 295
Bridgman, Laura, 220, 299
Bristed, Charles Astor, 254, 255
Brooklyn Daily Eagle, 250
Brooks, Preston, 194
Brothels, Depravity, and Abandoned Women (Schafer), 300
Brown, John, Jr., 227
Brown, Kathleen M., 301
Brown, Lois, 274, 275, 285n25
Brown, Rebecca Warren, 283n8
Brown, William Wells, 227
Buchanan, James, 199–200, 334
Buckley, Thomas E., 155, 303
Burke, Sarah Woods, 53–54
Bush, George W., 332
Butler, Fanny Kemble, 151
Butler, Judith, 325
Butler, Pierce, 151
Byars, Tom, 64n8
Bynum, Victoria E., 300
Byrne, Katherine, 266

Cain, Granny, 53
Caldwell, Charles, 239n21
Cameron, Alexander, 19n11
Camp, Stephanie M. H., 297
camp meetings, 103, 121
Cane Hill Female Seminary, 125
Carey, Matthew, 71, 72
Carnes, Mark, 324
Cashin, Joan E., 292, 332
Cass, Lewis, 200
Caulfeild, James, 85–86
"Caution to the Fair-Sex" (Rowe), 73
Cealia (enslaved), 123
Celia, a Slave (McLaurin), 299–300
Censor, Jane Turner, 146
Chandler, Richard, 76
Chapman, Maria Weston, 283n8
Charity and Sylvia (Cleves), 299
Charles (enslaver), 165–66, 175
Chauncey, George, 324
Cheathem, Mark R., 333

Cherokee, 7–17, 17n1, 18n7, 19n11, 35, 293, 298
Cherokee Women (Perdue), 9, 298
"Cherokee Women and the Trail of Tears" (Perdue), 293
Chesnut, James, Sr., 176–77
Chesnut, Mary Boykin, 176–77
Chicago Evening Press, 256
Chickamauga, 7–9, 12–14, 15, 16–17, 17n1
Chickasaw, 135n7
Chiles, Josh, 51–52
Chinese women, 33, 83, 84
Choate, Martha, 229
Choctaw, 35, 135n7
cholera, 271, 272
Christopher (paramour of Elleanor Eldridge), 272, 274
Church, Pharcellus, 33
Citizen Bachelors (McCurdy), 334
citizenship: Black Americans and, 57, 59, 97, 102, 104, 112, 175; as constitutional privilege, 69, 87n2; historiography of, 302, 303–4, 320, 334
City of Women (Stansell), 292, 300
Civilization Fund, 121
Claiming the Pen (Kerrison), 304
Clawson, Mary Ann, 326
Cleves, Rachel Hope, 299
Clinton, Catherine, 291
Closer to Freedom (Camp), 297
Cohen, Patricia Cline, 300
Colored Travelers (Pryor), 102
Combe, George, 238n8
Combs, Gilbert, 132–33
Combs, Mable, 132
Commodore (enslaved), 177
Compromise of 1850, 189–90
Compton, Dorcas, 98, 100, 110, 114n10
Compton, Harry (Putnam, Harry), 105–6, 109
Compton, Jude, 106
Compton, Kate, 106
Compton, Rachel, 106
Compton, Richard, 98, 114n10, 116n32

Confidence Men and Painted Women (Halttunen), 290, 325
Congregationalist American Board, 34–35
Connell, R. W., 324, 328
Constantinople, Ancient and Modern (Dalloway), 75
Constitution, 196
Constructing Brotherhood (Clawson), 326
consumption. *See* tuberculosis
Contesting Slave Masculinity (Doddington), 336
Cormany, Samuel Eckerman, 231
Cott, Nancy F., 290, 291
Counterfeit Gentlemen (Mayfield), 333
Courrier des États-Unis, Le, 258n1
coverture, 74, 82, 86
Cox, Thomas, 177
Cradle of the Middle Class (Ryan), 290
Craft, Ellen, 337
Craft, William, 183n23, 337
Cragin, Ellen, 61, 62
Craven, Elizabeth, 80, 83
Creek, 119–34, 135n7
Crenshaw, Kimberlé, 141
Crocker, William, 23
Cuffee, Paul, 103
cult of true womanhood, 213, 267
Cummings, Sarah, 37
Curtis, George William, 245
Cutts, Adele. *See* Douglas, Adele Cutts

Dalloway, James, 75–76, 79, 80
dandy. *See* avenoodle; macaroni; manhood: dandyism
Davenport, Charlie, 52
David, Rene Peter, 177
Davis, Angela, 64n9
Davison, Ellida, 157
Dean, William, 32–33, 38
Delany, Martin R., 190
Deleuze, Giles, 251
Democratic Party, 186, 191, 196, 199

Diament, Elizabeth, 124, 128
Dickens, Charles, 270
Diggs, Kittey, 56, 57
disease. *See* tuberculosis; typhus
Disorderly Women (Juster), 305
divorce, 74, 78, 82, 143, 148, 149–57, 161n24, 161n28, 177, 248, 284n15, 303
Doddington, David Stefan, 68n40, 336
domestic abuse, 62
Dorsey, Bruce, 302, 325, 335
Doublehead (Chickamauga), 15
Douglas, Adele Cutts, 191
Douglas, Ann, 304
Douglas, Martha, 195
Douglas, Stephen: contrast with Frederick Douglass, 185–86, 189, 198; as Democrat, 186–88, 189, 191, 192, 196, 199; as enslaver, 194–95; manhood of, 199–200, 201; spelling of name, 208n41
Douglass, Frederick: as abolitionist, 194, 227; contrast with Stephen Douglas, 185–86, 187–88, 198; idea of Black family, 46, 62; and interracial sex, 197; racial symbolism of, 201; and racism, 103, 198; as Republican, 192–94, 197; and self-making, 328–29
Dowd, Gregory Evans, 96–97
Dragging Canoe (Chickamauga). *See* Tsi'yu-gunsi'ni
Driven Toward Madness (Taylor), 297
Dublin, Thomas, 292
Dubois, Charlotte, 109
Dubois, Dominicus (Minical), 98–100, 104, 108–9, 114n10
Dubois, Dorcas, 109
Dubois, Elizabeth, 109, 111
Dubois, Elizabeth Scudder, 98–100, 101
Dubois, Judith, 109
Dubois, Moses, 109
Dubois, Rachel, 109
Dubois, Silvia: biography of, 95, 111–12; birthplace, 114n10; celebrity of, 103–4, 111; concept of citizenship by,

97; enslavement of, 98–101; enslaver's abuse of, 98–100, 108–9; inheritance, 106–7; mobility of, 101–3, 104; as mother, 109; as tavernkeeper, 108, 110
dueling, 149
Dueling Cultures, Damnable Legacies (Welborn), 335
Dunbar, Erica Armstrong, 297
Dunovant, Alexander Quay, 178, 179, 180
Dwight, H. G. O., 31

eagle-tail dance, 7–8
Eastman, Carolyn, 295, 334–35
Eaton, Charles, 50
Eddy, Daniel, 37
Edwards, Barrett, 64n8
Edwards, Laura R., 303
effeminacy. *See* fairy
Egyptian women, 71–72, 74, 87n2
Eldridge, Elleanor, 264, 271–74, 281
Elleanor's Second Book (Green), 273
Ellet, Elizabeth, 289
Ellis, Mary, 31
Emerson, Ralph Waldo, 328
Empires, Nations, and Families (Hyde), 298
evangelicalism, 21–39, 103, 110, 267, 281, 285n25, 305, 335
Everett, Seraphina Haynes, 38

fairy, 257
Family Venture, A (Cashin), 292
Faragher, John Mack, 324, 325
Farnham, Christie Anne, 297
Farnsworth, John F., 192–93
Farrar, Cynthia, 36, 38
fatherhood, 28, 46, 58, 60–61, 326, 332
Faust, Drew Gilpin, 321, 322
Federalist Papers, The, 69
female husbands, 337–38
femes sole, 155
femininity. *See* womanhood
feminism, 266, 290, 291, 302, 328
feminization of Christianity, 25, 39, 304

Fifteenth Amendment, 58
Fifth Avenoodle. *See* avenoodle
Fincher, Bill, 64n8
Finley, Alexandra J., 297
firearms, 46–62, 64n9, 67n34, 67n38
Fisher, Eliza Middleton, 144, 148, 151
Fisher, Joshua, 148, 149, 150
Fisher, Sidney, 149, 151
Fisk, Pliny, 24
Fogelson, Raymond, 10
Foreman, P. Gabrielle, 266
Forester, Fanny, 32
Forrest, Catherine, 152, 248
Forrest, Edwin, 152, 248
Forret, Jeff, 55
Forten, Charlotte, 225, 239n24
Foster, Abby Kelley, 226, 227, 231
Foster, George G., 253, 254
Foster, Stephen Symonds, 231
Foster, Thomas A., 336–37
Fouke, Philip B., 192
Foul Bodies (Brown), 301
Fourteenth Amendment, 58
Fowler, Lorenzo, 220, 226, 231
Fowler, Lydia Folger, 224
Fowler, Orson, 222–24, 225, 227
Fowler and Wells, 227–28, 231
Fox-Genovese, Elizabeth, 296
Francklin, William, 76, 81, 82
Franconi's Circus, 244
Fraser, Rebecca, 65n19
fraternalism, 326
Frederick (enslaved), 177
Frederick Douglass' Paper, 189, 194
Freeberg, Ernest, 299
Freeman, Joanne B., 327
Freemasonry, 326
Free Women of Petersburg, The (Lebsock), 291
Fugitive Slave Act of 1850, 189–90
Fulton, DoVeanna S., 96

Galaxy, 249
Gall, Franz, 238n8

360   INDEX

Gardner, Jared, 73, 87n2
Garrison, William Lloyd, 188, 196, 226
Gaskell, Elizabeth, 266
Gay American History (Katz), 321
gay history, 321–22
Gay New York (Chauncey), 324
gay rights movement, 328
"Gender" (Scott), 294
gender studies, 1, 95, 294, 323, 325
General Training, 103–4
Genovese, Eugene D., 330
Giddings, Paula, 292
Gigantino, James J., II, 101
Gillespie, Emily Hawlie, 232–33
Gillespie, Henry, 232
Gillespie, Michelle, 296
Gilliam, Joseph, 53
Ginzburg, Lori D., 302
Gladdy, Mary, 61–62
Glimpses of New York City (Bobo), 245–46
Glover, Lorri, 331–32
Glymph, Thavolia, 296
Gold Rush, 332, 337
Goodell, William, 63n1
Gordon-Reed, Annette, 300
gossip, 143, 151, 152, 161n32, 167, 176, 181
Graham's Magazine, 248
Grant, Asahel, 27–28
Grant, Judith Campbell, 28
Gratz, Rebecca, 238n9
Green, Charles, 284n15
Green, Frances Harriet Whipple, 271–74, 284n15, 284n16, 284n18
Green, Jennifer R., 335
Green, Sarah Margru Kinson, 225
Greenberg, Amy S., 332
Greenberg, Joshua R., 333
Greene, Hannah, 122
Grimké, Angelina, 302
Grimké, Sarah, 302
Griswold, Robert L., 150, 156, 328, 332
Gross, Kali Nicole, 297
Grossberg, Michael, 155

Haas, Lisbeth, 298
Hagins, Malachi, 56–57
Halbrook, Stephen P., 59
Hale, Sarah, 249
Half Has Never Been Told, The (Baptist), 333
Halperin, David M., 251
Halttunen, Karen, 290, 325, 327
Hamlin, Harriet Lovell, 38
Hammond, James Henry, 164, 321
Hannibal (enslaved), 50
Harris, Leslie, 155
Hartford Review, 248
Hartigan-O'Connor, Ellen, 301
Harvard College, 22
Harvey, Charlie, 48, 64n8
Hasselquist, Frederik, 79
Hawthorne, Nathaniel, 239n24, 328
Head, Caroline, 53
Healey, Caroline, 228–31
Hemings, Sally, 300
Hemphill, Kate M., 300
Henderson, Richard, 7, 11
Heroines of the Missionary Enterprise (Eddy), 37
heteronormativity, 141, 322, 325, 337
heterosexuality, 141, 147, 325, 337
Hewitt, Nancy A., 290–91
Heyrman, Christine Leigh, 304–5
Hilde, Libra R., 46, 47, 60
Hill, Frederic, 249
Hine, Darlene Clark, 181n1, 329–30
historiography, 1, 287, 289–306, 320–38
"History of Manhood in America" (Dorsey), 325
Hodes, Martha, 300, 329, 330
Hodges, Graham Russell, 104–5
Holden, Vanessa M., 297
Holmström, Bo, 64n9
Holt, Hines, 61–62, 68n40
Home Journal, 245, 246, 253, 254
Home Rule (Sachs), 333
homosexuality, 244, 257, 321, 334

homosociality, 321, 326, 331, 333, 334, 336, 337
honor: and family, 151, 173; as historiographical theme, 322, 323, 327–28, 329, 331–32, 333, 334, 335; and manhood, 154, 156–57, 165, 169, 170–72, 175, 181; and sex, 164
Horlick, Allan, 322
Horn, Alice, 50
Horn, Josh, 50–51
Horniblow, Molly, 61
Horowitz, Helen Lefkowitz, 331
Horton, James Oliver, 99, 329
Horton, Lois E., 99, 329
Hough, George, 34
Howe, Samuel Gridley, 220
Huger, Thomas, 151
Hunter, Tera W., 297, 304
hunting, 9, 50–52, 333
Hurlbut, Elisha, 228
Hurston, Zora Neale, 51
Hurtado, Albert L., 332
husbands: and adultery, 31, 78, 82; as companion, 328; and divorce, 78, 152, 154, 155–56; and domestic violence, 62; among enslaved families, 53, 123; and evangelicalism, 128; female husbands, 337–38; in Indigenous American cultures, 10, 131; as patriarch, 37, 130; submissive, 85, 223
Hyde, Anne F., 298

Incidents in the Life of a Slave Girl (Jacobs), 264, 278, 279, 280, 285n31
In Dependence (Beatty), 295–96
Indian (South Asian) women, 76, 84
Indigenous American men: Chickamauga, 7–11, 12–14, 16–17; Creek and Seminole, 119–20; historiography of, 330
Indigenous American women: Chickamauga, 8–10, 12–14, 15–16, 18n4; Creek and Seminole, 119–21, 123–25,

127–28, 129, 130–31, 133; historiography of, 298
infertility, 176
In Pursuit of Knowledge (Baumgartner), 304
intersectionality, 141–42, 289, 292, 293, 296, 304
Intimacy and Power in the Old South (Stowe), 327
Intimate Economy, An (Finley), 300
Isenberg, Nancy, 302

Jabour, Anya, 297, 328
Jackson, James, 274, 276
Jacobs, Harriet, 171, 172–73, 267, 276–77, 278–80, 302
Jacobs, Louisa, 279
James Henry Hammond and the Old South (Faust), 321
Jameson, Elizabeth, 302
Jane (mother of William Moore), 54
Jay, John, 69
Jefferson, Thomas, 252, 300, 320, 333
Jeffrey, Julie Roy, 302
Jenkins, Ernestine, 329–30
Jensen, Joan M., 292
Johns Hopkins University Press, 293
Johnson, Andrew, 193
Johnson, Hersel V., 191
Johnson, Michael P., 147
Johnson, Susan Lee, 332
Johnson, Willis, 59
Jones, Jacqueline, 292
Jones, Martha S., 302, 304
Jones-Rogers, Stephanie E., 296
Journal of Women's History, 293
Joyous Greetings (Anderson), 302
Judge, Ona, 296, 297
judicial patriarchy, 155–56
Judson, Adoniram, 32, 34, 38
Judson, Ann Hasseltine, 29, 30, 37, 38
Judson, Emily Chubbock, 32, 33, 38
Judson, Sarah Hall Boardman, 32, 38
Jumper, John, 130

362 INDEX

Junkin, James, 126, 131
Junkin, Mary, 131
Juster, Susan, 305
Juvenile Choir, 274–75

Kana'ti (Cherokee), 9
Kann, Mark E., 326, 336
Kansas-Nebraska Act, 186, 187, 189, 190, 194, 195, 199
Kaplan, Catherin O'Donnell, 334
Kasson, John F., 325, 327
Katz, Jonathan Ned, 321
Kelley, Mary, 291, 304
Kennington, Kelly M., 303
Kerber, Linda K., 291
Kerrison, Catherine, 304
Key, Philip Barton, 149
Kierner, Cynthia A., 296, 303
Killer, Whiteman, 15
Kimmel, Michael, 325, 336
King, William Rufus, 334
Kirk, John, 14–15
Klepp, Susan E., 96, 97, 109, 110, 295
Knickerbocker, 254
Knowles, James D., 30
Koschnik, Albert, 334
Kowetah Mission School, 119, 121–22, 123, 126–27, 129, 131–32
Ku Klux Klan, 48, 59, 60

Lacy, Aunt, 125–27, 138n22
Laqueur, Thomas, 213
Larison, Cornelius Wilson, 95, 96, 106, 108, 109, 110, 111, 112, 113n2, 116n32
Lasser, Carol, 266–67
Laurens, John, 56
Laurie, Thomas, 27–28
Laver, Harry S., 333
Learning to Stand and Speak (Kelley), 304
Lebsock, Suzanne, 291–92
Lee, Mattie, 53
Lemprière, William, 83
Lerner, Gerda, 290

Leverenz, David, 322, 324, 327, 328–29
Lewis, Charlene M. Boyer, 295
Lewis, Jan, 291
Lewis, Kizziah, 125, 128, 131
Liberator, The, 188, 226, 274, 275
Liberty's Daughters (Norton), 291
Lilley, John, 121, 123, 124–25, 127, 128, 129–30, 132, 137n15
Lily, The, 226
Lincoln, Abraham, 185, 188, 190, 196, 197
Lind, Jenny, 244
Little Owl, 15
Lobdell, Henry, 23
Lobdell, Jared, 109, 113n2, 113n3
Long Before Stonewall (Foster), 336
Long Fellow. *See* Tuskegetchee
Loosening the Bonds (Jensen), 292
Lord, Lucy Lyon, 32, 33
Loring, James, 268, 283n8
Lotty (enslaved), 177
Loughridge, R. M., 123, 127, 129, 131, 132
Love of Freedom (Adams and Pleck), 265
Lower Towns (Cherokee), 12, 13, 15, 19n14
Lowrie, John C., 29
Lowrie, Louisa Wilson, 29–30
Lowrie, Walter, 26–27, 29, 132
Lussana, Sergio A., 50, 336
Lyman, Henry, 25–26, 28
Lynn, Joshua A., 334
Lyon, Mary, 33
Lyons, Clare A., 214, 299
Lystra, Karen, 325, 327

macaroni, 243, 244, 245, 247, 251, 259n15
Macomber, Eleanor, 36–37, 38
Madison, Dolley, 296
Maffly-Kipp, Laurie F., 265
Manganelli, Kimberly, 266
manhood: and adultery, 149, 156; among Black Americans, 46–62, 57, 97, 189, 194, 200–201, 323; communal,

326, 334; contingent relationship with manhood, 7–17, 325; dandyism, 243–57, 258n3; and divorce, 156; enslaved, 49, 57; evangelical, 24–28; and firearms, 56; hegemonic, 324, 329; heroic, 28, 52, 55; historiography of, 320–38; among Indigenous Americans, 7–17; martial, 25, 147, 332; naval, 156; passionate, 326; and phrenology, 213–34; politicization of, 185–201; and procreation, 109; republican, 334; restrained, 25, 332; ruffian, 186, 191, 200; self-made, 28, 243, 326–27, 332; and sexuality, 336–37; tentative, 333; unrestrained, 190, 191, 199; among White Americans, 97, 143–58, 164, 165, 176, 188, 190, 195, 200–201
Manhood and the American Renaissance (Leverenz), 324
Manifest Manhood and the Antebellum American Empire (Greenberg), 332
Manion, Jen, 337–38
Manliness and Civilization (Bederman), 327–28
Mappen, Marc, 108
Marcy, William L., 199
marriage: among Black Americans, 63n1; companionate marriage, 75, 77, 82, 87, 145, 146, 158n5; contrast with non-Americans, 84, 85; between Edward and Edwardina Middleton, 147–48, 150, 156, 157; historiography of, 297, 304, 325, 327, 328, 332; as ideal, 76–77, 78; among missionaries, 34, 35; and phrenology, 223, 232
Martin, Joseph, 16
Martin, Martha, 208n41
Martschukat, Jürgen, 46
martyrdom, 21, 23, 25, 27, 29–30, 32, 33
masculinity. *See* manhood
masculinity studies. *See* men's studies
Massachusetts Baptist Missionary Magazine, 268

Masterful Women (Wood), 297
mastery, 164, 201, 328, 335
matriarchy, 84–85
matrifocality, 53
matrilineality, 9, 10, 13, 15, 16, 129, 130, 131, 333
Mayer, Holly A., 295
Mayfield, John, 333
McCall, Harry, 148, 149, 151
McCulloch, Samuel, Jr., 57, 66n29
McCurdy, John Gilbert, 334
McDougall, William, 284n15
McKissick, Amos, 64n8
McLaurin, Melton A., 299–300
McMahon, Lucia, 304
McPherson (enslaved), 67n34
Medical Bondage (Owens), 299
Medical College of South Carolina, 164, 166
Medical Society of South Carolina, 180
Melville, Herman, 328
Memoir of Elleanor Eldridge, The (Eldridge and Whipple), 271
Memoir of James Jackson (Paul), 276
"Memoir of Mrs. Chloe Spear, The" (unknown), 268
Men of Letters in the Early Republic (Kaplan), 334
men's studies, 1, 320–49
Mere Equals (McMahon), 304
Methodists, 121
Middleton, Arthur, 143
Middleton, Edward, 143–58
Middleton, Edwardina (Edda), 144–58
Middleton, Eliza. *See* Fisher, Eliza Middleton
Middleton, Henry, 143, 146
Middleton, John, 144, 149
Middleton, Mary, 144
Middleton, Williams, 148, 149
"Middleton Divorce Case" (unknown), 151
Middle Towns (Cherokee), 12
Miles, Tiya, 298, 302

Miller, Marla R., 301
Miller, Stephen Decatur, 176
Mills, Samuel, Jr., 23
Millward, Jessica, 297
missionaries, 21–39, 119–234
Missionary Herald, The, 35, 36
Missionary Sisters, The (Benjamin), 38
Mohawk, 11
Montgomery, Mary Virginia, 218, 225
Moore, William, 54
Morgan, Jennifer L., 267, 297
Morris, Aldon D., 329
Morris, Lewis, 107–8
motherhood: enslaved, 60–61, 98, 171, 175, 266, 267; evangelical, 30, 32; historiography of, 303, 304; Indigenous, 129–30, 132; mixed-race, 277; and phrenology, 231, 233; republican, 75, 84–85, 87, 176–77, 291; unwed, 278, 280
Mott, Lucretia, 226, 227
Moultrie, James, Jr., 163–81
Moultrie, Sarah Louise Shrewsbury, 166
Moultrie, William, 167
Mount Holyoke Female Seminary, 33
mulatta. *See* racial identity
Munson, Samuel, 23, 24, 25–26
Murder of Helen Jewett, The (Cohen), 300
Murray, Elizabeth, 296
Muslim women, 75–76, 81–82
My Brother Slaves (Lussana), 336
Myers, Amrita Chakrabarti, 297–98
Myth of Seneca Falls, The (Tetrault), 302

Nancy (Cherokee), 15
Nash, Margaret A., 304
National Anti-Slavery Bazaar, 275
National Manhood (Nelson), 326
Nation of Speechifiers, A (Eastman), 295
Native Americans. *See* Indigenous American men; Indigenous American women; *specific nations*
Ned (enslaved), 50

Needle's Eye, The (Miller), 301
Nelson, Dana D., 326, 329
Never Caught (Dunbar), 297
Newell, Harriet Atwood, 29–30, 37, 38
New Men (Foster), 336
Newton Theological Institution, 23
New Woman, the, 321
New York Herald, 196, 255
New-York Magazine, 87n2
New York Mirror, 248
Nielsen, Kim E., 299
Norcom, James, 171, 172
Norcom, Mary, 171
Normann, Edwardina de. *See* Middleton, Edwardina
Northern Baptist Education Society, 23
Norton, Mary Beth, 291
Nunley, Tamika, 297

Oak Ridge Mission School, 121, 123, 125, 127, 129, 130
Oberg, Barbara B., 295
Oconostota (Cherokee), 16
Old Tassel (Cherokee), 14, 15, 20n19
Olsen, Christopher J., 334
Opal, Jason M., 22, 331
orphans, 23, 129, 131
Osage, 35
Othering, 2, 72, 73, 74, 75, 86, 90n11, 323, 326, 328
Our First Families (anonymous), 256
Our Nig (Wilson), 277–78, 280
Out of the House of Bondage (Glymph), 296
Overhill Towns (Chickamauga), 11, 12, 14
Owens, Deidre Cooper, 299
Owl, The (Chickamauga), 15

Pace, Robert, 331
Pagan, Robert A., 169, 170, 172, 174, 175, 178, 180, 183n15
Painter, Nell Irvin, 297
pansy. *See* fairy

Parker, Alison M., 302
Parker, Laura Ramsey, 61
Parlor Politics (Allgor), 295
Parr, Joy, 321
Parson, Levi, 24
passing (racial), 337
patriarchy, 130, 155–56, 165, 192, 248, 305, 321, 322, 328, 333
Paul, Susan, 264, 274–76, 281–82, 284n25
Paul, Thomas, 275
Peace Came in the Form of a Woman (Barr), 298
Pearis, Richard, 19n11
Pencillings by the Way (Willis), 253
Penn, Mary, 131
People and Their Peace, The (Edwards), 303
Perdue, Theda, 9, 293, 298
Perkins Institution for the Blind, 220
Perry (enslaved), 177
Pethy, Marilda, 67n34
Petigru, James, 164–65, 166, 167, 168–72, 174–75, 177–80
Pettigrew, James, 168
Pettigrew, William, 168
Pflugrad-Jackisch, Ami, 335
Philadelphia Bulletin, 154
Philadelphia Young Ladies' Academy, 75
Phrenological Almanac for 1841, The, 220
phrenology, 211, 215–34, 236n4, 239n21
Pierce, Franklin, 200
Pinckney, Eliza Lucas, 296
Pitts, Reginald H., 96
Plantation Mistress, The (Clinton), 291
Pleck, Elizabeth H., 265
Poiret, Abbé Jean Louis Marie, 73, 80
Political Culture and Secession in Mississippi (Olsen), 334
Polk, Tom, 61
popular sovereignty, 186, 195, 199
Presbyterian Board of Foreign Missions, 26

Presbyterians, 37, 119–34, 135n7, 138n26
prescriptive literature, 73, 78, 325
Price, Mary, 120, 124, 128, 131, 135n5
Price for Their Pound of Flesh, The (Berry), 301
Princes of Cotton (Berry), 331
Private Woman, Public Stage (Kelley), 291
Proclamation of 1763, 7
Proctor, Nicholas, 47, 52
Pryor, Elizabeth Stordeur, 97, 102, 104
Pugh, David W., 322, 323
Pumpelly, George, 249
Pumpkin Boy (Chickamauga), 15
Punch, 245
Purvis, Robert, 199
Put, Harry. *See* Compton, Harry
Putnam, Harry. *See* Compton, Harry
Putnam, Rufus, 116n32

Queen Victoria, 143
queerness, 251, 257, 346n44
Question of Manhood, A (Hine and Jenkins), 329–30

racial identity, 83, 120–21, 175, 184n27, 198, 225, 264–82
racism, 96, 120–21, 141, 189, 191, 192, 234, 274, 281
Raimon, Eve Allegra, 265
Ramsay, James R., 122, 126, 127, 129, 130
rape. *See* sexual violence
Rape and Sexual Power in Early America (Block), 300
Ray (father of William Moore), 54
Reckoning with Slavery (Morgan), 267
Reforming Men and Women (Dorsey), 302
religion: evangelicalism, 21–39, 110, 119–34; feminization of, 304; and racial identity, 269, 277; and womanhood, 285n25, 304
"Republican Wife, The" (Lewis), 291
Republic of Men, A (Kann), 326

Revolutionary Backlash (Zagarri), 214, 295
Revolutionary Conceptions (Klepp), 295
Revolutionary War, 97, 106–7, 110, 295
Rice, Mary, 57–58
Rice, Spotswood, 57
Richmond, Stephanie, 302
Richmond Daily Whig, 256
Robert, Dana L., 30, 43n37
Robertson, Stacey M., 302
Robertson, William, 121, 129, 135n6
Rockman, Seth, 104, 301
Roll, Jordan, Roll (Genovese), 330
romantic friendship, 326, 328, 334, 335
Rosen, Hannah, 59
Rothman, Ellen, 145
Rothman, Joshua D., 146, 162n46, 300
Rotundo, E. Anthony, 324, 326–38, 332
Rudeness and Civility (Kasson), 325
Ruff, Joseph, 56–57
Rush, Benjamin, 75
Ruth Hall (Willis), 249
Ryan, Mary P., 290
Ryan, Susan M., 98

Sachs, Honor, 298, 333
Saints and Citizens (Haas), 298
Salmon, Maylynn, 303
Sam (of North Carolina; enslaved), 62
Sam (of Texas; enslaved), 54–56
Sánchez-Eppler, Karen, 266, 285n33
San Diego State College, 309n21
Sappho, 244, 247
Sargeant, Delight, 35
Sawyer, Samuel Tredwell, 171, 172–73, 279
Scandal at Bizarre (Kierner), 303
Schafer, Judith Kelleher, 300
Schultz, Martin, 150
Schwarzberg, Beverly, 154
Scott, Anne Firor, 321, 322
Scott, Ellison, 64n8
Scott, Joan W., 294, 331
Scraping By (Rockman), 301

Searching the Heart (Lystra), 325
Sears, Clare, 337
Second Great Awakening, 38, 121, 304–5, 335
second-wave feminism. *See* feminism
Secret Ritual and Manhood in Victorian America (Carnes), 324
self-divorce, 154
Selu (Cherokee), 9
Seminole, 119–34, 135n7
Seneca, 35
Seneca Falls Convention, 291, 302
separate spheres, 10, 213, 233, 234, 246, 290–91, 324–25
Setting Down the Sacred Past (Maffly-Kipp), 265
Sevier, John, 14, 15
Seward, William H., 192
sex: extramarital, 277, 279; interracial, 106, 120, 164–70, 197–98, 329, 330
Sex, Love, Race (Hodes), 330
Sex Among the Rabble (Lyons), 265
Sex and Citizenship in Antebellum America (Isenberg), 302
Sex and the Eighteenth-Century Man (Foster), 336
Sex and the Founding Fathers (Foster), 336–37
sexuality studies, 289, 294, 299
sexual violence, 171, 181n1, 182n3, 199, 278, 299–300, 336
Shaping of Southern Culture (Wyatt-Brown), 327
Shawnee, 11
Sheidley, Nathaniel, 9
Sheridan, Richard, 261n38
Shrewsbury, Stephen, 167
Sickles, Daniel, 149
Sierra Leone, 23
Silvia Dubois (Larison), 95, 111–12, 113n2
Sizer, Nelson, 221–22, 225, 227
Slave Power, 189–90, 191, 194, 195, 201
Slaves for Hire (Zaborney), 301
Sleeper-Smith, Susan, 298

INDEX 367

Smith, Gerrit, 193
Smith, Merril D., 151, 303
Smith, Millie Ann, 51
Smith-Rosenberg, Carroll, 323
Snorton, C. Riley, 337
Society for Historians of the Early American Republic, 5
Society for the Promotion of Female Education, 33
Sojourner Truth (Painter), 297
Sons of Liberty (Pugh), 323
South Carolina Historical Society, 164
South Carolina Medical Association, 164
South Carolina senate, 177
Southern Honor (Wyatt-Brown), 322–23
Southern Lady, The (Scott), 321
Spears, Chloe, 264, 265, 283n8
Spruill, Julia Cherry, 289
Spurzheim, Johann Gaspar, 238n8
Stansell, Christine, 292, 300
Stanton, Elizabeth Cady, 226, 227, 241n32, 302
Stedman, John, 77
Steele, Brian, 333
Stevenson, Brenda, 53, 61
Stewart, Maria W., 274, 284n22
Still, James, 102
Stone, Lucy, 302
Stowe, Harriet Beecher, 226, 279, 285n33
Stowe, Steven M., 147, 327
Stuart, Henry, 11
Sumner, Charles, 194
Surinamese women, 77
Surviving Southampton (Holden), 297
Suttee ritual, 76
Sutter, Brenann, 96
Sweet, John Wood, 214
Swift, Elisha P., 29
"Swing the Sickle for the Harvest Is Ripe" (Berry), 297
Sycamore Shoals Treaty, 7, 10, 11, 12
Syrett, Nicholas L., 335
Syrian women, 74, 77

Tail, The (Chickamauga), 20n21
tavern culture, 97, 106–8, 110–11
Taylor, Nikki M., 297
Templeton, William, 123–24, 127, 131, 132
Tetrault, Lisa, 302
They Were Her Property (Jones-Rogers), 296
Thirteenth Amendment, 49, 58, 101, 184n39
Thomas, Eliza, 132
"Thomas Jefferson's Gender Frontier" (Steele), 333
Thompson, William, 25, 26
Thomson, Aaron, 64n8
Thomson, Andy, 64n8
Thoreau, Henry David, 328
Ties That Bind (Miles), 298
Ties That Buy, The (Hartigan-O'Connor), 301
Tolstoy, Leo, 157
Touching Liberty (Sánchez-Eppler), 266
Tracy, Joseph, 35
"*Tragic Mulatta*" *Revisited, The* (Raimon), 265
Traister, Bruce, 322, 324
Transatlantic Kindergarten, The (Allen), 304
Transatlantic Spectacles of Race (Mangenelli), 266
transness, 96, 337–38
Transylvania Land Company, 7
Traub, Valerie, 244
Travels Through Syria and Egypt (Volney), 74
Treaty of DeWitts Corner, 12
Treaty of Long Island of Holston, 12
Treaty of Nanjing, 26
tribal sovereignty, 120, 137n15
Truth, Sojourner, 225, 226, 302
Tsi'yu-gunsi'ni (Chickamauga), 8, 10–11, 12, 15–16, 19n11
tuberculosis, 264, 266, 275, 277, 279

Tuberculosis and Victorian Literary Imagination (Byrne), 266
Tulane, Victor, 105
Tullahassee Mission School, 121, 123, 124, 126, 128, 129, 131
Turner, Anna, 124
Turner's Rebellion, 48, 56
Turtle-at-Home (Chickamauga), 15
Tuskegetchee (Cherokee), 16
typhus, 271, 273

Ulrich, Laurel Thatcher, 320
United States Democratic Review, 248
University of Virginia Press, 295
unmanliness, 243–57, 258n3

Vaillant, François le, 79
Valley Towns (Cherokee), 12
Van Buren, Martin, 252
Vann, Susan, 131
Varon, Elizabeth R., 296
Vesey, Denmark, 170
Vester, Katharina, 252
Vice President's Black Wife, The (Myers), 297
Volney, Comte de, 74, 77, 81
voyeuristic gaze, 79, 82, 101, 266, 267, 272, 278, 280

Walker, David, 47, 52, 62
Walker, Pamela, 96
Waller, Tom, 54–55
Ward, Elizabeth "Betsy," 16
Ward, Nancy, 16
Warren, Mercy Otis, 289, 296
Washington, George, 295, 320
Washington, Martha, 296
Watkins, William J., 189, 195
Watts, John, Jr. (Chickamauga), 15
Webb, Mary, 268–71, 274
Webster, Noah, 72
Weekly Museum, 73
Weems, Mason L., 320
Welborn, James Hill, III, 335

Welch, Kimberly M., 303
Weld, Timothy Dwight, 226
Wellman, Judith, 302
Wells, Charlotte Fowler, 224
Wells, Ida B., 48, 226
Welter, Barbara, 223, 304
Weston, Anne Warren, 275
Wheatley, Phyllis, 296
Whipple, Frances Harriet. *See* Green, Frances Harriet Whipple
White, Charlotte H., 34, 35
White, Deborah Gray, 292, 296
White American men: citizenship of, 69, 97, 107, 186, 188–89, 191, 192; and family, 25; and firearms, 25, 47–48, 49, 62; historiography of, 305, 322, 323, 327, 328–29, 330–31, 333–35, 337; independence of, 147; and interracial relationships, 54, 77, 95–96, 163–81, 183n23, 278, 279; mobility of, 103, 104; patriarchal culture of, 21, 95, 134, 243; and phrenology, 233; politicization of, 185–201; racial anxieties of, 201; in tavern culture, 106; violence against Black Americans, 55, 59, 61
White American women: as authors, 265, 277, 280; and education, 76; as enslavers, 87n2; historiography of, 290–92, 296, 297, 299, 300, 301, 302; and interracial relationships, 197–98, 269, 270–71, 278, 300; and missionization, 28–29, 30–31; and phrenology, 233; political rights of, 72; and reading, 71, 265; and republican motherhood, 75; sexual violence against, 80; in tavern culture, 106–7; as victims, 200; and voyeuristic gaze, 266
Whiteman Killer (Chickamauga), 15
Whiteness, 165, 173, 175, 192, 266, 329, 333
White supremacy, 46, 49, 111, 165, 169, 188
Whitman, Walt, 246, 259n13, 328

Whittier, John Greenleaf, 233
Wiesner, Caitlyn, 9
Wilde, Oscar, 247
Williams, Lewis, 55, 66n26
Williams, Timothy J., 335
Willis, Nathaniel Parker, 243, 244–49, 250, 253–54, 256, 260n25
Willis, Sarah Payson, 249
Wilson, Harriet E., 264, 267, 277–78, 280, 281, 282n2
Wilson, J. Leighton, 122, 128
Wilson, Louisa, 29
Wilson, William J., 227
Winslow, Harriet Lathrop, 31
Winslow, Miron, 31, 32
Wirt, Robert, 328
Wirt, William, 328
Within the Plantation Household (Fox-Genovese), 296
wives: and adultery, 78, 148–49, 152, 156; as companion, 328; compared to slaves, 31, 74, 76, 77; and divorce, 78, 152, 154, 156; among enslaved families, 123; and evangelicalism, 31, 32–33, 128; historiography of, 291, 328; ideal of good wife, 73, 148, 176; loss of status, 130; political influence of, 16; supported through hunting, 50
womanhood: and adultery, 148–49, 152, 156; among Black Americans, 95–112, 119–34, 163–81, 264–82; contingent relationship with manhood, 7–17, 325; and divorce, 155; evangelical, 21, 28–38, 39, 285; historiography of, 289–306, 321, 322, 326, 327; ideal of true womanhood, 213, 223, 229, 267; among Indigenous Americans, 7–17, 119–34; and phrenology, 213–34; and procreation, 109; republican, 110, 267; among White Americans, 71–87, 246
Women of the Republic (Kerber), 291
women. *See* Black American women; Chinese women; Egyptian women; Indian (South Asian) women; Indigenous American women; Muslim women; Surinamese women; Syrian women; White American women
Women and Men on the Overland Trail (Faragher), 324
Women and the Law of Property in Early America (Salmon), 303
Women in the American Revolution (Oberg), 295
Women's Activism and Social Change (Hewitt), 290
Women's Education in the United States (Nash), 304
women's history/studies, 1, 289–319, 309n21, 324, 325, 331
Women's Life and Work in the Southern Colonies (Spruill), 289
Wood, Fernando, 193
Wood, Kristen E., 97, 107, 297
Woods, Alex, 52
Woods, Cal, 49
Woods, Leonard, 29
Woods, Major, 52
Works Progress Administration, 49, 138n26
Wright, Sylvanus, 64n8
Wurteh (Chickamauga), 15
Wyatt-Brown, Bertram, 146, 147, 322–23, 327, 328, 329
Wylie, Alexander P., 166, 175, 178–79, 180

Yale College, 22, 248
Yancy, George, 101
Yankee Doodle (magazine), 245
"Yankee Doodle" (song), 245
Yates, Richard, 193
Yazoo Democrat, 250
Yee, Shirley J., 302

Zaborney, John J., 301
Zagarri, Rosemarie, 214, 295

RECENT BOOKS IN THE SERIES
Jeffersonian America

The Scientist Turned Spy: André Michaux, Thomas Jefferson, and the Conspiracy of 1793
Patrick Spero

Sacred Capital: Methodism and Settler Colonialism in the Empire of Liberty
Hunter Price

Empire of Commerce: The Closing of the Mississippi and the Opening of Atlantic Trade
Susan Gaunt Stearns

Black Reason, White Feeling: The Jeffersonian Enlightenment in the African American Tradition
Hannah Spahn

Replanting a Slave Society: The Sugar and Cotton Revolutions in the Lower Mississippi Valley
Patrick Luck

The Celebrated Elizabeth Smith: Crafting Genius and Transatlantic Fame in the Romantic Era
Lucia McMahon

Rival Visions: How the Views of Jefferson and His Contemporaries Defined the Early American Republic
Dustin Gish and Andrew Bibby, editors

Revolutionary Prophecies: The Founders and America's Future
Robert M. S. McDonald and Peter S. Onuf, editors

The Founding of Thomas Jefferson's University
John A. Ragosta, Peter S. Onuf, and Andrew J. O'Shaughnessy, editors

Thomas Jefferson's Lives: Biographers and the Battle for History
Robert M. S. McDonald, editor

Jeffersonians in Power: The Rhetoric of Opposition Meets the Realities of Governing
Joanne B. Freeman and Johann N. Neem, editors

Jefferson on Display: Attire, Etiquette, and the Art of Presentation
G. S. Wilson

Jefferson's Body: A Corporeal Biography
Maurizio Valsania

Pulpit and Nation: Clergymen and the Politics of Revolutionary America
Spencer W. McBride

Blood from the Sky: Miracles and Politics in the Early American Republic
Adam Jortner

Confounding Father: Thomas Jefferson's Image in His Own Time
Robert M. S. McDonald

The Haitian Declaration of Independence: Creation, Context, and Legacy
Julia Gaffield, editor

Citizens of a Common Intellectual Homeland: The Transatlantic Origins of American Democracy and Nationhood
Armin Mattes

Between Sovereignty and Anarchy: The Politics of Violence in the American Revolutionary Era
Patrick Griffin, Robert G. Ingram, Peter S. Onuf, and Brian Schoen, editors

Patriotism and Piety: Federalist Politics and Religious Struggle in the New American Nation
Jonathan J. Den Hartog

Becoming Men of Some Consequence: Youth and Military Service in the Revolutionary War
John A. Ruddiman

Amelioration and Empire: Progress and Slavery in the Plantation Americas
Christa Dierksheide

Collegiate Republic: Cultivating an Ideal Society in Early America
Margaret Sumner

Era of Experimentation: American Political Practices in the Early Republic
Daniel Peart

Paine and Jefferson in the Age of Revolutions
Simon P. Newman and Peter S. Onuf, editors

Sons of the Father: George Washington and His Protégés
Robert M. S. McDonald, editor

Religious Freedom: Jefferson's Legacy, America's Creed
John Ragosta

www.ingramcontent.com/pod-product-compliance
Lightning Source LLC
Chambersburg PA
CBHW021338300426